Also by Kurt Gray

*The Mind Club: Who Thinks,
What Feels, and Why It Matters*
(CO-AUTHORED WITH
DANIEL M. WEGNER)

Outraged

Outraged

Why We Fight About
Morality and Politics
and How to Find
Common Ground

Kurt Gray

Pantheon Books, New York

Pages 355–56 constitute an extension of this copyright page.

Names: Gray, Kurt James, author.
Title: Outraged : why we fight about morality and politics and how to find
    common ground / Kurt Gray.
Description: First edition. | New York : Pantheon Books, [2025] | Includes
    bibliographical references and index.
Identifiers: LCCN 2024023366 | ISBN 9780593317433 (hardcover) |
    ISBN 9780593317440 (ebook)
Subjects: LCSH: Ethics. | Polarization (Social sciences) | Self-righteousness. |
    Perception (Philosophy)
Classification: LCC BJ1031 .G725 2025 | DDC 170—dc23/eng/20241024
LC record available at https://lccn.loc.gov/2024023366

www.penguinrandomhouse.com | www.pantheonbooks.com

Jacket design by Chris Allen

Printed in the United States of America

First Edition

10 9 8 7 6 5 4 3 2 1

The authorized representative in the EU for product safety and compliance
is Penguin Random House Ireland, Morrison Chambers, 32 Nassau Street,
Dublin D02 YH68, Ireland, https://eu-contact.penguin.ie.

To everyone trying their best to understand

Contents

PART 3: BRIDGING MORAL DIVIDES

Outraged

Introduction

Swerve: The Power of Harm

People today are divided. We are filled with outrage. We fight about morality and politics at the polls, on social media, and at the dinner table. These clashes destroy friendships and threaten our democracy. Although some people are happy to be angry, most of us want less outrage and more understanding. This book is for everyone who wants to better understand the "other side" and the hidden psychology behind moral conflicts.

Deep in our minds, every fight about morality comes down to one thing: competing perceptions of harm. We get outraged at people when they deny our assumptions about what causes suffering and when they reject our views of victimhood. In politics and everyday life, we get angry when people disagree about who is "really" harmed in a situation. Competing perceptions of victimhood fuel conflict in the media, at work, and in road rage—like the night when someone threatened to kill me.

I was sixteen and had just gotten my driver's license, speeding through suburbia in my maroon Pontiac Grand Am—nickname Fireball—while my friends gossiped and blasted 1990s hip-hop. The rain had just stopped, and the roads were slick. We were late to the movie.

We raced around the corner, and I could see the lights of the theater way up ahead. I accelerated. Suddenly someone in the back shouted over the din; we were about to blow by the shortcut to the theater. It was a left turn, and we were in the right-hand lane, so I swerved across the road. I didn't see the brand-new Mercedes in my blind spot until I had completely cut him off.

Our tires squealed on the wet asphalt as we both spun and braked. Our cars sat in the middle of a deserted intersection, steaming in the night. There were no witnesses to my reckless driving or what happened next. I turned off the music and opened my window to apologize. The other driver got out of his car and slammed his door shut. He was in his twenties, wearing a track jacket and a thick silver chain. His eyes were dark with rage. He pointed straight at me and said, "I'm going to fucking kill you."

I panicked and stomped on the gas. Everything in the car was dead quiet; no one could believe what was happening, and no one knew what to do. The other driver got back into his car and roared after us. Within moments, he was riding my back bumper. My brain was blank, filled with nothing but fear.

Without thinking, I blindly took random turns through empty parking lots until we ended up behind a big-box store. On one side the loading docks loomed above us, and on the other side a steep hill rose. We were trapped in a dark canyon.

He weaved back and forth behind us, corralling us into the corner. He parked right behind me to cut off any escape. My friends and I felt like trapped animals. The guy got out of the car, shouted, "You're dead," and came toward us. One friend in the back seat shouted, "Lock the door!" It probably saved my life. I clicked the lock, and a second later he was hauling on the door handle, shouting, "I'm going to kick the fucking shit out of you."

I opened my window a bit to apologize again. He slipped his hand in through the narrow opening, grabbed my collar, and shook me. Then he reached down deeper, trying to unlock the door. I smacked his hand away while continuing to apologize, a mess of instincts—the raw animal drive of self-preservation and the human intuition that I had to talk with him to somehow defuse his anger.

Then the clearest thinking of my friends—the one who reminded me to lock the door—held up a cell phone (still uncommon in the late 1990s) she had borrowed from her mom that night. "Stop or I'll call the cops!" He kept shaking and slapping me for a few more moments, then paused and said something crazy. Filled with righteous outrage, he spat, "Call the cops—I'll tell them what you did."

It didn't make any sense. *I* was the one fearing for my life. *I* was the teenager trapped in the car. He was literally assaulting me and threatening to kill me, but he thought that the law would be on *his* side. How could he be the one outraged, convinced that *he* was in the moral right?

THE ROOTS OF RIGHTEOUS INDIGNATION

I couldn't stop thinking about the events of that night. In the shower, while trying to fall asleep, while waiting in line, I was plagued by the memory of it. I would see the emptiness of that loading dock under the glare of headlights, remember the feeling of panic and helplessness and then the relief when he finally walked away from my window, got into his car, and sped off into the night.

Eventually, the memories of terror faded, but I couldn't forget his indignation. How could he be so emphatic that I was wrong and he was right, when he was the one threatening me? How could he be angry at me when I should be furious with him? He was the villain, and I was the victim.

I remained confused for a long time, but the events of that night began to make sense once I started a PhD in social psychology at Harvard, studying how our minds make sense of right and wrong. I am now a professor of psychology and neuroscience at the University of North Carolina at Chapel Hill, where I direct the Deepest Beliefs Lab and the Center for the Science of Moral Understanding. My job is to make sense of moral disagreement and find ways to help people in conflict understand each other. After more than a decade of research and over a hundred published papers, I finally have enough distance from that night to see how he could be so outraged.

The other driver was morally righteous because *he* felt victimized. He felt as if he had been harmed. He had come within a razor's edge of being injured by my reckless driving.

From my perspective, I was the one being harmed, but from his perspective he was the one in harm's way. Because each of us felt endangered by the other, we both felt that we were morally right and the other person was morally wrong.

Harm explains more than road rage. It also explains why society is so angry today, with everyone arguing about who is truly a victim, and who is most vulnerable to suffering.

OUTRAGED POLITICS

People today are most obviously outraged when it comes to politics. Liberals and conservatives shout at each other at school board meetings, at political rallies, and on social media. Pro-choicers and pro-lifers call each other "monsters" and "murderers," and debates about immigration, racial inequality, and censorship focus less on policy and more on who is acting like a Nazi. Even friends and families demonize each other when it comes to moral differences. One 2021 study found that one in seven Americans ended a friendship because of arguments over COVID.[1]

Moral outrage also poisons our government. Since the 1940s, the Brookings Institution has been tracking legislative action on political issues and found that our government has acted on fewer and fewer of these issues over time. In the 1940s, Congress was gridlocked by disagreement on 30 percent of issues of public concern—like transportation, agriculture, and education—but today lawmakers are gridlocked on 75 percent of important issues.[2] Gridlock has many causes, ranging from the introduction of the filibuster to more competitive elections where legislators feel pressured to satisfy their voter base. But one critical reason is that many members of Congress are outraged at the idea of compromising with the "evil" people on the other side of the political divide.

Liberals and conservatives have always had different visions about how best to help the country, but today we often see the other side as lacking a basic moral compass. During the 2016 presidential campaign, the Democratic candidate, Hillary Clinton, described Trump supporters as a "basket of deplorables" full of racist, sexist, homophobic, and otherwise bigoted people.[3] On the right, the popular conservative commentator Matt Walsh called the Democratic Party "an abjectly evil institution" and said that Democrats' views on abortion made them "in favor of infanticide."[4] Work from my lab finds that it's not just politicians and pundits who endorse this cynicism: many everyday people believe that people on the other side view murder, embezzlement, and even child pornography as acceptable.[5]

But even though people on the other side can act in ways that seem immoral, the vast majority of people have a basic moral sense, and it's the same no matter whom you vote for. We all have the same moral mind, one wired to care about protecting ourselves, our loved ones, and society's most vulnerable. Everyone's heart aches when confronted with the suffering of something vulnerable, like an injured puppy whimpering in fright. Everyone gets outraged when someone victimizes someone innocent, like an angry stepfather abusing his terrified stepdaughter. No matter which bumper stickers we have on our cars, where we live, or how we were raised, all human morality is driven by the same concern: harm.

THE MASTER KEY TO MORALITY

Questions of morality can be complex. For thousands of years, philosophers from Aristotle to Rawls have been arguing about the right way to act and the best way to structure society, with no clear winner in sight. Likewise, there are no easy answers when it comes to which policies are best for our cities, states, and countries. Every political choice involves complex trade-offs, whose consequences are often revealed only decades later.

Although objective questions of morality are complex, here we explore a different area—our moral psychology. We put aside questions of how we *should* make moral judgments to examine how people *do* make moral judgments. This book is *descriptive* and not *normative*, exploring how our minds make sense of morality. Of course, these two ideas of "do" and "should" can intertwine, but here we focus on the scientific question of how our moral minds work. How do people decide whether something is immoral?

When we look at our moral psychology, the picture is surprisingly simple. Deep down, we all have the same moral cognition. We all have a harm-based moral mind. Harm is the master key that unlocks understanding across the messiness of human moral judgment.

Experiments consistently reveal that our moral judgments are driven by our perceptions of harm. We condemn acts based on how much they seem to victimize someone vulnerable.[6] Acts that seem completely harmless, like walking on the beach, are judged as morally permissible. Acts that seem moderately harmful, like embezzling from a big company, are judged moderately immoral. And acts that seem very harmful, like intentionally maiming a child, seem extremely immoral. Importantly, even acts that philosophers might call harmless—from breaking promises to the dead to participating in bizarre sex acts—are judged wrong based on how much they give us the feeling that someone is being victimized.

A moral master key of harm means that if you want to know how much someone morally condemns an act, ask them how much they view it as harmful. But unlike a physical key that everyone can see, harm is a matter of perception, and this perception may not always reflect reality. Of course, some acts (like murder) seem more obviously harmful than others (like double-parking), but reasonable people often disagree about the harmfulness of an act, like whether using drugs is a harmless personal choice or something that destroys societies.

Our perceptions of harm are grounded in how we were raised and our assumptions about how the world works, and these differing assumptions give rise to differing moral judgments. If you were raised in a culture that believes in witchcraft, like rural Uganda, then you might see harm—and therefore immorality—in performing a magic ritual intended to make a neighbor sick. The Aztecs believed that their god Huitzilopochtli required human blood to wage war against the darkness every night, allowing the sun to rise again in the morning. When the conquistadors arrived, they were horrified at these ritual sacrifices, but the Aztecs believed that they were necessary to prevent the far greater harm caused by an extinguished sun.

People today all condemn ritualistic human sacrifice, but progressives and conservatives have different perceptions of harm, and this explains many moral divides. With immigration, progressives focus on the suffering of innocent children fleeing war, while conservatives highlight victims murdered by drug smugglers. With abortion, progressives see the harm suffered by women lacking access to medical care, while conservatives see the harm suffered by fetuses.

The idea that harm is a kind of moral master key goes beyond understanding political division; it helps us make sense of all moral disagreements. The driver of that Mercedes-Benz and I were not political opponents, as far as I know. As young guys from the same Canadian city, we likely agreed on most political issues, but that night we were bitterly divided by morality, each of us convinced that we were the righteous victims of harm.

Recognizing the power of harm in morality helps us understand moral disagreements and those we disagree with. When confronted with someone with different views, ask yourself, "What harm are they seeing?"

In the upcoming chapters, we will see how conflicting perceptions of harm underlie modern clashes about morality and politics. We will also see how our worries about harm are as old as humanity—even older in fact. Our ancient hominid ancestors lived their short lives terrified of harm, of being eaten by predators or being beaten by other hominids. Even as *Homo sapiens* emerged, we remained easy pickings for hungry tigers and jealous neighbors, cementing our preoccupation with threats.

Today we are safe from being eaten, and safer from being beaten, but we still cannot shake our feelings of fear, like when we scroll through social media. Rather than worrying about obvious physical harm from predators, we fret over more subjective harms like the threat of political rivals gaining power or the wrong court decisions. The ambiguity over what is truly harmful to modern humans in our modern world creates ample space for disagreement and outrage. Take guns, for example. Some believe that handguns obviously hurt families, and others believe that handguns obviously protect families, and these different perceptions drive political division.

The argument of this book is simple: *We have a harm-based moral mind. Our evolutionary past makes us worry about harm, but people today disagree about which threats are most important or most real, creating moral outrage and political disagreement.* All people have the same human nature grounded in worries about ancient threats, and all people are concerned about the looming harm of modern threats. But while someone on the left might emphasize the threats of growing inequality between rich and poor, systemic racism, and the destruc-

**Our evolutionary past makes us all worry about harm,
but today we disagree about which threats are most real,
creating moral outrage and political disagreement.**

Figure I.1: We have a harm-based moral mind.

tion of the environment, someone on the right might emphasize the threats of banning firearms, restricting religious freedoms, and destroying sacred national symbols.

The key point is that perceptions of harm on both sides are *sincere*, even if they don't immediately make sense to you. It is tempting to dismiss someone's feelings of threat as misguided or exaggerated, but studies show that our moral convictions are underlain by genuinely perceived harms. Once you empathize with people's perceptions of harm—often by learning about their experiences of suffering—you can better understand people on the other side.

A BOOK TO BETTER UNDERSTAND OURSELVES AND OUR DIFFERENCES

In the coming pages, we will dive into our harm-based minds, exploring why harm is important in morality, how exactly perceptions of harm shape our modern moral world, and how to use the idea of harm to better bridge divides. Our discussions will be grounded in science, especially moral psychology and anthropology, but I'll take care to illustrate key points by using personal anecdotes because—as we'll see—stories can resonate more than raw statistics. By the end of this book, you will better understand your own moral mind and be better able to navigate moral differences.

I have seen firsthand how learning about the power of harm in our moral minds can foster "moral understanding," even in situations where understanding is rare. I have taught college students to have more meaningful conversations with their friends and family about contentious issues. I have taught faith leaders to turn down the dial on political conflict in their congregations as they navigate fights over affirmative action, pandemics, immigration, gender, and sexuality. Learning about the science and practice of our harm-based morality will help you become less outraged when people make different moral judgments.

This book covers three big ideas. First, we explore *why* harm drives our moral minds. We will delve deep into our evolutionary past, where potential harm was everywhere. Even though many modern humans live in safety, we are hardwired to perceive threats. Millions of years of being hunted have made us preoccupied with danger, but without saber-toothed cats to fear, we fret about elections, arguments in group texts, and decisions at PTA meetings.

Second, we will explore *how* harm fuels morality. We will see how harm underlies moral judgments about different kinds of acts, and how it drives disagreements between liberals and conservatives. Appreciating the power of harm in morality explains many quirks in human behavior, like why it's rare to think of victims as evil, or of villains as suffering. We will also examine why harms to ourselves seem more obvious than harms to other people, and why social media fuels the competition for victimhood.

Third, we will explore the *practical takeaways* of our harm-based mind—what can we do to better manage moral conflict? We will see how sharing stories about experiences of suffering can make people more willing to interact across moral divides and how affirming people's feelings of threat can reduce the temperature of moral outrage and bring people closer together.

The three parts of this book—"Human Nature," "Our Moral

Mind," and "Bridging Moral Divides"—focus on harms of the past, the harms we see in the present, and how the idea of harm can provide a better future. Each of these three sections is preceded by a myth, a popular but mistaken idea that prevents us from appreciating our harm-based moral minds. The next few pages provide a bird's-eye overview of these sections and the chapters within each.

PART 1: HUMAN NATURE

MYTH I: THE MYTH OF HUMAN NATURE: WE EVOLVED AS APEX PREDATORS

Many assume that humans—and our ancestors—are apex predators, aggressive primates who are more likely to kill than be killed. Modern humans are undoubtedly the masters of the natural world and the top of the food chain. But for most of history, as our minds were slowly evolving into what they are now, we were less predators and more prey. Chapter 2 explores how our ancestors were not the bloodthirsty "killer apes" that many believe them to be, but instead frightened creatures worried about being killed and eaten. These ancestral concerns about victimization shape our modern lives.

To protect themselves from predation, our ancestors banded together into groups and developed our trademark adaptation: big brains suited to social environments. But, as chapter 3 shows, living in groups posed a significant problem: we could be harmed by other people. To reduce the threat of this aggression, humankind developed a sense of morality and feelings of moral outrage. This moral sense allowed us to cooperate, paving the way for modern society, and allowed us to moralize many different values; but at its core our moral minds are grounded in avoiding harm.

Today society is safer than ever—in part because of our moral concern—but we remain vigilant for danger. Chapter 4 reveals that this increasing safety, when paired with our innate drive to detect harms, shifts the goalposts for what counts as "harmful." What once seemed innocuous decades ago, like rough-and-tumble games, can now seem traumatic.[7] This "creep" of harm is why we seem to coddle today's children, but it also drives moral progress as we continue to press for more protections. But even if modern society is safer than ever, one modern invention—social media—supercharges our perceptions of danger, helping to fuel online moral panics.

PART 2: OUR MORAL MIND

MYTH 2: THE MYTH OF THE MORAL MIND: THERE ARE HARMLESS WRONGS

One popular theory from moral psychology separates concerns about harm from other moral concerns, arguing for the existence of "harmless wrongs"—acts that people condemn despite seeming to harm no one, like breaking promises to the dead. Harmless wrongs seem to argue against a harm-based moral mind, but we will see how the idea of harmless wrongs is a myth. Chapter 5 charts the arc of the field of moral psychology and our changing understanding of the moral mind, first beginning with how children make sense of right and wrong, before examining how one sect of Brahmin Indians challenged Western-centric notions of morality. We then see how moral psychology mistakenly leaped from the idea of moral diversity across cultures—which is obviously true—to the idea that our moral minds are divided into separate little rooms.

Chapter 6 explains a new harm-based theory of moral judgment, grounded in a new understanding of harm. While past theories considered harm a matter of reasoning, it is better understood as an intuitive perception, something that we just feel in our gut. Studies show that feelings of harm are the master key of morality: all people judge acts as wrong based on how harmful they feel, explaining how even so-called harmless wrongs can be condemned based on harm. This finding provides a new understanding of morality and provides a powerful lingua franca to connect with others across divides.

Even if we all share a harm-based mind, people clearly disagree about morality. Chapter 7 reveals the roots of this disagreement: different people see different things as especially vulnerable to harm. Much of political disagreement between the left and the right can be explained by different perceptions of four clusters of entities: the Powerful, the Environment, the Divine, and the Othered. Zooming out from perceptions of specific groups, liberals tend to divide the world into two camps—the vulnerable oppressed versus the invulnerable oppressors—while conservatives see everyone as similarly susceptible to victimization. These differences in assumptions about vulnerability help explain many moral differences, especially reactions to social justice movements.

Chapter 8 explores how the judgments of everyone—whether you lean liberal or conservative—are lopsided when it comes to assigning blame. We all seek to simplify messy moral situations, seeing one side as 100 percent the righteous victim and the other side as 100 percent the blameworthy villain. Once we label someone the "true" victim, they seem totally innocent, and their victimizer seems cold and callous. This black-and-white distribution of victimhood is called moral typecasting, and it is why victims escape blame and why no one worries about the suffering of villains.

Even if we often disagree on questions of vulnerability and blame, chapter 9 shows that everyone agrees on the most obvious victim: themselves. Because we are best acquainted with our own suffering, our own victimhood seems more obvious than the victimhood of others. Luckily, most people do not walk around feeling like victims all the time, but once people start competing for victimhood, we almost always put ourselves first. Competitive victimhood can entrench and inflame conflicts, both around the world and in our everyday lives.

PART 3: BRIDGING MORAL DIVIDES

MYTH 3: THE MYTH OF BRIDGING DIVIDES: FACTS BEST BRIDGE DIVIDES

Ever since the Enlightenment, facts have reigned supreme. What is true is what is supported by facts. This explains why most people think the best way to bridge divides is to share facts with each other. Sadly, the power of facts to increase respect within moral debates is a myth. Flinging statistics at each other does not foster understanding when it comes to morality, because one person's facts are another person's lies, especially in politics.

Chapter 10 reveals how sharing personal experiences of harm—not facts—helps create common ground. Discussing the feelings of threat that drive your moral judgments makes you seem both more human and more rational, because everyone understands the desire to avoid suffering. Of course, it's not always easy to be vulnerable with someone you're arguing with, and so chapter 11 explores important wisdom about how to encourage opening up in conversations that make us want to shut down.

AN INITIAL STUMBLING BLOCK

These widely held myths about human nature, the moral mind, and bridging moral divides all stand in the way of truly understanding our minds and each other. But there's one more faulty preconception that is especially tenacious today. It's the idea that we shouldn't even attempt to make sense of the other side. When we are locked in a battle of us versus them, merely trying to understand "them" can feel like betrayal. In Chapter 1, we explore this feeling and the culture war that seems to rage around us.

Chapter 1

War: Is Understanding Betrayal?

It feels like we are at war. People on the left and the right battle over abortion, immigration, gender identity, multiculturalism, and race, with culture "warriors" on both sides using metaphors of war to rile up their side. We are each urged by our side to "fight" for the future, to "defend" crucial values, and to "win the battle" for our country.

The influential conservative political commentator Matt Walsh claims that "we are, after all, in a war and lives are at stake. We are in a war against the most deranged ideology ever invented by the human race, plain and simple. We are fighting to eradicate the ideological equivalent of a parasitic infestation."[1] Wajahat Ali, the progressive *New York Times* contributor, argues that American Democrats "must bring brass knuckles to the knife fight, take out the Republicans' knees if they go low, and fully engage in the culture war in defense of women, people of color, the poor, and other marginalized communities being steamrolled by the GOP hate machine."[2]

Comparing politics to war motivates people to donate to campaigns, but it is terrible for democracy, because democracy requires us to cooperate and compromise for the good of the country. In a war, we feel licensed to hate the other side, to attack them. Likening politics to war also hurts our mental health because we feel constantly worried about the next attack from the other side. This book tries to transcend the idea of the culture war and provide a more nuanced understanding of the other side's psychology. This sense of "moral understanding" can help us see the other side as decent people, which can defuse our collective hatred.[3]

But the problem with seeking understanding is that in a war, trying to understand the other side can seem like betrayal. When two sides are locked in an us-versus-them battle for survival, even the smallest amount of empathy can seem like treachery. When I mentioned to people—both progressives and conservatives—that I was writing a book on moral understanding, some bristled. They wondered why they should understand a group who seemed to hate them, who were trying to destroy their way of life.

The good news is that even in the heat of a real war people can rise above their differences. World War I witnessed 5.7 million deaths for the Allies and 4 million deaths for the Central powers, as well as the first widespread use of machine guns and poison gas. But during the Christmas season of 1914, following the pope's suggestion, soldiers stopped trying to kill each other and came together as fellow human beings for a "Christmas truce." Some German and English soldiers began exchanging seasonal greetings, songs, and even some gifts. When Christmas Day finally arrived, many soldiers climbed out of their trenches into no-man's-land, where they sang carols together and even played a game of soccer. Henry Williamson, a nineteen-year-old private in the London Rifle Brigade, wrote to his mother about the momentary cease-fire on Boxing Day:

> Dear Mother, I am writing from the trenches. . . . In my
> mouth is a pipe presented by the Princess Mary. In the
> pipe is tobacco. Of course, you say. But wait. In the pipe is
> German tobacco. Haha, you say, from a prisoner or found
> in a captured trench. Oh dear, no! From a German soldier.
> Yes, a live German soldier from his own trench. Yesterday
> the British & Germans met & shook hands in the Ground
> between the trenches, & exchanged souvenirs, & shook
> hands. Yes, all day Xmas day, & as I write. Marvelous,
> isn't it?[4]

Many were horrified at this goodwill. A young German soldier named Adolf Hitler scolded his fellow soldiers during the truce, "Such a thing should not happen in wartime. Have you no German sense of honor left?" and the British general Sir Horace Smith-Dorrien wrote in a confidential memo that "this is only illustrative of the apathetic state we are gradually sinking into."[5]

Hitler and Smith-Dorrien need not have worried, because the soldiers were soon back to killing each other. But this brief truce holds an important lesson for us today: even during war, we can take some space and time to recognize the humanity of other people. Connecting with the other side can prevent us from demonizing the other side, even when conflict is inevitable. Of course, not all of us can play soccer with our opponents, but learning more about them can reveal how they too are moral creatures, helping us refrain from viciousness even as we stick to our convictions. In this chapter, we start on this road to moral understanding, exploring the rise of hate in politics, and also how we widely overestimate this hate.

THE RISE OF HATE

Political animosity has been rising in many countries, especially in the United States, which I focus on here as a well-studied example. For decades, social scientists have been tracking cross-partisan feelings with an instrument called a feeling thermometer. Zero on the feeling thermometer represents feeling freezing cold toward the other side, and 100 represents feeling very warm and welcoming.

When the American National Election Survey used the feeling thermometer in 1978, the average rating of the other party hovered around 50, and even not that long ago, in the year 2000, Americans reported low 40s—feeling ambivalent. But today, Americans feel downright chilly about the other side, with an average score of about 20.[6]

One reason for this ill will is that we see the other side as less intelligent than our own side. Research from my lab finds that liberals and conservatives see each other as about half as smart as members of their own party.[7] People believe their own side votes for the best candidate based on rational deliberation but see the other side as mindlessly following the flock. Liberal media often portrays conservatives as easily tricked rednecks who vote against their self-interest, while conservative media paints liberals as foolish, out-of-touch urbanites who vote for policies that don't work in the real world.

My lab documented perceptions of unintelligence in our own back-yard using the 2018 midterm election as a backdrop. In North Caro-lina, six amendments to the state constitution were on the ballot. As amendments go, they weren't super controversial, revolving around protections for victims of crime, the size of ethics boards, judicial appointments, and state income taxes. Conservatives tended to be in favor of these amendments, while liberals generally opposed them, but we wondered if political labels had become so toxic that people would think those who disagreed with them about the amendments were idiots.

In a survey study, we told hundreds of North Carolina Demo-crats and Republicans how each party voted on the amendments.[8] Then they rated the extent to which members of the other party "were not smart," "were not thinking clearly," and "can't be reasoned with," from 1 (almost no one) to 7 (almost everyone). After learning about how the other side voted, Democrats and Republicans believed that people in the other party were about 2 points less intelligent (around 4 points out of 7) than their own party (around 2 points out of 7). In other words, voters on each side thought that the other side voted the "wrong" way because they were too muddled to make good decisions and too irrational to recognize what was best for themselves and the state.

We tend to think of our political opponents as stupid, but there is no consistent evidence of an association between political ideology and cognitive ability. Liberals and conservatives generally score pretty similarly on the SAT and ACT[9] and have similar college GPAs.[10] One study does argue that people with socially progressive and fiscally con-servative positions are higher in cognitive ability, but a closer look raises doubts about this conclusion.[11]

In this study, interviewers asked people about their political beliefs and then measured cognitive ability by assessing their vocabulary and by reflecting on how smart the participant seemed—did they *sound* intelligent during the interview? More socially progressive and fiscally conservative folks had larger vocabularies and were rated as sounding smarter, but only by a very small margin (just 4 percent). Importantly, impressing an interviewer with big words does not fully capture someone's intelligence. Liberals and conservatives perform similarly on comprehensive IQ tests and problem-solving tasks, whether they involve matching words to their meaning or solving statistical problems.[12]

There is, however, one robust association between intelligence and politics: we all get dumber when we think about politics because of a psychological process called motivated reasoning. Most of us are motivated to find support for our beliefs, which undermines our ability to accurately evaluate evidence and draw correct conclusions from data. One study suggests that Democrats and Republicans become worse at math when working through a problem when the answer contradicts their political views.[13]

In the study, participants were given a word problem that the researchers invented but that participants believed contained real statistics. They were told that a "city government was trying to pass a law banning private citizens from carrying concealed handguns in public," and that government officials were "unsure whether the law will be more likely to decrease crime by reducing the number of people carrying weapons or increase crime by making it harder for law-abiding citizens to defend themselves from violent criminals." Participants then had to work out which conclusion was supported—whether banning guns increased or decreased crime—based on the following data: Among cities that *did* ban concealed handguns in public, 223 saw crime increase and 75 saw crime decrease. In cities that did *not* ban concealed handguns in public, 107 saw crime increase and 21 saw crime decrease.

Determining the impact of the policy requires calculating some percentages. In this case, 25 percent of cities that banned handguns saw crime decrease (75/298), whereas only 16 percent of cities that continued to allow handguns saw crime decrease (21/128). Because crime decreased at higher rates in cities that banned handguns, this scenario supports the conclusion that banning guns was effective at reducing crime. Critically, some participants saw a version with the labels reversed so that the correct interpretation of the data was that banning handguns *increased* crime.

Whether you are pro–gun control or pro–gun rights is irrelevant to arriving at the correct answer. But the researchers discovered that political views, not mathematical ability, were the best predictor of who got the correct answer. Democrats were roughly 35 percent more likely than Republicans to answer correctly when the scenario showed that banning guns decreased crime. Conversely, Republicans were roughly 35 percent more likely than Democrats to answer correctly when the scenario showed that banning guns increased crime. In other words, members of each party were great statisticians when the answer supported their politics, but suddenly got worse when the correct interpretation of the data challenged their preexisting views—even though the math involved was the same.

Just as we are motivated to find evidence to support our views, we are motivated to view the other side as stupid. If they disagree with us, they must not really understand what is best for the world, right? But sometimes we believe that the other side *does* understand the best path, but willfully chooses the wrong option, opting for evil instead of goodness. It's easy to see how someone who takes a different position on a hot-button issue like abortion or immigration might seem immoral, but our research finds that these perceptions of malevolence

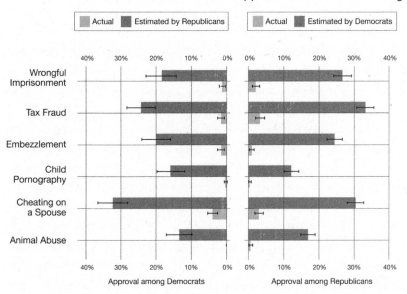

Figure 1.1: People believe that the other side sees obvious wrongs like child pornography, animal abuse, and embezzlement as much more acceptable than they really do.

go beyond these specific issues. People often think that the other side lacks a basic sense of right and wrong.

In one set of studies, we asked Democrats and Republicans whether they approve of acts widely viewed as wrong, like child pornography, animal abuse, and cheating on a spouse.[14] We then asked them to estimate what percentage of their political opponents approve of the same acts. The results were striking: people on both sides drastically overestimated the extent to which their opponents approve of blatant wrongs. For example, people thought that around 10–15 percent of those on the other side viewed child pornography as acceptable, even though almost everyone views it as immoral.

One alternative explanation of this finding is that people might have been using their responses simply to bad-mouth the other side. For example, sports fans are happy to say terrible and sensational things about players on rival teams without actually believing that they are evil. When I lived in Boston during grad school, I marveled at the cruelty of the Red Sox fans toward their New York City rivals. The first Sox game I went to was at home against the Seattle Mariners—no Yankees involved—so I was surprised to see someone wearing a shirt insulting Alex Rodriguez (A-Rod), who at the time was the Yankees third baseman. More surprising was that the shirt read, "A-Rod has AIDS," despite—to my knowledge—Rodriguez not having any sexually transmitted diseases at the time. Perhaps this Sox fan had some insider information about A-Rod, but I suspect he was just happy to slander him.

When political partisans claim that the other side approves of child pornography, maybe they are just slandering them. To address this concern, we ran another version of the study where we paid people to be accurate in their estimates: participants would get extra money if they correctly guessed the percentage of people on the other side who approved of these obviously evil acts. When we looked at the data from this version of the study, the results were identical. People legitimately believed that a sizable number of those on the other side were okay with adultery and child pornography.

If the other side is morally bankrupt, it is easy to spin a dark narrative for why they vote against you on policies and politics. Rather than human beings trying to do their best, people on the other side seem like comic book villains who inexplicably want to cause maximum harm. I call this story about the other side the *destruction narrative,* because we believe that they want to destroy the world.

Everyday people tend to see the actions of the other side through the destruction narrative. One of my collaborators, Daniela Goya-Tocchetto, asked Democrats and Republicans to consider some controversial government policies on taxation, gun control, environmental protection, and voting rights, passed either by their side or by the other side.[15] Like any policy, these policies had trade-offs, trying to achieve some good but at the cost of some negative consequences. Importantly, these negative effects are usually unintended and often regretted. For example, when Democrats lobby for tighter environmental regulations to protect ecosystems, they regret that blue-collar workers in the fossil-fuel industry will lose their jobs. Likewise, when Republicans support plans to ease environmental regulations, in order to provide more blue-collar jobs in the fossil-fuel industry, they regret the harm caused to the environment.

When people thought about their side's policy preferences, they explicitly argued that the negative trade-offs involved were unintentional: their political leaders didn't want to cause suffering; they were just making the best of a tough situation. But people thought that politicians on the other side *wanted* to cause suffering, that these harmful side effects were not side effects at all, but instead an intentional consequence of their malicious agenda. Republicans said that Democrats wanted to help the environment and also intended to destroy working-class jobs. And Democrats said that Republicans wanted to safeguard jobs and also intended to harm the environment. These perceptions are a perfect demonstration of the destruction narrative: they paint the other side as villains filled with hate who want to sow maximum damage, rather than decent people trying to balance benefits and costs.

The destruction narrative is alluring, but most people are not motivated to destroy. Another study conducted by Daniela Goya-Tocchetto and her team examined whether people cared more about making their own political party look good or making the opposing party look bad. They asked Democrats and Republicans to vote on which of two headlines should appear on the front page of an online news website, one praising the participant's own party and the other criticizing the opposing party.[16] For example, Democrats picked between the headlines "Democrats Making Strides to Fix Congressional Gridlock" or "Republican Offices Account for a Disproportionate Number of Financial Scandals," and Republicans picked between the same headlines with the party names switched. They found that two-thirds of people opted to publish a story that praised their own group, rather than maligning the other side.

Of course, people frequently disparage their opponents, and sometimes try to harm them, but when people lash out, it's usually because they feel threatened or scared. In another version of the headline-choosing study, the researchers first attacked participants' political identity. Before voting for which headline to publish, Democrats saw that an article titled "Democrats Violate Rules at Polling Sites, Studies Show," was getting a ton of upvotes on social media. Republicans saw the same headline but with "Republicans" as the party accused of cheating. The researchers found that when people felt threatened, they became more willing to lash out: the proportion of people deciding to publish the news story attacking the other side went from one-third to one-half.

The idea that people go on the offensive because they feel defensive helps explain the rise in anti-Asian sentiment during the COVID pandemic, when conspiracy theories wrongly blamed Asian people for the spread of the virus. A former member of my lab, Jake Womick, found that a strong predictor of anti-Asian prejudice among right-wing individuals was anxiety and fear about the disease. The more these people worried that COVID would harm them and their loved ones, the more they disliked Asian people.[17]

The destruction narrative is appealing because it reduces the complicated truth of political conflict into a simple black-and-white picture of good versus evil. But these studies show that people are less motivated by destruction than by *protection*. Rather than the destruction narrative, the thoughts and deeds of the other side are better described by the *protection narrative*. People are trying their best to protect themselves, their loved ones, and members of society, which explains why they prefer to help their own side rather than harm the other side and why lashing out is tied to feelings of threat.

The protection narrative is supported by studies with Democrats and Republicans, and with Palestinians and Israelis. Researchers asked people embroiled in these conflicts how much their side (versus the other side) was motivated by "ingroup love" versus "outgroup hate." In every case, people rate their group's behaviors as more driven by compassion and empathy toward their own side than by dislike and animosity toward the other side.[18] But when people rate the motivation of the other side, these perceptions are flipped; *we* just care about protecting our people but *they* hate us and want to harm us.

In political conflicts, the truth is that most people are focused on protecting themselves, even when they act aggressively. But it is hard to recognize that—like us—the opposing side is motivated by the desire for protection more than destruction. When we are locked in an us-versus-them conflict, it is much easier to see our own side as heroic victims and the other side as villains.

The destruction narrative spells trouble for democracy. If you believe that your opponents are trying to destroy democracy, then you might think the only way to save your democracy is to resort to antidemocratic practices yourself,[19] including illegal gerrymandering, restricting free speech, and forcing gridlock to hurt the other party. In one study, Democrats thought that the average Democrat valued democratic norms, like free and fair elections, 77 percent more than the average Republican, and in a mirror image Republicans thought that the average Republican valued the very same elements of democracy 88 percent more than the average Democrat. Importantly, the gap in these perceptions was wrong; both Democrats and Republicans say they highly value these core democratic principles.

Troublingly, once people believe that "the other side doesn't care about democracy," they too suspend the rules of democracy, becoming more likely to endorse statements like "[My party] should redraw districts to maximize their potential to win more seats in federal elections, even if it may be technically illegal." The destruction narrative leads both sides to self-righteously subvert democratic norms even though virtually everyone wants a healthy functioning democracy.

This study found that Republicans who endorsed the destruction narrative about Democrats were especially likely to be indifferent to Republican antidemocratic actions. In his speech on January 6, 2021, before the invasion of the U.S. Capitol, former president Trump connected the destruction narrative to breaking the rules of democracy, saying, "The Republicans have to get tougher. You're not going to have a Republican Party if you don't get tougher. . . . When you catch somebody in a fraud, you're allowed to go by very different rules."

But again, the good news is that the destruction narrative is wrong. Perceptions that people on the other side are dumb or evil are *misperceptions.* Most people stand firmly on the side of good and democracy and are more strongly motivated by protection than by destruction. In truth, most people are not even motivated by politics.

THE EXHAUSTED MAJORITY
AND THE MIRAGE OF HATRED

Given the sheer size of the United States—or any other country—one side or the other cannot be entirely evil. You might be able to imagine a conspiracy featuring a small cabal of left- or right-wing politicians, millionaires, and media elites. But it is harder to imagine an evil cabal of 36 million people (the number of registered U.S. Republicans) or 49 million people (the number of registered U.S. Democrats). It is also impossible that the other side lacks a basic moral compass. Our study found that respondents believed 15 percent of the other side approves of child pornography, but it is certainly false that 5.4 million Republicans or 7.4 million Democrats endorse the sexual exploitation of children. Even convicted murderers are disgusted by child pornography.

The truth is that most people who vote for either party are not trying to destroy the country. They are trying to get by and do right by their families and their country. And the very boring truth is that most people try to ignore politics. Social media might be filled with nonstop ideological firestorms, but in the offline world most people want to avoid the mayhem and the outrage.

A comprehensive report by the nonpartisan organization More in Common argues that 67 percent of Americans belong to the "exhausted majority." These 221 million people do not want to fight about politics or even think about politics. Compared with the remaining 33 percent of Americans who are more politically engaged—and who loudly dominate the conversation—these folks are pragmatic and ideologically uncommitted. This exhausted majority just wants its government to get things done and the economy to help people flourish. One woman interviewed by More in Common, a fifty-four-year-old moderate from New Jersey, sums up the feelings of many of the exhausted majority:

> What would make me excited again is if people would just give somebody a chance. People should realize that we are all Americans. We have to accept what we have been given, and we have to come together rather than divide, whether you are in agreement or not in agreement [with the choice of president or Congress].

The exhausted majority is usually silent when it comes to politics, lacking the inclination for moral outrage. This is hopeful because it means that millions of Americans want more civil discourse in their country. On the other hand, their absence from discussions lets the loudest people seize control of the conversation and creates "pluralistic ignorance," the belief that everyone thinks a certain way, when only the most visible or vocal do.

Pluralistic ignorance makes college students think that everyone on campus drinks excessively at parties, because the students who do are the loudest and most obvious. In a self-fulfilling twist, this illusion can change people's behaviors. First-year students on campus look around and see that "everyone" is drinking and think they should too. Likewise, when Americans see outpourings of outrage in politics, they infer that everyone is polarized and think that they too should hate the other side—not because they actually dislike them, but because it seems as if everyone is doing it.

Once people start down the slope of partisan animosity, the process of reciprocity helps hatred blossom. One of the most powerful drivers of liking and disliking between two people (or groups of people) is when one person thinks the other person likes or dislikes them. We generally reciprocate how someone feels toward us, so if someone compliments our fashion sense and praises our thoughtfulness, we tend to like them and treat them kindly. If someone tells us that our hair looks like a road-killed squirrel and that we have the intellectual depth of a birdbath, we usually dislike them.

The hitch is that while we often accurately guess what people think of us, we can be wrong. When you meet someone for the first time, things can accidentally start off on the wrong foot. You might misinterpret a lighthearted joke as a cruel remark and then become chilly toward them. They then reciprocate this chilliness, and become chilly back to you, and before you know it, you have developed a deepseated dislike of them.[20] All this because of a simple misunderstanding. Conflict also persists because people dislike revising their opinions of someone else; it means admitting that you were wrong, and no one likes being wrong.

Political animosity is especially entrenched because there are famous people telling us that we must hate the other side. The journalist and author Amanda Ripley has a great term for the elites spewing messages of discord and distrust: "conflict entrepreneurs."[21] They are the social media personalities, TV pundits, and politicians who profit from outrage, like the onetime Fox News host Tucker Carlson, whose business model thrived on sowing frustration. A *New York Times* analysis of 1,150 episodes of the former Fox News hit show found that his most prominent narrative was, "They want to control what you do, and then they want to control your children."[22] Liberals have their own conflict entrepreneurs who appear on outlets like MSNBC and Crooked Media and who reflexively frame any political issue not as a debate between competing goods but as a battle between progress (the liberal position) and the worst impulses of humanity (the conservative position).

Two social scientists have charted the rise of the "outrage industry,"[23] and their data show that rising outrage in political discourse is driven mostly by the inflammatory tactics of elites, not the political inclinations of everyday people. These researchers analyzed ten weeks of liberal and conservative political blog posts, cable news programs, and radio talk shows and found high levels of outrage: 98.8 percent of talk radio episodes contained an instance of outrage; 82.8 percent of blog posts had outraged writing; and every single political discussion on TV included outraged rhetoric, averaging one instance every ninety seconds.[24] These media pundits weren't just loudly shouting rational arguments at each other; their outbursts tended to be characterized by uncivil behaviors and logical fallacies, from insulting language to name-calling to slippery slope arguments. Although we cannot see into the minds of the famous people screaming obscenities and yell-ing urgent warnings, elites know that outrage captures people's attention, and they—and their advertisers—really want your attention. Many conflict entrepreneurs have gotten wealthy by popularizing the destruction narrative and repeating that "*they* hate *us.*"

Despite what the conflict entrepreneurs say, we vastly exaggerate how much the other side hates us. It might be human nature to disparage the out-group, to think of the other side as more stupid and evil than they actually are, but people hugely inflate how much *they* disparage *us.* Studies find that people's understanding of how the other side views them—what psychologists call meta-perceptions, or *our* perceptions about *their* perceptions—are overly pessimistic. In one study, both Republicans and Democrats overestimated how much the other side dislikes and dehumanizes them by 50–300 percent.[25] Because of the process of reciprocity, these misperceptions drive us to hate the other side in return, but in reality we are not "returning" their feelings, only acting on faulty assumptions. Thankfully, research finds that correcting these overly negative meta-perceptions decreases partisan animosity.[26] Once you know that *they* don't really hate *us,* you dislike *them* much less.

Not only are we wrong about how the other side feels about us; we're also wrong about *who* the other side is. Democrats estimate that 44 percent of Republicans earn more than $250,000 per year when in reality only 2 percent do, and Republicans estimate that 38 percent of Democrats identify as gay, lesbian, or bisexual when only 6 percent do.[27] While many stereotypes contain kernels of truth, people overestimate how much the other side fits various party stereotypes by a whopping 342 percent. When Democrats think of Republicans, they picture rich old evangelical southerners, and when Republicans picture Democrats, they imagine gay Black atheist union members.

When we caricature the other side in this way, it's easy to also overestimate the extremity of their political beliefs. In a report by More in Common, Democrats estimated that only 50 percent of Republicans think racism still exists in America, when polling data suggest that at least 75 percent do. On the flip side, Republicans estimated that half of Democrats think that "most police are bad people," but when researchers actually asked Democrats for their opinions, more than 80 percent disagreed with that statement. Of course, genuine political disagreement exists, but people on the left and right are more similar than we think.

Even when people do hold different political views from you, a key point of this book is that they endorse these positions not because they thirst for conflict but because they are trying to safeguard themselves, their families, and the country. The many people who belong to the "exhausted majority" loathe divisive debates, and when they reluctantly feel outrage, it is driven by the desire for protection, not destruction.

The upcoming chapters sketch out the evidence for this protection narrative, including how human nature revolves around threat, how morality is grounded in perceptions of harm, and how we often feel like victims. By exploring the power of harm in our nature, our minds, and our lives, I hope to paint a more promising picture of political division—one in which we can better talk to people who disagree with us.

I am deeply committed to redeeming our perceptions of the "other side" and helping us connect across divides. It's why I have published dozens of papers on understanding and overcoming political animosity, and why I teach the science of moral understanding to college students, community leaders, and nonprofit practitioners. There are two reasons for my commitment to bridging divides: One is my personal experience with my family, which we'll get to soon. The second has to do with what I see as the greatest threat to modern democracy—anti-pluralism.

WHY WE NEED THE "OTHER SIDE"

Modern democracies are founded on political pluralism, the coexistence of different ideas and ideologies within society. It only makes sense to vote and run for office if there are legitimately different political ideas and policies. Today, we bemoan our "political differences," but democracies function best when disagreeing ideas coexist and different groups compromise.

It surprised me to learn that once upon a time America did not have enough political differences. In the 1950s, the American Political Science Association's Committee on Political Parties famously complained about the lack of ideological polarization. It argued that a well-functioning democracy requires that its citizens distinguish between the positions of each party.[28] Appreciating the political differences between liberals and conservatives is important in society, because it helps to balance tradition with progress. As John Stuart Mill argued in *On Liberty,* "A party of order or stability, and a party of progress or reform, are both necessary elements of a healthy state of political life."

People today are less excited than Mill about political pluralism, believing that the country would be better off without the other side. According to data from two national surveys, 15 percent of self-identifying Republicans (7.9 million people) and 20 percent of self-identifying Democrats (12.6 million people) think the country would be better if members of the opposing party "just died."[29] But these opinions are grounded in misperceptions: people wrongly believe that the other side is anti-pluralistic and think—in an imagined race to the bottom—they need to oppose pluralism too.

As we covered above, both Democrats and Republicans support core democratic elements like free and fair elections, but dramatically underestimate how much the other side supports them.[30] Misperceiving that the other side is motivated by destruction leads people to bend the rules, because, as they see it, desperate times call for desperate measures. When Democrats or Republicans gerrymander districts into bizarre shapes, it is not because they want to watch the world burn but because they are trying to save their state and their country from the evil policies of the other side.

Even if people's anti-pluralism is motivated by a desire to protect themselves, it is still a threat to our nation. But the good news is that most of us today—along with the Founding Fathers—agree that America is a better place when people can freely discuss competing ideas about politics and morality. I have seen firsthand the benefits of open discussion in the course I teach at UNC, called the Science of Moral Understanding, where students discuss hot-button issues like abortion, taxes, and racism. Defying the complaints that college students are too fragile to engage in these conversations, my students are hungry to be challenged and are excited to learn about competing perspectives, even if it makes them uncomfortable.

Some people are less excited about pluralism. One frequent objection I hear is the "KKK counterargument." Do we really want an America where people with repugnant ideas—like White supremacists—have a seat at the table? Does pluralism mean we have to support those who are anti-pluralists, who want to deny the free expression of other people? The short answer is no. In a pluralistic society, anti-pluralists—as fellow human beings—should enjoy the same fundamental rights as everyone else, including free speech. But any ideologies that involve stripping others of their basic rights because of their race, beliefs, or anything else should be doubted and opposed. In the quest for a thriving democracy, we should seriously consider only ideas that affirm democracy.

Despite my commitment to free speech, I have a hard time finding patience for KKK members and others with anti-pluralist ideologies, but some people are stauncher pluralists than I. For example, Daryl Davis, an R&B and blues musician and activist, has personally befriended more than two hundred KKK members despite being Black and therefore a target of their hate.

Davis is immensely patient as he kindly but firmly challenges the Klansmen's misconceptions over shared lunches and cups of coffee. One of these faulty ideas is that Black men are genetically violent and therefore innately threatening to themselves and the social order. Davis risks his own safety to meet with these Klansmen and then risks backlash among the Black community to speak on their behalf—revealing how their behavior is described less by the destruction narrative than by the protection narrative. Davis, in his 2017 TED talk, mentions that, like everyone else, these KKK members say they want to promote what they believe is best for all races, but their assumptions about race are both wrong and odious.[31]

Research reveals the benefits of Davis's approach: respectful conversations make people more pluralistic. In 2014, Miami-Dade County in Florida passed a law prohibiting discrimination against transgender people in housing and employment. Anticipating that the law might result in a reactionary increase in anti-transgender prejudice, volunteer canvassers and LGBT organizers, many of whom were transgender themselves, went door-to-door to talk with Miami-Dade voters.[32] The canvassers were trained to listen deeply as voters explained their views, to refrain from condemnation, and to humbly offer their experiences during the ten-minute conversation. They also encouraged voters to engage in perspective taking by imagining a time that they felt judged for being different and connecting that experience to the experience of transgender people.

The outcomes of these conversations were encouraging, because they increased support for the nondiscrimination law. They also decreased transphobia as measured by the "feeling thermometer" we introduced earlier, a 0–100 scale of how warm people feel toward (in this case) transgender people. People who talked with a canvasser felt, on average, 10 points warmer than people who didn't. Ten points is a lot—it is 1.5 points greater than Americans' average decrease in homophobia (8.5 points) from 1998 to 2012, a time period lauded for huge strides in increasing acceptance of gay people, when ten states legalized same-sex marriage. When researchers followed up with people three months later, they found that this reduction in transphobia had lasted.

Daryl Davis is convinced of everyone's inner goodness, and this helps to draw out the best versions of the KKK members. Most of us are less excited to talk to extremists, but research finds that we generally all share Davis's conviction that people have a good "true self."[33] Even when people do bad things, we tend to believe that in their heart they still want to do the right thing. This is why we nod along in movies when the villain—despite perpetrating horrible deeds—redeems himself at the end. We believe that almost everyone is good deep down.

I am convinced of the ultimate inner goodness of others not only because of my work as a social psychologist but also because of my first-hand experience with my family of conservative evangelical Christians.

MY NEBRASKAN FAMILY—
DIFFERENT BUT STILL MORAL

When I was five, my dad married my stepmom. She comes from a large conservative and evangelical family in Nebraska.

My Nebraska family and I are very different. I am a scientist who started college as an earth science major, where I learned about how fossils can reveal the ancient age of Earth. In contrast, one of my cousins believes that dinosaur bones were put into Earth as a test of our faith, seeing if science might lead us astray from the biblical truth. On Sundays, we might both listen to church music, but I do it while making French toast for my kids, while they are sitting in pews. On American political issues, I lean more left, like most people born in big Canadian cities, and they lean more right, like most people born in small-town Nebraska.

Although my Nebraska family and I may disagree about politics, I have never applied the destruction narrative to them, because it is obvious that they are good people. They help their community, they support their friends and co-workers, they give to charity and speak up for what seems right. And consistent with the protection narrative, they do their very best to protect their loved ones. I have always felt immensely loved by them, even though I wasn't born into their family, and even though I'm a relative outsider as a stepchild and a foreigner. Usually, these acts of love and protection are obvious to everyone, like making my favorite meal and giving thoughtful gifts, but sometimes they are more particular.

When I was ten, I was in Nebraska, staying with my aunt and uncle—an uncle who later became a pastor. Sunday morning came around and we all went off to church, with the adults attending the service upstairs and us kids heading down to the basement for Sunday school. We sat in a circle on the floor, surrounded by brightly colored walls and posters about how God has the whole world in His hands. The lesson of the day was baptism, and after a brief discussion of John the Baptist and the purpose of baptism, the teacher asked, "What happens to people who aren't baptized?"

I don't know if the Sunday school teacher knew that I wasn't baptized, but I suspect she did. It was a small community, and everyone in my family definitely knew that I had not been. I was the only one in that entire building who had not been baptized, and so the Sunday school teacher's question seemed too convenient. One of the kids stuck up his hand, and the teacher nodded approvingly at his enthusiasm. He shouted out his answer: "They go to hell!" It was hard not to be offended at this kid's confidence that I was destined for eternal damnation. I also felt irritated at my family for what seemed like a setup, a spiritual ambush.

But it didn't take too long for me to see that Sunday school lesson in a warmer light, especially once I learned that my aunt, uncle, and cousins prayed for me daily. It is true that they were trying to make me feel uncomfortable, but not out of cruelty. Instead, their actions were motivated by love. They were authentically worried that my lack of baptism would harm me and wanted to protect me from that harm. Of course, compared with my ten-year-old self, they had different assumptions surrounding harm, believing in the existence of eternal souls, the weight of sin, and the redemptive power of baptism. But the important point is that their actions were driven by genuine perceptions of harm. Throughout this book we will see how the key to morally understanding the other side is appreciating how they make sense of harm.

Not only did my Nebraska family love me when I was a kid, but I've felt loved as an adult, too. They have made sure to invite me to every big family occasion. A big wedding? Invited. A graduation party? Invited. Engagement party? Invited. They have been so generous with invitations that I'm ashamed to admit that I seldom go to these events. Not because I don't want to go, but because there's always some work commitment or other travel booked in advance.

Despite my constantly declining these invitations, they still came to my wedding, held in Cambridge, Massachusetts—sometimes called the People's Republic of Cambridge for its leftist leanings. My Nebraskan family drove days to get there and were nothing but gracious at an event that had lots of alcohol and no mention of Jesus, until the breakfast that they hosted for us. My pastor uncle gave a heartfelt prayer and blessing before we ate. It was a beautiful moment, and I'm glad they came, even if we often don't agree on politics.

Not all family interactions are as lovely as sharing a blessing before a marital meal. I will admit that when politics comes up—especially in online conversations—discussions with my relatives have gotten heated. People say cutting things that hurt feelings. But everyone always moves past these bursts of outrage because we appreciate that each other's true selves are good. They know I don't have evil intentions, and I can say the same about them.

It is not always easy to appreciate that those we disagree with have good true selves, especially if someone has been selfish, mean, or—God forbid—violent toward you. But even that driver who slapped me in that dark parking lot did not wake up that morning filled with hate.

With distance from that night, it is clear to me that his actions were better described by the protection narrative than by the destruction narrative.

One reason why we neglect the protection narrative is that it is easier to assume our political enemies are enemies of *everything*—of truth, justice, and kindness. It simplifies our moral world to split people into all good or all evil, and it is mentally taxing and emotionally uncomfortable to recognize that those who disagree with us might also be good people.

The other reason we fail to appreciate the protection narrative is because of a myth about human nature: the faulty idea that, deep in our hearts, we are killer apes.

In Sum

- A culture war is raging in America, with politicians and "culture warriors" urging their side to fight tooth and nail. This fight is fueled by the false perception of people on the other side as stupid and evil. Both Democrats and Republicans incorrectly think that 10–30 percent of their opponents approve of obvious wrongs like child pornography and animal abuse, when virtually none of them do.
- These misperceptions play into the "destruction narrative": each side believes that the other wants to harm them. The destruction narrative is the natural way to view moral opponents, but telling ourselves this story about the other side creates animosity and undercuts our support for democracy.
- Fortunately, the destruction narrative is wrong. Instead, people's thoughts and behaviors are better captured by the "protection narrative." People are primarily motivated to protect themselves and their loved ones from harm. This book will provide evidence for the protection narrative, starting with evidence from our ancient past.

PART 1

HUMAN NATURE

Harms in the Past

Humans Evolved as Apex Predators

We human beings are unique mammals who "live in nearly every major ecosystem on earth, create vaccines against deadly plagues, explore the ocean's depths, and routinely traverse the globe at 30,000 feet in aluminum tubes while nibbling on roasted almonds."[1] But despite our achievements, we are still animals, and animals are categorized as either predators or prey.

Of course, any animal can technically be both. A pack of hyenas will occasionally hunt down an old, sick, or wounded lion, but we still acknowledge that lions are fundamentally predators. Healthy adult lions are fearsome hunters with large fangs, sharp claws, and the cold patience for calculated murder. On the other hand, field mice are fundamentally prey. Even though mice eat insects, they spend most of their lives fleeing and hiding from the many creatures who like to eat them, including owls, foxes, cats, and big lizards. Mice spend most of their time out of sight, while lions laze out in the open.

Humans are neither lions nor mice, but are we mostly predators or prey? Knowing where we are on the food chain is essential to understanding our modern moral minds and political conflict. It is easy to think that we have transcended our animal nature because we wear performance fabrics and prompt artificial intelligence to help with our "knowledge work," but all our thoughts and feelings arise from a mind that evolved eons ago. One evolutionary psychologist succinctly summarizes this idea: "We have stone-age brains in modern environments."[2]

Our evolved human nature shapes our responses and decisions even today, often in counterproductive ways. One obvious impact of these Stone Age brains is our unhealthy addiction to processed foods. We evolved in environments where fat and sugar were scarce, and so we are programmed to binge on fatty and sweet foods when we can. Now that these foods are ubiquitous, we eat too much of them, explaining why worldwide obesity rates have tripled since 1975.[3] Food companies also use our evolved Stone Age preferences to supercharge their food with chemicals that make us want more, like artificial flavors and MSG. Doritos were never encountered in the wild, but our love of them can be explained by looking to our past.

The foundations of human nature are also essential for understanding moral outrage. Our ancestors never had the chance to yell at each other on social media, but we can learn about modern moral conflict by understanding how they lived and who they were. Morality helped us transcend some of our animal nature, including—as we will see—suppressing our most selfish instincts so that we could live among other people. But morality can also be a tool harnessed to serve our crueler impulses, licensing violence and vengeance, complicating the simplistic idea that our morals make us the saints of the animal kingdom.

Even if the purpose of morality is to regulate our social behavior, nudging us toward kindness, it is important to explore what hominids were like before we developed our modern moral sense. Evolution always builds on top of preexisting mental structures rather than replacing them. If we are going to understand the moral minds of today's *Homo sapiens,* we need to make sense of how we lived in the distant past.

There are many books that explore how ancestral environments shaped human nature, exploring questions about knowledge (how much are we born with it versus acquire it through learning?) or violence (were prehistoric humans peaceful or warlike?), but these investigations often overlook one of the most fundamental questions about human nature—whether we are more predators or prey. One reason for this neglect is that this question seems so "animalistic." When we are thinking about the human mind and its marvelous adaptations, it seems too reductive to wonder about what kind of beast we might be—whether we were more bloodthirsty hunters or dinner for other animals. But the line dividing predator from prey is perhaps the most important one in the animal kingdom, because it reveals such a wealth of information about an animal's anatomy, behaviors, and psychology.

Most important, answering the question of predator versus prey helps us understand why our species developed morality and why we sometimes act cruelly. If we are predators, then morality might have evolved to make sure that the spoils of the hunt were evenly distributed. Predators are confident killers, but—as the argument often goes—humans (like lionesses) need to work together to bring down big game, so morality ensured a peaceful distribution of meat between members of our group after a successful hunt.[4] The morality of predators balances the interests of aggressive individuals who live together in groups to magnify their hunting power.

On the other hand, the morality of a prey species is more defensive, geared toward guarding individuals from the many threats surrounding them. Prey are constantly at risk of being harmed or attacked, and so their morality would be driven by these concerns. A prey-based morality would focus more on preventing people from exploiting our vulnerabilities. The story behind a prey-based morality would be a narrative of protection, and I believe this story is a better fit for our behavior, even though it challenges past wisdom about human nature.

HUMANS AS HUNTERS

Scientists long believed that deep in our hearts humans are predators. Humans have killed and eaten members of almost every other living species, from the tender turtles of the Galápagos Islands during the expeditions of Charles Darwin[5] to the brains of monkeys during banquets of the Qing dynasty.[6] Humans today stalk wild boar with giant knives and shoot bears with sophisticated compound bows. We design elaborate systems to birth, grow, and kill billions of cows, pigs, and chickens. It's no wonder that we label ourselves "apex predators."[7] We stand at the very top of the food pyramid. We hunt any animal we please, and no animal hunts us in return.

Scholars argue that we are apex predators because of the unique abilities of our body and brain. We are good at throwing spears (to kill animals)[8] and endurance running (to exhaust animals),[9] and we have amazing brains that allow us to coordinate and plan with other people (to hunt). It's been argued by the evolutionary anthropologist Richard Wrangham that our ability to provide ourselves with a steady diet of meat—especially cooked meat—provided humans with the caloric surplus needed to grow our trademark big brains.[10]

I was nine years old when my family took me to Head-Smashed-In Buffalo Jump, and I too became convinced that humans are predators. This UNESCO World Heritage Site sits on the prairies of western Canada, underneath a huge open sky, not far from where I grew up in Calgary, Alberta. The buffalo jump is a large cliff in the middle of an otherwise unbroken expanse of plains.

Six thousand years ago, the indigenous Blackfoot people recognized the potential of this cliff to kill, and it's now considered by one archaeologist "the most productive food-getting enterprise ever devised by human beings."[11] The work for the Blackfoot people began months before the day of the hunt. First, the tribe would burn a large plot of grass at the "gathering basin" above the cliff, so that months later a plot of lush, thick regrowth would entice buffalo to graze close to the ten-meter drop. When an appropriately sized herd was in position, the hunters (some disguised in wolf skins, others disguised in buffalo skins) would shout and run, sending the buffalo into a panicked stampede over the cliff to their death.

As a kid, I stood there in awe of human ingenuity, imagining the sounds of the buffalo slamming against the earth after plummeting thirty-three feet. I pictured the tribe celebrating as they collected their bounty of meat, cooking what they could eat right then and preserving the rest as jerky, which could be carried by hunters as they hunted more animals in an endless cycle.

This creative system of hunting convinced me that we are essentially fearsome predators, but there's one problem with using Head-Smashed-In Buffalo Jump to argue about our human nature: it is too recent in human history. To understand human nature, we need to look at our distant evolutionary past, before we were *Homo sapiens.*

To make sense of our psychological and physical roots, it is obvious that we cannot look at modern humans who can snipe wolves from helicopters. But we also can't look at humans from the recent past, especially from North America, where humans migrated only about thirteen to fifteen thousand years ago. Human history has a much longer shadow, and in this shadowed past we might not always have been hunters.

In *Sapiens,* an expansive account of human history, Yuval Noah Harari argues that to truly understand the roots of human history, we need to look far beyond the last few thousand years.[12] We even need to look beyond the last 300,000 years of the existence of *Homo sapiens,* past all remnants of human civilization, like pottery shards, papyrus, or any other artifacts. To discover how we lived, felt, and thought when humans were first becoming *Homo sapiens,* we need to examine the fossils of our primate ancestors from millions of years ago. A set of these fossils was discovered in the early twentieth century by one anthropologist, who thought they proved that our ancient hominid ancestors were ruthless hunters.

BONES OF KILLER APES

One hot day in the summer of 1924, a shipment of bones arrived on Raymond Dart's driveway in Johannesburg, South Africa. Dart was an anthropologist specializing in hominid fossils; he spent his days carefully examining the bones of our ancient primate ancestors. But right then, he and his wife were busy getting their house ready for a wedding. Not only was Dart hosting the wedding, but he was also the best man, and was in the middle of putting on his fanciest suit when he noticed the crate arrive. It was sent from a limestone mine just outside Taung, a mining town four hundred kilometers west of Johannesburg.

Knowing that Taung was a hotbed of fossil discoveries, Dart was eager to open the box. Mrs. Dart was less enthusiastic, telling her husband, "Now, Raymond, . . . the guests will start arriving shortly and you can't go delving in all that rubble until the wedding's over and everybody has left. I know how important the fossils are to you, but please leave them until tomorrow."[13] He agreed with his wife and continued putting on his suit.

But as soon as Mrs. Dart was out of sight, Dart raced outside and started digging through the dusty crates. The first box was disappointing—just tiny bone fragments, some fossilized turtles, and eggshells. But in the second crate, he found anthropological gold. On top of a rock was an endocranial cast, a mold from the inside of a skull. To the untrained eye, it might have looked like a big monkey skull, but Dart recognized it as a new species of hominid—a human ancestor. The skull's spinal opening was at the bottom (like humans), showing it walked upright with the spine vertical, rather than in the back, which would have meant the creature walked on all fours with its spine horizontal.

Dart called this new species *Australopithecus africanus,* "the southern ape from Africa."[14] He reasoned that it was "an extinct race of apes *intermediate between living anthropoids and man,*" a missing link in the chain between human beings and other primates. He identified this set of bones as juvenile—a child—because of its small teeth and shallow face, and because it was found close to Taung, South Africa, Dart nicknamed it the "Taung child."

The Taung child shook the world of anthropology by providing proof of a human ancestor in Africa that walked upright, like modern humans. Most anthropologists at the time were European, who believed that humankind had emerged in Europe, both because of previous anthropological finds—like "Piltdown Man," the British hominid skeleton that turned out to be a fraud—and because of the self-serving assumption that Europe just had to be the birthplace of humanity. How could White Europeans claim to belong to "the master race" if the original cradle of mankind was Africa?

There was something else shocking about the bones of the Taung child, which were discovered in a pit along with the skeletons of other animals, including baboons. Dart noticed that all the bones were marked with a pattern of grooves that could come only from being scraped with something hard. He deduced that all the creatures in that pit—both hominids and baboons—had flesh scraped off their bones by tools. These tools for butchery could only have been designed and handled by other hominids,[15] which meant that ancient *Australopithecus africanus* killed and butchered both other animals *and their own kind.*

Based on this logic, Dart concluded that our ancestors were killers and cannibals. He imagined the uncle of the Taung child sitting in a cave, butchering his nephew and then eating his flesh before tossing the bones into a pit of garbage, along with the bones of other devoured animals. In his scientific writings, Dart suggested that the Taung child represented the "predatory transition" from fruit-eating monkeys to "killer apes." This discovery fit well with centuries of thought about human nature. We had always known that "nature [was] red in tooth and claw,"[16] and now we had proof that early humans embraced violence.

The idea of humankind as cruel predators animates stories of human ruthlessness from *Lord of the Flies* to *Heart of Darkness*. The evidence of the Taung child also seemed to square with early psychology. Sigmund Freud believed that the human psyche was fueled by the id, a primitive animalistic mind fixated on sex and aggression. In *Civilization and Its Discontents*, Freud wrote that "men are not gentle, friendly creatures wishing for love, who simply defend themselves if they are attacked, but . . . a powerful measure of desire for aggression had to be reckoned as part of their instinctual endowment."[17]

If Dart and Freud had been asked to choose whether human beings were better described by the destruction narrative or the protection narrative, their answers would be obvious. Both believed that we were natural-born predators, driven by destruction. If humans are killer apes, it offers a clear explanation for our constant warring, our conflicts over morality, and our penchant for political violence. A species motivated by domination and destruction should often be at each other's throats. When we shout over politics at the dinner table, it is a wonder that we only shout, when we could be trying to cannibalize each other.

But the idea of humankind as "killer apes" is wrong. There is no doubt that today's modern humans are apex predators, and that our hominid ancestors were capable of brutal violence and calculated aggression.[18] However, our hominid ancestors were *not* apex predators. Dart made a mistake when interpreting those bones. Ancient hominid life did involve substantial harm, but our ancestors weren't the ones doing the harm; they were the ones being harmed. A growing body of scientific work shows that our minds and bodies evolved to help us escape threats, not be the threat. We were less hunters and more *hunted*.

In the full spectrum of the animal kingdom, species range from obvious predators like tigers and obvious prey like deer. We flatter ourselves by seeing humans like tigers, but the truth is that our species is more like deer. Millions of years of evolution built us to detect danger, to run, and to flee. We are constantly vigilant to the threat of harm, and this concern about harm structured our mind and our morals.

In Sum

- The myth of human nature is that we are—deep down—more predator than prey.
- The assumption that we are "killer apes" was solidified by Raymond Dart's discovery of the Taung child, who was apparently butchered by another *Australopithecus africanus*.

Chapter 2

Prey: The New Human Nature

Most modern humans walk around feeling like apex predators. Even if you haven't heard of Raymond Dart, the Taung child, or "killer apes," our everyday experience shows that we are the monarchs of the animal kingdom. We can easily prey upon other animals and never worry about getting eaten.

If there are any animals around you, you either have dominion over them—your pet cat or dog—or they are small enough, like squirrels, that you could easily kill them with a snare or a slingshot. When you take a walk in the woods, everything seems to flee as you approach, whether it is deer, birds, or foxes. When talking to kids about animals, we say "they're more scared of you than you are of them," even when discussing snakes, bears, and pumas. We assume that other animals must have some reason to fear us.

This assumption shapes how we view both woodland creatures and other people, especially moral opponents. Predators are typically on the offensive, roaming confidently, easily using violence. If humans are predators, then in modern life, when someone roars their moral outrage at us, it is because they are aggressive and trying to be threatening. Humans as predators means that groups of people on the other side—whether they are posting on social media or voting for rival candidates—are like prides of lions or packs of wolves, intent on stalking and hunting us.

But if humans are less predators and more prey, it gives a very different explanation for their behavior. A prey animal is typically on the defensive, often afraid, and always vigilant for danger. If humans are prey, then modern moral outrage is just people trying to protect themselves from threats.

Centuries of philosophy and theology reinforce the idea that humans are apex predators, depicting humans at the top of the great chain of earthly beings. Genesis states, "And God blessed them, and God said unto them, Be fruitful, and multiply, and replenish the earth, and *subdue it:* and *have dominion* over the fish of the sea, and over the fowl of the air, and over every living thing that moveth upon the earth." This quotation—especially the part I emphasized with italics—argues that creatures of the earth are under our control; we can hunt them, use them to plow our fields, and snuggle with them in our beds.

Many prominent nineteenth-century scientists might have disagreed with a literal reading of Genesis, but they almost certainly shared the intuition that humans had dominion over beasts. Scientists like Charles Darwin and Alfred Russel Wallace, who both independently developed theories of evolution by natural selection ("survival of the fittest"), were wealthy landowners or the good friends of wealthy landowners. They could spend an afternoon hunting pheasants and foxes from horseback, letting servants and dogs flush out frightened game, which they shot from the comfort of their tweed suits.

As the scientific evidence of evolution accrued, scholars continued to write about humans as hunters by virtue of our ancestral heritage. The American writer Robert Ruark eloquently captured this idea when he wrote, "Deep in the guts of most men is buried the involuntary response to the hunter's horn, a prickle of the nape hairs, an acceleration of the pulse, an atavistic memory of his fathers, who killed first with stone, and then with club, and then with spear, and then with bow, and then with gun, and finally with formulae."[1]

The story of ancient humanity was written mostly by scholars sitting safely in strong houses, whose dominion over the natural world was unquestioned. Even today, scientists who study human nature live dozens of miles from the wilderness. One wonders what these scholars and scientists might think about the essence of humankind if they were stripped of their safety, their cities, and their weapons, and were left to fend for themselves in unfamiliar wilderness. When I was nineteen—ten years after seeing Head-Smashed-In Buffalo Jump—I found myself stranded in the wilderness, and it changed my perspective on human nature.

STALKED BY LYNX

All five of us were wearing bright-blue flame-resistant Nomex coveralls, but there was little risk of fire standing in the middle of a frozen swamp, knee deep in snow. It was 4:00 p.m. in northern Canada in March, and the sun was already setting. The cold was coming on fast. We huddled around a single walkie-talkie held by Ian, our crew chief. He was tall and confident and had years more experience than the rest of us. He had just turned twenty-four.

"Exploration crew here. Ready for pickup. Over," said Ian. Then, more tentatively, "What's the weather like there?"

We all looked around. The sky up north was almost always clear, such a delicate blue it was easy to believe that only a few miles of atmosphere separated us from space. But today we could see only a dozen blurry feet in front of us. A surprise storm had swooped down, bringing low clouds, fog, and snow. We were waiting for a helicopter to pick us up.

"Chopper pilot here. Getting hit by the storm." That was our pilot, Caleb, who ferried us to and from the exploration site every day. He was radioing from the helipad in Rainbow Lake, Alberta (population about a thousand), twenty-five miles away with nothing but frozen wetlands and scrubby, snow-laden trees between us.

Caleb was not a risk-averse man. He had chosen a life of flying helicopters in the far north, slinging snowmobiles, chain-saw teams, and geophysical exploration crews out to remote locations. His favorite phrase was "eight hours, bottle-to-throttle," which meant he could drink aggressively until midnight every night and still legally fly us to the site every morning. We were normally uncomfortable with his laissez-faire sense of safety, but today we were hoping it would work in our favor, giving him the courage to take off.

"Visibility is really low here." We all held our breath. "Too dense to fly. Going to have to pick you all up tomorrow. Over." Our eyes widened, and the four of us junior crew members all looked at each other, trying to figure out whether this was really happening.

Ian's face was impassive, impressively calm. He blinked hard, twice. "Please repeat. Over."

Caleb preferred to speak in radio staccato even in person, but when he radioed back, he sounded more human than I had ever heard before: "Sorry, guys. I can barely see my hand in front of my face. We're up on a hill here, and right in the middle of the storm. Night is falling soon. Even if I could take off, it would be hard to find you, and impossible to make it back. Hunker down, and I'll come get you as soon as I can see. Over. And good luck."

Ian paused for a moment. "Understood. Over."

Before I was a social psychologist, I thought I wanted to be a geophysicist, exploring the wilderness looking for oil and natural gas. That's why I spent the winter of my sophomore year of college working for a geophysical exploration company and why I was standing in the northern Alberta wilderness with a crew of other college students.

We were all Canadian, and all used to the cold, but we were very far north. We had little food, no water, no shelter, and no plan, and it would soon be dark for the next fifteen hours. Ian pointed to a spot on the edge of a nearby forest and said that it looked like a good spot to set up camp. Grateful for something to do, we all started our snowmobiles and roared off. Once there, we built a lean-to and started a fire with the help of a hefty pour of gasoline.

After the excitement of building camp, we settled in to wait. And wait. After we had exhausted all conversation and our few snacks, we decided to go to bed, all spooning next to each other in the lean-to. Cuddling was still too cold, so we all got up and curled around the fire, falling asleep when the fire was high and warm and waking up again when the flames dwindled.

In the middle of the night, we all woke up feeling uneasy. It was hard to put a finger on what exactly was wrong because everything was so miserable, but it felt as if we were being watched. It was a ridiculous feeling; this was no horror movie forest with a nearby insane asylum.

The next person was twenty-five miles away. But we still felt as if something were menacing, lurking in the darkness just outside our tiny bubble of light. There was nothing to do but fall back asleep and hope our fears were unfounded.

As the dawn broke, our hearts felt lighter. But this happiness was quickly tempered. As we looked around our campsite, we noticed pawprints all around us. They crept from the forest, circled our campfire, and seemed to pause behind us. Ian bent down to inspect them. "Lynx."

I shuddered. I always lived in cities and never even considered the possibility of wildlife threatening us, but in a dark forest it was obvious that we were easy targets for predators. Of course, lynx are small cats who usually hunt hares and squirrels; they pose little threat to five adult men. But there are bigger predators; Alberta also has grizzly bears and wolves.

Caleb eventually picked us up that morning, but not until almost noon, and back in Rainbow Lake we all ate a huge meal. Bacon, ham, and sausage. I devoured meat like a predator. But as I sat in the safety of a cheap hotel, it was hard to shake the feeling of being prey.

Weeks later, I was working on another site up north, where the snow had been falling for weeks. I had to install some gear about a hundred feet into the forest, and there was too much brush for the snowmobile to make it through. I had to get off and walk into the woods alone. Just as I was finishing up with the gear, I heard a noise. I looked around but didn't see anything. Nothing was moving. No birds, no other sounds. The forest seemed to be waiting for something. The rest of my crew was far away; I doubt they could hear me if I screamed. The snow was too deep to run. I felt as if something were waiting for me to turn my back so it could devour me.

Nothing happened, but every time I went out with the crew after that, I found myself wondering about the place of human beings in the food chain. I had been to Head-Smashed-In Buffalo Jump and taken a college course in ecology, and both suggested that humans were at the top of the food chain. But it didn't match my experience. Of course, I felt like a predator when I was in the grocery store, picking out slabs of meat to cook on the grill; but in the wilderness, where humans evolved, it seemed as though we were more prey than predators.

WHY SCIENTISTS ASSUME THAT
ANCIENT HUMANS WERE HUNTERS

Anthropology shows that for the last fifty thousand years, *Homo sapiens* have been more than excellent hunters; we have been super-predators. Between 52,000 and 9,000 BC—a period called the Quaternary megafauna extinction—we hunted more than 178 species of large animals to extinction.[2] Wherever humankind migrated, anthropologists find a flood of extinctions.

While fifty thousand years ago seems like deep history, our brains and bodies were forged over eons. If the span of human history was the ocean, the last fifty thousand years would be the shallows of the beach we can see from shore. The rest of human history—the millions of years that determine who we really are—is the dark water of the rest of the ocean, stretching far beyond the horizon. Because there are no written records from these times, we understand the environment of our prehistoric ancestors through three main sources. One source is the fossil record of hominids, which Raymond Dart consulted. Another source of evidence is examining our closest living primate relatives, like chimpanzees, which primatologists study to draw inferences about our evolution. The final source we can consult to get to the bottom of our human nature is our own bodies and minds. Our anatomical, physiological, and psychological adaptations shed light on our lifestyles millions of years ago, and we examine these adaptations now.

PHYSICAL AND MENTAL ADAPTATIONS

Anthropologists often point to two specific adaptations that seem to demonstrate that ancient humans evolved as predators: our ability to throw things (at prey) and our ability to run long distances (after prey). We will first explore the evidence for why scientists believed that these adaptations made us hunters and then see why newer research raises doubts about these ideas.

The world record for throwing a javelin is 98.48 meters—almost an entire football field. Compared with the throwing ability of other animals, this achievement is amazing, and even if we are small for an apex predator (compared with a lion), we are fearsome when armed with a set of metal-tipped spears. Human beings can also be incredibly accurate at throwing. The best NFL quarterbacks throw footballs at sixty miles an hour and can hit a small target forty yards away, all while running and dodging. It doesn't take much imagination to switch out footballs with spears and wide receivers with antelope and see our predatory potential.

Of course, not many of us can throw with the accuracy and speed of professional athletes, but our species is unarguably better at throwing than any other species.[3] Unlike every other predator, which has to get close to their prey to actually scratch or bite them, we can kill from a distance. Imagine a group of prehistoric humans creeping up on a herd of unsuspecting deer and then unleashing a barrage of spears.

Our ability to throw stems from the most unique of human biological adaptations—standing upright. Other animals walk on all fours, but we walk only on two feet, which keeps our hands free for throwing. Bipedalism also allows us to scan the horizon for potential prey. We can rise above the tall grasses to detect animals we want to attack, getting close enough to throw our spears.

Although this story about standing and throwing for hunting seems intuitive, it doesn't square with the broader picture of hominid evolution. Our earliest human ancestors evolved to stand upright somewhere between four and six million years ago, long before hominids were ruthlessly hunting species to extinction.[4] One of these early bipedal species, *Australopithecus afarensis,* could not even eat meat. Its blunt teeth were too dull to rip apart animal muscle, suggesting that it subsisted mostly on a diet of fruits and nuts.[5]

When bipedal hominids did start hunting, they did so long before footballs and javelins, both of which are deliberately manufactured to be very aerodynamic. Ancient spears were designed with much less precision and therefore were much less accurate, and they also lacked the one feature that would have made them effective: hard tips.

Prey animals often have thick hides, so a prehistoric hunter would need to be outfitted with metal- or stone-tipped spears to efficiently hunt. Some scholars argue that stone-tipped spears were first invented about 500,000 years ago,[6] quite recent given the millions of years of hominid evolution, but even this estimate is misleading. Despite one tribe having stone-tipped spears half a million years ago, they were not ubiquitous until about 100,000 years ago, a very brief time in the scheme of our evolution.

Anthropologists argue that the mere invention of a technology is not enough to influence human evolution; it has to be widespread.[7] Before the advent of social media, books, and structured trade routes, technology spread slowly, in fits and starts. When one tribe discovered a better way of doing something—stitching clothing, making tools, or making spears—the lack of efficient travel or communication meant that there was no systematic way to spread the word. In the archaeological record, inventions commonly popped up and then fizzled out because of the lack of interconnectivity in prehistoric life.

For millions of years of our evolution, our species could throw only sharpened sticks, which were neither very straight nor very heavy. Unless you threw these sticks perfectly, they were very unlikely to kill animals and more likely to anger them, prompting them to charge or attack back. Imagine yourself and a group of friends taking some sharpened sticks and trying to kill a buffalo or an elephant, both of which have hides thick enough to resist the claws of an aggressive lion. Futile at best and, more likely, extremely dangerous.

If throwing does not make us apex predators, then how can we explain our ability to walk upright? One theory is predator avoidance: standing up helps us keep our heads high so we can better scan for threats.[8] Many other prey species, like meerkats, frequently stand on their hind legs to look for threats. Standing up also helps prey animals look bigger, which can scare off predators.[9] Another theory suggests that bipedalism evolved because of the benefits of hands-free walking, which allowed our ancestors to carry food and babies as they walked from place to place, searching for new sources of fruits and nuts, and perhaps even scavenging from the leftover meats of other animals.[10]

Neither standing upright nor throwing seems to make us ruthless hunters, but perhaps we don't need to spear our prey; maybe we just need to run them to exhaustion? Our ability to run long distances has been celebrated as a predatory adaptation. Daniel Lieberman, a paleoanthropologist at Harvard University, argues that our legs are finely tuned for endurance running, with muscles and joints that act like springs and efficiently conserve energy over long distances.[11] Today's ultramarathoners, who compete in races between 26.3 and 200 miles, seem to be living proof that we're "born to run."

Our bodies' internal air-conditioning system also seems uniquely designed to help us run. When any mammal runs, metabolic reactions produce excess heat that the body must expel. Most mammals cool down by panting, but panting is inefficient—water evaporates only from the tongue—and it is hard to sprint and pant at the same time. If you are a dog owner, you might have noticed how your pet needs to sit and pant for a while after running full tilt. The human internal cooling system is better than this; we sweat across our entire body to efficiently lower our temperature even while running.

Predators like cheetahs hunt by outsprinting their prey, but humans are slow sprinters compared with other animals. It is our capacity for long-distance running that is thought to make us hunters. The story goes like this: Humans intimidate a prey animal by standing tall and throwing something. The prey sprints off, expending much energy. Meanwhile, humans pursue the prey at a steady pace, following the tracks of the animal while carrying water with our free arms. Eventually, we catch up to the animal and then spook it again. Our prey sprints off again, using more energy. We follow relentlessly. Eventually, these spells of sprinting overwhelm our prey, and it collapses, exhausted. We kill it with a club, then bring its body back to camp for a feast.

Some evidence advanced for humans evolving as "persistence hunters" is that running can be immensely pleasant. Our nervous system rewards long-distance running with a "runner's high," courtesy of our internal endocannabinoid system—our bodies' own THC, the active ingredient in marijuana. As the neuroscientist and runner Arnold Mandell described in the 1970s, "Colours are bright and beautiful, water sparkles, clouds breathe, and my body, swimming, detaches from the Earth." If we feel good running, we are more likely to practice it and be fit, giving us a better chance at running down prey when the chance arises.

Of course, many people think running feels terrible, and it seems to destroy our bodies—at least how we do it today—but even if you love running, the evidence that early humans evolved as persistence hunters is slim. When researchers scoured through ethnographic accounts of modern hunter-gatherers—ranging from the sixteenth to the twenty-first century—they found that tribes persistence hunt very infrequently,[12] suggesting that this technique could not have shaped human evolution.[13] These societies also all had modern stone-tipped weapons, which our early ancestors lacked. Most anthropologists therefore argue that the modern existence of endurance hunting means little for the evolution of our species.[14]

Even today, persistence hunting is an exhausting and uncertain endeavor. One BBC camera crew followed a set of Kalahari Bushmen who chased down some kudu, a species of antelope, for eight hours until one collapsed in the sand. But the problem with extrapolating from this one case backward into human history is that the conditions in the BBC documentary were ideal—and they have to be ideal for persistence hunting to work. In this example, it was very hot out—104 degrees—with few trees to shade the kudu when it stopped to pant and cool off. The terrain was very soft, so the kudu tracks would be deep and easy to track. In the documentary, you can see that the Kalahari Bushmen were wearing modern running shoes to protect and cushion their feet and had modern steel knives.[15] It also seems that the jeeps of the camera crew were carrying the many and heavy liters of water each man needed to survive a day of desert running.

Our ancient ancestors lacked support crews and evolved in environments that did not support persistence hunting. Two anthropologists at the University of Wisconsin suggest that the 1.5–2.3-million-year-old African environments of our hominid ancestors were not deserts but savanna woodlands, which makes persistence-hunting strategies challenging.[16] First, the soils of savanna woodlands are more compact than the loose sands of arid deserts and tend to be covered by thick grasses, which makes tracking difficult. Second, savanna woodlands have regularly spaced trees, forests, and thick grasslands, providing ample places for prey to rest and hide. And even if our ancestors could run down an antelope, one glaring issue is what to do with a hundred-pound dead animal when you are exhausted and thirsty, miles away from your tribe.

The endurance running hypothesis also neglects the idea that running ourselves ragged in an open field might make *us* more vulnerable to predation. Humans were not the only species out hunting in deserts and savannas. Packs of wild dogs have both excellent stamina and impressive sprinting speeds, and if a human endurance hunter happened to encounter a pack of them after five hours of running in the hot sun, they would be an easy meal.

Throwing and running long distances are two human adaptations that first seem to make us fearsome hunters, but a closer look at these abilities raises doubts. Even if modern humans can use these skills today to hunt animals, they do not obviously qualify our ancestors as apex predators. Simple observations about our bodies also suggest that we are biologically more prey than predators. We lack fangs, we lack claws, we cannot jump high, and we cannot run fast. We're not very strong. Compared with our cousins, like chimpanzees, we are laughably weak. For our size, we are one of the weakest, slowest, and most defenseless species around.

That said, we do have one more advantage that no other species has. We have incredible minds that allow us to coordinate and plan. We can work together with other people to herd animals into bad situations where their innate physical superiority is useless. That's exactly what Stone Age humans did at Head-Smashed-In Buffalo Jump about five thousand years ago.

Although our ability to plan and coordinate helps modern humans hunt, it might not have initially evolved for this reason. Our cleverness could also have evolved primarily to help us avoid the more physically imposing animals that were hunting us, and there was certainly ample evolutionary pressure for ancient hominids to avoid predation. In the 1920s, anthropologists discovered a cave just south of Beijing with the remains of forty-five ancient hominids, all of whom had gaping holes in their skulls. They were eaten by the now-extinct *Pachycrocuta*, a 440-pound hyena.[17]

Giant hyenas were not the only ones making the forests more treacherous. In the book *Man the Hunted*, two anthropologists, Donna Hart and Robert Sussman, provide a laundry list of predatory species that used to eat hominids, from man-eating bear-dog hybrids and saber-toothed tigers to 260-pound eagles with twenty-three-foot wingspans.[18] The environments of our ancestors were rife with hominid-hunting predators, and before stone-tipped spears and accurate arrows to fight off these predators, we relied upon our wits to avoid becoming dinner. Our burgeoning intellectual skills, like the ability to plan and communicate, helped us understand the habits of predators and anticipate their behaviors to stay alive.

Of course, once we developed stone-tipped weapons, we could use our powerful minds to better hunt; but in the scheme of human evolution the latest 100,000 years of being semi-confident hunters cannot overturn the 4 million years where we were frightened prey. It was these 4 million years of being prey that shaped our minds. Psychological traits can evolve rapidly, even within 100,000 years[19]—including abilities that make us better hunters—but there is little impetus for evolution to remove our innate fear of predators. Even in this more modern historical period of humans as hunters, we remained stalked and killed by predators, which makes it useful to stay afraid of them. In other words, there is good reason for much of our prey-based nature to persist even as we evolved into the humans we are today.

CLUES FROM OUR PRIMATE COUSINS

New insights into our primate cousins also support the idea that humans are more prey than predator. For a long time, primatologists saw our closest primate relatives as apex predators, which supported the argument that we too are apex predators. When the legendary Jane Goodall studied chimpanzees in Gombe National Park, she was struck by their excellent hunting skills and their capacity for chimp-on-chimp aggression.[20] These "killer apes" would ruthlessly murder and even dismember other chimps.

Despite this aggression, viewing chimps as more predators than prey is based on a flawed set of data. Most primatologists study chimpanzees in sanctuaries—literally, "a place of refuge or safety"—like Gombe National Park where these creatures are safe from human poachers. These sanctuaries also keep chimps safe from other predators, who shy away from the constant presence of armed guards. When chimpanzees are not constantly protected by humans with guns, a different picture of their lives emerges. They are very likely to get eaten by big cats like leopards and panthers, who wait until night, then creep up trees into the nests of chimpanzees. While the family is sleeping, the leopard will grab a baby in its mouth and run off into the jungle to devour it.

Primatologists in Senegal's Parc National du Niokolo-Koba[21]—not a sanctuary—noted that chimpanzees there behave much differently than Goodall's chimps because of the constant threat of predation from lions, leopards, spotted hyenas, and wild dogs. Compared with the Gombe chimps, the Senegal chimps build nests much higher in the trees and rarely engage in hunting behavior because of the danger posed by leaving the trees to walk on the ground. When chimps do walk through the forest, they try to keep safe from predation by maintaining a constant lookout and staying in large packs, which makes it difficult for them to hunt.

Similarly, Japanese researchers who have studied chimpanzees in the Mahale Mountains in Tanzania suddenly recognized that lions were hunting chimps when they discovered that four out of eleven samples of lion feces they collected contained chimpanzee hair, bones, and teeth.[22] These researchers estimated that 6 percent of the chimpanzee population was murdered by lions during their yearlong research visit.

Chimpanzees are also predators themselves, killing and eating small mammals like monkeys, rodents, and the occasional other chimp, but primates generally seem to be more victims than perpetrators. In their book *Man the Hunted*, we already saw how the anthropologists Hart and Sussman critically evaluated the evidence for ancient humans as hunters. They also explored how much our primate cousins were predators or prey, and they estimate that—across many species of primates—rates of them being preyed upon are much higher than assumed. Some smaller primate species have predation rates as high as 25 percent, and even in larger species it is not uncommon for one in ten animals to get eaten by a predator each year.[23] Perhaps this predation rate does not seem extreme, but it is high: imagine that every year 10 percent of everyone you knew got eaten.

Another reason that primatologists failed to recognize this predation of chimpanzees is that they study them in the daylight. Researchers obviously want to see what they are studying, but the daytime is also when many predators sleep. Leopards and other big cats most often hunt at night, relying on their exceptional night vision and stealth to snatch unsuspecting prey in their sleep.[24]

Primatologists also underestimate how much primates are prey because the simple presence of a group of modern humans and their vehicles makes predators skittish. But if you're willing to hike by yourself, you can find good evidence of primates being eaten.[25] One National Geographic explorer, Michael Fay, went on a two-thousand-mile trek across the African tropics to study gorilla populations and discovered consistent evidence of gorillas being preyed upon, including whole gorilla toes in leopard scat. If gorillas—which are even bigger than chimpanzees and roughly twice the size of early hominids—are vulnerable to predation, then it seems likely that our much smaller and weaker ancestors were subject to predation as well.

The fact that wild primates are consistently preyed upon makes it no wonder that human children (and sometimes their parents) are afraid of sounds that go bump in the night. If our closest—and much stronger—cousins are stolen by leopards from the safety of their beds, then our kids' nighttime fears start making sense.

There is one more piece of evidence we need to explore when making sense of human nature: the fossil record. What did Raymond Dart really discover when he dug through those crates of bones?

THE REAL TAUNG KILLER

Raymond Dart was convinced that the fossil record painted ancestral hominids, and therefore modern humans, as predators. The patterns of grooves on the bones of the Taung child reveal that it was butchered, and Dart reasoned that the butcher was another Taung person. Dart was aware that big cats like leopards often ate ancient hominids, but he believed that the mix of bones in those crates argued against that possibility. He wrote,

> Examination of the bone deposit at Taung shows that it contains the remains of thousands of bone fragments. It is a cavern lair or kitchen-midden heap of a carnivorous mammal. . . . The bones are chiefly those of small animals like baboons, tortoises, rodents, bats, and birds. Eggshells and crab shells have also been found. This fauna is one which is not characteristic of the lair of a leopard, hyena or other large carnivore but is comparable with the cave deposits formed by primitive man.[26]

Not only was this "primitive man" responsible for the deaths of hominids and other beasts, but Dart further deduced that the killer "must have been powerful, and he must have used sticks or stones to have killed baboons, and I think he probably hunted in packs." As evidence, he pointed to the fact that the hominid hunter expertly smashed open skulls to eat the brains waiting inside.

For years, most scientists were convinced by Dart's interpretation, but more recently two paleoanthropologists disagreed. In 1995, decades after Dart's idea of "killer apes" had taken hold, they published an important reanalysis of the Taung child, spurred on by one curious fact—the presence of eggshells. Why would a ruthless killer ape, capable of killing whole animals, bring little eggs back to its lair to smash apart? Another curious fact was that the eggshells were eagle shells, which are hard to acquire in the large quantities found in the nest. Why would primitive killer apes spend their days scouring the landscape for eagle eggs?

These anthropologists came up with a simpler explanation: the eagle eggs came from hatching eagle chicks. Dart had found an eagle's nest, not a hominid cave. Modern humans are too big to be carried off by an eagle, but prehistoric hominids—especially children—were certainly small enough to be picked up by large carnivorous birds.

Modern eagles are a major predator of primates today, and harpy eagles can pick up a twenty-pound animal, even if it is writhing in the grip of their talons. These birds can reach speeds of forty to fifty miles an hour and deliver an impact force of 13,500 foot-pounds on their prey, about triple the muzzle energy of a bullet from a rifle.[27] Ancient eagles were definitely big enough to pick up a hominid child, and a fresh look at the marks and grooves on the bones of the Taung child found markings suggestive of talon damage. What about the opening of the skull and the removal of the brain? Birds of prey eat the insides of the cranium. And when these researchers examined the Taung skull themselves, they found V-shaped nicks consistent with an eagle beak.

Dart built a whole view of human nature based on the idea that the Taung child was killed by another human being. But these modern researchers argue convincingly that the Taung child was a victim not of a cannibalistic human but instead of a hungry bird.[28] Other anthro-

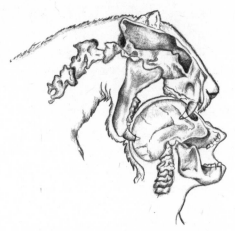

Figure 2.1: Anthropologists have discovered that early
hominids were often preyed upon by big cats. This
artist's rendition reflects the specific pattern of holes
found in the skull of one fossilized *Australopithecus*.

pological work reveals more hominid victims of predation preserved
as fossils. One team of researchers discovered a 1.75-million-year-old
hominid fossil skull, one of humanity's earliest ancestors, with two
round holes in the top—exactly fitting the size and location of a saber-
toothed cat's fangs.[29]

These scientific studies reveal a very different picture of human
nature from what Dart assumed. The idea that we evolved more as prey
than predator is less thrilling and empowering than the "killer ape"
idea, but it is more consistent with the scientific evidence.

Our ancestors were likely often filled with fear, worried about being
harmed. They might have enjoyed relative safety in the daytime as
they walked through the savanna or the forest in large, noisy groups,
searching for fruits and nuts to eat. But when darkness came, they
would be blind, especially on moonless nights. As they waited for the
sun to return, they would huddle close and try to sleep, straining their
ears for any sounds of approaching predators. But the predators that
stalked them were silent. A panther could sit unseen mere feet away,
watching and waiting for a mother to take her arm from around her
baby, and then suddenly snatch the infant and run into the night. The
terrified cries would jolt awake the entire family, but they could do

nothing but listen to the screaming in the blackness, hoping the cat didn't return for another of them.

This ancient fear of predation might be hard for modern urban humans to imagine. Today, we live in relative safety, but this safety is only possible because we have confined all the predators to zoos and wilderness reserves or forced them to extinction. When you walk in the woods, it's just you and the forest, and perhaps some small squirrels or foxes. It is very rare to run into the occasional bear or puma. But only 100,000 years ago, there were wolves, big cats, and other menacing giant beasts lurking among the trees, explaining why scientists argue that our recent ancestors were very vulnerable to predation.[30]

Even today, in some regions of the world, humans aren't safe from predation. Despite a dwindling population of tigers, one hundred people in India and Nepal are eaten by these big cats every year. There are even occasionally lethal animal attacks in North America. In 2009, the nineteen-year-old Canadian pop singer Taylor Mitchell decided to go for a relaxing hike through the forest in Cape Breton Highlands National Park but never made it back to her car. She was hunted down and killed by a pack of wild coyotes.

NATURAL-BORN VICTIMS

For millions of years, humans have been the victims of predation, and this legacy has shaped our psychology, instilling in us a powerful vigilance against threats. Of course, there are many people today who are excellent hunters, and some who thrive on the thrill of wilderness survival. Think of Arnold Schwarzenegger in the movie *Predator* as he stalks through the forest in tattered camo. The internet celebrity the Liver King, a tanned, muscled Mongolian man, seems to be another example of a modern predator. He claims that humans are naturally alpha hunters and takes his name from his penchant for eating raw liver and animal organs, which he claims give him an incredible—and ancestral—physique. But if you look closer, the truth isn't what it seems. The Liver King got his muscles from anabolic steroids, and the whole point of *Predator* is that Schwarzenegger's muscular character is the *prey*, chased through the jungle by a ruthless alien hunter. Stories of being chased and stalked resonate with us because we can all relate to the premise. Our evolutionary legacy means that we viscerally understand what it is like to be threatened and hunted.

Why does it matter that we were more prey than predator? It matters because it fundamentally changes who we think we are and how we understand moral conflict. If you think that people are predators, then it reinforces the "destruction narrative" of moral conflict. Imagine someone attacking your moral convictions. If you see them as a predator, you assume that they are coming from a place of cold confidence, watching from the darkness, waiting for the best time to hurt you and your children—an assumption all too common in politics today with accusations of brainwashing, grooming, and the like. On the other hand, if people are scared deep down, then their attacks are driven more by desperation than a drive for dominance. They are asking themselves not "how can I hurt the other side?" but "how can I protect myself from them?"

Consider the enraged driver from the opening of the book. He was not driving around the mall like a predator, looking for someone to attack. Instead, he was driven to violence by a dangerous near miss. Viewing his actions through this more accurate lens of human nature helps me better understand his motivation, which helps me forgive him. Knowing the truth about human nature can also facilitate understanding—and perhaps even some compassion—across political divides. When trying to make sense of people who disagree with you, ask yourself, "What are they afraid of?"

It may seem odd that people on the other side are afraid of anything. Don't most of us today enjoy unprecedented safety? The problem is that our Stone Age minds, long afraid of predators, are still vigilant to threats, even if we are surrounded by manicured lawns and suburban sidewalks rather than untamed forests. Chapter 4 will explore how this vigilance causes the concept of harm to creep, leading us to see dangers even in mild harms, like social media posts or free-range childhood. But before we explore how our minds discount our safety, we must first understand how we became safe in the first place. How could we protect ourselves from being eaten by predators? We had to become *social* and band together into big tribes with many people. Unfortunately, group living introduced new threats—like murder.

In Sum

- Humans today are the most powerful hunters on Earth, which makes it easy to assume that we evolved as killers. The assumption that humans are predators makes our moral opponents seem predatory—cold and calculating—when they do bad things.
- Scientists initially believed that we evolved as predators because of the discovery of the Taung child, the fossils of a juvenile ancestral hominid that was brutally butchered. But it was not butchered by another human. Instead, it was devoured by an eagle. This was not an isolated incident; our ancient ancestors were frequently preyed upon by large predators.
- Scientists also once thought that our evolved bodies and minds provided evidence of our hunting prowess, but we are a weak species, and newer work reveals how our physical and mental adaptations are better suited for migration and for avoiding predators.
- Analyses show that early humans were preyed upon at rates similar to other primates and even deer. Our modern primate cousins also provide a window into human nature, and research finds they are more preyed upon than scientists once assumed.
- Our evolution as a prey species means that our actions are better described by the protection narrative than by the destruction narrative. Even today, we remain powerfully motivated to protect ourselves from threats.

Chapter 3

Social: The Rise of Morality

As a species, humans are physically unimpressive. We are weak and lack big teeth and big fangs. This weakness helps explain why, as we saw in the last chapter, scientists estimate that 10 percent of ancient hominids would have been eaten by predators each year, a rate similar to other grazing species. How can our vulnerable species defend itself?

A common strategy for prey species is to look for safety in numbers and form large groups, and humans clearly live in groups. Our species has undergone a "social transition." But group living brings with it another big problem: other people can take advantage of us. They can murder us, steal from us, lie to us. How can we reap the anti-predation benefits of group living—staying safe from lions, tigers, and bears—without being harmed by other people within our groups? To reduce the threat of other people acting selfishly or impulsively, we needed a sense of morality. This ancient sense of morality roots our modern explosions of moral outrage, and so we need to understand the genesis of our feelings of right versus wrong and their foundation in our species' quest for protection.

GROUP LIVING TO AVOID PREDATORS

Being in a big group helps protect prey animals, explaining why scientists find that nearly every prey animal forms groups. At first, group living sounds like a bad idea because big groups are easy for predators to find, but one of its simplest advantages is "dilution." Group size dilutes the risk of attack to any individual by having many others who might get eaten first. If your herd has fifty members rather than twenty, your chance of being the unlucky animal that gets eaten decreases from 5 percent to 2 percent. Big groups are also confusing to predators, especially when prey animals run in different directions. Zebras are masters at creating confusion: when a zebra herd is in full sprint, their stripes all blend together, creating a flickering "motion dazzle" effect in the eye of the predator.[1]

When animals are in a herd, they can also better protect themselves by clumping tightly together. A lone straggler on the edge of a group is an easy target for a predator, but getting closer to its friends helps transfer its own risk onto them, increasing the likelihood that the predator will go for one of its nearest neighbors instead. This "selfish herd theory" was most convincingly proven in the great-white-shark-infested waters of False Bay, South Africa. Researchers built a series of rafts that had differently spaced fake Styrofoam seals (some in a tight herd, some in a looser herd) and then towed them behind their boat as they drove around the bay. The researchers counted thirty-six different white shark attacks on their fake seals and found that seals in the tightest herds offered the best chance at survival.[2]

These anti-predation strategies may make sense for other prey species, but how did group size keep our hominid ancestors safe? Our ancestors lived not in running, jumping, and diving herds but in slower-moving troops, tribes, and clans.

Hominids benefited from a larger group size in a few ways. First, numbers offer more eyes to improve predator detection. Many predators rely on the element of surprise to hunt, sneaking up and then pouncing, and more vigilance can deter these hunters. Big enough groups can also have rotating sentries, a division of labor that allows other group members to focus on gathering food on the ground. If the designated sentry sees a predator, it can shout an alarm call, alerting the other animals to the danger, who then scramble to safety.

Vervet monkeys (among other monkeys) use distinct alarm calls for different predators. Eagles get a two-syllable cough, leopards or other big cats get a bark, and pythons and other snakes get a "chutter" call, which sounds halfway between a rapid growl and the clicking of a camera shutter. The rest of the troop understand these different calls: after hearing the eagle call, monkeys look up and find cover; after hearing the leopard call, they climb up trees; and after hearing the snake call, they stand on two legs and look around.[3]

Sophisticated communication helps keep group-living primates safe, and humans have the most sophisticated communication system in the animal kingdom. With language, early humans could provide specific details about where the predator was spotted, what kind of threat is lurking, and what other members of the group should do to prepare.

Beyond avoiding predators, group living allowed us to share food (helping to prevent starvation), share childcare (allowing more time for hunting and gathering food), and share technologies (like medicine and methods for preparing food). Stable group living also allowed for the systematic division of labor, where people could specialize and gain expertise in a task. Someone could be a hunter and someone else could be a gatherer, and this specialization—if you connect the dots far enough—eventually fueled events like the Industrial Revolution.

Group living was so beneficial that it became a defining feature of *Homo sapiens.* More than any other species, our ancestors underwent a *social transition,* banding together in big groups while simultaneously developing uniquely powerful brains to help us reap the benefits of social life. This idea is called the social brain hypothesis and argues that the pressures and opportunities of social living catalyzed the neural expansion of our species.

Our minds are so attuned to social life that we can keep track of approximately 150 different people in our environment, far more than many other animals as far as we know. Robin Dunbar, a British evolutionary psychologist, found evidence for the social brain hypothesis when his studies revealed strong correlations between a primate species' average group size and its brain size. Out of all primates, we grew the thickest cortices, which also supported our most powerful social innovation—language—which allows us to share ideas about how to keep ourselves safe and productive, and to effectively pass those ideas down through generations. The anthropologist Joseph Henrich calls social living and our social brains "the secret of our success."[4]

The mental bandwidth provided by our big brains allowed humans to outcompete other hominid species, like the Neanderthals. *Homo neanderthalensis* was more physically powerful than *Homo sapiens,* with a stockier build and a barrel shape, better fitting the ideal of "man the hunter" than our ancestors. Neanderthals were also excellent tool manufacturers, which helped them hunt large prey up close, but despite these advantages humans eventually emerged victorious, in part because of our social prowess.[5] With the ability to infer the intentions, motivations, and goals of our fellow sapiens, our species could gradually build more useful innovations that helped us survive and thrive. Scholars point to the many impressive cultural adaptations provided by our social brains, including religion and storytelling, which helped us work together to achieve our collective goals.[6]

Our big social brains also helped us better achieve the goal of escaping predators. Scholars highlight how fish and birds with larger, more social brains tend to take more precautionary anti-predator measures than their smaller-brained, less social counterparts.[7] Although there is little study of predator-avoidance techniques among ancient humans, you can see the ingenuity of modern *Homo sapiens* in avoiding predation. Indian people who live in areas with roaming tigers discovered that wearing a mask of a face with open eyes on the backs of their heads could keep them safe. Tigers like to sneak up on unsuspecting prey, and these masks make the tigers think that humans are always looking. Another tiger-deterrent technique involves putting human mannequins in fields of tall grass and wiring them to give electric shocks to anything that touches or pounces on them.[8]

These clever anti-predation solutions can only emerge within a social species that can take the perspective of predators: "Tigers will think I'm looking at them" or "Tigers will confuse this mannequin for me and learn not to pounce on people" are thoughts about the minds of other entities, which requires a social brain. Humans can then use these social brains to take the perspective of other people when they share these predator-avoidance techniques within their tribes. As Dunbar, the proposer of the social brain hypothesis, argues, "Predation is the principal survival problem that animals have to contend with."[9]

Group living undoubtedly kept us safer—especially from predators—but there are some big problems with living with other people. They can hurt you.

WORRIED ABOUT OTHER PEOPLE

Social living was good for our species because we could work together with other people to keep ourselves safe from wild animals, and as our groups got bigger, we could achieve more than just staying safe. We could construct buildings, build irrigation systems, and develop advanced weapons to finally become apex predators. But stable groups are precarious things, and societies can easily dissolve into anarchy because of unrestrained selfishness, megalomaniacal leaders, and the constant threat of people harming each other.

One well-studied problem of group living is the rise of "free riders," tribe members who live off the labor of others while doing nothing themselves. Free riders are the people in group projects who don't bother replying to emails or attending meetings, knowing that the more conscientious group members will work to earn everyone an A plus. Even if you are not a deliberate loafer, experiments show that everyone has the tendency to relax in large groups.[10] This effect was discovered in the early twentieth century by the French agricultural engineer Maximilien Ringelmann, who was studying how best to maximize the agricultural output of humans, oxen, and horses. He found that people pulled less hard in tug-of-war when there were more team members: in a one-on-one match, men pulled with a force of 85.3 kilograms, but that output dropped to 65 kilograms in a seven-man team and to 61.4 kilograms in a fourteen-man unit.

Left unaddressed, the free-rider problem can destroy societies, if everyone decides to do the bare minimum while still reaping the benefits of other people's labor. Our resulting animus toward free riders is reflected in modern worries about people who exploit social welfare policies.

Another problem of group living is the rise of megalomaniacal alpha-male leaders. Leaders arise naturally within any social group and have power to decide who gets what. They can use their power for the good of the group, promoting a fair distribution of resources, but leaders can also act selfishly, keeping more for themselves. This selfishness can fuel a feedback cycle where power begets more resources, which begets more power, until the influence—and the ego—of the alpha male (and it is almost always a male) swells so much that they deem themselves the absolute authority, like a king or dictator. This alpha male can then harm other group members with impunity, taking all the resources and potential mates for himself. This unchecked power is bad for almost everyone in the group except the leader and undermines the growth of society—think North Korea—and so societies need a way to dampen rampant selfishness.

But the most basic problem of group living is simply that we can harm each other. Even if people are generally more motivated by protection than by destruction, people can—and do—use violence against each other. Anthropologists have documented interpersonal and intergroup violence in all tribal societies, but exactly how much violence existed within ancient groups of *Homo sapiens* is debated. Some scholars see ancient human tribes as idyllic communities of cooperation and compassion. They take inspiration from philosophers like Rousseau, who saw human nature as fundamentally kind and peaceful but as easily corruptible by society and hierarchy. To support their arguments of kindness, these scholars cite the low levels of violence in modern-day hunter-gatherer societies.[11]

Other researchers see ancient human tribes as violent. The psychologist Steven Pinker looked across several sources to argue that there were high rates of conspecific violence (violence between members of the same species) in ancient human groups, ranging between 25 and 40 percent annually.[12] This means that every year held up to a 40 percent chance that you could be killed by another human. This evidence supports the view of human nature espoused by Thomas Hobbes, who said that life in a state of nature was "nasty, brutish, and short." But some have suggested that Pinker cherry-picked his tribes, selecting groups that had a reputation for being unusually violent and leaving out the most peaceful groups from his analysis.[13]

What seems clear is that interpersonal violence existed in early tribes, and its exact amount varied from group to group. One of the most comprehensive studies of human-on-human violence was published in the journal *Nature,* where the authors used complex evolutionary diagrams to compare six hundred human populations ranging from the Paleolithic era to the present.[14] These researchers not only analyzed an especially broad sample of early human tribes but also weighted the influence of each tribe by its size, ensuring that a very small but very violent or peaceful tribe could not skew the results. These analyses arrived at an authoritative estimate of the annual rate of human deaths caused by interpersonal violence: 2 percent. Across our ancient past, every year held a one-in-fifty chance of being murdered by another human.

A 2 percent rate of interpersonal homicide in ancient human society is small compared with some social species. The most blood-soaked mammals are meerkats, with an estimated conspecific death rate of 19.36 percent. But 2 percent is much higher than the rate of homicide and other violent crimes in society today. In 2020, the FBI estimated the U.S. violent crime rate (including homicide, rape, robbery, and aggravated assault) at 0.4 percent, and the homicide rate at 0.0065 percent. This means that in 2020, you had only a one-in-fifteen-thousand chance of being killed.

People today might be afraid of crime—of muggings and kidnappings and mass shootings—but if you were living in ancient society, you had much better reason to be afraid of violence. In Hobbes's famous quotation, before mentioning how our lives were nasty, brutish, and short, he begins by saying, "No arts; no letters; no society; and which is worst of all, continual fear, and danger of violent death." We can argue about how much ancient humans had arts, letters, and society, but it seems clear that ancient humans—now less worried about animal predators—remained worried about being harmed by other humans.

How could people manage this very reasonable fear while also solving the issue of free riders and megalomaniacal leaders? They couldn't simply leave their tribes and venture alone into a wilderness filled with predators, because avoiding those predators was the whole reason they formed tribes in the first place. Instead, humans needed a way to live together in relative harmony—a system that encouraged people to suppress their most violent and selfish impulses. Humans needed morality.

THE FUNCTION OF MORALITY

Morality is the most fundamental of human social contracts. Morality is a set of norms (expectations about behavior) shared by a group. These norms revolve around encouraging cooperation and kindness and discouraging selfishness and aggression. Morality inhibits people from taking advantage of others, especially through violence. When people break these moral norms, others react strongly, becoming outraged and ostracizing or punishing the offender. Morality restricts the realm of acceptable behaviors that people can do, but we generally accept this reduced personal autonomy because it helps protect the overall interests of the group and allows us all to enjoy the benefits of communal living. It's nice to have complete freedom, but it's even nicer to live in groups where people generally don't steal or assault us.

All moral norms are social norms—rules of a society—but not all social norms are moral norms. Wearing pajamas to work violates a social norm but not a moral norm; attending meetings in your favorite plaid PJs feels very different from kneeing your co-workers in the groin. Of course, your boss might scold you if they think your unorthodox outfit undermines productivity, but it wouldn't generate outrage or punishment like doing violence. In practice, the line between a moral norm and a nonmoral norm can be blurry, but it is still useful to distinguish between them; the convention of setting a table with forks on the left (a social norm) is very different from a rule against theft (a moral norm).

In some modern societies, moral norms are explicit (for example, a set of laws) or revolve around the declarations of a holy text (such as the Bible). But all human societies have nuanced moralities, even if they lack a Model Penal Code—the blueprint for many U.S. states' criminal codes—or a religious doctrine such as the Ten Commandments. There are many similarities across the moral norms of societies, especially around prohibitions against harming other people. There are also interesting differences.

In *Don't Sleep, There Are Snakes,* the linguist Daniel Everett recounts his experience of living with the Pirahãs, a remote Amazonian tribe with a unique language. Everett was trying to learn the grammatical rules of these people, but he and his family also ended up learning their moral rules. Just like in America, where he grew up, Pirahã parents thought it was their duty to help their family. "A Pirahã father would paddle for days for help if he thought he could save a child,"[15] but Pirahãs also show little sympathy for others who suffer loss. In modern Western culture, if a loved one dies, you are allowed to take a break from the daily grind to grieve. People might bring you casseroles or other comfort food, but not among the Pirahãs: "If your mother dies, if your child dies, if your husband dies—you still have to hunt, fish, and gather food. No one will do this for you."[16] Not allowing space for grief initially seemed callous and even immoral to Everett, but he then realized it simply acknowledges the realities of life. When you are isolated in the jungle, your survival depends on people doing their share of work, every single day. This extreme emphasis on self-reliance seems cruel to Americans who have freezers and pantries filled with food, but Pirahãs lack ways to reliably store food, and without these caches have nothing to spare for others in times of grief.

Moral norms also vary across more industrialized cultures. For example, in Singapore, both vandalism and importing dangerous fireworks are punishable by caning—getting beaten by a thin rattan cane—whereas Scandinavian countries shy away from direct corporal punishment. In fact, in 1979 Sweden became the first country in the world to ban all corporal punishment toward children, while some American families still see spanking children as an important way to correct behavior. Part of growing up in a society is learning exactly which acts are permissible, obligatory, and forbidden. An only child growing up in upper-crust England will learn different moral norms from a kid growing up in a big family in rural Alabama.

Despite this variation in moral norms, much morality is common across cultures. For example, virtually every society values group loyalty, respects property rights (some things belong to me, and it is wrong for you to take those things), and prohibits assault and murder.[17] Although not every culture forbids all kinds of violence in all circumstances, if there were a consistent core of morality across cultures, it would be this: it is wrong to intentionally harm vulnerable people within your group. Where such harm is allowed, it is because people in the culture feel that it offsets some greater harm. For example, those who endorse capital punishment argue that it deters crime across society.

Societies prohibit harm for many reasons. The genes of all people want to survive and reproduce, and suffering violence makes that difficult. Being stolen from also makes it harder to survive, but even lying, disrespect, and unfairness can reduce people's chances of survival because these acts destabilize the group. It is challenging enough for groups to work together to protect themselves from external threats like wild animals and rival human groups, and almost impossible to meet these challenges if you are also worried about being lied to, being exploited, or getting clubbed in the back by a neighbor. The specter of neighborly harm decreases trust, and the dissolution of collective trust spelled disaster for ancient human groups—and for modern human groups, too—causing a descent into violence and anarchy.[18] Achieving harmonious and violence-free groups is so important to societies that its pursuit can override other moral prohibitions, like incest.

Most human societies have moral norms against brother-sister or parent-child incest,[19] because kids born from these relationships usually have a lower chance of survival. When very closely related people procreate, it increases the likelihood that harmful genetic traits get expressed, leading to children with heritable diseases, lower intelligence, and infertility. Parents who saw incest as immoral were more likely to have healthy surviving kids, who in turn were taught that incest was immoral, who in turn had healthier kids than those who engaged in incest, resulting in a continuing cycle that reinforced this moral judgment. That said, there can be benefits to marrying your relatives.

The house of Habsburg achieved a centuries-long reign in what is now Germany and Austria by strategically marrying close relatives like cousins and nieces together to consolidate their power and literally "keep it in the family."[20] This was a winning strategy because alliances on paper can always be violated for personal gain, but you're less likely to raid the castle next door when it's owned by your uncle. Evolution endowed us with a strong aversion to hurting our own family because they are walking copies of our own genes, which also helps explain why stepchildren are a hundred times more likely to be victims of abuse than biological children.[21] The Habsburg family epitomized the incest-as-peacemaking strategy with their motto "Let others wage war. You, happy Austria, marry!"

By reducing the likelihood of violent infighting, the Habsburgs helped to create an environment where people could better survive and thrive. Historians argue that their cousin-marrying dynasty ushered in exceptional political stability, which helped create economic growth through public works, like roads and railways, which all require large-scale cooperation between different regions.[22] Of course, having children with your cousins also increases the chances of inheriting two copies of harmful recessive alleles. For the Habsburgs, recessive alleles led to a massive chin coupled with an unflattering underbite, later termed the Habsburg jaw. One team of researchers cross-examined the Habsburg family tree with their depictions in royal portraits and found that the more inbred they were, the more deformed their chins.[23] The Habsburgs' unorthodox strategy to achieving political power got them only so far; the Spanish lineage died out with King Charles II, whose extreme physical and intellectual disabilities meant that he couldn't have children.[24]

Another consequence of inbreeding is hemophilia, a genetic disorder sometimes called the royal disease. People with hemophilia have deficiencies in the proteins that help their blood clot, which means that even the slightest cuts can lead to fatal bleeding. Hemophilia was a major issue for the Romanov family, an inbred Russian dynasty that ruled from 1613 until they were murdered in the Bolshevik Revolution of 1917. After the bodies of the last Romanovs were rediscovered in an unmarked grave several decades ago, forensic analysis confirmed that they had the genetic markers of a rare form of hemophilia found in only one in twenty-five thousand (0.0038 percent) people.[25]

These royal dynasties highlight how there are always trade-offs when it comes to morality as societies struggle to balance competing harms. Is it worth having your national leader bleed out from an accident if you can avoid war and help your society flourish? Of course, the blind process of evolution does not explicitly weigh these decisions, but instead shapes our moral judgments over generations as people try to minimize the many harms we face, both personally and in society.

Moral psychologists all agree that humans developed a sense of morality to protect people and their genes and their groups from harm. But they quibble about how to divide up and label the many harms faced by social-living human beings. One theory called moral foundations theory outlines five or six different ways that people and groups can be harmed[26]—by direct violence like murder, by unfairness in which people receive help but do not help others in return, by betraying your group to rival groups, by disobeying authorities that are tasked with maintaining social order, and by acting in impure ways, like engaging in incest. Each of these harms involves a different kind of act—sleeping with your sibling is clearly different from murder, which is different from talking back to a tribal chieftain—but underneath these differences is a common core: they all undermine peaceably living together.

Another theory called morality as cooperation highlights that a crucial function of a society is to encourage cooperation among its members.[27] As we briefly touched on above, one reason why group living is so beneficial to humans is that we can work together to achieve common aims, like hunting big game, dividing labor, and protecting ourselves from rival tribes. With enough cooperation, we can also build public works, develop electricity, build hospitals, and construct a network of millions of computers. But there are many ways to undermine cooperation in human society, and this theory highlights seven of them including neglecting loyalty, not deferring to authority, not respecting property rights, and not safeguarding family values. These values overlap somewhat with those of moral foundations theory, because both theories focus on the elements that make the difference between a safe thriving society and violent chaos.

Yet another theory, the model of moral motives,[28] argues that morality revolves around avoiding three kinds of harms. These include avoiding harm to your future self, like being lazy and not studying for an important exam, avoiding harm to a specific other, like committing murder or assault, and avoiding harm to society at large, like having widespread anarchy. This theory, like those of moral foundations and morality as cooperation, highlights the importance of encouraging positive virtues to safeguard against harm. By celebrating examples of loyalty, heroism, industriousness, justice, bravery, and cooperation, societies nudge people to act morally.

These three theories disagree about the name and number of the specific challenges faced by humans in social groups, but all of them emphasize that morality is ultimately rooted in concerns about protecting ourselves, our families, and our societies. They also argue that morality is both innate and learned: we are born with a fundamental concern for following rules—especially moral rules—but exactly which norms become moralized is something we acquire through cultural learning. This learning is based on the specific threats that people generally agree are important in their cultures.

In cultures facing a constant threat of starvation, norms surrounding food sharing will be more moralized because they are necessary to protect people and the group.[29] Someone who hoards food in a famine is not simply selfish but likely to kill other people. The East African nation of Ethiopia is often threatened by famine and also has a strong tradition of communal eating, where friends and family share food by eating out of the same large bowl.[30]

In cultures engaged in war, whether battling tribes in Papua New Guinea,[31] or the Allies versus the Axis in World War II, extreme loyalty and valor in battle are both celebrated. Without these heroic acts, your culture is more likely to be harmed by losing the war and being enslaved or totally annihilated.

Like any set of human rules or norms, morality is not a perfect system for preventing harm. Even people in societies with very explicit moral rules can harm each other, as evidenced by the approximately twenty-six thousand murders per year in the United States. The voice of our moral conscience can be shouted down by both rampant selfishness and powerful emotional reactions. Even if we know that we *should* pay taxes to support the social infrastructure upon which we all rely, people frequently fudge their tax forms. Even if we know that we *should* turn the other cheek after someone gives us the middle finger in traffic, our anger can compel us to retaliate with violence. But even acts that might seem like failures of morality can be "moral" if we take a broader perspective about the purpose of morality. Sometimes people commit harm *because* of morality.

VIRTUOUS VIOLENCE

Morality, as a rule, dampens our tendency to harm others, but every rule has exceptions. Acts of "virtuous violence"—like war and honor killings—seem to contradict the harm-reducing function of morality,[32] but killing in war allows people to protect themselves from foreign threats. Aristotle wrote that "we make war that we may live in peace," and Thomas Jefferson proposed that "from time to time, the tree of liberty must be watered with the blood of tyrants and patriots."

Even attacking others who affront your sense of honor may help mitigate broader harm; that's the argument advanced by a team of psychologists who studied the "culture of honor" in the American South. They found that men who grew up in the rural areas of Kentucky and North Carolina got aggressive when their honor was insulted, and they argued that this aggression served as an effective deterrent against those who might harm them.

Researchers from the University of Michigan recruited men who were from either the American South or the North and then had an accomplice bump into them while they were walking. After the bump the participants usually mumbled an apology, but instead of returning this apology, the accomplice called them an asshole. No one likes being insulted, but the researchers reasoned that people from a culture of honor should get especially offended. They were right. Southern men were more than twice as likely as northern men to become visibly angry at the insult (85 percent versus 35 percent).[33]

The researchers also reasoned that these southern men should be vigilant for a chance at violent redemption to reestablish their honor. To test this hypothesis, they had the recently insulted participants walk down a narrow hallway and then rigged it so that a different accomplice would be walking toward them. In contrast to the first accomplice, who was a normal-sized guy, this second accomplice was a University of Michigan football player. He was *big*, and his job was to walk straight ahead and give no quarter to the participant. The hallway was very narrow because the researchers lined it with surplus furniture and discarded desks, leaving barely enough space to fit the football player.

Unless they wanted to be completely flattened, the insulted participants had to dodge out of the way and hide among the little alcoves created by the piles of furniture. Even though everyone yielded to the football player, not everyone moved at the same time. Some stepped aside as soon as they saw the giant coming down the hall, and some waited until the very last second, barely avoiding the collision. The researchers hypothesized that the southern men stung by an insult would wait longer to move than the northern men, trying their best to stand their ground and force the football player to move. As expected, the southerners played this reputational game of chicken for longer, only giving way when they were an average of three feet away, compared with the northerners who moved aside at five feet.

How can this urge for retaliation help prevent harm? The American South, especially North Carolina, was settled by herders from the hilly highlands of Scotland who—now in their new hilly American homes—continued their animal herding lifestyle, keeping sheep, pigs, and cows.[34] The problem with keeping animals is that it's relatively easy for people to "rustle" them—to steal them from you—especially under the cover of darkness, and so animal herders needed a psychological adaptation to discourage others from thievery. What they needed was a way to get so outraged that they would be willing to retaliate with violence when people tried to take advantage of them. Of course, retaliating with violence is dangerous because you could be injured or killed, but if other people know that you are *generally* the kind of person who is willing to kill after being merely insulted, they will think twice before provoking you in more substantial ways, like stealing your animals.

The threat of violence is also an effective deterrent in prison, where many prisoners foster a reputation for craziness to deter other prisoners from messing with them. In one analysis of the American prison system, a criminologist found that 70 percent of inmates reported getting aggressive with another prisoner primarily to avoid seeming weak.[35] Of course, showcasing violence can deter others, but it also brings a risk of being grievously injured in a fight. This explains why many prisoners opt for *self*-harm as a less costly signal of their proclivity for irrational violence. Inmates with no prior history of self-harm will decide to headbutt walls and cut themselves in the solitude of their cell and then flaunt their scars in the daytime to give off the aura of a seasoned fighter.[36] These gruesome examples show that in unstable environments violence to the self and others serves as a strategy to prevent greater violence in the long run.

Thankfully, in modern stable societies, few of us face the constant threat of theft or violence, and so have less need to deter others through harm. Institutions like the police enforce moral codes, and the courts punish those who perpetrate harm. If someone steals from you, or threatens your safety, it is usually best to call the cops. Admittedly, the justice system may not always be just, but relying on them is statistically safer than doing vigilante justice.

In the distant past where human nature evolved, there were no separate police forces or an impartial judicial system. These institutions require a large society with enough division of labor and surplus resources to allow some people to spend their days enforcing order, rather than hunting or farming. Small hunter-gatherer tribes like our ancestors and like the current-day Pirahãs of the Amazon have to mete out justice among themselves. But trying to punish thieves or murderers yourself is dangerous, especially because these offenders have already shown that they are willing to inflict harm. How can a small group of law-abiding citizens punish a remorseless thief or a remorseless killer? As with the culture of honor, this challenge of motivating people to punish others was solved with moral outrage.

MORAL OUTRAGE

Moral outrage is the psychological tool that motivates people to punish wrongdoers, even at cost or risk to themselves. It is a "commitment device," something that commits people to punishment, even though trying to punish someone can be dangerous. When we witness unjust harm, whether someone committing interpersonal violence or blatant cheating, we have an embodied physical reaction. We get angry, our blood pressure spikes, our heart beats faster; we thirst for retribution. Outrage leads us to ignore the irrationality of risking our own safety to punish someone. In any single situation, there is rarely an immediate personal benefit for meting out punishment, and often there is real risk, because the person you are serving justice against could lash out at you or retaliate in the future. But the powerful feeling of outrage leads us to momentarily forget this unfavorable calculus and get involved in a situation we would be better off avoiding, and science reveals how this feeling and forgetting is essential for maintaining a cooperative society.

A series of studies has used "public goods games" to reveal the benefits of outrage. In these games, all players start out with some resources (for example, $20), and they can choose to contribute some or all of their money to the common pool, or just keep all their money for themselves and give nothing. The total common pool, which is all of people's donations combined, is then multiplied (for example, tripled) and redistributed equally among *all* participants. This means that even those who did *not* contribute to the common good get an equal share of this tripled pool of common resources. This setup encourages personal selfishness. The people who make the most money in this scenario are free riders, those who encourage everyone *else* to give the maximum amount of money to common resources but who personally decide not to give anything.

These games capture the tension of living in society. All people are better off if everyone cooperates, contributing to public goods like roads and libraries by paying their share of taxes. But each person is individually better off if they avoid paying taxes and enjoy the benefits of other people's contributions to public goods. All of us see the allure of being selfish, but our moral sense nudges us toward cooperation—at least until we witness other people failing to contribute to the public good. For example, when kids on Halloween see an unattended candy bowl that says, "Please take only one," most trick-or-treaters take only one piece of candy, until one kid takes a fistful; then it's everyone grabbing for themselves. Order collapses and there's no more candy.

You can see this pattern in public goods experiments, where "society" can quickly go from stable to shambles. Once a norm of selfishness has been established, with a few people keeping their money, others decide that they too should keep their money. Soon everyone keeps their money, and the whole public goods system collapses. This is the "free rider problem" that plagues many countries with strong social safety nets but also endemic tax evasion. For example, Italy allows citizens to retire at sixty-seven with 20,000 euros a year, but also has a tax evasion rate of about 70 percent, a combination that challenges its national finances.

Economists thought that outrage-driven punishment could be the key to maintaining cooperation in public goods games.[37] They compared people's behavior under two key conditions: In the standard public goods game, people could donate up to $20 each round to a central pool, which would then be tripled and evenly distributed among all the players (again, even among those who did not donate). In the "altruistic punishment" condition, people played the same public goods game but could also spend a dollar of their own money to punish anyone who they felt didn't give enough to the common good. For every dollar people paid to punish, the impact was tripled with free riders being docked three of their dollars.

Economists are quick to point out that within any given round it is technically irrational to pay to punish because it reduces your money without providing a tangible benefit to yourself. But 84 percent of people paid to punish at least once, and many people felt inspired to punish again and again. In fact, roughly 10 percent of participants punished more than ten times. Why? Because the punishers were *outraged* at free riders who enjoyed undeserved rewards and who ultimately threatened cooperation within their group.[38]

The more outraged people felt, the more likely they were to punish, and despite its short-term irrationality this outrage-fueled punishment was rational in the long term because it protected cooperation from destruction. Groups that could altruistically punish maintained their cooperation after many rounds, while groups that could not translate people's moral outrage into punishment witnessed the death of cooperation. Outrage toward free riders allowed people to avoid the very real harm of cooperative collapse.

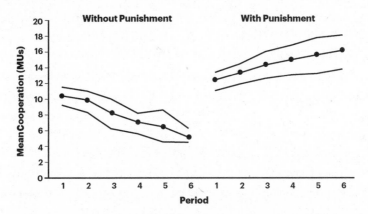

Figure 3.1: Groups where people can punish others ("with punishment") get more cooperation over rounds ("periods") of investment. "MUs" represent "money units." I use "dollars" in the text description for simplicity.

Feelings of moral outrage also help to solve the problem of tyranni-
cal alpha-male leaders I introduced earlier. Humans get outraged when
a leader's ambition and selfishness threaten the rest of society—and
so do chimpanzees. Similar to humans, chimps live in complex status
hierarchies where a tyrant alpha male sometimes emerges and tries to
exploit everyone else. Primatologists have discovered that when the
alpha is too strong and ruthless to be challenged by any individual
chimp, groups of lower-ranking chimpanzees often band together to
dethrone the alpha, sometimes murdering him by ripping his body
limb from limb, and even cannibalizing him.[39]

In his book *Hierarchy in the Forest,* the anthropologist Christopher
Boehm argues that this collective compulsion to revolt when the powerful exploit the weak is exactly what allowed early egalitarian societies
like hunter-gatherers to form.[40] We see the remnants of this in modern
societies where disenfranchised people foment revolution against leaders who seem to have amassed more wealth than they deserve. Consider
the grisly fates of the tsar of Russia and the king of France, who incited
outrage for living lavish lifestyles while common people starved.

Morality is a set of group norms, and so moral outrage is most
powerfully felt in groups, when everyone agrees that someone did
something wrong. Punishing others in outraged mobs—whether in
person or online—is easier because many hands (or fists) make light
work, and it is safer because it is difficult for recipients of punishment
to retaliate against a whole group of people. Showing up at someone's
hut to take back your stolen property will go better if you have a dozen
neighbors with you.

Although moral outrage evolved when we lived in small groups and
had to enforce justice ourselves, today we are still filled with moral
outrage. We seem constantly angry, despite having a justice system
to punish wrongdoers and despite being relatively safe from violence
and the impacts of free riders. Current murder rates are a thousand
times lower than when humans first grouped together in tribes, and
so it's fair to ask whether our modern moral outrage is still motivated
by avoiding harm.

It is true: we are safer today than we were at the dawn of humanity.
But we don't *feel* safer. The problem is that the human mind is a threat
detector; we continue to see harm everywhere we look. Ironically, we

are especially likely to see innocuous things as harmful and evil when we live in safety.

In Sum

- Eons ago, our ancestors underwent a "social transition," banding together in larger tribes to protect themselves from predators. This social transition occurred together with the evolution of our big social brains, which allowed us to better navigate group living and devise creative solutions to avoiding predators.
- Social living helped us avoid getting eaten, but it introduced a new source of potential harm: other humans. Free riders could take resources from the group without contributing anything; megalomaniacal alpha-male leaders could amass power and exploit others; disgruntled neighbors could hurt or kill us.
- We developed a rich sense of morality to keep everyone in line and discourage antisocial behavior. Morality encourages cooperation and kindness, discourages selfishness and aggression, and provides the psychological basis for punishing and exiling wrongdoers.
- Our sense of morality ultimately evolved to help us avoid harm. While moral norms vary across cultures, they all generally prohibit direct interpersonal harms like assault and murder. When harm seems acceptable (for example, honor attacks), it is because it discourages other harms.
- One way that we enforce moral rules is through outrage. When someone violates our moral sense, we bristle with anger and thirst for retribution. Moral outrage mobilizes us to incur personal costs—and to band together—to combat the many types of harm that threaten us in group living.

Chapter 4

Dangerous: Ignoring Our Obvious Safety

Our modern world would be unrecognizable to our prehistoric ancestors, and even to human civilizations from just a few thousand years ago. Not only do we have conveniences like memory-foam pillows and heated car seats, but also we are incredibly safe. Ancient hominids feared getting eaten alive, and our more recent ancestors worried about being killed by other people. Thankfully, almost no one today is concerned with getting eaten, and relatively few people are at risk of murder, and yet we still panic about threats and become outraged over immorality. Some of these targets of panic and outrage—like authoritarianism and war—would make sense to our ancestors, but some would seem incomprehensible, like social media controversies.

In one infamous example from 2013, a thirty-year-old woman named Justine Sacco made a joke on Twitter just before she boarded an eleven-hour plane ride to Cape Town: "Going to Africa. Hope I don't get AIDS. Just kidding. I'm white!" She thought her joke was well meaning, believing it highlighted the unfairness of racial inequality, but people on Twitter were not amused. By the time she landed, the tweet had gone viral, with thousands of people condemning her for racism. Because of this outrage, Sacco was fired from her job, and in a later interview she discussed how this tweet turned her into a complete pariah.[1] Even her closest friends villainized her. Most of the people outraged by Sacco's joke were liberals, but conservatives were outraged too—at the overblown outrage of liberals.

How did humans evolve from a species terrified about the obvious harm of predation and murder, to a species outraged over online jokes and other people's reactions to online jokes, neither of which would seem harmful to our ancestors? Understanding our outrage over minor harms—at least compared with those humans have historically faced—is important because it illuminates the psychology of moral division. One intuitive explanation for why moral outrage is everywhere is that things are bad today: perhaps harm is on the rise and morality is on the decline. But although many people *think* this is true, it is not. Instead, the real reason we get outraged at fairly innocuous offenses is that people are *more* moral than ever, and we are safer than ever before.

SAFE AT LAST?

Scholars debate whether "progress" in human civilization is true.[2] Some argue that technological achievements only perpetuate inequality[3] and chain us to our work. There is some truth to this argument. The Pirahã people, whom we met in the last chapter, have a society with less "progress" but enjoy a lifestyle that modern urbanites might envy. Although they work hard gathering food and maintaining their villages, the Pirahãs also spend hours each day relaxing and chatting with each other as the Amazon River flows by.[4] In contrast, many people in industrialized countries have little time to rest, spending their days grinding at jobs and then commuting to and from those jobs. Most of the value from their labor is then absorbed into the multinational companies who employ them.

But those who argue for the benefits of progress point to one undeniable feature of modern human life: safety. Compared with any time in the past, we are much safer today; our species has undergone the *safety transition.*

Last chapter we saw how humanity underwent the *social transition,* where we moved together into tribes to avoid predation and developed big social brains to cope with group living. In the more modern safety transition, occurring mostly over the last hundred years, societies have changed to protect people from harm, passing laws and implementing policies to help us all avoid suffering and victimization. As we'll see, this safety transition has powerfully affected our moral judgments and laid the foundation for modern outrage, including on social media.

To get a sense of modern safety, we can take almost any statistic from today and compare it with the past. Consider deaths from infectious diseases, like COVID-19. Figuring out the official infection mortality rate (the likelihood of death given infection) of COVID-19 is surprisingly hard, but most experts agree it was somewhere between 1 and 2 percent. This means that one or two in a hundred people died after being infected with COVID. This seems high until you consider that the infection mortality rate of the bubonic plague was between 30 and 60 percent when it ripped through Europe in the mid-fourteenth century. Almost every family buried at least one loved one to a disease that could have been easily treated with modern antibiotics.

Moving from the Middle Ages to Victorian England, we can see that death was still everywhere. Let's look at the number of accidental deaths, starting with those popular puffy cloth skirts, crinolines, buttressed by giant metal and wooden frames. These beautiful dresses are often featured in historical dramas, but these television shows fail to highlight that they are highly flammable. Because the lightbulb wasn't invented until 1879, candles were everywhere in Victorian life, and one scholar estimates that up to three thousand women died in crinoline-related fires just in 1860.[5]

What if you wanted to become safer by leaving the Old World and its dangerous dress codes? Unfortunately, migrating to a new country used to be very dangerous, especially if it involved a long ocean voyage, where approximately one in five passengers died at sea either from starvation or from diseases that thrived on overcrowded ships. The dangers of picking the wrong cruise line were much greater than the inconvenience of picking a less reliable airline. In 1846, when the Irish potato famine killed nearly a million people, many survivors fled for the New World. Those who bought tickets with one company died at a rate of nearly 10 percent, while those who sailed with another company had a one in three chance of dying because those ships had poor food rations and defective ventilation.[6]

Critics might argue that human-caused climate change is an obvious example of progress making the world more dangerous. Global warming has increased the number and size of natural disasters, but our ability to protect ourselves from threatening weather has improved dramatically over the last several decades. Data from the World Meteorological Organization show that while the number of natural disasters has grown fivefold in the past fifty years, fatalities have decreased by two-thirds.[7] In the early twentieth century, disaster deaths (including those from droughts, storms, and flooding) exceeded a million annually, but as figure 4.1 shows, by the 1970s these fatalities dropped to around 100,000 per year. Today, they are only a fraction of that amount.

Consider wildfire responses: California had a record-high number of wildfires in 2022, but only nine people died thanks to the efforts of the National Interagency Fire Center in the United States, which releases seasonal fire outlooks, carries out fire prevention efforts, and coordinates firefighters. Globally, the United Nations and the World Meteorological Organization are committing even more resources to safety, launching a $1.5 billion program to ensure that everyone on Earth is covered by a disaster early warning system within five years.

Beyond natural disasters, just going about life was remarkably dan-

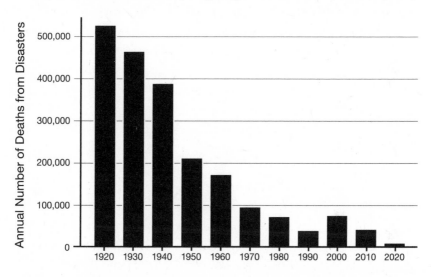

Figure 4.1: Global averages of annual death rates from natural disasters from each decade between 1920 and 2020. Disasters include all geophysical, meteorological, and climate events including earthquakes, volcanic activity, landslides, droughts, wildfires, storms, and flooding. Decadal figures are measured as the annual average over the subsequent ten-year period. In 1920, there were 2 billion people in the world, compared with today's 7.8 billion. *Data source:* Our World in Data, based on EM-DAT, CRED / UCLouvain, Brussels, Belgium.

gerous two generations ago. In the United States, worker protections were minimal for dangerous jobs like mining, railroad construction, and manufacturing. Cars had no safety features, and half a dozen U.S. commercial airplanes crashed every year, usually killing everyone on board. A little while ago, I was talking with my mom, who grew up in the 1950s and 1960s in Sudbury, a small city in northern Canada built around a nickel mine. I was shocked when she started casually recounting all the people who had died as she was growing up. One family on her street had real candles on their Christmas tree, and two of their kids died when the tree caught the house on fire. Another neighborhood family had a three-year-old burst into a fit of rage as they drove on the highway. He opened the back door of the car and flew out onto the road at full speed. No child lock on the door, no car seat, and no seat belts. Kids used to die by drowning in pools, asphyxiating after getting trapped in fridges, and choking on food before Henry Heimlich came around in 1974.

Although no community today is a stranger to misfortune, preventable deaths are much rarer than they used to be. There is simply no debating that our lives are *much* safer today than they have ever been throughout human history. Part of this safety is because, as Steven

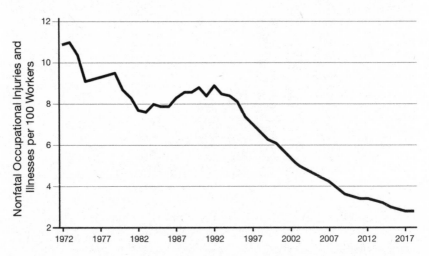

Figure 4.2: Incidence rates of nonfatal occupational injuries and illnesses among private industry workplaces from 1972 to 2018. Incidence rates are measured in cases per 100 full-time equivalent workers. *Data Source:* U.S. Bureau of Labor Statistics, Survey of Occupational Injuries and Illnesses.

Pinker points out in *The Better Angels of Our Nature,* we are less violent toward each other. But the safety transition is also driven by technology and policies that make us safer at work and home. You can see in figure 4.2 that the rate of injuries and illnesses at work has plummeted over the last forty-five years. Our cars have child locks, seat belts, and airbags, our Christmas trees have LED lights, our pools have safety fences and lifeguards, and babysitters now take first-aid courses that include the Heimlich maneuver.

But here's a puzzle: if you look at how parents treat their kids, you would be convinced that the world is more dangerous than ever. Parents don't let their kids walk to school or play outside. Some parents are so worried about their kids' safety that they microchip them, putting an Apple AirTag on their clothes so that they can see where they are at all times, just in case a van pulls up to kidnap them. Parents who dare to buck this trend are villainized and even arrested. In 2021, Heather Wallace, a thirty-seven-year-old mother of three, was driving home through her neighborhood. Her eight-year-old son, Aiden, was having a tantrum, and Wallace pulled over half a mile from home. She told Aiden to walk the rest of the way home so he could calm down. Their neighborhood was extremely safe; there were sidewalks next to manicured lawns and no traffic.

Wallace got home, and fifteen minutes later there was a knock on the door. It was not her son but instead two police officers, who had Aiden in a patrol car parked across the street. A neighborhood woman, who lived just one block away, had asked Aiden where he lived. After the neighbor confirmed that he was heading just down the street, she called the police to address the danger. The officers asked Wallace whether she would let her son walk home again after they had informed her about the general dangers of sex trafficking, which had never been a problem in their suburban neighborhood. Wallace, knowing she lived in a safe place, said, "I don't know." Then the cop replied, "I'm going to have to arrest you." The officer handcuffed her hands behind her back and escorted her to the back seat of the police vehicle while her child watched.

Wallace took a plea bargain to avoid a potential twenty-year sentence for felony child endangerment. She completed her court-mandated sixty-five community service hours at an early childhood care center, but only during the weekends, when the children weren't around—because she was now officially a "danger to children." She also had to resign from her job at a pediatric sleep consulting business, because their patients were children. As a part of her rehabilitation, Wallace had to submit to eight random drug tests where she had to pee into a cup as an officer watched to make sure she didn't tamper with the urine.[8]

If you think this is an extreme punishment for a well-meaning mom, you are not alone. Many people lament losing the days of free-range childhoods and get outraged at helicopter parents. Books like *The Coddling of the American Mind, I-Gen,* and *The Rise of Victimhood Culture* argue that this oversensitivity to harm is making our kids less resilient,[9] and the evidence seems to back up this claim: teens and young adults today are more susceptible than ever to debilitating anxiety and depression.[10]

As a parent, I'm sympathetic to concerns about over-coddling. I want my two daughters to feel comfortable walking through the neighborhood and to feel confident navigating the problems of young adulthood. I want them to be resilient. But I can't deny my uneasiness when I imagine them living like a kid in the 1980s. When I was growing up, I rode my secondhand BMX (no helmet) through the city of Calgary—population approximately 700,000—until it got dark. I occasionally wiped out and got injured far from home. I sometimes had suspicious characters follow me. I often got lost. These experiences helped me grow into a resilient adult, but it is hard to be excited about my kids risking getting injured or stalked or lost.

Whether you find parenting today to be overly coddling or appropriately protective, the undeniable truth is that our idea of what counts as "harmful" toward kids has expanded. We let our kids do less on their own, and we see more danger in things that used to seem safe. Even though the world is safer, we remain afraid of danger—and perhaps even *more* afraid. Parents during the Industrial Revolution had to worry about their child being dismembered by dangerous machinery while working twelve-hour days in hot, dark factories. Parents today worry about the harm of walking home, or the trauma caused by the cruel comments of other kids. The concept of harm has crept.

CONCEPT CREEP

The Australian social psychologist Nick Haslam coined the term "concept creep" to describe how harm-related concepts—including abuse, addiction, mental illness, trauma, bullying, and prejudice—have crept to encompass broader meanings. Historically, the definition of each of these words was relatively tight, referring to a small set of severe harms, but over time these definitions have expanded to include a greater set of less severe examples. The concept of abuse was once understood to involve only physical assault, but now some consider it abusive to let your kid walk home alone. The concept of addiction used to involve dependence on chemicals like alcohol or drugs, but has now expanded to include addictions to sex, social media, or work. The concept of trauma once focused on directly experiencing or witnessing violence, like surviving a massacre, but has expanded to involve watching violent movies or even having your values challenged.

I have seen firsthand how the concept of bullying has crept. When I was thirteen, I went to live with my dad in England. He was in the Royal Canadian Navy and got posted to Bristol to help design a new class of frigates. Our flat was in nearby Bath, a charming Georgian town of limestone with a beautiful abbey and its namesake, a set of historic Roman baths. Because of a set of arcane rules governing military postings and school equivalencies, the Canadian government funded my tuition at King Edward's School, an esteemed all-boys private school founded in 1552. We wore gray wool suits—perpetually damp and itchy in the rainy British winter—while dragging around the classics of literature in our bags. We listened to dry recollections of Napoleonic battles from a teacher who offered us snuff.

Between classes, we played a soccer game called headers, volleys, and beats. The aim of the game was to score three times in a row on the same person by either heading or volleying the ball into the goal behind him. If someone gave up three goals in a row, the game was paused, and everyone playing lined up for the opportunity to "beat" the unlucky goalie, punching him in the arm as hard as they could. As the newest, poorest, and most foreign kid at this fancy school, I was singled out by the other boys. I was frequently scored upon and frequently received beats. Sometimes the boys would slightly angle their knuckles to give me a "dead arm" for the entire next class period.

The question is whether these beats count as "bullying." Sure, my left arm often hung limply by my side while I took notes, and sure, I often had black, brown, and yellow bruises blooming like mold under my skin, but I never considered it bullying. My teachers certainly did not see it as bullying, because they happily watched all this punching, seeing it as good schoolyard fun. But today, I'm certain that teachers—and especially parents—would think otherwise. If my kid came home with bruises all over their arm and told me about a game where everyone punched them, I would probably call the principal. Over the past thirty years, the concept of bullying has crept.

You might argue that it's only the weak or the soft who show concept creep. Studies show that left-leaning folks are more likely to be "concept creepers,"[11] but even people who advocate for free-range kids, and who rail against the creep of harm, are guilty of concept creeping. Think about it: compared with the threats faced by past generations of children, like getting caught in farm machinery or drowning in the local pond, the threat of coddling—of too much protection—seems mild. Ironically, worrying about the harm caused by trigger warnings, microaggression training, and political correctness requires an expanded conception of harm.

Whether you lean left or right, it makes little sense to point fingers about the creep of harm. Concept creep is no one's fault because it is unavoidable and occurs anytime two conditions are met. The first condition is that people are motivated to find a "thing," and the second condition is that this "thing" is becoming (or has become) less prevalent. For example, consider food. We are powerfully motivated to find food because our body needs it to survive, meeting condition one. Now imagine that food has become much scarcer than it is today, meeting condition two. Rather than living in a world of easy takeout and giant grocery stores, you're in some postapocalyptic wasteland where fresh food has all but disappeared.

As you shuffle along the deserted streets between decaying buildings, you spy a can of Friskies cat food in an alley. You might have never considered eating cat food in the glorious past of abundant meals, but in this scarce future chances are you would greedily slurp it down.

Because of your continued motivation to find food and its relative rarity, the concept of food has crept to encompass more questionable examples.

Scholars have observed the concept creep of food in real-life situations of scarcity. During famine in Haiti, Zambia, Guinea, and Cameroon, mud cookies are sometimes eaten by the poorest people to avoid starvation. The recipe for mud cookies is simple. Step 1: Collect some dirt. Step 2: Strain the dirt to remove rocks and clumps. Step 3: Mix the wet dirt with salt and vegetable shortening or fat. Step 4: Compress the mud into a ball and press gently, forming the mud into flat disks. Now dry your mud cookie in the sun, and a few hours later it will be ready. Those who eat mud cookies describe them as having a dry consistency with a pungent aftertaste that lingers for hours.[12] The fact that people feel compelled to use this "recipe" is tragic, but nevertheless mud cookies are a real meal to them. It is hard to be pedantic about what counts as "real" food if you are desperate to survive. Of course, these famished folks would rather consume something other than mud cookies, but when people are hungry and food is scarce, the concept of food creeps.

Now consider the creep of harm. Humans are extremely motivated to detect harm (meeting condition one). Our ancestors were constantly worried about threats, and our brains carry this legacy. We evolved to proactively find threats and protect ourselves from them, whether those threats are predators, other people who might harm us, or environmental risks. The foundations of this harm-avoidance motivation are fear and anxiety, feelings that serve an extremely useful survival purpose. If you stayed worried about wild animals and immoral people, you were more likely to take precautions like staying inside or running away, and therefore more likely to avoid death. These worried ancestors passed on their concern to their children, who passed them on to their children, and so on, baking them into human genetics.

Research shows that our attentional system is biased to detect threats and continues to focus on them even after the threat disappears— sometimes literally. In one set of studies, participants looked at a small cross in the middle of a screen when two pictures of faces suddenly appeared, one to the left of the cross and one to the right.[13] One of these faces had a neutral expression, looking vaguely bored, and the other face had a threatening, angry expression. Then both pictures disappeared, and a dot appeared on the left or the right, smack in the middle of where one of the pictures used to be. Participants were asked to quickly press a button to indicate the location of the dot: left or right?

When the dot popped up in the place where the threatening face used to be, people were very quick to indicate its position, which shows that they continued to focus on that spot. Their attention lingered on the location of the "threat," their minds vigilant to the return of danger. On the other hand, when the dot replaced the neutral face, people were slower to indicate its position, for the same reason. People had a hard time disengaging their attention from the "threatening" side of the computer screen, even after the picture had vanished, revealing that we are wired to remain vigilant to threats.

Our sensitivity to danger goes beyond merely focusing on people with threatening expressions. Our big social brains are attuned to information revealing how much a potential threat is actually threatening. A pair of face-perception researchers[14] designed a study that used two sets of pictures. One set of pictures featured people looking ahead, as if they were looking straight at you; this is the standard face set used in psychological research. But the researchers also created another set of pictures, where people were looking off to the side. They reasoned that angry people might seem especially threatening with a direct gaze because it seems as if they were coming to attack you, while a fearful person might indicate the most threat with an averted gaze because it looks as if they detect some unseen threat in the environment, like a predator or a killer.

The study came out as predicted: although people were overall quite quick to detect negative facial expressions of both fear and anger, they were quicker to label anger expressions that were direct (862 milliseconds) rather than averted (914 milliseconds), and they were quicker to label fear expressions that were averted (891 milliseconds) rather than direct (944 milliseconds). This study shows how our innate sensitivity to threat is bound together with our social minds, which focus on the thoughts and feelings of other people.[15]

Although we remain vigilant to potential harms, for concept creep to occur, the prevalence of threats must be declining. As explored at the beginning of this chapter, threats *are* declining: we are much safer than we used to be because of workplace reforms, consumer protections, and safety regulations. We are also much less likely to be victimized by violence compared with our ancestors. As mentioned in chapter 3, the average murder rate within early groups of *Homo sapiens* was 2 percent,[16] meaning that there was a one-in-fifty chance every year of being murdered. Today, the world's most violent cities are much safer than this. One of the most dangerous cities in the world is Tijuana, Mexico, a border town just south of San Diego. It has a murder rate of around 120 for every 100,000 people,[17] or 0.12 percent, an order of magnitude less than the average early hunter-gatherer society. You are ten times safer living in one of the modern world's most dangerous cities than in a random ancestral tribe.

Despite our substantial safety, people are still anxious about crime. In a 2022 Gallup survey, 53 percent of Americans said they worry a "great deal" about crime, and another 27 percent said they worry a "fair amount"—a total of 80 percent of Americans worrying about something relatively rare in society.[18] Interestingly, people living in the safest of suburbs were almost equally worried about violent crime as those living in big cities, even though murder and aggravated assault are extremely rare in the suburbs.

The legacy of evolution means that no matter how much crime is actually occurring, our minds remain set to high alert. The disconnect between *worries* about crime and the *actual prevalence* of crime is caused by concept creep: the safest people remain motivated to find threats, and so their concept of crime expands. Without the sound of gunshots echoing through the suburbs, people see kids walking home by themselves as an example of child abuse.

Beyond people's constant worries about crime, there is good experimental evidence of concept creep. Researchers from Harvard devised a set of simple experiments to induce concept creep—experiments that contained the two conditions we've been discussing: the motivation for detection and reduced prevalence. They reasoned that you could create concept creep in even banal and uncontroversial circumstances, like asking people to find a certain kind of dot.[19] In the actual study, the researchers used different-colored dots, but we can just as easily use shades of gray.

Figure 4.3: Mostly dark dots with some light ones. When you are motivated to find dark dots, it is easy to find them. The four lighter dots clearly do not count as "dark dots."

It's simple: your job is to find all the dark dots. In the figure above, this task seems easy enough, because there are many dark dots (sixteen) and just a few lighter ones.

Now, do the same dot-detection task in the diagram on the next page, which has the same array of dots, but with many lightened. You remain motivated to find dark dots, but now there are fewer of them. This reduced prevalence of dark dots compels you to shift your criteria: the same three or four dots that once seemed light now seem dark, because they are surrounded by even lighter dots. The concept of dot darkness has crept because people's constant motivation (find dark dots) is operating in a context of reduced prevalence (fewer dark dots). Just as people who live in a big city with substantial crime (many assaults and thefts) might scoff at the worries of suburbanites (many fewer assaults and thefts), people who look at the darker picture of figure 4.3 might scoff at the dot detection of those looking at the lighter picture of figure 4.4. But in all cases, our constant motivation for detection adapts to different circumstances, leading people to make more lenient judgments of what "counts" as a concept.

Figure 4.4: A similar diagram to Figure 4.3, but now there are mostly light dots with some darker ones. Now the four dots on the right seem like "dark dots," especially if you are motivated to detect them.

Finding that concept creep occurs with basic perception is important because it reveals that this psychological process is deep and automatic. Pundits often blame concept creep on people's political agenda, and while people's convictions might shape concept creep, it is mostly driven by the simple mechanics of cognition and context: our minds are wired to be vigilant to threats and also to adjust to the surrounding setting.

It is fair to wonder whether dot-detection experiments extend to questions of harm. Another research team at Harvard explored the concept creep of trauma, asking people to rate whether various events were "traumatic," to create a motivation to detect trauma.[20] They had people read scenarios that varied widely in severity, ranging from benign things like "walked up a flight of stairs" to pretty bad things like "broke an ankle while running" to awful things like "having your tongue cut out by a stranger."

The researchers wanted to see if people's concept of trauma would "creep" when they were exposed only to mild events—in other words, when the prevalence of severe trauma was relatively scarce. To test this, they focused on the ratings of two groups of people: one group that saw only mild examples, where the most severe example was something like "was not hired after a job interview," and another group that saw only severe events, with the mildest example being something like "received chemotherapy."

People's ratings revealed evidence of concept creep. People who saw only mild events were looser in rating them as "traumatic" compared with the people who saw just the severe events. One way to capture this shift in ratings is to examine the threshold where participants in each group became more than 50 percent likely to rate an event as traumatic—in other words, how severe an event needed to be for most participants to agree that "yes, this is trauma."

For the group exposed only to severe events, this threshold was high. The label of trauma wasn't consistently applied until events like "listening to an audio tape of a stranger being raped" or "witnessing a corpse unexpectedly in the street." But for the group that saw only mild events, the trauma tipping point was much lower, starting around events like "being publicly scolded by a teacher" and "witnessing a deer killed by a hunter." Their concept of trauma had crept.

This study shows that harm-related concepts can creep, but it also shows that concepts can *un*creep when people are exposed only to severe examples. Our minds categorize events based on the context, and this context can cause us to both relax and tighten our judgments of what counts in a category. When your frame of reference for trauma includes witnessing a murder in a refugee camp, getting your wisdom teeth out doesn't seem so bad. But when those severe cases go away, even minor events can seem traumatic. These findings help explain how our modern society can fixate on relatively minor threats, even though the world is safer than ever. We fixate on these minor threats *because* our world is so safe.

Broadening what counts as harmful or traumatic can spell trouble for people and their mental health when those milder "traumas" are experienced. In a follow-up study, the same team of researchers experimentally manipulated the scope of participants' ideas about trauma, either narrowing their understanding by telling them that scientists consider traumatic events "very rare, horrifying events such as witnessing the murder of innocents" or broadening their understanding by telling them that scientists define trauma subjectively as "any event that could cause intense distress to a person."

Once the researchers shaped people's sense of trauma, they showed them a brutal and gory movie clip—a scene from *The Last King of Scotland* that includes images of a mutilated pregnant woman—and then examined how they reacted. They found that those whose concept of trauma had "crept" in the lab reported being more distressed by the movie clip, were more likely to classify it as a personal trauma, and had more intrusive thoughts (a symptom of PTSD) in the following days.[21]

These results, together with the societal creep of harm, may explain a puzzle in the prevalence of PTSD. Within the United States, Canada, and Europe, PTSD rates have remained stable despite steady decreases in the most common causes of PTSD like violent crime and rape.[22] People get PTSD not necessarily based on the objective violence of an event but instead upon whether they *experience* an event as traumatic—and what events seem traumatic shifts over time.

Creeping concepts of harm (and increasing vulnerability) may also help explain why PTSD rates are higher in affluent countries than in countries that face higher rates of adversity and violence; for instance, the PTSD rate is six times higher in Canada than Mexico,[23] despite Canada's being objectively safer. The clinical psychology professor and PTSD expert Richard McNally writes, "Improvements in standards of living, including reductions in violence, may render people sensitive to stressors that would have seldom affected their grandparents. Perhaps the better things get, the more sensitive we become."[24]

When our mind is motivated to detect something, it will usually find it, even if it means shifting the criterion of detection, whether that's changing what counts as "dark" dots or what counts as "harmful." Of course, you might argue that there is still some objective truth external to our perceptions of these concepts: some dots are physically brighter than others, some foods are more or less nutritious, and some acts cause more or less physical damage. But the objective, physical world is always filtered through the subjectivity of our minds. The concepts of darkness, food, and harm are all ultimately psychological concepts, and as with all concepts what counts as a member of each category is influenced both by our internal motivations and by our external context.

THE CREEP OF OUTRAGE

Just as harm creeps, so does evil. When we expand notions of harm, we also expand notions of harm *doers,* those immoral people who victimize others. If an act seems to hurt children or weaken society, we try to identify the people who enable those harms, and we usually find them. We see well-meaning moms as criminals when they tell their kid to walk home through the suburbs, or British private school boys (or perhaps their teachers) as villains when they play a schoolyard game with ritualized punching.

As we saw in chapter 3, we become outraged when confronted with immorality, and so the yoked-together creep of harm and evil holds powerful consequences for society. As harm seems more ubiquitous, so do evildoers, driving us to feel more morally outraged. We lash out at others as we try to uphold what seems like slipping standards of morality. The creep of harm and evil compels us to feel righteous indignation at even small slights to prevent moral decay from spreading.

Political philosophers have long recognized the paradoxical connection between increased safety and greater perceptions of evil. The "Tocqueville paradox," named after the nineteenth-century French diplomat Alexis de Tocqueville, argues that as societies enjoy more economic and moral progress, people get more frustrated at injustices. Tocqueville understood the subjectivity surrounding which acts are judged as "injustices," and that these judgments hinge on people's reference points. The less overall injustice in a society, the more that unjust acts should stand out—thereby inciting outrage. As Tocqueville puts it, "It is natural that the love of equality should constantly increase together with equality itself, and that it should grow by what it feeds on." As society gets less unjust, people demand even more justice.

The Tocqueville paradox nicely captures the idea of concept creep and explains how people today can be outraged at (historically speaking) minor social injustices, despite being surrounded by (historically speaking) unprecedented equality. People feel outraged not *despite* increasing equality but *because* of it.

The trouble with the creep of harm and evil is that our fixation on smaller and smaller injustices may lead us to destroy institutions that work to keep us safe, like the courts and the police. This is the conservative argument against concept creep, and it should be taken seriously because these institutions (like the rule of law) generally do make us safer—at least much safer than our ancestors, who lacked these institutions.

At the same time, if concept creep is a problem, it is surely a problem of progress. The concept creep of harm reveals that society is getting increasingly safer. Concepts creep when instances of the concept become less prevalent, and so the creep of harm signals that violence is becoming rarer. People labeling offhand comments and unintentional slights as "harmful" might be frustrating, but it means that blatant cruelty is less pervasive than before. Of course, it bears acknowledging that much cruelty exists today, and any amount of cruelty is too much. It is also true that our institutions are imperfect and often biased, but for many people in the world safety is increasingly the norm.

Concept creep also explains why it always *feels* as if the world were getting less moral, even if people have been getting less violent over time. In a paper called "The Illusion of Moral Decline," a team of researchers gathered large-scale surveys from around the world and identified fifty-eight different questions focusing on perceptions of morality in society.[25] Approximately 354,000 participants from sixty different nations answered these questions, which included "Right now, do you think the state of moral values in this country as a whole is getting better or getting worse?" and "Considering just the moral climate of the country today, do you feel things in this country are generally going in the right direction, or do you feel things have pretty seriously gotten off on the wrong track?"

People's responses across a twelve-year span from 1996 to 2007 showed a clear trend: for 86.21 percent of these items, people thought that morality had declined. When researchers cross-checked their findings with an American data set of 220,000 people from 1949 to 2019, their results replicated. People believe that morality has been declining, at about the same rate, for as long as researchers have been asking.

When these researchers asked Americans living in 2020 why they thought society was less moral than it was fifteen years earlier, most people volunteered two explanations. The first explanation was interpersonal change: respondents believed that the people who were alive in 2005 had become less kind, honest, nice, and good as they've aged. The second explanation was generational change: respondents believed that compared with the people who died in the past fifteen years, the new generation that replaced them is crueler and less moral. This belief was endorsed most strongly by older generations, like boomers and Gen X, but even Gen Z somewhat agreed with the idea of generational decline. Even someone just turning eighteen shakes their head at "kids these days."

People believe that others are getting less moral, but is this true? To test this question, the researchers turned to a Gallup survey that spanned fifty-five years from 1965 to 2020, with almost four and a half million respondents. This survey contained questions asking people about their own moral behavior and the moral behavior of those around them, and each person took the survey twice (or more), with at least ten years between them taking and retaking the survey. The questions included "Have you helped a stranger or someone you didn't know who needed help in the last month?" or "Within the past 12 months, have you been assaulted or mugged?" or "During the past 12 months, have you let a stranger go ahead of you in line?"

Over the decades, people's answers to these questions remained the same; there was no moral decline. Other data showed evidence of moral improvement: people's rates of cooperation in the prisoner's dilemma game from 1956 to 2017 increased. The prisoner's dilemma is a simple two-player game used in economic experiments. It is like the public goods game described in the last chapter, where cooperation leads to a better outcome for both players, but each player has an incentive to betray the other for individual gain. In this big data set spanning seventy-one years, people have become increasingly likely to choose cooperation over betrayal.[26] All these data convincingly show that—luckily—moral decline is an illusion, but it is a particularly powerful illusion that distorts our perceptions, making us worry about the fate of society and the intentions of strangers.

It is all but impossible to escape our constant concern about harm, but in a strange way there is another reason to be grateful for the existence of concept creep. Although it makes the world seem worse, it helps drive society toward increasing safety. As our moral minds become increasingly intolerant of danger and injustice, we move the goalposts of what counts as truly "safe" or "fair" and then try to change the world to meet those goalposts. Consider the safety of cars. Once Volvo invented the three-point seat belt in 1959 and shared it with the world, humanity could have just high-fived each other and stopped worrying about car safety. After all, the seat belt reduces fatalities in collisions by 45 percent. But the human motivation to protect ourselves pushed engineers, designers, and policy makers to make ever safer vehicles, creating airbags (which save an additional 2,756 people annually), antilock brakes, and dozens of smaller but important safety innovations.

Perhaps the best example of the creep of harm is our expanding compassion for animals. Not so long ago, animals were simply fleshy resources to be exploited by people. We kept dogs for protection, horses for transportation, oxen for plowing fields, and other animals just to eat. Animals were chattel, mere possessions to be bought and sold, to be hit if they disobeyed and killed once they outlived their usefulness.[27] But as we got safer and better fed, our concerns about suffering no longer extended to merely our family and fellow humans; they jumped species.

As we reduced many of the most salient threats to our own safety, we started expanding our moral circle, worrying more about the safety and rights of animals, wondering whether livestock are happy and whether our pets are depressed. If you told someone seventy years ago that Americans today spend nearly $7 billion annually on pills for pet anxiety, depression, and OCD,[28] they would laugh in disbelief, wondering how people could care so much about the feelings of mere beasts. The explanation is the creep of harm. Just as many people today would see the private school game of headers, volleys, and beats as bullying, they would also see it as animal abuse to leave a dog chained up outside in the rain. We care so much about the well-being of all living creatures because society today is so safe.

Just as we should be happy that the world is getting safer, it might make sense to dispel the illusion of moral decline. Wouldn't we all be happier to appreciate the more optimistic truth behind our pessimistic assumptions? The website HumanProgress.org, a project of the Cato Institute, aims to create gratitude and resilience by spreading awareness about many often-ignored positive trends in society. The goals of this project are admirable, but face psychological headwinds because focusing on threats and evil is part of human nature. Becoming more aware of social progress will provide only a temporary guard against feelings of moral decay, especially because of the power of one modern institution: social media.

On social media, feelings of threat can spur full-blown moral panics. To manage this panic, we react with the best tool available—moral outrage.

ONLINE MORAL PANICS

Modern life is filled with moral outrage, especially on social media. *Slate* magazine nicknamed the year 2014 "The Year of Outrage," documenting an online controversy for every single day of the year.[29] But soon *Slate* had to admit a sadder truth: there was nothing special about 2014, because "every year is the year of outrage."[30] Every day of every year, people are incensed on social media. Why?

Many features of social media make it perfect for expressing outrage. Anonymity turns people callous and bold,[31] making them comfortable saying cruel things to others. One reason you don't often scream at people in real life after they make a bad joke or express an unpopular opinion is that you're engaging with a human face, and you can see firsthand when that person winces and cries. But social media connects distant strangers, each of whom is represented with an abstract avatar, making it easy to forget that there is a real human being receiving your attacks.

Another related reason that people are aggressive on social media has to do with social diffusion: platforms allow you to hide in a crowd. If you shouted at a stranger on the street about how their clothing offends you, you would be accountable to everyone else watching, but social media allows you to just be one of hundreds of angry comments on a post, hoisting your digital pitchfork in an internet mob.

Expressing outrage is also encouraged on social media by design: the algorithms that fuel various platforms are fine-tuned to capture people's attention, and research finds that few things are more attention grabbing than moral outrage. A study of 563,312 political tweets found that people engaged most with posts that included emotional words related to morality. For every extra outrageous word, including "hate," "violent," and "destroy," posts were 20 percent more likely to be shared.[32]

Because we intuitively appreciate the attentional appeal of moral outrage, we often exaggerate moral outrage in posts, claiming that people are "monsters" or "pure evil." It is like typing "LOL" in a reply to a friend's text, even if you didn't actually laugh out loud at all. You know that "LOL" will win you more points with your friend than writing, "That was kind of humorous."

One popular theory argues that vying for attention is the main driver of expressing outrage online. This idea is called moral grandstanding and suggests that people express moral outrage to look good to their fellow group members. If you are a member of one political party and aggressively rage against the other party, then other members of your party see you as morally upstanding. The more outrage you express, the more social points you get—sometimes literally when it comes to "likes" or "shares"—and these social points make you look good, helping you to gain friends or impress potential dates.

Moral grandstanding suggests that moral outrage is like a peacock's tail—less about expressing deep moral convictions and more about looking nice. There is some evidence for moral grandstanding. In one study, researchers measured people's tendency to express moral outrage online, and also how much they thirsted for fame and power. The study showed that the more people reported a strong desire to lead, dominate, or be respected, the more they admitted to getting into online fights about politics.[33]

Moral grandstanding certainly exists, but it seems unlikely that people express outrage online primarily to win social rewards. The big problem is that social media is *un*rewarding. The more that people use platforms like Facebook, the worse their mental health.[34] Of course, correlation is not causation, but it seems clearly soul-wrenching to compare the monotony and indignities of your own offline life with everyone else's magical, angel-blessed online highlight reel. You're sitting in sweatpants at your messy kitchen counter, looking at your phone while eating dusty bottom-of-the-bag cereal. Online, other people are laughing with attractive friends about inside jokes as they drive to a secret beach in a retro convertible, sunshine glinting off their wind-swirled hair.

Social media seems especially bad for your mental health when you are engaging with politics. My postdoctoral researcher Curtis Puryear and I measured the mental health of people who used Twitter to engage with either politics or nonpolitical content like memes, hobbies, and entertainment. We also looked at how much attention people paid to metrics, including retweets and likes, because presumably people who are fixated on gaining social attention notice metrics related to social attention.

Once you crossed the distinctions between those who looked at politics (versus not) and those who checked metrics (versus not), it left four different groups of people. We were most interested in the mental health of people who were engaging with politics and looking at social media metrics. As predicted, these folks were the most stressed out. In fact, many of them reported a clinically significant level of PTSD symptoms, like feeling constantly on guard, having random outbursts of anger, and having recurrent thoughts about stressful events.

If engaging with politics on social media impairs our mental health, then why do people spend hours each day on these platforms, getting outraged at strangers? Consistent with everything we've been discussing, we find that outrage on social media is driven by feelings of threat—the threat of harm and the threat of evil. At its core, moral outrage is a response to the feeling that others are acting immorally and that their immorality is destroying society. We yell at people so that we can call out evildoers to others so that we might collectively punish and exile them.

Perhaps it seems far-fetched that screaming at someone on social media can result in exile, but there are many cases, like Justine Sacco, of people being "canceled" from society. Of course, being canceled is a subjective term that might mean losing your job, getting shunned by your friends, or getting kicked off social media. These punishments instill fear in the minds of other people, discouraging their acting immorally in the future.

In other words, humans express outrage online for the same reason they expressed outrage in Stone Age tribes: to guard against societal harm and reinforce moral norms. People scream at others on social media not primarily to win points but because they feel threatened. This idea is supported by a series of studies we ran examining mass outpourings of moral outrage—moral panics. The term "moral panic" was coined by the sociologist Stanley Cohen to describe large-scale mobilizations of outrage targeting apparent societal threats like witches (in 1692 Salem) and marijuana (from the 1930s onward).

One of the biggest American moral panics happened in the 1980s in response to kids playing Dungeons & Dragons (D&D), the imaginative tabletop role-playing game where players go on fantasy quests together. One Christian right organization, BADD (Bothered About Dungeons and Dragons), launched an intensive media campaign falsely linking role-playing games to youth suicide, drug use, and satanism. After someone spread these allegations on the widely watched news program *60 Minutes,* moral panic ensued. Horrified suburban parents wrote letters to Congress trying to get the game banned, and the game became contraband among teens in the late 1980s.

Although the claims of BADD were discredited, some still worry about the impact of these games. In 2010, Kevin Singer, a prisoner at the Waupun Correctional Institution in Wisconsin, decided to pass the time by introducing his fellow inmates to D&D. Kevin grew up loving the game, but could no longer play after he was sentenced to life in prison for brutally murdering his sister's boyfriend, so he decided to make his own version of D&D, complete with a ninety-six-page manual of stories and characters. It might be funny to imagine hardened criminals role-playing as wizards and mythical creatures, but the prison guards didn't find it amusing. They promptly shut the operation down, arguing that it could make the prisoners more violent and give them ideas about escaping.[35]

With all moral panics, D&D included, the perception of threat is clear and these perceptions feature prominently in Stanley Cohen's definition of the term: "A condition, episode, person, or group of persons emerges to become [collectively] defined as a threat to societal values and interests." Curtis Puryear and I wondered if feelings of threat might also fuel moral panics on social media. We reasoned that social media should be an especially fertile place for moral panics, because it pairs an infinite source of threats—from the deadliness of gas stoves to the destruction of democracy—with social proof of the danger.

As a social species, we humans rely on other people for information. We wear clothing brands that other people wear and we watch the TV shows other people watch, because questions of what makes for good fashion or solid entertainment are ambiguous. When other people think or act a certain way, it provides proof that we should think or act that way too. It is easy to be cynical about this conformity, but it also makes good sense. If everyone in your tribe is eating one kind of mushroom, it is probably safer to eat that mushroom than something you randomly pick in the forest.

Social proof is especially powerful with threats. If you're standing in the street and you see a flood of people running away and screaming, you would decide to run too. It is reasonable to assume that something dangerous is coming. Social proof is one reason why threats in crowded public places can be so deadly, even when there is no real threat. In 1913 one man shouted "fire!" at a crowded union miners' Christmas party in Calumet, Michigan. There was no fire, but this man's perception of imminent danger killed seventy-three men, women, and children, all trampled as the crowd rushed frantically toward the single exit.

Our minds evolved to panic when other people detect threats. Consider our primate cousins, who react similarly to social proof. If a few members of a monkey troop make the "leopard" alarm call, other monkeys seldom pause to ponder whether there is *really* a leopard, at least not until they are hidden within a tall tree. Instead, they scream, holler, and sprint for safety.

In social media, this social proof is provided by people's outraged replies and also by explicit virality metrics like reposts and retweets, which provide concrete markers of how many people are talking about various threats. Curtis and our team reasoned that these virality metrics might accelerate moral panics as we mapped out a model of how online moral panics occur: first, some potential threat (danger?) is identified; second, warnings about the threat go viral (social proof: danger!); third, people personally feel threatened (I feel threatened by danger!); and, fourth, people express moral outrage (punish people responsible for danger!) in an attempt to protect themselves and society from the threat.

As a first test of this model, Curtis used an algorithm to collect and analyze hundreds of thousands of tweets about three political topics that often create outrage: climate change (97,088 tweets), immigration (43,531 tweets), and COVID-19 (96,611 tweets).[36] He then looked at whether those tweets that went viral (those in the top 10 percent of virality with more than 7,495 retweets) generated more moral outrage than nonviral tweets (those in the bottom 10 percent of virality with fewer than 2 retweets). For the least viral tweets, 25 percent of replies were morally outraged, as measured by levels of anger, disgust, contempt, and blame. But when tweets went viral, 40 percent of replies used emotionally outraged language.

I've been suggesting that virality causes people to spew angry comments, but there could be another explanation for this effect: the content of highly viral tweets could simply be more outrageous, and this alone could be driving outraged replies. We know from other studies that outrageous content is more likely to go viral, so perhaps people respond to viral tweets like "This politician killed a kitten!" just because they are intrinsically outrageous, not because they are going viral.

To rule out this competing explanation, we can compare tweets that contain similar content (and outrageousness) but have different levels of virality. Would the exact same tweet have more outraged replies when it goes more viral? When we reran our analyses controlling for the content, the predicted effect held strong: more viral tweets were more likely to have outraged replies. The more any dangerous idea seems to be spreading in society, the more people try to combat its spread with outrage.

We also tested the idea that moral panics are driven more by feelings of danger than by moral grandstanding. People in our study read fake tweets designed to be threatening based on their political orientation: liberal participants read about the threat of police violence and environmental catastrophe, and conservative participants read about the dangers of critical race theory and the flood of illegal immigrants crossing the border.

We manipulated the virality of these threatening tweets, showing people that they had either gone viral (a thousand retweets) or not (just a dozen retweets), and then measured people's feelings of threat by asking whether the topic of the tweet "is a dangerous issue" and "poses a serious threat to this country." Finally, we measured how much people planned to express moral outrage about the tweet. As we predicted, increasing the virality of the threatening tweet made people feel more threatened, and these feelings of looming danger most strongly drove people's desire to respond with outrage.

My favorite study by Curtis examined people's reaction to the worrying trend of *dizzydogging*—when people use laser pointers to make their dogs run in circles until they get dizzy, and then laugh as their dizzy dogs stumble into objects, and perhaps even tumble down the stairs. Don't worry about the dogs—dizzydogging was a fake trend invented by Curtis to test whether our model of moral panics applied to new threats. We showed participants a photo of what looked like a dizzy dog, along with this accompanying tweet: "I got him dizzy as hell with this laser pointer. Wait till he starts crashing into everything at the end haha #dizzydogging."

We varied the virality metrics of these dizzydogging videos, giving them a few or thousands of retweets. As expected, people who saw it going viral were more likely to see danger in society and more likely to express outrage about that danger. We again found that people's willingness to express outrage—to rant and rage about the evilness of the dizzydoggers—was best predicted by feelings of danger. These data are consistent with a harm-based moral mind and support the "protection narrative." When people lash out online, it is not because they are aggressively trying to destroy the other side but instead because they are fearfully trying to protect their children and society—and dogs—from perceived threats.

Social media companies understand this model of online moral panics but have a different name for moral panics: "engagement." Their algorithms promote content that is both threatening and viral, a recipe for constant feelings of danger and moral panics. Exacerbating these feelings of danger is *where* we often look at social media: on the toilet or in bed. It's hard to imagine a more vulnerable situation than sitting with your pants down or lying alone in the dark. Both situations left our hominid ancestors exposed to predators, so is it any wonder that we get panicked about moral predators and the collapse of civilization while reading about them in our bathrooms and bedrooms? Social media may theoretically hold unparalleled promise for connecting humankind, but to our ancient harm-based minds it is mostly terrifying.

FROM THEN TO NOW

Humanity has come a long way from little *Australopithecus* cowering from predators in caves. We now live in cities and towns that protect us from animal attacks, and we have a powerful sense of good and evil—along with strong institutions to help enforce our morals. At the same time, we just can't shake our fear of harm and evildoers. Now that we live in relative safety, our concepts of harm creep to include milder situations, and we fixate on viral threats on social media.

Concerns about harm have driven much of our ancient evolution and continue to drive our modern moral judgments—even toward acts that seem harmless to some.

In Sum

- Just as our ancestors underwent a "social transition" by moving into big groups, modern humans have undergone a "safety transition," eradicating many threats. Today, we are safer than ever from diseases, natural disasters, and interpersonal violence.
- Despite this safety, we cannot relax. Because our minds are wired to scan for threats, we still see danger everywhere. As our environment becomes safer, we broaden our concept of what counts as harmful. The "concept creep" of harm leads us to see relatively mild harms as traumatic.
- When harm creeps, so does evil. Our moral minds are grounded in concerns about harm, so when we expand our perceptions of harm, we also see more immorality. The creep of evil explains why we see well-meaning moms as criminals and why society (wrongly) always seems to be in moral decline.

- Social media makes us feel even more threatened and drives record levels of moral outrage. Online platforms provide a limitless supply of potential threats and concrete evidence—virality metrics—that other people are worrying about these threats. These are the perfect conditions for moral panics.

PART 2

OUR MORAL MIND

Modern Harms

Harmless Wrongs Exist

In part 1, we saw how the threat of harm has shaped human nature. Because we evolved as a prey species, we are wired to remain vigilant for danger. To avoid getting eaten by predators, we moved into groups, which also kick-started the development of our powerful social brains. Living with so many other people helped to keep us safe, well fed, and prosperous, but other people also posed a threat.

Our fellow humans could hurt us, and so we developed a moral sense—and a sense of outrage—to maintain cooperation and safety. Human cultures evolved to condemn the many acts that might directly or indirectly cause harm, and to get outraged at those who perpetrate these acts. No matter what or whom our moral condemnation was targeting, it was always driven by the same underlying concern about threat and danger.

All moral psychologists agree that morality evolved to help us avoid harm, but there is a big debate about how much our moral judgments are—in the present—*psychologically* rooted in perceptions of harm. Evolutionary pressures compelled humans to develop a sense of right and wrong because it protected our ancestors, but how much does harm matter when our modern minds make moral judgments? In this book, I argue that we have a harm-based moral mind and that *all* moral judgments are psychologically grounded in harm, no matter whether you lean left or right. To answer the question "How morally wrong is this behavior?" people intuitively ask themselves, "How harmful does this behavior seem?" In the end, there is no moral judgment that does not somehow psychologically revolve around harm.

However, there are moral psychologists who believe that only *some* moral judgments are driven by concerns about harm. They reject the idea of a harm-based moral mind, and instead argue for a moral mind that is carved up into different little mechanisms, only one of which revolves around harm. Which view of the moral mind is correct matters not only for science but also for how we understand and bridge moral divides. And so we will dive deeply into moral psychology. But first a little story.

To support the claim that harm matters for only some of morality, researchers point to people's reactions to a short scenario, the most famous in the history of moral psychology. Be warned, it's a bit gross:

> Julie and Mark, who are brother and sister are traveling together in France. They are both on summer vacation from college. One night they are staying alone in a cabin near the beach. They decide that it would be interesting and fun if they tried making love. At the very least it would be a new experience for each of them. Julie was already taking birth control pills, but Mark uses a condom too, just to be safe. They both enjoy it, but they decide not to do it again. They keep that night as a special secret between them, which makes them feel even closer to each other. So what do you think about this? Was it wrong for them to have sex?[1]

This scenario was constructed by today's most famous moral psychologist, Jonathan Haidt. You might know Haidt today for his thoughtful indictments of modern society, including the harm caused by coddling American youth or the suffering caused by social media. But before this work, he argued for a model of the moral mind that locked harm into a little box.

Haidt's idea was that the moral mind is divided into distinct sections, like a building partitioned into different rooms, each opened by its own unique key. One room was opened by a harm-based key, but he was certain there were other rooms that this key could *not* open. He argued that some kinds of morals were completely disconnected from concerns about harm and that unlocking the door of these morals required other non-harm keys, including special keys for loyalty, authority, and purity.

To the question "How do concerns about harm matter for morality?" Haidt's answer is that worries about victimization matter only when people are judging acts that cause obvious physical or emotional harm, like assault or abuse. When it comes to acts that are not obviously harmful, like "talking back to an authority figure" (a violation of authority), Haidt argues that considerations of harm are irrelevant; people condemn this act based only on its amount of disrespect.

To argue against the sweeping importance of harm in our moral judgments, Haidt devised some scenarios that he believed to be "objectively harmless," where something wrong happens without causing obvious physical or emotional harm. The Mark and Julie scenario is the most famous of these harmless scenarios. When Haidt and his colleagues asked University of Virginia undergraduates about Mark and Julie, many of them said that the siblings were doing something wrong by making love.

When Haidt followed up on these judgments and asked why these students saw consensual incest as immoral, participants initially provided harm-based explanations: these siblings might have children with disabilities, or ruin their relationship, or cause their parents anguish. But Haidt pointed to elements of the scenario that explicitly ruled out this harm, reminding them that Mark and Julie used two forms of birth control, the incest brought them emotionally closer together, and they forever kept it a secret from their parents.

After people's initial harm-based explanations had been defeated, many students still saw Mark and Julie's tryst as wrong. The durability of their moral condemnation, even after their harm-based explanations had been refuted by reason, led Haidt to conclude that harm could not be the master key of morality. Here was a room carefully designed to be off-limits to harm—*an objectively harmless wrong*—and yet people still saw what was inside that room (that is, Mark and Julie's lovemaking) as immoral. He reasoned that this provided evidence of one or more moral keys in addition to harm, especially a separate purity key that—at least for conservatives—is used to condemn bizarre and "impure" sexual behavior.

The existence of harmless wrongs seemed to argue against a harm-based moral mind and kicked off a whole movement in moral psychology, a movement that culminated in the idea of "moral foundations theory." This theory partitions our moral mind into five different psychological rooms, two used by both liberals and conservatives (care/harm, fairness), and three used only by conservatives (loyalty, authority, purity). We will explore the claims of moral foundations theory in the upcoming chapters, but the essential idea is that different moral concerns are deeply and fundamentally distinct. This theory animates Haidt's best-selling book *The Righteous Mind* and is popular because it seems to make sense of the divides between liberals and conservatives.

As a junior graduate student, I was enamored with moral foundations theory, and not just because my adviser and Haidt were great friends. I appreciated how it gave a language to describe the values that people cared about and fought over. I also appreciated the elegance of moral foundations theory. Few things in nature or in the mind are so tidy that they can be neatly divided into a whole number, but moral foundations said there were just five moral concerns—of which harm was only one.

The Mark and Julie scenario was the key piece of empirical evidence used to argue for the existence of harmless wrongs and to advocate for a mind that divided harm from other moral concerns. This story of consensual incest was not the only "harmless wrong" that existed. Philosophers have long discussed the immorality of other harmless wrongs, like white lies and breaking promises to the dead, and now moral foundations theory seemed to provide a psychological framework to make sense of these harmless wrongs.

But the more I studied morality, the more I thought that "harmless wrongs" might be a myth. The whole idea of harmless wrongs argues that—psychologically speaking—people are willing to condemn an act as immoral while also genuinely seeing it as harmless. In other words, in people's minds there should be a clean break between what people see as harmful and what they see as wrong. To explore the idea of "harmless wrongs," we can study two kinds of people: those who see Mark and Julie's actions as harmless, and those who see their actions as wrong.

Who sees Mark and Julie's actions as harmless? Mostly the moral psychologists who designed the scenario with circumstances that seldom exist in the world. Real-life examples of sex between family members are seldom harmless and typically involve large power differences, lack of consent, destroyed families, social disapproval, and children with disabilities. Of course, there may be some very well-kept cases of incest that are beautiful, fun, and consensual, but we can all agree that the story of Mark and Julie is atypical—explaining why people generally find the premise of "harmlessness" very hard to believe.[2]

The moral psychologists who see Mark and Julie's actions as harmless also seem *not* to see consensual incest as wrong. For unclear reasons, moral psychologists tend to lean libertarian, believing that people should be free to do whatever they like so long as it doesn't cause immediate physical or emotional harm, whether that's using drugs, indulging in bizarre fetishes, or engaging in consensual incest.

Perhaps my colleagues and I are born with blunted senses of moral outrage, and so are fascinated by other people's strong moral reactions. This is called the deficit theory of research—that people are drawn to study what they lack. It's why people who feel loneliness might study social connection, or why people with trouble reading might decide to study the psychology of language comprehension. But whatever drives people to study morality, my colleagues generally do not see Mark and Julie as doing something heinous. So from the perspective of my fellow moral psychologists, consensual incest is both harmless and permissible. To put it succinctly, morality researchers judge Mark and Julie's behavior as a "harmless right," or at least a "harmless okay."

Who are the people who see Mark and Julie's actions as wrong? They include some of the college students from Haidt's studies (and most other people too). Crucially, these students also feel that consensual incest is harmful, as revealed by how they initially explained their moral outrage toward Mark and Julie: these siblings would destroy their family, have deformed children, and be filled with the emotional pain of regret. Of course, Haidt and his colleagues designed these scenarios to not include these harms, but—in the pits of their stomachs—these students did not believe these contrived safeguards.

In fact, in follow-up studies using this same scenario, participants remain convinced that Mark and Julie's actions will cause harm, believing that there is still a chance that Julie could get pregnant, no matter what the scenario says.[3] In another study, participants believed that Mark and Julie's actions *could have* caused harm, even if they got away with it in this instance. Just as people condemn drunk driving even when someone makes it home from the bar without incident, these participants condemned incest because of its potential for harm.[4] These studies show that people who see incest as wrong do not accept that sex with your sibling is completely harmless. Their intuition is that consensual incest is both wrong *and* harmful—not a harmless wrong but a "harmful wrong."

Let's revisit the question of who sees Mark and Julie as a "harmless wrong." It's not the moral psychologists, who see consensual incest as harmless but not wrong, and it's not the student participants, who see it as both wrong and harmful. Psychologically speaking, *no one* sees it as a harmless wrong. In people's minds, harm and immorality seem to be tightly connected, whether you are a laissez-faire moral psychologist or a condemning college student.

Haidt might argue that the students are wrong in their intuitions of harm: the story of Mark and Julie was designed to be objectively harmless. But what if questions of harm are more subjective than objective?

Even if some acts might be more or less obviously damaging, I'm proposing that harm is better understood as a perception, especially when it comes to morality. Rather than being objectively present or absent, harm should be understood as a subjective perception that varies from low to medium to high. Acts can seem more or less harmful to different people, and these perceptions are what drive our moral judgments. Moral psychologists might view consensual incest as low on harm, and college students might view this act as medium harmful, and these relative differences in perceived harm might explain why college students condemn this act more than moral psychologists.

If psychology teaches one truth, it is that our minds take the outside world as only a starting point, filtering "objective" external information through our idiosyncratic perceptions, our intuitive assumptions, and our cultural lens. We saw the subjectivity of harm when we talked about concept creep in the last chapter, how people living at different times disagree about which acts are truly harmful, including bullying or trauma.[5] The subjectivity of harm means that before we make blanket assertions about whether an act is harmless or harmful, we need to ask, "According to whom?"

In the quest to understand people's inner worlds, modern moral psychology does a decent job of asking, "According to whom?" when it comes to judgments of right and wrong. All moral psychologists—whether my team or supporters of moral foundations theory—argue that moral judgments are subjective. There may be moral absolutes underpinning the universe, but moral psychology puts aside this question to study how different people make sense of good and evil. As I mentioned in the introduction, moral psychology is a *descriptive* science when it comes to morality, not a prescriptive one. Rather than studying which deeds are actually good and evil, moral psychologists study people's *perceptions* of which deeds are good and evil.

But although all scientists agree that moral judgments are subjective, my team and I disagree with supporters of moral foundations theory about one crucial thing—harm. We argue that *harm is also subjective* and that questions of threat, danger, suffering, and vulnerability are ultimately in the mind of the beholder. In fact, we claim that harm is just as subjective as morality and that our intuitive perceptions of harm drive our intuitive perceptions of immorality. "Harmless wrongs" do not exist in the human mind, because perceptions of harm and judgments of immorality are inextricably linked. As we will see, this deep link between harm and morality explains both our moral disagreements and how best to bridge them.

The key claim we explore here in part 2 is that people's moral condemnation of an act hinges on its harmfulness—and its harmfulness is a matter of perception.

Of course, there are many acts that many agree are obviously harmful and obviously wrong, like murder or abuse. There are also many acts that—despite violating social norms—seem obviously harmless and obviously permissible, like reading a book upside down. But there are other acts—like having an abortion or opening up a country's borders to immigrants—that lie in the murky area where wrongness and harmfulness are ambiguous. When we look across the whole spectrum of morality, we will see evidence of a harm-based mind. All people—liberals and conservatives—condemn acts based on how harmful they seem.

In Sum

- The myth of our moral minds is that harmless wrongs exist. Because people condemn "objectively" harmless acts like consensual incest, some moral psychologists partitioned harm from other moral concerns.
- The idea of harmless wrongs rests on the false assumption that harm is objectively absent or present, rather than a subjective perception from low to medium to high.

Chapter 5

Legacy: A Recent History of Harm

This book is about the power of harm in our minds, in morality, and in society. It is about how concerns about victimization drive our moral disagreements and how stories of suffering can bring us back together. By emphasizing the importance of harm, we follow a path laid down more than fifty years ago by the moral psychologist Elliot Turiel and his colleagues. These researchers studied not adults' judgments of consensual incest but instead how children made sense of rule violations, like whether it was morally acceptable for a kid to punch a classmate or to wear pajamas to school.

Lots of work from developmental psychologists (psychologists who study children) finds that even before children learn to speak, they have strong intuitions about who is good and who is bad.[1] Understanding how children think about morality helps to reveal the building blocks of our moral minds.

Elliot Turiel works at the University of California, Berkeley, and in the 1970s, he invited three- and five-year-olds into his lab to get their moral judgments about everyday scenarios. When Turiel asked kids about punching a classmate or a sibling, they almost always said that it was wrong.

When he tweaked the scenario, now asking if this violent act would be okay if a teacher gave permission, kids said it was still wrong. In the language of moral psychology, the wrongness of these acts was "universal and authority-independent." Whether you were at home, at school, or on vacation in a foreign country, kids said it was always wrong to punch your classmate, even with the permission of an authority figure.

Kids made very different moral judgments when it came to wearing pajamas at school. They usually said it was not allowable if the teacher forbade it, but that it was okay if their teacher allowed it. Wearing pajamas to school might sometimes be "wrong," but it isn't *morally* wrong in the same way as punching a classmate. Based on these interviews with kids, Turiel discovered that our moral minds distinguished between acts that were truly immoral and acts that merely violated social conventions (also called social norms, as we saw in chapter 3).

Turiel argued that truly immoral acts were seen by people as immoral across cultures, places, and times, while acts that violated social conventions were more context dependent, like whether you could eat French fries with your fingers, which is probably okay at McDonald's but not at dinner with the British royal family. In the language of moral psychology, merely counter-normative acts—those that just break social norms—are neither universal nor authority independent. The wrongness of these acts depends on who you are, where you are, and who says it's okay. Of course, immoral acts like punching an innocent person are both immoral *and* counter-normative, because they violate the rules of society, but some acts like impolite behavior are *just* counter-normative.

By interviewing many kids about many different scenarios, Turiel discovered what separated immoral acts from violations of mere social convention: harm. Acts that seemed immoral to kids were those that seemed to victimize other people. Kids thought that it was wrong to intentionally cause damage to someone vulnerable. When acts broke social norms but did not cause harm—like not setting the table the right way—kids did not judge them as immoral.[2]

Future studies built on Turiel's initial findings, and eventually it became clear that harm was the central criterion that kids used for making moral judgments. Yet more studies extended this theory to adults, demonstrating that if you want to know what someone sees as *wrong,* your best bet is to figure out what they see as *harmful.* The discoveries of Turiel and his colleagues pointed to a harm-based moral mind, but others had doubts.

BEYOND WEIRD

By the beginning of the 1980s, Turiel seemed to have moral psychology all wrapped up. There was a bright line—harm—separating acts that are morally wrong from acts that are merely socially wrong or just counter-normative. But some people wondered if this line was a little too bright. Perhaps a different set of people would condemn acts that did not involve obvious physical violence. Perhaps some people would judge harmless norm violations as morally wrong.

The problem with Turiel's studies is that they all focused on "WEIRD" people. They didn't have green antennae or extrasensory perception; instead, they were all from societies that are "Western, educated, industrialized, rich, and democratic." Although WEIRD people represent most of the people in psychological experiments—including college sophomores—cultural anthropologists are quick to point out that they are unrepresentative of the rest of the world. Most people on Earth live in societies that are not Western and that are less educated, less industrialized, less rich, and less democratic.[3] Because Turiel focused on kids in Berkeley, California—which today is still an extremely WEIRD and politically progressive place—scholars were skeptical of his claim that his theory explained all human morality. They argued that to really understand morality, you had to study different groups of people. It helped if you were willing to travel.

One of Turiel's skeptics was an anthropologist who traveled to Bhubaneswar, India, in 1987. There he studied the moral judgments of Brahman Indians, testing how much they matched (or didn't match) the moral judgments of Americans. Brahmans are the "priestly" caste within Hindu society and are expected to serve as religious teachers and to preside over sacred ceremonies within temples. Because of this focus on sacredness and religion, this anthropologist—named Richard Shweder—thought that these Brahman Indians might have moral concerns that kids in Berkeley lacked. Rather than asking Brahmans about wearing pajamas and punching your classmate, Shweder asked about the morality of eating chicken.[4]

Americans might see eating chicken as immoral if they are vegetarians or vegans. After all, a chicken dies so you can eat it. But Shweder asked them a slightly different question: Is it *especially* wrong to eat chicken after a funeral? Your first reaction is probably confusion. The question seems odd, because, to Westerners, nothing about funerals seems to forbid eating chicken. I recently went to an American funeral that served fried chicken, and no one shouted in outrage. In fact, the author of a funeral food cookbook from the American South agrees that fried chicken is an especially great food to serve the grieving because it is comforting and almost everyone likes it.[5]

But the actual question Shweder asked them was even more specific: Is it especially wrong for an *eldest son* to eat chicken after his *father's* funeral? Again, this question seems strange. If it is generally okay for people to eat chicken after a funeral, then why not the deceased's eldest son? But these Brahman Indians were insistent that this act was immoral.

When Shweder asked this priestly caste to explain their judgments, they talked a lot about "purity." They believed that death creates a kind of impurity called "death pollution" and that the eldest son was responsible for processing (or sublimating) his father's death pollution by eating a pure vegetarian diet. The idea is that spiritual toxins build up in the father's spirit after death, and the son must use his own body as a filter. To be effective, this filter must be kept clean by refraining from meat eating. Processing the death pollution was thought to take twelve days, during which the spiritual toxins would grow out in the son's fingernails and his hair. On the twelfth day the son would cut his hair and fingernails, where the death pollution had accumulated, and take a final "purifying" bath.[6] Until his father's death pollution was properly processed by the son's body, it was wrong for him to eat chicken or cut his nails or hair.

This purity-focused justification provided by Brahmans seemed hard to reconcile with how Turiel—and most other Americans— seemed to think about morality. American morality revolves around harm and victims, with laws focusing on autonomy and rights because, as we saw in part 1 of this book, those concerns are important to preventing us and our loved ones from being harmed. But Shweder found that Brahman Indians cared about more than just rights and autonomy; they also cared about the sanctity of rituals and the purity of souls. Eating chicken after a father's funeral was not a direct physical harm, but neither was it merely a violation of conventional norms. It seemed to be a harmless wrong.

Looking at the world through the eyes of Brahmans, Shweder saw a world divided into two elements: the sacred and the profane. The sacred part of the world stemmed from the divine; it was pure and holy. The other part of the world was mere earthly matter; it was dirty and impure. In their philosophy, the sacred part of the world was not supposed to mix with the profane. For example, Brahmans, thought to be holy people, were not supposed to mix with contaminants from the outside world, and their children were taught to remove their "polluted" outside clothes immediately upon returning from school. Brahmans were so close to the gods that they were thought to have special powers, including purifying the impure, like a father's death pollution.

Based on his findings in Bhubaneswar, Richard Shweder developed a theory that extended morality beyond concerns about physical harm. He called it the "CAD" hypothesis, arguing that discussions of morality (especially in non-WEIRD cultures) tended to revolve around three themes: community, autonomy, and divinity.[7]

Community is about respecting social arrangements, including being loyal to your family and respecting your elders. Concerns about community focus on maintaining the stability and cohesiveness of the groups that humans depend upon. Autonomy is about respecting personal choice and preventing interpersonal harm, which is what most laws in the West revolve around. Obvious interpersonal harm is what Turiel focused on with his question to kids about punching classmates. Divinity is about respecting the natural order of the world and maintaining the purity of sacred rituals, including funeral rites.

As with Turiel, Shweder argued that concerns about autonomy were important because everyone wanted to be protected from suffering direct harm. But he also argued that autonomy was only part of the puzzle in how different cultures talked about morality.

There was a lot to like about Shweder's idea of the three different conversational themes of morality. He broadened the concept of morality beyond conventional Western definitions and blurred Turiel's bright line between acts that seemed morally wrong and those that seemed to violate only social convention. One person's mere social convention violation—a son eating chicken after a funeral—seemed to be another person's act of immorality.

Shweder emphasized that morality was in the eye of the beholder and that people's moral judgments could be understood only by considering their culture-bound understandings of the world. This meant that human morality was more flexible than psychologists had assumed and that people could see immorality in acts that did not cause obvious physical violence, including those that undermined the social and religious order.

Some researchers—like Haidt, whom we will soon hear more about—saw Shweder's work as a death blow to Turiel and the overarching importance of harm in our moral minds. Harm was linked to autonomy, and autonomy was a separate theme from the two other moral concerns of community and divinity.

But this conclusion against harm was too quick. First, a close look at Shweder's ethnographies reveals no clean separation between the different themes when Brahmans discussed morality. Conversations about whether an act was wrong could flow back and forth between any and all themes. An act could be seen as violating autonomy while also sullying someone's divine spirit and undermining community cohesiveness.

Second, even if concerns about autonomy—individual rights—could be separated from concerns about community and divinity, worries about harm could underlie them all. If you dig deeper into Shweder's work, you can see that Brahman Indians do connect the theme of divinity/purity to harm, even for acts that seem harmless to Americans. This sect of Indians cared deeply about purity after a funeral because they wanted to protect the deceased from harm. Processing the father's death pollution is the only way to ensure that his soul can successfully move to the afterlife. When the processing of death pollution is prevented—by eating chicken—the father's soul becomes stuck in a purgatory-like realm where he suffers for eternity.[8]

Elliot Turiel, the champion of harm within moral judgment, actually saw Shweder's work as supporting his broader hypothesis. Turiel acknowledged that Brahman Indians discussed concerns of divinity, but argued that they were grounded in a deeper desire to protect people from suffering.[9] He emphasized the importance of the "informational assumptions" that Brahmans make about how people suffer harm.[10] Brahmans make radically different judgments than Americans about eating chicken after a funeral—and about many other acts, too—but Turiel argued that this did not demonstrate that the Brahmans had a different sense of morality. Instead, he insisted that they had the same fundamental sense of morality, one revolving around harm, but they had different assumptions about which kinds of acts were likely to cause harm.

To see how a culture's "informational assumptions" about harm connect to their moral judgments, let's consider an analogy.

Imagine an anthropologist living in 6000 BC in ancient Mesopotamia. She stumbles upon a time machine and travels to the year AD 2020 to study the morality of the future. She finds that most people are obsessed with purity, especially the purity of the air. Everyone is wearing masks, opening windows, buying air purifiers, and standing six feet away from each other. People condemn those who break these rules, getting outraged at anyone who sullies the purity of their air.

Nothing about these breathing rituals seems to be about harm, so the anthropologist concludes that people are moralizing issues of purity and not harm. When she asks people from 2020 to explain their purity judgments, they tell her that the world is filled with tiny, invisible creatures called germs that can make you sick and even kill you. The most fearsome of these germs is "COVID-19." She nods along and writes it all down, but chuckles knowingly to herself because she knows that there are no such things as tiny, invisible creatures that make you sick. "What an interesting religious superstition!" she says.

She returns home and argues that the people of 2020 are concerned about the morality of purity, telling her fellow Mesopotamians about the futuristic people who get worried and angry about the cleanliness of their air. She also concludes that this purity-based morality is disconnected from harm, because there's no obvious violence in breathing air.

In one sense, this ancient anthropologist is correct, because people from 2020 condemned acts that tainted the purity of air, or that violated people's invisible "personal space," and these acts seem very different from an act of violence, like a Mesopotamian child hitting their classmate. But in a deeper sense, the anthropologist is wrong. Modern people condemned these impure acts because of a deeply held belief about how the world works—that coughing and sneezing could harm people. Getting a lungful of the COVID virus could be lethal, especially in early 2020. These people from 2020 were condemning these acts because they saw them as harmful.

Turiel would argue that these two moral judgments—mask wearing during the time of COVID-19 and processing death pollution after a funeral—both revolve around harm, even if they initially seem quite different from physical violence, and even if they involve conversations about purity. They are both focused on *perceptions* of harm and protecting people from the threats they *assume* exist.

If anthropologists acknowledge that perceptions of morality can vary across cultures, they can also acknowledge that perceptions of harm might vary across cultures. It makes no more sense to talk about "objective" harm or harmlessness in the case of chicken eating than it does to talk about "objective" morality. Both are in the eye of the beholder.

For a while, it seemed as if moral psychology were about to accept a view of morality that emphasized harm and its various cultural manifestations, a hybrid between Turiel and Shweder. People's moral minds could generally revolve around perceptions of harm, but these perceptions of harm were shaped by different assumptions about what is harmful, giving rise to a diversity of moral themes.

In fact, a decade after Shweder wrote about visiting the Brahmans, he wrote about how cultures have different "causal ontologies of suffering." Ontologies are beliefs about reality, and "causal ontologies of suffering" are beliefs about causes of suffering—specifically which kinds of acts might lead to different kinds of harm.[11] Acts that seemed to cause harm to the soul might prompt conversations about divinity and purity; acts that seemed to cause harm to the group might prompt conversations about community; and acts that seemed to cause harm to an individual might prompt conversations about autonomy. Different ontologies of suffering generate different moral concerns.

But a student of Shweder's, Jonathan Haidt, believed that these cultural understandings of harm did not drive morality, but instead were just-so stories told by people to make sense of their judgments. Haidt thought that morality was subjective and in the eye of the beholder but that harm was an objective fact. He argued that some acts are objectively harmful, like punching someone, and some acts are objectively harmless, like eating chicken after a father's funeral. His theory was that Brahmans condemned the latter act because they cared about divinity/purity in itself, and their conversations about harm were just post-hoc sense-making. Never mind that Brahmans grounded their divinity-related judgments in an ontology of suffering that linked spiritual impurity to harm. Haidt thought that people invented harms after the fact to justify their moral judgments. He thought you could prove that even WEIRD harm-focused Americans could morally condemn harmless acts if you designed the right scenario.

MORAL FOUNDATIONS THEORY

When one constructs a big building, like a skyscraper, it takes surprisingly long to get above the ground. Construction crews seem to take forever digging into the ground, laying rebar, and pouring concrete to make sure that the building has solid footings in the earth. They need to lay a strong foundation.

The depth and solidity of the word "foundation" is something that Haidt capitalized on when he called the theory "moral foundations theory," sometimes abbreviated as MFT. These moral foundations are not huge blocks of concrete but rather hypothesized chunks of mental machinery. Haidt argued that we had multiple—and fundamentally separate—pieces of machinery, each corresponding to a different kind of moral concern, that arose from threats that people might face in group living. For example, one proposed foundation or mechanism is "authority," which grew out of Shweder's "community" theme. Haidt argued that it is morally important to respect authority because failing to listen to leaders, like elders, tribal chieftains, or the police, can create anarchy and violence. To support this idea, he pointed to the many people across cultures who think it is immoral not to listen to authorities, and the obvious risk to society of lacking social order.[12]

There is no doubt that people morally condemn those who deny legitimate authorities, but Turiel would explain this moral condemnation by referencing harm: people who condemn defying authority see it as causing harm, tipping society toward anarchy. Haidt would agree that the *ultimate* purpose of human morality is to protect us from harm, but he would also say that perceptions of harm are not *psychologically* involved in many moral judgments. Whether people perceived harm in acts that violated the value of authority was beside the point because, in Haidt's view, authority violations were condemned by a separate piece of mental machinery—a little room in the mind—that specialized in detecting authority violations.

In Haidt's formulation, harm was like a distant god that set up the moral mind and then retreated to the heavens. Morality was instilled in our minds by various threats from our ancestral past, both direct physical harms, like violence, and indirect harms that threatened the cohesion of the group. But now that we had fully developed psychological mechanisms that help guard against these ultimate threats, our moral judgments were disconnected from the potential harmfulness of these acts. Our minds could instead focus directly—and specifically—on whether acts violated "foundational" values, like authority and purity, that grew out of Shweder's conversational theme of divinity.

We already saw from Shweder that people condemned more than just violence and abuse, with some immoral acts prompting discussions about divinity and community. Haidt's new idea was to interpret these conversational themes as evidence of separate psychological mechanisms and to argue that acts of impurity and disobedience were seen as wrong *only* because of their impurity or disobedience, without any connection to harm. Of course, we know from Shweder's conversations that the people who discuss disobedience as immoral also discuss it as harmful, but Haidt suggested that these perceptions of harm were just empty rhetoric—something people say but do not genuinely believe.

Haidt and his colleagues suggested that there were five separate moral foundations—five separate blocks of mental machinery, or locked doors in the moral mind, each with separate keys. Here is a list of their names and definitions, along with a brief question designed to capture each one.

1. Care: Concern for physical suffering and the protection of the vulnerable. Is it wrong to kick a dog?

2. Fairness: Concern with equity and proportionality. Is it wrong to cheat on a math test?

3. Loyalty: Concern about your community. Is it wrong to publicly renounce your country?

4. Authority: Concern about respecting hierarchy. Is it wrong to disrespect your mother or father?

5. Purity: Concern about sanctity and contamination, not only with food, but also spiritually. Is it wrong to burn a Bible?

If Haidt's foundations were simply an expansion of Shweder's conversational themes from three to five, we could stop our discussion here, because any conversational theme could coexist with a moral mind driven by deeper concerns about harm. But there are two crucial—and unique—claims about moral foundations theory. The first claim is that while conservatives are concerned about all five moral foundations, liberals understand only the first two. Liberals are said to understand care and fairness but are blind to loyalty, authority, and purity. Haidt has termed this difference a "conservative advantage" in morality, and it is something we will explore in chapter 7.

The other key claim, as we've discussed, is that each of these moral concerns is caused by separate psychological mechanisms. In some versions of MFT, these mechanisms are argued to be separate "switches in the brain,"[13] but there is no evidence of separate foundations in the brain. Modern neuroscience shows that our brains are not divided into different little parts,[14] but instead are composed of interconnected functional networks. These networks operate at very general scales. For example, the "salience network," which includes the amygdala and the insula, orients attention to surprising stimuli ("snake!"), and the "default network," which includes the dorsomedial prefrontal cortex and the posterior cingulate cortex, helps people to rehearse plans for the future (for example, daydreaming) and recollect and learn from the past (for example, "Was I weird in that conversation yesterday?").

Our moral judgments are underlain by two different large-scale networks: the social cognition network, which helps us think about other people and includes the temporoparietal junction and the anterior cingulate cortex; and the affective network, which helps us feel things and includes the orbitofrontal cortex and the ventromedial prefrontal cortex. These networks are used in many judgments, because there are many times in life we think about other people while feeling something. Research reveals that there are no specific functional bits of our brains dedicated to morality, let alone specific moral concerns like authority or loyalty.[15]

Setting aside the strong claim about neural distinctness, there is also no robust evidence for the softer claim of psychological distinctness—that people separate these concerns in their moral judgments. Some of the best proof against this separateness comes from one of the original MFT papers published by Haidt and his colleagues,[16] where they report correlations of the overlap between judgments of different foundations.

In general, correlations range from −1 to 1, with 0 suggesting no overlap between two judgments, 1 suggesting a perfect overlap between them, and −1 suggesting a perfect opposite overlap. For example, there is no correlation between my cat's napping behavior and the temperature of Jupiter's moons, but there is a very strong correlation between the presence of the sun and the presence of outdoor light. In fact, the correlation between the sun and light is so high that we might argue that they are basically the same thing—that when we say that it is "bright" out, what we are really saying is that the sun seems very strong.

This MFT paper reports correlations between how people judge scenarios specifically designed to capture *only* authority (like disrespecting community leaders) and scenarios specifically designed to capture *only* loyalty (like burning a flag). It shows that the correlation between judgments of authority-only scenarios and those of loyalty-only scenarios is 0.88, suggesting that people respond to authority almost identically as they respond to loyalty. If these are separate foundations, there should be some clear differences between how people react to these scenarios—someone's judgments of authority should be reliably separate from their judgments of loyalty. But instead their correlation is so high that most scientists would say that these scenarios measure virtually the exact same thing, like the presence of the sun and daylight.

A correlation of 0.88 is like paying a contractor to pour two separate foundations for two different buildings and then coming back to find only one foundation with twice as much concrete. Likewise, purity correlates with authority at 0.80, suggesting one big clump of loyalty/authority/purity scenarios rather than separate foundations. This clump of scenarios arguably revolves around indirect harms that undermine group cohesion, by fraying the social and spiritual structures that bind tribes together.[17]

But as we'll see in chapter 7, rather than impartially capturing a constellation of moral values across cultures, these MFT scenarios tap into a clump of conservative concerns. It has long been obvious that U.S. conservatives care more about sexual chastity, religion, and flag-waving patriotism, and these are the kind of scenarios used to capture purity, authority, and loyalty. Because conservative concerns are baked into how these foundations are measured, it is hard to argue that conservatives but not liberals care about values like loyalty. Instead, the more accurate claim from MFT data is that conservatives care most about the conservative formulation of these values—a circular argument.

But leaving aside the conservative leaning of how moral foundations are measured, the key point here is that "foundations" are not foundations at all, because they are not separate psychological mechanisms. When confronted with this clear overlap, advocates of MFT usually double down on one argument for separateness: people condemn wrongs designed to be objectively harmless, like the Mark and Julie scenario of consensual incest described earlier.

Whether these acts are "objectively harmless" is therefore critical to moral foundations theory because if an act is harmless but still morally condemned, there must be some reason *other than harm* for its moral wrongness. If perceptions of harm do not help explain the moral condemnation of consensual incest or Brahman post-funeral chicken eating, then harm is not the master key of morality. Instead, the mind requires some additional moral mechanisms independent of harm, like a purity foundation.

Of course, when people explain their moral judgments, even for "harmless wrongs," they almost always mention harm or potential harm, just like Brahman Indians explaining why purity is important after a funeral. These explanations of harm seem to support the idea of a harm-based mind, but Haidt argued that these harms were merely invented and that people were mistaken about the roots of their beliefs. Morality may be a subjective matter of perception, but Haidt thought that questions of harm were objective—and reasoned.

REASONED HARM?

The idea that morality is subjective but harm is objective shows that Haidt understood the nature of harm to be very different from the nature of morality. He argued—with good evidence—that much moral judgment is intuitive, driven by quick judgments and feelings. When you see someone doing something wrong, you don't need to think hard about your judgment; instead, you immediately "feel" moral disapproval.[18]

In contrast to our intuitive perceptions of morality, Haidt argued that harm is something people must think about—they have to ponder, rationalize, and consciously invent the suffering behind immorality. If moral judgment was like a visceral feeling of anger or disgust, concerns about harm were more like how people talk about their emotions to their friends or a therapist—as a sense-making process that happens after the fact.

This distinction between the idea of intuitive morality and reasoned harm maps on to the distinction between automatic and deliberative processing, one of the most famous dichotomies in psychology. Daniel Kahneman, the late Israeli American psychologist, spent his career (alongside his colleague and best friend, Amos Tversky) upending everything economists believed about human behavior. Humans were once assumed to be rational beings who made logical decisions by carefully analyzing information. Kahneman and Tversky proved this assumption wrong. They showed that human decision making relies on intuitive heuristics—shortcuts for thinking—that make them irrational. Nearly a decade after winning the Nobel Prize, Kahneman popularized his work in his best-selling book *Thinking, Fast and Slow*.

Kahneman argued that we have two ways of thinking: the fast "System 1" and the slower "System 2." System 1 operates automatically and intuitively, with little or no conscious effort. For example, when you read the equation $2 + 2 = \_\_$, the answer "4" appears in your mind automatically. System 1 is acting when you read the term "pink elephant" and an image of a florid pachyderm immediately springs to mind, or when your ears perk up after hearing your name mentioned at a party. By operating subconsciously, System 1 allows us to respond to our environment quickly and efficiently.

System 1 is fast, but System 2 is slow. It is characterized by deliberative, conscious reasoning. We use System 2 to weigh different options, search through our memories, and perform cognitively demanding tasks, like counting the number of times the letter *a* appears in this sentence. System 2 requires dedicated cognitive resources to achieve its goals—time and thought—and because these attentional resources are limited, it can only focus on one demanding task at a time. Counting *a*'s is time-consuming but doable, but now try it while counting backward from a hundred by threes. Because System 2 requires conscious effort, it comes to conclusions more slowly than System 1.

For the last twenty years, many moral psychologists believed that thoughts about morality were grounded in System 1 and thoughts about harm were grounded in System 2. Morality seemed intuitive, but harm seemed reasoned. One explanation for why harm was linked to reasoning was that it was often referenced in thoughtful discussions about morality. When judges provide commentaries on laws, they frequently reference harm and its related concepts of damage, suffering, and victimization.

Another explanation for why harm was connected to conscious reasoning is that people often appeal to harm as the "reason" behind their moral judgments. In the psychology experiments run by both Turiel and Haidt, people volunteered harm-based reasons to make sense of their moral judgments, so in a sense their expressions of harm were literally "after" their moral judgments. They intuitively condemned an act like consensual incest and then explained that it was harmful. But does this prove that harm is System 2 and morality is System 1? Harm is certainly present in System 2 thinking, but this doesn't show that it's *absent* from System 1. As the saying goes, "where there's smoke, there's fire," and it may be that harm is reliably present in people's reasoning (the smoke) because it is powerfully present in people's intuitions (the fire).

I too initially believed the idea that morality was intuitive and harm was reasoned. I began graduate school focusing on a fringe topic in social psychology—people's beliefs about the minds of machines—and just accepted this common view, but as I began to do more research on the nature of moral judgment, my doubts grew. Study after study consistently revealed that harm was best understood not as a reasoned rationalization, but instead as an intuitive, quick gut feeling, just like our moral judgments. More than that, my research revealed that this intuitive feeling seemed to be the master key of morality. People condemned all acts—whether they involve violence, unfairness, disloyalty, disrespect, or impurity—based on how harmful those acts *feel*.

In Sum

- All moral psychologists agree that morality ultimately evolved to protect humans from harm but disagree about how much harm matters within our moral minds today. Is harm important for all moral judgments, or only a narrow subset of them?
- Initially, moral psychology believed that all moral judgments revolved around harm. The work of Elliot Turiel in the 1970s suggested that harm separated immoral acts (for example, punching your classmate) from acts that merely violated social norms (for instance, wearing pajamas to school).
- In the 1980s, the anthropologist Richard Shweder discovered that Brahman Indians morally condemned acts that seemed harmless to Americans, including an eldest son eating chicken after his father's funeral. These Brahmans also frequently mentioned "purity" in moral conversations, especially when discussing religion, revealing that people have moral concerns beyond obvious physical harm.
- In the first decade of the twenty-first century, the moral psychologist Jonathan Haidt proposed moral foundations theory, which turned Shweder's conversational themes of morality into cognitive mechanisms, arguing that our mind has separate moral processes—locked rooms—one for each of five evolutionary concerns faced by our ancestors: care, fairness, loyalty, authority, and purity. But there is no consistent evidence for these separate "foundations."
- Core to moral foundations theory is the idea of harmless wrongs. Because people morally condemned "objectively harmless" acts

like consensual incest, Haidt reasoned that there must be additional drivers of moral judgment beyond harm (for example, a purity mechanism).

- However, people *do* see some amount of harm in "objectively" harmless wrongs. Those who see consensual incest as immoral also see it as harmful. Likewise, the Brahman Indians who condemned after-funeral chicken eating saw it as harming the soul of the deceased. Different people from different cultures have different "informational assumptions" about what causes harm.

- Haidt dismissed these perceptions of harm as being merely after-the-fact rationalizations. He believed that moral condemnation was an intuitive "System 1" feeling, but harm involved only careful "System 2" reasoning. But perhaps perceptions of harm, like moral condemnation, are also best understood as intuitive feelings.

Chapter 6

Intuitive: The New Harm

For the last ten years, my colleagues and I have been developing a harm-based theory of our moral minds. This idea builds on a growing body of research about how the mind works, and it has benefited from the feedback of many moral psychologists, especially Jonathan Haidt, the architect of moral foundations theory. He served as a reviewer for many of the peer-reviewed papers where we scientifically tested the hypotheses of a harm-based moral mind. His thoughtful criticism and insightful prodding were crucial to making the theory strong.

The reason we advanced this theory was not merely to challenge the status quo in morality. Nor was it to turn back the clock in moral psychology to the 1980s, when harm was seen as central to our minds. Instead, we developed this idea to help people better understand themselves and modern moral disagreement. We also wanted a theory that squared with one important underappreciated fact about human nature, covered in part 1 of the book: we evolved as a prey species that was constantly concerned about harm, and remain powerfully motivated to protect ourselves, our families, and our society. We are hardwired to be vigilant for harm and danger, and we can feel threatened—deep down in our gut—even when we are safe. A harm-based mind allows us to connect the dots from humanity's past into the present. If our mind evolved to worry about harm, to avoid harm, and to talk about harm, then it seemed natural that our moral mind also functioned based on harm.

My research suggests that a harm-based mind can explain all human moral judgment—but only if harm is correctly understood. To do this, we must incorporate important insights made by past scholars. Shweder found that culture matters, and that people morally condemn more than just direct physical violence, and so a harm-based theory of morality must acknowledge these facts. Haidt found that morality was grounded more in intuitive feelings and less in calculated reason, and so a harm-based theory of morality must acknowledge that as well.

The idea of a modern harm-based mind respects these insights and is relatively simple. It does not require arguing for some set number of moral concerns or little boxes in the mind. It argues that moral judgments are based on intuitive perceptions of harm. How much people condemn an act is based on how much an act intuitively seems (or feels) harmful. These intuitions of harm stem both from evolution, which results in similarities between people, and from culture, which can create differences across people.

Of course, not all forms of suffering harm are immoral. Stubbing your toe is upsetting but not immoral, and getting injured from driving off the road in a car crash is sad but not immoral. The kind of harm to which our moral minds are attuned is *victimization,* when one person unjustly harms another vulnerable person. When I say "harm," what I really mean is the perception of interpersonal harm—mistreatment, not mere suffering. But for the sake of concision, we will mostly discuss "harm."

Just as Turiel argued fifty years ago, a harm-based morality suggests that perceptions of harm distinguish acts that are morally wrong from acts that merely violate social norms, both in the West and in other cultures. We all make moral judgments based on harm, but different people in different cultures—including secular Californian kids and Hindu Brahmans—have different assumptions about what causes harm and who or what is vulnerable to suffering. For example, if you think that eating chicken after a funeral causes your father eternal suffering, you will see that act as immoral.

One reason why moral psychology missed the broad importance of these informational assumptions is that people seldom articulate the core assumptions—the "ontologies"[1]—of their cultures. Just as we take for granted the air that we breathe, people take for granted their deepest beliefs about how the world works. Uncovering how exactly people make sense of harm requires investigation, whether you are a cultural anthropologist traveling to India or just someone willing to ask those on "the other side" to discuss their beliefs about what causes suffering.

Although both Turiel and I agree that harm is central to moral judgment, the difference between his theory and mine is I emphasize that both morality and harm are more about intuitive feelings than deliberate reasonings. Another key point of my theory is that harm is a continuum; people see harm not as just present or absent but instead as present to some degree. Categorizing any act, whether murder or consensual incest, as either "harmful" or "harmless" collapses the rich variation that people see. It's true that some acts seem very harmful (like genocide), and some seem very *not* harmful (like taking the bus), but many more acts sit somewhere in between these extremes, like insulting someone or shoplifting from multinational corporations.

Questions of relative harms—which harms are worse—are what create difficult moral dilemmas. Killing a cat for fun might be obviously harmful and wrong, but what about euthanizing an old cat to free up space in a shelter for a kitten? Does protecting the kitten from harm justify harming the old cat? Likewise, it is clearly immoral to take away someone's hard-earned money, but what about taking away a percentage of that money—via taxes for healthcare—to help those who are suffering? It is how our minds intuitively make sense of these competing harms that determines our moral judgments.

This continuum of harm can make sense of the continuum of moral judgment. When we're being dramatic, we might talk about something being "completely wrong" or "perfectly fine," but people naturally distinguish between heinous crimes and minor misdeeds. We condemn theft more than double parking, and we condemn murder more than theft, and these distinctions are driven by differences in perceived harm.

These simple truths about our minds—that perceptions of harm happen intuitively, that perceptions of harm differ by cultures, and that perceptions of harm vary along a continuum—are the core claims of my harm-based theory of morality, which suggests that harm is the master key of morality. This theory also provides simple advice for understanding the moral judgments of other people: if you want to understand how much someone will condemn an act, figure out how

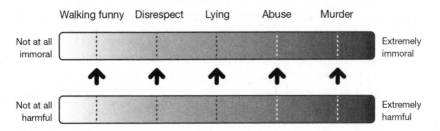

The more harmful it seems, the more immoral it seems.

Figure 6.1: From harm to immorality. Many acts seem to break some kind of social norm, but how much these acts are seen as immoral hinges on intuitive perceptions of harm or victimization. People condemn acts based on how harmful they seem—or feel. The more that people feel an act is harmful, the more they see it as immoral.

much they feel that act is harmful. In figure 6.1, you can visualize this key idea.

There is extensive evidence of the link between harm and moral condemnation. Even Haidt would agree: As the perceived harmfulness of an act increases, the more people will judge it as more immoral. Consider a thought experiment with two scenarios. Which is more wrong: punching a child with brass knuckles or flicking the ear of a Navy SEAL? The first scenario seems much more wrong than the second, because it causes more harm.

The connection between harm and moral judgment in many cases is uncontroversial, but what about the moral condemnation of "harmless" consensual incest between Mark and Julie? My co-authors and I, including my first graduate student, Chelsea Schein, argue that people can intuitively *feel* that these acts are harmful, even when they are designed to be "objectively" harmless.

FEELING HARM DESPITE OBJECTIVE SAFETY

We have discussed how our mental experiences are often only loosely connected to objective facts. In part 1 we saw how our brains can distort the world, especially when it involves potential threats, because of our evolutionary heritage as a prey species. Our genes have programmed us to be "better safe than sorry," and this includes the visceral belief that even objectively safe situations might be harmful.

A good example of the intuitive force of harm comes from the Yale philosopher Tamar Gendler, who describes an experience that many people have when they visit the Grand Canyon Skywalk.[2] This awe-inspiring *transparent* bridge hangs out over the canyon. Standing on it feels as if you were hovering impossibly in the air, with the canyon floor far below. The Skywalk website reads, "There's simply no thrill like stepping out on glass thousands of feet in the air, yet there's no need to be nervous—Skywalk is strong enough to hold seventy fully loaded 747 passenger jets."

The Grand Canyon Skywalk is objectively safe, yet people are still terrified. If you ask people standing on it *why* they feel terrified—why their heart is pounding and why their hands are sweaty—they will tell you it's because they are afraid of dying, of plummeting thousands of feet below. Of course, these people can also reason (System 2) to tell themselves that they are objectively safe, but their intuitions of threat (System 1) persist.

When it comes to the fear of heights, our intuitions of harm defy rational reason, and in our experience of the world intuitions are in charge. The same is true when it comes to morality, where people get a robust sense that an act like consensual incest is harmful despite it being "objectively" harmless. Both these indelible feelings of harm—heights and immorality—arise because of our evolutionary past.

Humans innately believe that heights are dangerous, because our ancestors who didn't believe this were more likely to mess around by the edge of cliffs and fall to their deaths. Likewise, we have deep evolutionary beliefs that it is harmful to have sex with your sibling, because our ancestors who engaged in incest were less likely to pass on their genes. These intuitive beliefs remain even though we have ultra-strong skywalks and modern contraceptives because we still think and feel with our Stone Age minds. And so just because a psychologist tells you that an act is "objectively" harmless does not mean that you intuitively believe them, and it is these intuitive feelings of harm that drive our moral judgments.

Because harm is intuitive, we do not need something like a "purity foundation" to explain our moral judgments of "harmless wrongs" like consensual incest. Instead, we can just say that people do not intuitively accept that incest is harmless, and condemn this act based on their intuitive perceptions. Consensual incest does not seem as harmful as murder, of course, but we see—and feel—harm along a continuum. If people feel that an act is somewhat harmful, they will condemn it as somewhat immoral.

To hit the point home, let's take the logic of Haidt's "objectively harmless" wrongs toward those afraid of heights on the Grand Canyon Skywalk. Imagine you come across a terrified tourist moaning and crying on the skywalk. You ask them why they're afraid, and they tell you that they are worried about falling into the void. But then you pull out your arsenal of facts. You tell them about the many true reasons why the skywalk is objectively safe. They nod along, and yet they remain afraid.

You are puzzled. How can they remain afraid of heights despite your calm explanations of the harmlessness of the skywalk? Then you have an idea! You make the same logical leap as Haidt: because the tourist remains scared despite acknowledging the objective truth of its harmlessness, you assume there must be some reason *other than the threat of harm* for why they are afraid. It simply *can't* be that the risk of falling is making them cry, because they know they are objectively safe. So then you posit that there must be some separate part of the human mind that makes this tourist afraid. Perhaps they feel that the skywalk places them too high up in the sky—so close to heaven that it affronts God—and their fear is driven by a concern for divinity or purity. This "purity" mechanism explains their fear of heights on the skywalk, separately from their normal harm-related fear of heights in other legitimately dangerous situations.

But of course, there is no need for a distinct heights-related purity mechanism to explain their fear on the safe skywalk. Instead, this tourist's fear can remain driven by gut feelings of danger when they look four thousand feet straight down into the canyon below. Yes, you might have told them about their objective safety, and they may even explicitly agree with you, but deep down, they still feel the danger. With morality, the intuitive feeling of harm in "harmless wrongs," like consensual incest, cannot be easily shaken with a set of facts. Deep in their gut, people intuitively believe that Mark and Julie are doing something that could result in harm.

You might find the Grand Canyon scenario rhetorically compelling, but still wonder, "Are people actually doing this?" That is, do people intuitively perceive harm when they think about Mark and Julie and other "objectively harmless" scenarios? One study from my graduate school days shows that yes, people viscerally feel the persistence of harm even in harmless wrongs.

In this experiment, Harvard undergraduates came into the lab, and we measured their physiology as they performed acts designed to be objectively harmless. These acts were harmless imitations of typically harmful acts, like shooting someone in the face or smashing someone's leg with a hammer.[3] In this way, these acts were similar to the Mark and Julie scenario, which modified a typically harmful act (incest) to be harmless.

The "victim" of these harmless acts was always an accomplice of the experimenter, and when we designed this study, we tried to think like Hollywood directors, keeping the feeling of violence even as we made the acts objectively safe. When participants were asked to shoot the accomplice in the head, we gave them a heavy, realistic prop handgun. When participants smashed the accomplice's "leg" with a hammer, they were smashing a piece of PVC pipe hidden under a pant leg.

Participants knew with 100 percent certainty that these acts were

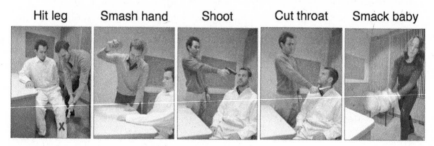

Figure 6.2: Participants performed five different "harmless" acts. Despite knowing that the acts objectively caused no harm, they still intuitively felt harmful to participants. The author is pictured getting "shot in the head" and his neck "slashed." (The other man is the moral psychologist Fiery Cushman. The woman smacking the fake baby is my wife, neuroscientist Kristen Lindquist. We have two kids together.)

fake, but we wanted to know what happened in their bodies when they performed these acts. Would their bodies intuitively believe that they were harmless? We hooked participants up to sensors that measured their physiological threat reactions via their heart rate and blood pressure. As we predicted, these sensors revealed a whole-body negative threat reaction in participants who "killed" and "harmed" other people. Although they could explicitly reason with their reason-based System 2 that these acts were harmless, their intuitive perceptions of harm from System 1 disagreed, creating a visceral reaction in their bodies.

Just looking at these participants, it was obvious that these acts still felt harmful. They would freeze while holding the gun to the other person's head, breathing shallowly and sweating. They willed their finger to move the trigger but seemed unable to do it. Their intuitions of harm were so strong that participants wanted repeated reassurance from the experimenter that the act was actually harmless.

Importantly, for both the scientific conclusion of the study and the well-being of participants, people rationally accepted that these acts were harmless. When we debriefed participants after the study, none seemed to suffer any lasting mental anguish. In fact, the typical reaction of participants was surprise; they were surprised that the actions were so hard to do, despite knowing that they were "objectively" harmless. The reasoning part of themselves knew it was all a ruse, but their intuitions seemed to defy this reasoning. As with the terrified tourists on the Grand Canyon Skywalk, objective facts pale against the vividness of our emotional gut reactions.

Importantly for the harm-based theory of moral judgment, another study in this same paper showed that these negative intuitive feelings can drive moral judgments. In this study, participants were subjected to a stressful and socially threatening task: doing a difficult math test in front of a stony-faced experimenter in a white coat. Imagine it: you're doing mental calculations under the withering glare of an unimpressed scientist. It's not a nice experience.

We measured people's physiological threat reactions during this task and then asked them to rate the immorality of questionable moral decisions, like throwing people out of a sinking lifeboat to prevent it from fully sinking. Analyses revealed that the more participants' bodies felt threatened, the harsher they were in their moral judgments, becoming more condemning of the idea of killing people to save the lives of others.

Together, these studies connect the dots to support a harm-based theory of morality. In the first "Hollywood harms" study, we found that objectively harmless acts of violence remain intuitively harmful to people, as indexed by their physiological threat reactions and their reluctance to carry through with the action. In the second study, we found that these physiological threat reactions drive people's moral judgments. People can still intuitively infer the presence of harm even when actions are objectively safe, and intuitive inferences of harm drive moral judgment. But there is one limitation with these studies—these acts still resemble real forms of harm, rather than something "impure" like sexual indecency, and we are trying to explain how people judge acts like consensual incest.

How much do people have an intuitive sense of harm when it comes to the "harmless" wrongs of impurity? One compelling way to test this would be to bring people into the lab with their siblings, and encourage them to make love to each other, providing ample contraceptives and thorough after-the-act counseling. But that experiment would clearly be unethical, so instead, we turned back to the kinds of studies used by Haidt and other moral psychologists—ratings of scenarios.

My team and I had people rate scenarios of harmless wrongs used in other studies, including watching animals have sex to become sexually aroused, and having sex with a corpse. Of course, we already knew from past studies that people initially volunteered harm-based explanations for their moral condemnation of these acts, but researchers like Haidt argued that these explanations were merely fabricated justifications. We needed a way to ensure that people could rely only on System 1 intuitions and not on System 2 rationalizations.

There are many methods to "deactivate" System 2 and prevent people from reasoning. The easiest is to put people under time pressure. When you force people to provide answers quickly, they give you their gut feelings. This is why people blurt out what they *really* think if you give them almost no time to answer, explaining how people say inappropriate things during think-quick game shows like *Family Feud*.

The power of time pressure to make people respond intuitively has been used by social psychologists in many different areas,[4] so we were on firm ground with this kind of method. We reasoned that if we gave people scenarios designed to be morally wrong but objectively harmless, and then forced them to quickly rate their harmfulness, we could determine whether their perceptions of harm are intuitive or merely reasoned rationalizations. Inventing and rationalizing anything takes time, and so—if harm is just rationalization—people should be less likely to see harm in "objectively harmless" wrongs while under time pressure. On the other hand, if people robustly see harm in harmless wrongs, even with little time, it suggests that their perceptions of harm are intuitive, like their feelings on the Grand Canyon Skywalk or in the lab study with fake face shooting and smashed PVC legs.

The study was simple. People read about different kinds of acts, including the sexual "harmless" wrongs but also acts that were obviously harmful (for example, murder) and obviously harmless (like taking the bus). After they read these scenarios, we asked people how much there was a victim harmed by the act.[5]

Everyone answered the same questions about harm, but we split participants into two conditions. The first "time pressure" group read the scenario and gave their answer as quickly as possible. Based on some pretesting, we determined that seven seconds was just enough time for participants to read it and respond with their gut feeling. These pretests found that with only seven seconds people do rather poorly at answering math questions (for example, 137 + 53), demonstrating that this condition deactivated System 2 reasoning and forced people to answer with System 1.

The second "unlimited time" group had as much time as they wanted to read the scenario and answer the question about harm. In fact, to encourage System 2 reasoning in this condition, we allowed people to rate the harmfulness of the scenario only *after* a seven-second delay, where we also told them to think carefully.

What did we find? Let's start with the obviously harmless scenarios. People didn't see any harm in taking the bus, whether they were under time pressure or not, which makes sense. You don't need careful reasoning to tell you that it's harmless to ride public transportation. What about the obviously harmful wrongs, like murder? People always said these acts were harmful, regardless of time pressure, which also makes sense. You know immediately that it's wrong to kill people.

But what about the "harmless" wrongs like having sex with a corpse? In the unlimited time condition, when people had lots of time to reason, people saw some victims. When asked whether the act had a victim on a scale from 1 (definitely not) to 5 (definitely yes), they reported the harmfulness at about a 2. This finding shows that harm is perceived along a gradient; consensual incest is less harmful than murder but not as harmless as taking the bus.

But the real question: How do people rate the harmfulness of sexual impurity when forced to answer with their gut feelings in the time pressure condition? If Haidt is right, then perceptions of victimhood should mostly disappear when people are put under time pressure, because they cannot use reasoning to invent harm. But if we have a harm-based moral mind—if harm is intuitive—then perceptions of harm will remain despite people lacking time to reason.

People's perceptions of harm did not stay the same under time pressure, but they also didn't disappear. Instead, perceptions of harm *increased*. People were more likely to see harmless wrongs like consen-

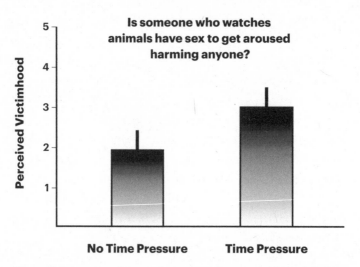

Figure 6.3: Impact of time pressure on the perception of victimhood in scenarios of "harmless" wrongs. People see *more* victimhood when denied the time to rationalize and reason, suggesting that harm is intuitively perceived in these scenarios, consistent with the idea of a harm-based moral mind.

sual incest as victimizing people when they didn't have time to reason. So, contrary to what Haidt initially assumed, perceptions of harm are intuitive. He was right that reasoning can affect perceptions of harm, but reasoning does not lead us to invent harms. Instead, reasoning seems to *dampen* perceptions of harm. Our rational mind functions like the experimenter from the original Mark and Julie study, insisting that these acts are harmless despite our visceral conviction that incest is going to hurt someone.

Both Haidt and I agree that our intuitive "System 1" mind is running the show when it comes to moral judgments, and this study demonstrates that our intuitive mind is also what perceives harm, especially in scenarios designed by experimenters to be "objectively harmless."

Finding that harm is intuitively perceived is the key piece of evidence for a harm-based moral mind, and therefore the key piece of evidence against the idea of a mind divided into different moral foundations. Harm can serve as the master key to morality and can unlock even moral judgments that seem "objectively harmless."

One question that often comes up when I describe these data is who exactly is harmed by these acts? Who are the victims in apparently victimless acts like consensual incest. When we asked people to explain their judgments of sexual impurity scenarios like Mark and Julie, they emphasized three kinds of possible harms.[6]

One possible harm is to their future selves: Imagine the shame! Not only will you be racked with guilt, but people won't want to hire someone who sleeps with their sibling. No one will want to date you. Just as many people look back with regret at not saving more for retirement, our participants believed that people might regret degrading acts of sexual depravity.

Second is harm to people's relationships: You just had sex with your sister! It will blow up in your faces and destroy your family. Your parents will be horrified, and your mom will cry every time she sees your old family portraits. Family reunions will be painful places.

Third is harm to society at large: What if everyone started engaging in incest! How would we raise children? And once consensual incest seems normal, other, more harmful kinds of incest will become acceptable. Sexual abuse will become the norm.

Of course, these are harmful outcomes that Haidt's original scenario was designed to rule out, but that's the point: people's intuitive minds simply cannot believe that harmless wrongs are harmless. They might understand that engaging in sibling incest is less obviously harmful than suffering from murder or abuse, but that still fits with the idea of a harm-based mind because it suggests a gradient of intuitively perceived harm. The more harmful something intuitively seems, the more immoral it seems.

The intuitive persistence of harm explains not only the results of psychology experiments but also reactions to Supreme Court decisions.

HARMLESS WRONGS IN REAL LIFE

In June 2015, the U.S. Supreme Court was deciding on the case of *Obergefell v. Hodges* about whether the Fourteenth Amendment of the U.S. Constitution guarantees same-sex couples the right to marry.

Americans were divided. Liberals saw gay marriage as a fundamental right that allowed gay people to express their love, and perceived substantial harm in denying this right. Even beyond the insult of having your love delegitimized, being forbidden to marry would have clear economic harms: gay people would be denied the advantages of jointly filing taxes and would not receive death benefits if their partner died. Without marriage, gay couples would have a hard time adopting and be unable to achieve their dream of creating a family.

Many conservative Christians were outraged at the idea that gay marriage might be allowed. Gay marriage contradicted what they saw as God's word. A translation of Leviticus 18:22 reads, "You shall not lie with a male as with a woman; it is an abomination," and right-leaning Christians often saw same-sex relationships as immoral, as going against the natural order of God's creation.

Moral psychologists like Haidt saw gay marriage as a textbook demonstration of the different moral foundations of liberals versus conservatives. To liberals, the denial of gay marriage seemed to be a harm-based violation. But many scholars argued that conservatives condemned gay marriage because they saw it as (only) a violation of purity. Their hypothesis was that right-leaning people saw gay marriage as immoral because they were disgusted about gay sex and not because of any perceptions of harm.

But there are two important counterpoints to the moral founda-tions idea of a conservative opposition to gay marriage grounded in disgust and not harm. The first is that the mere existence of disgust is not sufficient to explain moral judgments. Many things are disgusting but not immoral, including stepping on a piece of your dog's poop or accidentally taking a bite of moldy bread.

If you've ever taken care of kids, you are an expert in disgust. One day, my five-year-old daughter was home sick with a stomach bug. As I sat next to her, she told me that she needed to get to the bathroom *now.* I scooped her up in my arms and hustled to the bathroom, but we didn't make it in time. She vomited and had diarrhea at the exact same time. The puke hit me in the chest, and the diarrhea shot out of the back of her pants, covering my arm before dripping down my legs onto the floor.

You might be grossed out after reading about me being covered in slimy foul-smelling effluvia. But I'm guessing you don't see me as a moral monster. You are not outraged at the situation, despite being disgusted. More likely, you'll sympathize with my taking care of a sick child.

Disgust does not lead inevitably to moral condemnation. In our studies, we have separated acts that are merely disgusting (like finding a hair in your food) from acts that some people think are both disgust-ing and wrong (like having sex with animals).[7] We find that people's moral condemnation is best predicted by their perceptions of harm. Of course, negative feelings of disgust might cue people to look out for something harmful, but these feelings alone do not fuel moral outrage.

The second reason we shouldn't consider gay marriage a disgust-ing but harmless wrong is that moral psychologists have again con-fused their own perspective for those of people they study. Progressive moral psychologists argue that gay marriage is harmless—or even beneficial—but they do not see it as wrong; instead, they see allowing gay marriages as a "harmless right." So, when these psychologists used the term "harmless wrong," they were not speaking from their own perspective but assuming how Christian conservatives saw it. Were these assumptions correct? Did conservative Christians actually see gay marriage as a harmless wrong, as something that was impure and forbidden by God, but hurt no one?

Just before the U.S. Supreme Court decision, one conservative evangelical pastor from North Carolina wrote an op-ed that outlined the consequences of failing to ban gay marriage. He argued the harm caused would be "equivalent to a nuclear holocaust,"[8] creating widespread destruction across the country. I will admit that this pastor was likely exaggerating, but behind this metaphor was the sincere belief that gay marriage was harmful and would inevitably lead to suffering. He argued that gay marriage would undermine the functioning of the heterosexual family, the essential social structure for protecting children.

This pastor is not alone; many opponents of gay rights have argued for their harmfulness in good faith, including Anita Bryant, the one-time famous country singer turned antigay activist. Bryant sacrificed her entire music career to combat the harms that she saw in the advance of gay rights, which suggests that she really *felt* those harms. In her book *The Anita Bryant Story: The Survival of Our Nation's Families and the Threat of Militant Homosexuality,* she argued that gay rights pushed society down a slippery slope: "If we label homosexuality a civil rights issue, what is to stop the murderer from shouting 'murderer rights'?"[9] She saw gay rights as a threat to children, the most vulnerable of potential victims: "Homosexuals cannot reproduce, so they must recruit. And to freshen their ranks, they must recruit the youth of America."

I am not saying that these fears are well founded. What I am saying is that fears about the harms of gay marriage were (and still are) sincerely held by many conservative Christians, who see the advance of gay rights as both wrong and harmful.

Soon after the *Obergefell* decision, I co-authored an op-ed in *The New York Times* with Chelsea Schein where we used our scientific studies to argue that many conservative Christians intuitively perceived harm in gay marriage. After this piece was published, I got a lot of pushback from gay rights advocates, who accused me of being antigay or being in league with conservatives. I truthfully replied that I was trying to use science to better understand people's conflicting moral positions.

I also received an email from a conservative pastor, who thanked me for recognizing the authenticity of his moral stance and his perceptions of harm. He acknowledged that he did talk about God's word when condemning gay marriage, but he also believed that God forbade gay marriage because He was trying to keep the souls of His people safe.

As Turiel long ago suggested, this pastor had different informational assumptions about what was harmful, and these drove his moral judgments. As Shweder also noticed, this pastor spoke about divinity when discussing this moral judgment, because divinity is a crucial cultural theme in Christian thought. But in contrast to Haidt's arguments, this discussion of purity and immorality was not separate from harm. Instead, concerns about purity and morality were fundamentally grounded in intuitions of harm. The pastor was making sense of his intuitive perception of harm through the lens of his faith.

THE NEW MORAL PSYCHOLOGY: DIVERSITY AND HARM?

My work supports a harm-based understanding of our moral minds, but other scholars have published recent research that seems to argue against this idea, showing that people condemn acts of impurity despite their harmlessness. But this work is plagued by the same problem as older studies like the classic Mark and Julie scenario: they fail to measure people's intuitive perceptions of harm, instead simply assuming that some scenarios are "objectively harmless."[10] Some other studies do better and solicit people's perceptions of harm, but force them to reason about whether an act is harmful or harmless,[11] ignoring that harm is an intuitive continuum rather than a reasoned dichotomy. Importantly, when studies measure these intuitive perceptions of harm, they find robust support for a harm-based moral mind.[12]

Perhaps the most striking vote for a harm-based moral mind is the change in how Haidt and his co-authors now discuss moral foundations theory. In its initial formulation in *The Righteous Mind*, moral foundations were described as "cognitive modules," distinct mechanisms defined as "little switches in the brain." But years later, after we published our studies on intuitive harm, writings on moral foundations theory have largely jettisoned this talk of distinct mechanisms—of separate rooms with separate keys.

Now values like care, loyalty, and purity are merely "developmental constructs"—general themes that kids are likely to moralize as they grow up and learn about morality.[13] This is a far cry from the deep "foundations" suggested by that name, and it's much closer to the moral themes outlined by Shweder. Importantly, any theme or "developmental construct" can be moralized by connections to harm, like when the children of Brahman Indians are taught to condemn purity violations by connecting them to spiritual suffering.

In fact, studies show that the best way to teach kids that something is wrong is to tell them that it causes harm.[14] In one of these experiments, researchers told young children about a "harmless" wrong like when the "Bonzers [a group of pretend creatures] fill the forest with cotton balls." Children thought these actions were okay until they learned that "it really hurts others" when the Bonzers do this; then they readily condemned these formerly harmless acts.

This weakened argument about moral foundations as mere developmental constructs—which are easily moralized via harm—brings us full circle to where we first began with Turiel, who used studies with children to argue that harm was central to all moral judgments. Of course, we also have the work of Shweder and Haidt that reveals the diversity of morality and the power of intuitions. And so we now need to reformulate Turiel's theory of moral judgment to highlight the importance of a continuum of intuitive, perceived harm.

This convergence in moral psychology allows us to draw a line from the *evolutionary* importance of harm, where morality evolved to protect us from being victimized, to the *psychological* importance of harm, where morality revolves around concerns about protecting victims from suffering. One recent study by a researcher at Duke University named Nicolas Ochoa nicely illustrates the consilience between different moral values and a harm-based moral mind. He gave both liberals and conservatives twenty-five scenarios to evaluate, five from each of the five moral foundations, including students cheating on a test (fairness), a man who votes against his wife in a beauty pageant (loyalty), and marriage between cousins (purity).[15]

Ochoa assessed people's judgments of harmfulness and immorality across these twenty-five scenarios and then tested the relationship between those judgments. The results of this study are striking and provide better evidence of a harm-based mind than I could have imagined. No matter what "foundation" the scenario was drawn from, and

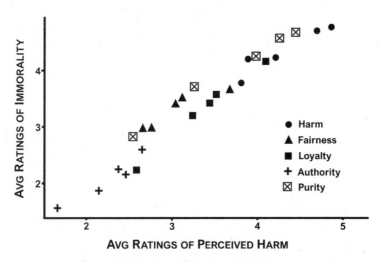

Figure 6.4: Ratings of perceived harm and immorality of actions that violate each of the five moral foundations. As acts seem more harmful, they seem more immoral, regardless of what "foundation" the acts are drawn from.

no matter whether people are liberal or conservative, people's moral wrongness judgments were predicted by their perceptions of the scenario's harmfulness. The gradient of harm predicts the gradient of immorality.

Understanding the importance of harm to different moral values helps us connect them to our evolutionary heritage and explains when people get most outraged at violations of values: when they see those violations as causing the most harm. Haidt and his co-authors have usefully highlighted five values, but I think this focus is too narrow. Humans care about countless different values—all varieties of social norms—from property ownership to humility to self-reliance. These many social values become *moral* values when connected with harm.

Consider punctuality, a value whose importance varies widely among people. People in southern Europe (for example, Greece) care less about punctuality than people in northern Europe (for instance, Germany), explaining why deliveries arrive on time more often in northern Europe.[16] Despite caring more about punctuality, most people in northern Europe do not think that late people should be morally condemned—unless it causes harm. Both northern and southern Europeans would still judge lateness as immoral if it caused obvious suffering, like a surgeon whose tardiness caused a patient to die. Social values are merely guidelines until suffering seems to be at stake, at which point they become moral imperatives.

VIRTUES: THE GOOD SIDE OF MORALITY

When I discuss our harm-based mind, people frequently ask about virtues. They rightly point out that moral values are many and frequently positive. Morality is not just about evil but also about goodness; not just about how people *shouldn't* act but also how they *should* act. Punctuality, respect, compassion, temperance, thoughtfulness, and charity, these are all *moral* rather than immoral. How can we square a moral mind focused on avoiding victimization with values celebrating virtue?

There are two ways to connect harm with virtues. The first is to recognize that virtues outline ways of acting that prevent salient harms in society. In chapter 3, we learned about the "morality as cooperation" theory, which argues for the universal importance of seven cooperative virtues including helping kin, helping one's group, respecting prior possession, and caring for offspring. All these virtues help to safeguard people from suffering and protect groups from decay. Groups that consistently defy these virtues find themselves quickly slipping down the dangerous slope to infighting and anarchy.

Research by my former colleague Michele Gelfand, now a Stanford professor, also connects the moralization of virtues to harm. She and her co-authors find that acting virtuously is especially important within societies frequently facing threats, like natural disasters, disease, or war. If there's a big flood coming, it's essential that everyone cooperate to help build a wall of sandbags, rather than doing their own thing. One person's failure to help could spell death and disaster for many others. In contrast, in societies with fewer natural disasters or enemies to worry about, cooperative virtues become less moralized,[17] and people can focus more on making their own choices. For example, Japan is more likely than Norway to suffer from earthquakes and tsunamis and is also more likely to moralize values of collectivism, group harmony, and respect for authorities. Japan also gives out stricter punishments when people violate these values.[18]

The second way that a harm-based mind understands the importance of virtues is that virtues compensate for harm. We celebrate good behavior that not only prevents future wrongs but also corrects past wrongs. Consider the virtue of charity. We might praise someone—but only a little—if they gave money to a random wealthy person walking around Wall Street. But we give much more praise to those who help the needy—people suffering from past harm. We often donate to charities that help victims of disasters, crime, or diseases because our harm-based minds care about making amends for past harms. We seldom donate to charities that help middle-class folks take an extra vacation.

Our minds understand goodness in contrast to harm. Just as we enjoy food most when we are starving and appreciate heat most when we are freezing, we appreciate goodness most when it offsets the evil of victimization—whether by preventing or redressing it. This is why every true hero needs a victim to protect. Storybook knights are virtuous when they kill a dragon that has murdered townspeople (redressing past harms) and plans on devouring a captured damsel (preventing future harms). A knight who kills a dragon living quietly alone in the forest is not a hero but a hunter.

Discussions of virtues inevitably connect with religion, which seems to argue that virtues are intrinsically important. Some moral psychologists see the religious commitment to acting virtuously as evidence of the disconnect between virtues and concerns about harm. For example, one biblical virtue is unquestioning obedience to God, exemplified by the Genesis story of God commanding Abraham to sacrifice his innocent son Isaac, which seems to be a flagrant harm. But we need to consider the broader context. .

The Christian philosopher Søren Kierkegaard discussed this biblical event in his book *Fear and Trembling,* a title that reflects the deep emotional states associated with Abraham's act of obedience and the difficulty of causing such harm. To nonbelievers, Abraham's obedience seems cruel and callous, but closer examination reveals that this virtue is rooted in a deep belief about how the world works—and how to best prevent suffering.

Christians (along with Jews and Muslims) believe that God's understanding is "infinite" (Psalm 147:5) and good, so trusting him will lead to an ultimate good, as evidenced by verses in the Bible like Proverbs 3:5–6, "Trust in the Lord with all your heart and lean not on your own understanding; in all your ways submit to him and he will make your paths straight." Christians see their own moral intuitions as flawed or incomplete and believe that by outsourcing their conscience to a higher and more knowledgeable power (a core virtue), they can better alleviate pain and create a better world.

You cannot make sense of the Christian belief in obedience by simply referencing the value of "authority." Instead, you must recognize that Christians have different informational assumptions from atheists, perceiving that the best way to safeguard themselves and society is by being obedient to God. Understanding someone's perceptions of harm unlocks our understanding of their moral judgments.

RESPECTING THE WISHES OF THE DEAD

Despite all the published research and logical arguments collected above, not everyone is convinced that we have a harm-based moral mind. Some years ago, I was talking to a moral philosopher who was a staunch believer in objectively harmless wrongs. Like many moral psychologists, this philosopher rarely felt personally outraged and saw many morally debatable acts as both harmless and permissible. But he was convinced that other people condemn acts that they acknowledge are harmless. To support his position, he talked about his mom, who strongly condemned when people dishonored the wishes of the dead—a classic example of a "harmless wrong" in philosophy.

His mom lived in Philadelphia, which houses the Barnes Foundation, a vast collection of impressionist, postimpressionist, and modern art, including masterpieces by Gauguin, Henri Rousseau, van Gogh, and Modigliani. It is named after Albert Barnes, a self-made multi-millionaire who was an eclectic collector of art. Barnes wanted the collection to be open to the public after his death, but he stipulated that it always remain in his house, where his specific arrangement could live on forever and blend perfectly with his mansion's unique architecture, which included sprawling fireplaces hand cut from Parisian stone, a library, and a twelve-acre arboretum.

The collection stayed in the house for many years, but eventually the trustees of the Barnes Foundation decided to move the art to

Philadelphia so many more people could enjoy it. They built a whole new building to showcase the paintings, one that reflected the general design of Barnes's house. But it was *not* Barnes's house, and therefore it rejected Barnes's last wishes.

The philosopher said that his mother thought moving the Barnes collection was outrageous and clearly immoral. He also argued that his mother saw moving the collection as a harmless wrong, since Barnes was long dead. I suggested that the philosopher was confusing his mother's perceptions with his own, much like the many progressive moral psychologists who studied the moral judgments of conservatives and Christians. He saw it as a "harmless okay," and I argued that if his mom saw moving the art as wrong, then she would also see this act as harmful. The philosopher countered: obviously she saw the act as harmless because it was objectively harmless. Who's the victim? Barnes was long dead.

But I stuck to my guns, and to my harm-based theory of morality. We were at an impasse; it was his word against mine. I suggested that we call his mom. It was ten o'clock in a noisy pub, but he was game. He called her and, thank goodness, she was still awake. After the usual motherly pleasantries (nice to hear from you, where are you, what's going on, are you okay?), the philosopher launched into his question. He did a fantastic job of not "leading the witness" when he prompted her to think about the Barnes case, before asking her the two key questions.

The first question: Was it wrong for the Barnes Foundation to move the art into Philly? Her answer was a resounding yes. The second question: Was it harmful for the Barnes Foundation to move the art collection? (These may seem like weird questions to ask your mom, but as the mother of a philosopher she seemed accustomed to strange thought experiments.) The philosopher smirked as he anticipated her answer. After all, this was his mother, and he knew her well.

But he was wrong. She was emphatic: Moving the collection *was* harmful. She thought it harmed the memory of Barnes, whom she still imagined as being upset with the decision. She thought it paved the way for future harm, setting a precedent for ignoring the wishes of all of us who will one day die. And she thought it would harm everyone who attended the museum because they wouldn't see the collection as it was meant to be seen; they would get a distorted sense of the art and the museum.

We can argue about whether her perceptions were true. You might think that Barnes, as someone long deceased, would not be objectively victimized by disobeying his wishes. You might not perceive the same slippery slope of legal precedent created by moving the art. But the potential for disagreement is the entire point. Harm is perceived, and each of us—whether liberals or conservatives, philosophers or their mothers—sees it in our own way, shaped by our assumptions and our culture.

In this chapter, we saw how all our moral judgments are grounded in intuitive perceptions of harm. Because harm is the master key of morality, it can provide common ground between political opponents today. But an important question remains: If we all have the same harm-based moral mind, how is it that liberals and conservatives disagree? If we are all motivated to protect those we care about from suffering, why do we have different moral judgments?

The answer is straightforward: people disagree in large part because they make different assumptions about who or what is especially vulnerable to harm.

In Sum

- A harm-based theory of our moral minds argues that all moral judgments revolve around perceptions of harm. This theory also provides a new understanding of harm that reconciles Turiel's historic harm-based theory of morality with Richard Shweder's evidence about moral diversity across cultures.
- Harm is a matter of intuition, not just careful reasoning. The apparent harmfulness of something is felt deeply, viscerally, and automatically. People rate "objectively harmless" acts like consensual incest as more harmful when placed under time pressure, despite having less time to rationalize and invent harms. Just as people fear the Grand Canyon Skywalk even when they know it is objectively safe, people who condemn "harmless" wrongs continue to feel deep down that they are harmful.
- Perceptions of harm exist on a continuum. Acts can seem more or less harmful, and this perceived level of harmfulness predicts

people's level of moral condemnation. Many acts that research-ers have labeled "harmless" wrongs are seen as both moderately harmful and moderately immoral. Consensual incest seems less harmful and less immoral than genocide, but more harmful and more immoral than singing show tunes in an elevator.

- Although there are many values that people discuss when it comes to morality, from punctuality to honor to the sanctity of the soul, these values become *moral* values when they are connected to harm. Moral diversity arises not because different cultures or people have different moral foundations but because they have different assumptions about what is harmful.

- Morality is about punishing wrongdoers, but it is also about being virtuous. The positive side of morality can also be under-stood through a harm-based mind. Just as storybook villains are those who victimize the vulnerable, storybook heroes are those who valiantly protect the vulnerable from harm or redress past injuries. Across cultures, values and virtues emerge to protect us from danger. Cultures that face many ecological threats, like Japan with earthquakes, develop strict moral values to keep society safe.

Chapter 7

Vulnerability: Explaining Political Differences

Political divisions over morality are obvious. Liberals and conservatives argue over dozens of issues, including climate change, health care, unemployment, immigration, and the idea of systemic racism. This disagreement makes it easy to assume that we must have deep mental differences—that left- and right-leaning people rely on different moral mechanisms, foundations, or brain switches. But moral disagreements can still arise even if we all share a harm-based moral mind, because liberals and conservatives disagree about who is especially vulnerable to victimization, and therefore who most urgently needs protection from harm. People who lean left versus right make different *assumptions of vulnerability.*

The most obvious example of this difference in assumptions of vulnerability is fetuses. Conservatives are more likely than liberals to view a fetus as a human baby, which is extremely vulnerable to victimization—at least more vulnerable than the adult women who hold fetuses in their womb. On the other hand, liberals tend to see early-stage fetuses as much less vulnerable to victimization, placing them somewhere between a human baby and a mindless mass of rapidly dividing cells. Even though left-leaning people see fetuses as having some susceptibility to suffering, they perceive mothers as being more vulnerable to victimization. These different assumptions of vulnerability explain political differences. If fetuses are more vulnerable than mothers, then abortion seems immoral, but if mothers are more vulnerable than fetuses, then abortion seems permissible.

Assumptions of vulnerability help make sense of debates surrounding hot-button issues because these issues all involve trade-offs about harm—questions about who *really* needs protection. Abortion is a trade-off between the vulnerability of the mother and that of the fetus; illegal immigration is a trade-off between the harm faced by the immigrants in their homeland and the harm they could cause to the citizens of their new country; taxation is a trade-off between the harm of taking money earned by richer people and the harm of failing to help poorer people.

Although we usually agree that all human beings are generally susceptible to harm, political debates pit competing narratives about victimhood and suffering against each other. Everyone agrees that both American citizens and undocumented immigrants can be victimized, but if you see illegal immigrants as—on balance—causing harm to American citizens by taking jobs or increasing crime, then you will be attracted to tighter immigration policies. On the other hand, if you focus on the vulnerability of undocumented immigrants, emphasizing the heightened suffering of people detained at the border or fleeing violence in their homeland, you will find looser immigration policies more appealing. Of course, there is more nuance to debates about immigration—and to debates about abortion and taxation—but we will soon see how much perceptions surrounding harm explain arguments about morality and politics.

There are two reasons why we should be pleased that assumptions of vulnerability drive moral disagreement. First, assumptions of vulnerability provide a more *parsimonious* way to explain divisions than different mental mechanisms. In science, parsimony means preferring the simplest explanation for a phenomenon without sacrificing necessary complexity. The idea is captured by Occam's razor, sometimes stated as "plurality should not be posited without necessity" and other times said as "entities are not to be multiplied beyond necessity."

In the case of morality, this "plurality" or these multiplied "entities" are cognitive mechanisms: we should not posit additional cognitive mechanisms (or foundations) beyond harm-based morality unless it is necessary. Whether it is necessary depends on whether we can explain the diversity of moral judgment with a common harm-based mind. In the previous chapter we saw how there is no need to invoke a "purity mechanism" to explain moral judgments of acts like consensual incest, because people intuitively perceive these "harmless" acts as harmful. The argument explored here in this chapter is that assumptions of vulnerability can explain moral differences across politics without multiplying mental mechanisms.

Beyond scientific parsimony, the second benefit of using assumptions of vulnerability to explain moral disagreement is that it helps bridge divides in the real world. Because we are all deeply motivated to protect ourselves from suffering, we can easily understand why people on the other side worry about harm. A shared harm-based morality across politics provides a lingua franca that allows us to better translate between our own moral positions and those we disagree with. When someone has an opinion we find immoral, we can ask ourselves, "What harm do they see?"

Although a shared harm-based mind helps to clarify moral conflict, it runs counter to the impulse to explain differences between people with something deep in our minds. When men and women have trouble understanding each other in relationships, it's easy to say that they have different brains, as the book *Men Are from Mars, Women Are from Venus* proposes.[1] While men and women may differ in obvious biological ways, most people substantially overestimate sex differences when it comes to the mind. Even superficial differences are scarcer than we believe. For example, most people believe that women are more talkative than men, but when researchers tested this assumption by listening to 396 people's daily interactions after fitting them with microphones, they found that both sexes used the same number of words per day: about 16,000.[2]

Like men and women being from different "planets," moral foundations theory argues that differences between liberals and conservatives are rooted in deep psychological differences. It also argues that conservatives have a moral advantage: liberals are said to be sensitive to care and fairness, while conservatives are said to have a more well-rounded moral palette of care, fairness, loyalty, authority, and purity.

One problem with the claim of a "conservative advantage" is that Haidt and his colleagues designed their studies to *confirm* this hypothesis. The confirmation bias—when people seek information to support their intuitions—is a problem in many areas of life. In police work, cops can act in ways to confirm their "hunches" about a suspect's guilt, which is one reason innocent people can be arrested and convicted.[3] In medicine, a doctor's initial guess about a diagnosis can lead them to selectively look for symptoms that confirm the presence of that disease instead of other likely candidates.

The confirmation bias is also a problem in science.[4] After all, scientists are human, and all humans have cognitive biases. But this bias can create faulty conclusions when researchers design experiments to reveal their favored effects, as seems to have happened with the "conservative advantage."[5] The values of loyalty, authority, and purity could be tapped with many different scenarios. For example, purity could be measured by having people rate the importance of eating only organic produce (a more liberal concern), but instead it is measured by having people rate the importance of sexual chastity, and it has long been obvious that conservatives care more than liberals about teenagers practicing abstinence.[6]

Other scenarios that tap the cluster of loyalty, authority, and purity include the acts of mocking America, burning a flag, and defiling a Bible. We have long known that conservatives are more explicitly patriotic[7] and more religious,[8] and—as expected—conservatives reacted more strongly to these scenarios. But what happens to this apparent conservative advantage when researchers use different scenarios to represent the ideas of loyalty, authority, and purity?

Studies show that liberals care more than conservatives about loyalty and authority when asked about respecting civil rights leaders or staying loyal to union leaders.[9] What is "solidarity" with the labor movement but loyalty to fellow workers? In President Biden's 2023 State of the Union address, it was conservatives who booed him, despite his occupying the highest position of authority in the land. Likewise, although conservatives do care more about the purity of sex and souls, liberals care more about maintaining purity when it comes to the environment,[10] health, and New Age spirituality.[11] Other studies confirm that using a broader set of scenarios to measure loyalty, authority, and purity reveals a more balanced picture, with both liberals and conservatives caring about many different values.

The many studies from the last chapter also show that even if liberals and conservatives might sometimes disagree about moral values, there is no evidence of separate mental mechanisms or brain switches.

People's intuitive perceptions of harm almost perfectly predict how much they condemn acts across all five of the moral foundations.[12] This harm-based nature of morality means that if we want to understand moral disagreement, we need to understand how liberals and conservatives see harm and whom they see as vulnerable to victimization. But there's a big problem: other people's perception of vulnerability is ambiguous.

THE PROBLEM OF THE VULNERABILITY OF OTHER MINDS

"This will be the most vulnerable thing I'll ever share," began a social media post by Braden Wallake, the CEO of a small company called HyperSocial. Wallake had built up HyperSocial, a marketing services agency based out of Columbus, Ohio, after dropping out of college in 2010. His company enjoyed success in the tech boom leading up to 2022, allowing him and his wife to travel full time, running the company out of a Ford Transit van plastered with HyperSocial decals.

He was living his dream, but then the market changed. Stocks were dropping, and the big tech giants—Amazon, Google, and Facebook— were laying off employees. Wallake first cut his own salary and then tried making cuts around the edges of his company, but eventually had to face the reality that HyperSocial needed layoffs. Wallake shared on LinkedIn that he had let go of two of his seventeen employees. He wrote that firing them was "the toughest thing I ever had to do" and lamented the strength of his own compassion, saying, "I wish I was a business owner that was only money driven . . . but I'm not." He wanted to make sure that people knew that "not every CEO out there is coldhearted" and that he loved those he had laid off "from the bottom of my heart."

Wallake ended his post with "I can't think of a lower moment than this," and included a high-resolution headshot of himself. This picture was not of Wallake in a power suit in a boardroom, looking like a determined leader, but instead showed him in a green T-shirt sitting at his home office desk, crying.

The post went viral on LinkedIn. Many people praised Wallake for showing his humanity and vulnerability, but others were in complete disbelief, arguing that he was showcasing narcissism, not compassion. Skeptics said that if he really cared about his employees, he would have found ways to keep them, or at least used his LinkedIn posts to try to get them another job, not to take self-pitying selfies. Others were even more cynical, wondering whether Wallake was actually upset. One person commented, "If you're truly upset, you don't think to open the camera on your phone and take a photo of your face," and another wondered, "How many crying selfies did that CEO take before he picked one to post?" Some argued that even if he was legitimately suffering, what was his sadness compared with that of his newly job-less employees who were suddenly without a salary or health insur-ance? Whether or not Wallake was truly suffering, different people on LinkedIn made very different assumptions about his vulnerability.

How can some people look at Wallake's photo and see only croco-dile tears, while others see evidence of deep pain? People's assumptions of vulnerability can vary so much because of the philosophical "prob-lem of other minds." The "problem" is that other minds are ultimately inaccessible. You can never know other people's feelings beyond what they tell you or what you infer from their facial expressions or other behaviors. You can't know if bananas taste the same to someone else as they do to you, or what the color green looks like to a stranger. If you're a man, could you really know what it's like to give birth? If you are a woman, could you really know what it's like to get kicked in the testicles? You might argue yes, but it is hard to prove it. Other people's experiences are ultimately inaccessible.

The problem of other minds creates a fundamental ambiguity about the feelings of other people. It creates doubt. When you tell someone "I love you" and they say it back, do they love you as much as you love them? Perhaps they want to break up with you but are too afraid of hurting your feelings. Perhaps when they look at you, your partner's heart feels nothing but mild contempt, but they are afraid of dying alone. I am not suggesting you should panic about your relationships, but only that you can never *really* know someone else's mind.

Some philosophers suggest that the problem of other minds means that other people might not have feelings at all. The philosopher David Chalmers asks us to consider whether the people around us—people who tell us about their thoughts and feelings—might be "zombies."[13]

These philosophical zombies are not brain-eating plague spreaders, but instead people whose minds are empty of "qualia," a word used to capture the hard-to-describe quality of having conscious sensations and feelings. Qualia include that inner sense of "redness" when you see a red apple, the inner sense of joy when you see a funny movie, the inner sense of physical suffering when someone slams your finger in a door, and the inner sense of sadness when you fire employees. You can only experience your own qualia from the inside of your own mind.

Most of us do not worry about philosophical zombies, jolting awake in the night with the sneaking suspicion that other people might not have subjective experiences. But the kernel of truth in this idea is undeniable. We remain fundamentally uncertain about the minds of everyone, including our closest friends but especially strangers on the internet. The problem of other minds means that each of us must merely *perceive* other people's experiences, thoughts, or feelings—and this is a crucial idea for making sense of moral disagreement. Because we must make our own assumptions about someone's capacity for suffering, each of us can legitimately see different people as more or less vulnerable to harm. Someone crying on social media can be seen as either truly suffering or crying fake tears, and it is hard to ever know which perception is correct.

Judgments about professional soccer players is an obvious case where people have different perceptions about suffering. Research shows that if a player from *your* team is on the ground, clutching their leg after getting pushed by the other team, you see them as filled with pain and you get outraged at the player who pushed them. But if you cheer for the other team, you might see that player as a whiny pretender trying to get an undeserved penalty kick.[14]

Of course, we agree that soccer players have the general capacity to feel, but how do people perceive different kinds of minds like those of animals and fetuses? In addition to studying morality, I have spent more than a decade making sense of how people perceive the mental worlds of other entities—the phenomenon of "mind perception."

Mind perception matters because we treat entities differently depending on whether they have a mind. Entities with minds deserve moral protection and compassion, but entities without minds are simply "things" that can be bought, sold, and destroyed after you're done

Figure 7.1: The soccer player Andy Carroll grimaces after tumbling in a 2014 match. Is he really in pain or faking it? It is hard to tell because of the problem of other minds. Behaviors and facial expressions are an unreliable guide to someone's internal mental state.

using them. When slave owners in America wanted to justify their cruel treatment of African Americans, including whipping and raping them, they argued that slaves lacked the mental capacity to feel powerful emotions. The American physician and slave owner Dr. Samuel Cartwright argued that African Americans had smaller brains and that "their organization of mind is such, that if they had their liberty, they have not the industry, the moral virtue, the courage and vigilance to maintain it, but would relapse into barbarism."[15]

Cartwright notoriously pushed pseudoscience to justify slavery, arguing that African Americans suffered from "*Dysaesthesia Aethiopis*," a unique disease that made them "insensible to pain when subjected to punishment,"[16] and the mental illness "*Drapetomania*," which caused them to run away from slave owners (in his view, most African Americans loved being enslaved). He also noted that African Americans had smaller lungs, which he interpreted as meaning that they didn't need as much fresh air as White people and could be in hot, tight spaces for longer.

In contrast to the dehumanizing slave owners, abolitionists emphasized the obvious mental capacities of African Americans. The famed abolitionist Frederick Douglass argued for the emancipation of slaves by saying, "What is this but the acknowledgement that the slave is a moral, intellectual, and responsible being?"[17] Because slaves possessed rich minds capable of thinking, feeling, and suffering, they deserved the freedom enjoyed by White Americans.

Mind perception can also explain differences in how people treat animals. If you see animals merely as machines made of meat—as the philosopher René Descartes did—then you will see no real harm in eating them or having them fight for our amusement.[18] But if you see animals as having rich personalities—as many people do with their pets—then you will feel compelled to protect them from harm, buy them fancy food, and pay for their medical care.

In our first foray into the scientific study of mind perception, my collaborators and I asked 2,399 people to evaluate the minds of different entities, including a baby, a chimpanzee, a dead person, a dog, a fetus, a frog, a girl, God, and a robot.[19] Participants compared the mental capacities of these different entities, rating their ability to feel hunger, fear, pain, pleasure, and rage, to exert self-control, to remember things, to plan, to communicate, and to have thoughts. For example, in one trial, participants were asked whether a dead person or a dog was more capable of feeling hunger. (The typical answer was "dog.")

When planning the study, we thought that people's ratings of mental capacities might all group together. Past work in psychology and philosophy, as well as arguments from theology, sketched a single sense of "mind-having," a great "chain of being" ranging from rocks to plants, animals, people, and God.[20] In other words, scholars assumed that there might be one general dimension of mind perception: if someone perceives an entity as high in some mental capacities (for example, feeling pain and pleasure), they should also perceive that entity to be high in other mental capacities (for instance, exerting self-control or remembering things).[21]

However, when we looked across people's many thousands of ratings, we found evidence of *two* dimensions of mind perception, which you can see in figure 7.2. The first dimension of mind perception revolved around being a *vulnerable feeler*—whether someone or something could feel pain, pleasure, and fear and experience other emotions. How much something is a "vulnerable feeler" determines how much they can be harmed or victimized and how much they deserve special moral protections from harm.

The second dimension of mind perception revolved around being a *thinking doer*—whether someone or something was capable of planning, communicating, exerting self-control, and remembering. This dimension of mind perception is connected to someone's general competence in the world and their ability to get things done. When it comes to morality, perceiving someone as a "thinking doer" is a prerequisite to viewing them as a legitimate villain who perpetrates evil. For someone to earn our moral outrage and be worthy of punishment, they must be capable of acting intentionally in the world and appreciating the moral weight of their actions. This is why societies reserve their worst punishments for grown adults who understand the consequences of their deeds, rather than children, who we see as lesser thinking doers.

On the graph below, you can see how people perceive the minds of all the entities we included in the study. Human adults are seen as both vulnerable feelers and thinking doers and so they are capable of being legitimate victims and perpetrators of harm. Dead people are generally seen as neither vulnerable feelers nor thinking doers, making them neither legitimate victims nor legitimate perpetrators of harm. Of course, some people imagine dead people as ghosts or souls in heaven, earning them some mind and moral status. The mother of the philosopher discussed at the end of the previous chapter clearly perceived some mind in Albert Barnes when she condemned the trustees for moving his art collection.

Babies and animals are seen as vulnerable feelers but not thinking doers, explaining why we worry about the victimization of our pets but not their capacity for evil. God has the opposite mind perception profile, being seen as a thinking doer but not a vulnerable feeler. We think of God as a powerful doer, seldom wondering whether He might be hungry, happy, or embarrassed. We worry much more about God's wrath than about whether He might be victimized.

To double-check our hunch about the connection between mind perception and morality, we asked participants two questions about moral status. One question was, "If you were forced to harm one of these characters, which one would it be more painful for you to harm?" This tapped into how much people would be distressed by mistreating an entity. As you might expect, people's answers to this question were

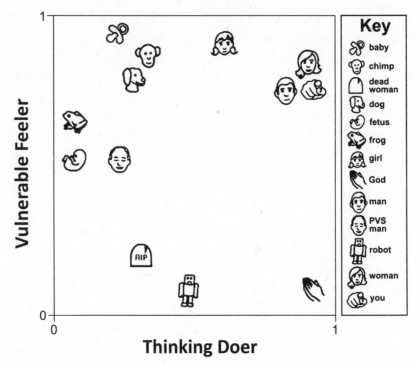

Figure 7.2: The map of mind perception. Mind perception is measured on the dimensions of thinking doers and vulnerable feelers. (Note: PVS man is a patient in a persistent vegetative state.)

highly correlated with their perception of someone or something as a vulnerable feeler. People expect to feel bad when harming something that can feel and suffer, explaining why they thought it would be more painful for them to harm a baby than a robot. We all assume that babies are more vulnerable to victimization than robots. It feels most distressing—and immoral—to harm entities that have the mental capacity to be legitimately victimized.

The other question asked, "If both characters had caused a person's death, which one do you think would be more deserving of punishment?" This assessed people's perception of moral responsibility, which is closely connected to the idea of being a thinking doer—a legitimate perpetrator of harm. In our study, people thought that adult humans were more deserving of punishment than dogs, and in real life more people get angrier at murderous humans than at murderous animals, because humans are more thoughtful. It feels most immoral when a fully thinking doer commits an act of harm.

Different perceptions of entities as vulnerable feelers and thinking doers explain why everyone gets more outraged at a father kicking a baby than at a baby kicking a father; babies are seen as more vulnerable feelers and less thinking doers than dads. In fact, people universally agree that babies and toddlers are vulnerable to harm, and that it is therefore immoral to harm them.[22] The clear vulnerability of kids is why "think of the children" is one of the most frequent rallying cries of any moral movement. For example, when opponents of legal marijuana want to build support, they point to stories of harmed children, like a three-year-old girl hospitalized after eating marijuana candy.[23] Children are the perfect victims within our moral minds, seen as capable of being harmed by evil but not capable of doing evil. Whichever side convinces the public they are the true protectors of children often wins moral debates.

Although everyone cares about kids, people differ in their assumptions about who else is especially vulnerable to harm, and these differences explain moral disagreement.

DIFFERENT ASSUMPTIONS OF VULNERABILITY

Our moral judgments are clearly connected to our political leanings, but what explains this difference? As we have seen, there is little evidence that liberals and conservatives have different moral foundations. Instead, we condemn acts based on how harmful they seem; this "seem" part is crucial for understanding political disagreement. Even though we all get outraged at norm violations that seem to victimize, people make different assumptions about who is most vulnerable to mistreatment. In chapter 5, we saw that Brahman Indians assumed that a father's soul was vulnerable to harm after his death, which led people in this culture to condemn a son who defies a vegetarian diet after the father's funeral.

A team of my collaborators and I wondered if assumptions of vulnerability might explain the moral divide between liberals and conservatives. This team included my post-doctoral researcher Jake

Womick, who studies politics and morality, the moral psychologist Daniela Goya-Tocchetto, who studies the roots of political animosity, and the sociologist Nicolas Ochoa, who has studied the importance of harm in moral cognition.

Studies on mind perception already revealed that debates over abortion could be explained by differences in assumptions of vulnerability, with conservatives seeing fetuses more as vulnerable feelers than liberals. We wondered whether assumptions of vulnerability might explain more political differences in moral judgments, which would provide additional evidence for a harm-based moral mind. Different assumptions of vulnerability could transform shared concerns about harm into different moral positions.

To test this idea, we needed to assess people's assumptions of vulnerability (abbreviated as "AoVs"), and so we developed a set of simple questions that measured them.[24] These questions went beyond the mind perception questions about whether an entity *can* feel pain or be harmed, instead asking whether an entity was *especially vulnerable* to harm.

We thought that these relative perceptions of vulnerability would better explain political debates because hot-button issues revolve around trade-offs about harm. People may agree that Black men and White police officers are both capable of being harmed, but which group seems *especially* vulnerable seems essential for whether someone supports Black Lives Matters or Blue Lives Matter. These AoV questions were each answered on a 5-point scale from 1, not at all vulnerable, to 5, completely vulnerable, with "the following" being a specific entity.

1. I believe that the following are especially vulnerable to being harmed.
2. I think that the following are especially vulnerable to mistreatment.
3. I feel that the following are especially vulnerable to victimization.

These AoV questions have "face validity" because they appear—on their "face"—to measure what they should. They are supposed to measure vulnerability, and the word "vulnerable" is in every question. Despite their common focus on vulnerability, these questions tap different elements of people's assumptions—their thoughts, feelings, and beliefs—and different shades of harm. As we discussed earlier, the mere existence of suffering is not necessarily immoral; instead, our moral minds are most likely to react with outrage when we see a thinking doer intentionally victimizing or mistreating a vulnerable feeler. We therefore asked people about harm, mistreatment, and victimization.

These AoV questions also demonstrate "construct validity," the technical term for how well a measure assesses the concept it was designed to evaluate. A measure of vulnerability should have high scores for entities thought to be very vulnerable to harm (like babies) and have low scores for entities thought to be relatively invulnerable (like professional wrestlers). In our pilot studies, we had people use the AoV questions to rate targets including babies and professional wrestlers, and reassuringly found that people had high AoVs about babies and low AoVs about wrestlers.[25]

Liberals and conservatives may have similarly high AoVs about babies and similarly low AoVs about wrestlers, but we expected more disagreement about entities connected to politically charged topics, like undocumented immigrants. Compared with conservatives, liberals seem to see undocumented immigrants as especially vulnerable to victimization, pointing out how detention scars young children by separating them from their parents. In contrast, conservatives paint undocumented immigrants as invulnerable people who harm others, highlighting people like Juan Garcia-Gomez, a.k.a. Scooby, a twenty-six-year-old from El Salvador and a soldier for MS-13, the Latin American gang notorious for murdering teenagers. Scooby killed nineteen-year-old Jose Urias-Hernandez in New Jersey as an initiation into the gang. We wanted to know if our AoV items would pick up on these and other political differences.

Much scientific work starts with informal pilot studies to get the lay of the land. Just like a prospector digging little holes to figure out where gold might lie, we ran many small studies exploring assumptions of vulnerability about seventy different entities. We tested which targets might be seen differently by liberals and conservatives and which targets might connect with hot-button debates. Eventually, we homed in on four clusters of targets:

1. The Environment
2. The Divine
3. The Powerful
4. The Othered

Before we explore these clusters, a quick note: these four clusters do not represent deep mental "foundations" in the way that Haidt might argue for them. We did not spend the last couple chapters arguing against a divided moral mind just to reintroduce divisions. Harm remains the master key of morality, and these groups are merely ad hoc clusters of convenience: collections of entities where assumptions of vulnerability vary by political affiliation and help to explain moral judgments. You could think of them like Shweder's three themes of moral discourse; these are four themes of entities that commonly feature in moral debates.

The Environment is one cluster. It could have included many different entities from the natural world, but we picked three that seemed to be at the center of debates: rain forests, coral reefs, and planet Earth. Rain forests are home to more than half of the world's biodiversity, produce about 20 percent of our oxygen, and help process more than two billion metric tons of carbon dioxide every year.[26] They are also the setting of movies like *FernGully* and *Avatar* that pit corporate interests against environmental protection. We picked coral reefs because many scientists argue that they are vulnerable ecosystems that provide a bellwether for climate change,[27] and we picked planet Earth because it captures a scope of concern broader than specific habitats.

The Environment AoVs capture how much natural ecosystems seem vulnerable to harm and mistreatment. We thought that both liberals and conservatives would generally agree on the vulnerability of specific animals or plants, seeing polar bears and California redwoods as being fairly vulnerable to harm, but would disagree on the vulnerability of more complex systems—especially their potential to be harmed by human intervention through logging, fishing, or climate change.

We thought that assumptions of vulnerability for the Environment could help explain the large partisan gap in support for policies that provide environmental protections and reduce the impacts of climate change. While 74 percent of Democrats said that protecting the environment should be a top priority for the American government, only 31 percent of Republicans agreed.[28] Republicans are more likely to advocate for drilling new oil wells in Alaska, and Democrats are more likely to advocate for bans on drilling. This difference is not because the actions of conservatives are described by a destruction narrative. We all want to protect ourselves and our world, and conservatives would rather not harm the environment, but they prioritize competing harms.[29] Drilling wells in Alaska helps America avoid being dependent on foreign governments for oil, which could lead to harm if these governments decided to suspend sales or attack.[30]

The Divine is another cluster. It focuses on entities thought to be imbued with supernatural power or divinity, especially within Christianity: Jesus, God, and the Bible. Of course, other religious traditions also believe in God and hold texts as sacred, and also sometimes nod to the importance of Jesus, such as Muslims who see Jesus as a prophet. However, our goal for these AoV items was to explore mostly American political disagreement, and Christianity is either explicitly or implicitly central to much of American political discourse.[31]

Both liberals and conservatives can be religious, but conservatives are statistically more likely than liberals to believe in the God of the Bible (70 percent versus 45 percent).[32] Questions surrounding the vulnerability of these religious entities can be tricky; Christian theologians have debated for centuries about whether God can suffer,[33] and our own work on mind perception finds that God is seen as less vulnerable to suffering than people.

Nevertheless, many everyday Christians believe that sin hurts God, and emphasize how Jesus suffered on the cross.[34] Many believers also see the Bible as being mistreated or harmed if it is damaged, set on fire, or defiled, like if its pages were used as toilet paper.[35] Christians do not see the "suffering" of the Bible as equivalent to the suffering of a child, but part of their faith is seeing the material world as infused with spiritual entities that are, in a powerful sense, "alive." For example, 30 percent of Catholics report that the Eucharist literally transforms bread and wine into the body and blood of Christ.[36]

Different AoVs about the Divine likely explain differences noticed by Shweder and Haidt on the theme of "Divinity." We saw in chapter 5 that Brahman Indians considered it immoral to disobey spiritual guidelines—in large part because disobeying these guidelines caused harm to spiritual entities like the souls of the deceased.

The Environment and the Divine both focus on entities that are not human—ecosystems and religious entities—which helps explain how liberals and conservatives can see them so differently. Unlike other human beings—with brains and bodies like us—it is not obvious how much coral reefs or supernatural agents can be victimized, leaving people plenty of space to inject their own beliefs into these perceptions. The other two clusters, the Powerful and the Othered, focus on people's AoVs about other humans.

The Powerful are those who occupy positions of power in society and enforce order: authority figures, corporate leaders, and police officers like state troopers. People think that the powerful are generally unlikely to be victims because they can use their power to protect themselves, but our research reveals political differences in these beliefs. Compared with those who lean left, right-leaning folks tend to see powerful individuals as more vulnerable to harm and victimization, including corporate leaders.

One conservative professor, an economist at George Mason University, explicitly argued for the vulnerability of corporate leaders in a book called *Big Business: A Love Letter to an American Anti-hero*,[37] where he points out ways that CEOs of multinational corporations have been mistreated by the public. Many evangelical conservatives sympathized with Dan Cathy, the chairman of Chick-fil-A, when he and his family were besieged by activists for supporting a "biblical definition of the family unit" that excluded same-sex marriages. Other conservative commentators have argued how businesses can be hurt by public backlash and invasive scrutiny.[38]

Police officers are another good example of powerful people whose vulnerability is perceived differently by conservatives and liberals. We selected state troopers for our AoV questions because they provide a specific example of police officers. If we asked simply about "the police," someone could picture anyone ranging from a high school resource officer to FBI special agents, and we wanted people to rate similar entities. State troopers also connect with AoVs because they frequently perform highway traffic stops, which can be dangerous for both them and those they stop—especially African Americans. One study examined 100 million traffic stops across the United States and found that African American drivers were 3–6 percent more likely than White drivers to get stopped, a disparity that decreased after dark when it was harder for police to identify a driver's race.[39]

Any interaction with law enforcement can end with either side—the civilian or the cop—becoming a victim. In 2023, at least 1,243 people were killed by police in America, and 108 of these deaths (roughly 9 percent) were traffic stops that turned deadly.[40] Police often fear for their lives in these interactions too, and with good reason: FBI statistics show that in 2022, 3,061 law enforcement officers were assaulted with firearms in the line of duty, and 49 were fatally shot.[41]

Conservatives seem to perceive the police as significantly more vulnerable than do liberals, and when an officer shoots an unarmed civilian, conservatives often note the vulnerability of police who risk their lives every day to safeguard society.[42] One reason conservatives worry about protecting the police and other authority figures is that they help maintain social order, and part of the definition of "conservatism" is "conserving" stability and order.[43] This conservative preference for preserving the traditional social order may also shape political differences in AoVs toward our last cluster: the Othered.

The Othered are entities that sit outside the traditional center of American society, including Muslims, illegal immigrants, and transgender people. The term "othering" was popularized by Simone de Beauvoir, the famous feminist writer and philosopher.[44] She divided society into the categories of dominant, or default, groups and those who are seen as different from these groups—the "other." She argued that this othering was both a cause and a consequence of having less access to power or influence compared with more dominant or default groups. Beauvoir was thinking mostly about men as the dominant group and women as the "other," but other scholars have extended this idea to other social groups.

Today, someone might call these "othered" groups "marginalized" or "disadvantaged," but I believe the term "othered" is good for multiple reasons. First, its historical roots are less tied to the partisan terminology of any modern moment. Second, liberals and conservatives argue about who exactly is marginalized and by how much, but both sides can agree that people like Muslims, undocumented immigrants, and trans people are outside the traditional center of American society. Some on the right might argue these "othered" groups deserve to be outside this center, because they reject the tenets of the traditional American way of life, which they view as the best way to maintain a stable society. Conservatives fighting against the idea of open borders believe that a country with more of the othered will undermine the success of citizens. In 2015, Trump said, "When Mexico sends its people, they're not sending their best. . . . They're bringing drugs. They're bringing crime. They're rapists."[45]

In contrast, liberals argue that these "othered" groups are placed outside the center of society for misguided and malevolent reasons, including racism, xenophobia, and transphobia. They highlight how being pushed toward the fringes of society causes increased harm and discrimination. Liberals see people within this category as less threatening to the country and, if anything, see broad inclusiveness as helping America thrive. Compared with conservatives, liberals seem to see people from the Othered as more vulnerable to victimization.

One debate about the Othered unfolded in my home state of North Carolina in 2016. The conservative-backed legislature passed House Bill 2, or HB2, which banned transgender people from using the bathroom of their choice. These legislators argued that trans women would be tempted to rape young women using the bathroom, by virtue of their innate male impulses for sexual aggression. Liberals argued vehemently against this claim, citing statistics that transgender people are much more likely to be victims of violence than perpetrators.

A similar disagreement about the vulnerability of the Othered focuses on Muslims, with conservatives pointing to examples of Muslim extremists perpetrating violence such as the 9/11 attacks, and progressives pointing to the many examples of innocent everyday Muslims being targets of hate crimes simply because of their religious beliefs.

Now that we have mapped out these four clusters—the Environment, the Divine, the Powerful, and the Othered—we are ready to dive into the data.

THE DIFFERENCE BETWEEN LIBERALS
AND CONSERVATIVES

Based on anecdotes, quotations, voting behavior, and polling data, it seemed as if liberals and conservatives make different assumptions of vulnerability about the Environment, the Divine, the Powerful, and the Othered. But there is a difference between these sources of information and scientific experiments, so we conducted three studies examining American political differences across these four AoV clusters.

In the first study, we asked 1,008 Americans about their assumptions of vulnerability on an online research platform. This was a sample of convenience, where we relied on whoever signed up to take the study. Participants answered each of our three AoV questions, which again assessed whom they saw as especially vulnerable to harm, to victimization, and to mistreatment, concerning all three targets from each of the four clusters. These were coral reefs, the rain forest, and Planet Earth for the Environment; transgender people, Muslims, and illegal immigrants for the Othered; authority figures, corporate leaders, and state troopers for the Powerful; and God, Jesus, and the Bible for the Divine. This meant that each participant answered thirty-six questions about their assumptions of vulnerability—three questions times three entities in each of four clusters—before reporting their demographics including political affiliation, education level, income, and race.

Samples of convenience are useful, but make it difficult to generalize the results to the wider population, and so for our second study we recruited a sample of 1,832 people who were broadly representative of America in terms of race and political affiliation and who included people from across the South, Northeast, Midwest, and West of the country. The sample contained participants who were 73.2 percent White, 12.1 percent Black, 4.6 percent Asian, and 10.2 percent other. The highest level of education of participants spanned from elementary school through PhD, and their income ranged from under $25,000 to more than $150,000 per year. The most frequently reported highest education level was some college (30.9 percent), and the median income was $25,000–$50,000 per year. Online samples tend to skew liberal, but our average political affiliation was slightly conservative—a

5.41 on a 9-point scale where 1 equals very liberal and 9 equals very conservative. This representative sample also oversampled religious Christian participants so we could compare their judgments with those of more secular Americans.

In the third study we recruited another sample of convenience, this time 1,011 Americans, and assessed people's AoVs at two separate time points, one week apart, to test whether they were consistent over time. Across all three studies—and across the two time points in the third study—the results were nearly indistinguishable from each other.

The first set of analyses assessed whether people's ratings clustered together into our four clusters of the Environment, the Divine, the Powerful, and the Othered. For example, were people's ratings of one Powerful entity, like corporate leaders, correlated with their ratings of another Powerful entity, like state troopers? And did these ratings of targets within the Powerful show a higher correlation than ratings of targets within different clusters, like the Environment? The answer is yes. Unlike with measurements of moral foundations, ratings of AoVs are highly correlated within clusters, which shows they are coherent themes, but these correlations are much lower across clusters, which shows that these themes are separate from each other.

We were pleased that each of the four clusters seemed to be coherent and fairly distinct, but the key question is whether there were systematic differences between the AoVs of liberals and conservatives. The short answer is yes, but before we explore these differences, I will note that the studies used different-sized scales to assess political affiliation. For simplicity, in describing results, we always use a 7-point scale where 1 equals very liberal and 7 equals very conservative. In all of these samples, middle-of-the-road centrists (who score 4 on a 7-point scale of conservatism) saw moderate differences in vulnerability between the clusters. As you can see in figure 7.3 (drawn from the first sample), centrists assumed that the Environment and the Othered were most vulnerable to harm, mistreatment, and victimization, followed by the Powerful, who they assumed were more vulnerable than the Divine.

Across all our studies, the overall ranking of AoV clusters is generally the same across all people: the Environment and the Othered were nearly tied at 1 and 2, followed by the Powerful at 3, and the

Divine at 4. All people also had stable AoVs across time, with their ratings at Time 1 and Time 2 correlated with each other at 0.88—high enough to assume that we are measuring the same thing at each time. Of course, a week is not an especially long time, but it is enough to ensure people are not giving the same answer from memory but instead making a fresh judgment.

Despite similarities in the overall rankings of the four clusters, our data revealed clear differences. For example, in our nationally representative sample that contained more Christian participants, the average rating of the vulnerability of the Divine was 2.46 out of 5, but in our less religious sample, the average rating was just 1.78 out of 5. This speaks again to the validity of our AoV measure: people who are more religious are more likely to feel as though God, Jesus, and the Bible can suffer mistreatment.

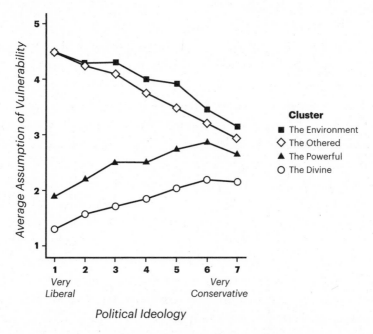

Figure 7.3: Assumptions of vulnerability (AoVs) are measured on a scale from 1 to 7, with 1 representing not at all vulnerable and 5 representing very vulnerable. Liberals *amplify* group differences, dividing the moral world into the very vulnerable (the Environment and the Othered) and the very invulnerable (the Powerful, the Divine), whereas conservatives *dampen* group differences, seeing more similarity among different clusters of entities.

The biggest differences were left-right disagreement about the Othered and the Environment versus the Powerful and the Divine. Extreme liberals (1 out of 7 conservatism) significantly *amplified* differences in assumed vulnerability, seeing the Othered and the Environment as *very* vulnerable to harm and the Powerful and the Divine as *very* invulnerable to harm. Conversely, extreme conservatives (7 out of 7 conservatism) *dampened* differences in assumed vulnerability. They still usually saw the Othered and the Environment as more vulnerable to harm than the Powerful and the Divine, but these differences were quite small.

In the graph above, you can see how the distance between AoVs about the Othered and the Powerful for extreme liberals is much bigger (a difference of about 2.5 points) than for extreme conservatives (a difference of less than 0.25 points). This ten-times difference is a huge gap in perceptions.

Overall, these data show that assumptions of vulnerability are stable perceptions that explain political differences. Compared with conservatives, liberals have higher AoVs about the Environment and lower AoVs about the Divine, which explains why they see more immorality in Arctic drilling, but less immorality in burning a Bible. Compared with liberals, conservatives have lower AoVs about the Othered and higher AoVs about the Powerful, which helps explain the many debates revolving around social justice.

Liberal advocates of social justice argue that people from marginalized groups—including religious, racial, sexual, and gender minorities—need additional protections and that we should restructure social systems to address modern power imbalances stemming from historical inequality. An obvious example of this restructuring is the policy of race-based affirmative action, which helps African American students gain admission into college, providing them with a stepping-stone to upward economic mobility. In arguing for affirmative action, liberals point to the pernicious effects of discrimination, starting with slavery and then Jim Crow laws, redlining, and the mass incarceration of Black men.[46] These arguments all revolve around the suffering of African American people and their continued vulnerability to victimization and mistreatment.

Of course, any policy has trade-offs, and the downside of affirmative action is denying admission to more White and Asian students, who may have higher grades or test scores than the Black students who are admitted in their stead. In the argument against affirmative action, David Cao of Houston Chinese Alliance cynically paraphrased George Orwell's novel *Animal Farm* by saying, "All animals are equal, but some animals are more equal than others. . . . In admission to the American elite universities, it is no secret that Asians are less equal."[47] Similarly, Coleman Hughes, a popular African American critic of affirmative action, argues that these policies harm the students they are intended to benefit: students "feel insecure and unprepared" within selective programs when they lower their admission standards to increase diversity, and these admits "end up struggling more than their peers."[48]

We can see that people's moral stance on affirmative action depends on how they perceive the relative harm to Black, White, and Asian students. People's assumptions of vulnerability determine how much they believe each group can be harmed. In terms of our four clusters, African Americans are relatively more "Othered," whereas White Americans and—arguably—Asian Americans are relatively more "Powerful." Of course, some Black individuals are more powerful than some White people; Barack Obama is a powerful man, but statistically speaking Black Americans have less wealth and influence in America. The median household income of Black families is $52,860, whereas the median household income of White families is $81,060,[49] and Black people are much less represented than White people in the corporate C-suite.

Regardless of statistics and the true state of the world, AoVs are perceptions, and because liberals see the Othered as much more vulnerable than the Powerful, it means that harm to Black Americans looms much larger to liberals than harm to White Americans. With this balance of perceived harm, it is natural that liberals want to protect Black Americans at a cost to White Americans. On the other hand, conservatives see the Othered and the Powerful as more similarly vulnerable, explaining why they are hesitant to restructure the admissions process to disadvantage White and Asian students, who also have hopes and dreams for their future.

The tension between the Othered and the Powerful also explains debates between Black Lives Matter and Blue Lives Matter. Liberals

are concerned about the vulnerability of Black men, who are dispro-
portionately the victims of gun violence in America, at the hands of
both police and other civilians.[50] Conservatives are concerned about
the suffering of Black men too, but they prioritize the vulnerability of
police officers who risk their lives to protect society and who are four
times more likely to be killed on the job compared with the average
occupation.[51] Most conservatives generally want to protect Black men
and most liberals generally want to protect the police, but when these
interests are pitted against each other, left-right differences in assumptions of vulnerability about the Othered and the Powerful drive different moral positions, leading liberals to support Black Lives Matter
and conservatives to support Blue Lives Matter.

AoVs explain political differences in many other issues. In debates
about trans rights, liberals emphasize how trans women are vulnerable
victims, while conservatives emphasize how they could be threatening
to other women. In debates about taxation and minimum wage, liberals emphasize how poorer people are especially vulnerable to suffering,
while conservatives emphasize how legislating a higher minimum wage
and higher taxes takes away money from hardworking business owners. Even debates about climate change touch on the Other versus the
Powerful, because liberals argue that the impacts of extreme weather
are most keenly felt by people in marginalized groups.

If you zoom out from specific issues, the overall pattern of AoVs
across politics makes sense of societal narratives on the left and the
right. The liberal tendency to amplify differences in vulnerability—
especially between the Othered and the Powerful—explains why they
often divide the historical and modern world into oppressors (very
invulnerable Powerful people) and oppressed (very vulnerable Othered
people). The left-leaning amplification of AoV differences can be seen
when Karl Marx described society as a struggle between the exploited
proletariat and the exploiting ruling class,[52] and when Martin Luther
King Jr. wrote, "Freedom is never voluntarily given by the oppressor;
it must be demanded by the oppressed."[53]

Meanwhile, the conservative tendency to dampen differences in
vulnerability explains why they are likely to see society as a collection
of consenting individuals, each of whom is personally responsible for
their outcomes. This right-leaning dampening of AoV differences is

captured by this quotation from John Locke: "We are born free, as we are born rational."[54] By not mentioning different human groups, but only a broadly collective "we," he emphasized the common freedom of all people and our shared capacity for reason and responsibility.

Of course, both liberals and conservatives believe in human rights and the importance of fighting for freedom, but liberals are more likely to see society through the lens of group-based inequalities, where some people are much more vulnerable to harm based on their identity and group membership, whether race, religion, gender, or sexuality. For liberals, protecting these especially vulnerable groups of people requires transforming the status quo, even if it means causing some harm to the very powerful, whom they view as relatively incapable of suffering.

In contrast, conservatives are more likely to see society as a contract between free individuals, viewing everyone as the master of their own destiny and attributing successes and failures primarily to people's choices. In this view, whether you're born poor or rich, you are an individual who can both commit harm against other people and be harmed by other people.

Amplifying versus dampening the differences in vulnerability between the Othered and the Powerful explains why liberals accuse conservatives of denying obvious social inequalities and why conservatives accuse liberals of exaggerating differences and creating division. The Fox News anchor Laura Ingraham complained in her podcast about the "Othered" getting special treatment by society: "Because you're a minority, you get special standards, special treatment."[55] Conservatives everywhere oppose what one *National Review* columnist refers to as the liberal tendency to organize "these groups into a hierarchy of victimization and grievance."[56] In the minds of committed conservatives, everyone suffers similarly, and the liberal exaggeration of the victimhood of the Othered actually makes them more likely to be victimized.

Liberals take the opposite stance, arguing that conservatives should spend less time ignoring group differences and accept that some people are more vulnerable to harm by mere accident of birth. Ibram X. Kendi writes in his book *How to Be an Antiracist,* "There may be no more consequential White privilege than life itself. White lives matter to the tune of 3.5 additional years over Black lives in the United States, which is just the most glaring of a host of health disparities, starting from infancy, where Black infants die at twice the rate of White infants."[57]

Whether you are more sympathetic to liberal or conservative positions, the key point of this chapter is that assumptions of vulnerability help explain moral disagreement. Despite us all sharing a harm-based mind, differing ideas about who or what is especially vulnerable to harm, victimization, and mistreatment drive divergent moral judgments. We all care about protecting the vulnerable from harm, but we disagree about which entities most need our protection. Even minor differences in AoVs can spark intense debates when people are forced to make trade-offs about whom to prioritize for protection.

Looking across all four clusters of entities we examined—the Environment, the Divine, the Powerful, and the Othered—explains many political debates, but other kinds of moral disagreements revolve around additional AoVs beyond these ad hoc categories. When people are arguing about foreign wars, about what happened at their homeowners' association meeting, or who is to blame for a family meltdown, different assumptions of vulnerability are likely lurking in the background. If you assume that your sister-in-law is impervious to emotional injury, but your spouse sees her as deeply sensitive to suffering, you will have different opinions on the morality of hurting her feelings. Importantly, these AoVs are not little boxes in the brain or separate mental mechanisms, but instead cultural assumptions woven into people's beliefs about morality and harm.

In the first part of the book, we saw how people are fundamentally compelled to protect themselves and others from harm, and in the previous chapter we saw how people's specific moral judgments are driven by their intuitive perceptions of harm. Assumptions of vulnerability are the cultural ideas that connect our general harm-based worries to specific intuitions about harming specific entities, and it is these specific intuitions that drive moral disagreement and outrage.

We all rely on the common moral language of harm, but differing AoVs cause us to talk past each other. This divide is not insurmountable, because we can always ask people about their beliefs, as we explore in part 3 of the book. But—as we will now see—it can be hard to discuss morality with people who seem to confuse absolutely evil villains with obviously suffering victims.

In Sum

- Liberals and conservatives have the same harm-based moral mind, grounding their moral judgments in intuitive perceptions of harm, but political disagreement is real. Moral divisions arise because liberals and conservatives have different *assumptions of vulnerability* (AoVs). They disagree about who is especially vulnerable to mistreatment and victimization.

- Assumptions of vulnerability vary widely because we can't truly know others' feelings, only perceive them externally. This subjectivity explains why sports fans might disagree on whether an "injured" player is genuinely suffering or faking it.

- Much political disagreement is driven by liberals and conservatives having different assumptions of vulnerability about four entities: *the Environment* (for example, Planet Earth), *the Divine* (for instance, God), *the Powerful* (for example, state troopers), and *the Othered* (such as undocumented immigrants). Compared with conservatives, liberals tend to view the Environment and the Othered as more vulnerable to victimization and the Powerful and the Divine as less vulnerable.

- There is a general pattern in assumptions of vulnerability across politics: Committed liberals *amplify* differences in vulnerability, splitting the world into the very vulnerable (the oppressed) and the very invulnerable (oppressors). Committed conservatives dampen differences in vulnerability, seeing all people as relatively similar in their vulnerability, believing that no matter their identities all people can be both victims and victimizers.

- Liberals' and conservatives' different assumptions of vulnerability help explain many modern culture-war debates, including about race and policing, affirmative action, taxation, and the environment. These assumptions of vulnerability explain how moral disagreement can arise even if we are all motivated to protect the vulnerable.

Chapter 8

Blame: Moral Typecasting

No one ever thinks of Hitler's inner pain. Fair enough: he was a monster who did monstrous things. But people forget that young Adolf's father was physically abusive, relentlessly beating him throughout his childhood.[1] For at least some part of his life, he was more victim than villain, and yet people bristle at portrayals of Hitler that show him as a human being with the capacity to suffer.

The movie *Downfall* depicted the true story of Hitler's final days in his underground bunker as Allied forces closed in around him. It was nominated for an Oscar because it powerfully depicted Hitler's vulnerabilities, fears, and emotions, which also explained why the movie incited so much outrage. People rejected the idea that a ruthless dictator could be sad and afraid. We might explicitly recognize that Hitler, as a fellow human being, can suffer, but his villainy makes it hard to see him as a victim.

In contrast to Hitler, consider Cody Posey, a boy from New Mexico. When Cody was ten years old, his parents were fighting in divorce court about who would get custody. As the proceedings dragged on, his father became abusive, taking out his rage on Cody by berating and beating him. Thankfully, Cody's loving mother was finally awarded custody, and Cody was able to avoid all contact with his dad. A few months later, Cody's mom decided it was time for a fresh start. As they packed up the car and headed from New Mexico to Washington state, Cody felt relief: he was free. But on the freeway their pickup collided with another vehicle, killing Cody's mother.

Custody laws in New Mexico meant that Cody was returned to

his cruel father, who lived with his new wife and her daughter on a secluded ranch. Cody was constantly abused[2] and forced to work on the ranch, often without food, water, or rest. He was awoken daily with an electronic cattle prod. His father routinely beat him with whips, shovels, a hay hook, rocks, and other farm tools. Cody's stepmother also participated in his mental and physical abuse, and his stepsister, Marilea, was encouraged to tattle on him and rewarded whenever Cody made a mistake.

One night, his dad tried to force fourteen-year-old Cody to have sex with his stepmother. When Cody refused, Cody's dad branded him with a red-hot iron. The next day, in desperation and despair, Cody took a .38 revolver and killed his father, his stepmother, and his thirteen-year-old stepsister.

There is no doubt that Cody is a murderer, but our moral mind treats him differently than Hitler. Rather than an insensitive villain, he is seen as a suffering victim. We empathize with his suffering, which makes it hard to see him as morally responsible for killing his dad and stepfamily. The tendency to see Cody as only a victim of harm explains why he mostly avoided punishment for the murders. In 2010, just six years after killing his entire family, Cody was released from prison.

Hitler and Cody are extreme caricatures of villains and victims. Most of us are much less evil than Hitler and much less victimized than Cody; our moral characters are blends of mild villainy and mild victimhood. We occasionally harm others and are occasionally harmed by others, placing us somewhere in the gray middle between pure victimhood and pure villainy.

Even people whose lives are touched by trauma are often combinations of villains and victims. The Lehigh Longitudinal Study illustrates this moral complexity. In the 1970s, a team of researchers at Lehigh University started tracking kids born into rough situations, focusing particularly on those in child welfare programs. Most (63 percent) of the families studied made less than $700 a month, and 42 percent of children lived in homes with frequent abuse.

The researchers found that a significant minority of all children—both those who suffered abuse and those who did not—eventually committed some kind of crime, including felony assault, which involves seriously hurting another person. The study also revealed that children who were abused or assaulted had a higher likelihood of engaging in felony assault: 47 percent of them committed this crime compared with 36 percent of those who weren't abused as children.[3] These results suggest a positive correlation between victimhood and villainy, illustrating the quotation "hurt people hurt people."

Despite the real-life association between being victimized and victimizing others, our minds struggle to accept the idea that people are mixes of victims and villains. Instead of shades of gray, we try to simplify the moral world into a tidy diorama of black and white. We want to overlook people's complicated lives and assign them to a one-sided moral role as *either* a villain *or* a victim. With morality, we typecast people with the confidence of a Hollywood director, caricaturing people as either sympathetic sufferers or vile perpetrators.

Moral typecasting is the idea that just as we typecast famous actors into certain roles, we typecast people into specific moral roles. It's hard to see the late actor Alan Rickman, who played two classic villains—the wormy and dour Severus Snape from *Harry Potter* and the callous and calculating Hans Gruber from *Die Hard*—as someone fun-loving and happy-go-lucky. Likewise, it's hard to see child actors—who act in roles that emphasize their vulnerability and cuteness—as ruthless villains. It is hard to imagine young Judy Garland from *The Wizard of Oz* strangling a Munchkin to death.

Typecasting in Hollywood is a problem for actors because they are trapped in a narrow set of roles, unable to explore their full acting range. Moral typecasting is a problem for everyone because it takes complicated moral issues, where truth is muddled, and simplifies people within them into two exaggerated sides—blameless victims versus invulnerable villains—paving the way for more moral conflict.

Central to the phenomenon of moral typecasting is *simplification.* Our minds may be incredibly powerful, but the natural and social worlds that surround us are dizzyingly complex. To help reduce this complexity, we have developed a suite of heuristics, also called rules of thumb or cognitive shortcuts, that help us make sense of the world. As I mentioned in chapter 5, the idea of heuristics was pioneered by the late psychologists Amos Tversky and Daniel Kahneman, whose book *Thinking, Fast and Slow* explains how these System 1 cognitive shortcuts help us to rapidly process information. Rather than effortful

System 2, we use the quick-and-intuitive System 1 to perceive harm and make moral judgments.

Moral typecasting is a heuristic about our moral world; it simplifies judgments of someone's moral character after they have either been victimized or perpetrated harm. Someone who has been harmed is flattened into a person who is—at their inner core—a complete victim and not at all a villain. In contrast, someone who perpetrates harm is flattened into a person who is—at their inner core—a complete villain and not at all a victim.

This either-or view of the moral world distorts how we make sense of conflict and the people within it, transforming well-meaning but imperfect people into Hitlers and Codys. These black-and-white perceptions can make it hard to have nuanced—or even civil— conversations about moral issues. Moral typecasting is surely one driver of Godwin's law, the adage about conversations on the internet stating that "as an online discussion grows longer, the probability of a comparison involving Nazis or Hitler approaches one."[4]

Godwin's law is why I started this chapter with the question of Hitler and his pain: in today's conversation about politics, the Nazi leader is never far from people's lips as they typecast the other side as pure villains. One study[5] found that no matter what side you're on, you think that Hitler shared the beliefs of your political opponents. These researchers asked liberals and conservatives to place where Hitler stood on a scale of political ideology ranging from extremely left-wing to extremely right-wing. They found that 75 percent of liberals ranked Hitler as right-wing as possible, and 50 percent of conservatives ranked him as left-wing as possible. We can debate about what Hitler really believed, but the truth is that people on neither the left nor the right are actually Hitler. Unfortunately, it is all too easy for our moral minds to slide down a slippery slope from "you believe something wrong" to "you are no different from the architect of genocide."

Moral typecasting means that different people live in different moral worlds, where one person's villains are another person's victims. In one study, college students wrote down their thoughts about undocumented immigrants, including their "social, political, moral, and economic views,"[6] and as the researchers predicted, the student responses showed clear evidence of moral typecasting. Out of eighty-five students, fifty (59 percent) discussed how undocumented immigrants perpetrated immoral deeds, arguing things like "immigrants come into our country, [and] they take away from the limited job opportunities" or "I think that illegal immigrants are taking away from the immigrants who are actually coming to this country legally." Thirty-seven students (44 percent) discussed how undocumented immigrants were victimized and highlighted their "desperation" and "dire situation." Importantly, only six students (7 percent) saw undocumented immigrants as mixes of both villainy and victimhood. Ninety-three percent of people simplified their moral world via moral typecasting.[7]

Imagine that you knew nothing about undocumented immigrants before reading these thoughts. Depending on which student's responses you picked up, you would get a completely different sense of the people coming to the United States outside legal immigration routes. Because 93 percent of people mentioned either only victim or only villain themes, you might not even realize that these students were all talking about the same group of people. This is the crux of moral typecasting; these students reduced moral complexity into a simplistic caricature.

THE DISCOVERY OF TYPECASTING

Moral typecasting is everywhere in conversations about morality and politics. Now that you've learned about it, you'll notice it all over the place, like when a family member sees their thoughtless relative as completely evil, or when your co-workers see a colleague as a complete victim of your heartless manager. Typecasting explains why a "canceled" pundit on the other side seems like a villain finally getting their comeuppance, but why someone canceled on your side seems like an innocent victim of a rabid online mob.

Although moral typecasting is everywhere, I stumbled on it by accident (as often happens with scientific discoveries), a surprise finding buried in failure during my first year of grad school. After arriving at Harvard, I was feeling like a complete impostor. My friends already had productive lines of research, and I had discovered nothing interesting. I was trying to explore the mysteries of the human mind by asking people to rate the minds and morality of people and robots, but nothing was noteworthy. For example, I found that people think that robots like Roombas deserve less moral protection than children. Not exactly shocking.

One winter evening during this spell of failure, I was staying late on campus. It had already been dark for hours—Boston in February—and I left my office and roamed the halls, trying to clear my mind. A friend of mine named Carey Morewedge, now a professor of marketing who studies perceptions of AI, was also working late. Carey had a knack for designing interesting studies, and always kept his overhead lights off, so his office was dark except for the glow from a dim desk lamp and the computer monitors shining on his face. As I hovered in the doorway, his office seemed like a cave of wonders where clever science grew out of darkness. I confessed my feelings of defeat.

He dropped what he was working on and told me to send him my surveys. I did, and he immediately dug in, slicing pages, tightening questions, and overhauling scenarios. In the end, he had turned a bloated twelve-page questionnaire into two clear pages. This revised survey now asked about how much two different targets—adults and robots—were capable of suffering harm (how much pain would they feel if cut) and how much each was morally blameworthy for wrong-doing (how much blame they would deserve if they hurt someone).

Carey also suggested that I go beyond looking at robots and typical adult humans, perhaps exploring how people perceive someone with developmental disabilities, like a person with Down's syndrome. I thought it was worth shaking it up and followed his suggestion, but I had low hopes. The next day, I took the stack of surveys and swiped into the subway station, asking commuters to fill them out as they waited for the train. We weren't allowed to collect data in the subway, but the transit cops rarely came to crush the scientific hopes of graduate students.

When I analyzed the data, most of the effects were again obvious. Compared with robots, people thought a typical human adult was more capable of experiencing suffering and would also be morally blameworthy for causing harm. Also obvious was that typical adults were seen as more morally blameworthy than people with Down's syndrome. After all, the law treats having a developmental disability as a mitigating circumstance for criminal punishment. If someone lacks an intellectual understanding of the moral weight of their actions, we hold them less accountable.

But there was also an odd finding: people with developmental disabilities were seen as more sensitive to pain than typical adults. This is strange because, as it was understood at the time, all mental and moral capacities were thought to cluster together.[8] This was before we did the mind survey (discussed in the last chapter), which revealed how perceptions of someone as a thinking doer could be separated from perceptions of them as a vulnerable feeler. At the time, the prevailing view of mind perception was that if someone seemed more intellectually sophisticated, they should *also* seem to have more powerful emotional experiences. If a typical adult was ascribed more moral responsibility than someone with Down's syndrome, shouldn't they be attributed more capacity for pain and suffering?

But I found a disconnect between perceptions of moral blameworthiness and their capacity to be harmed. The person with Down's syndrome was seen as less capable of being a villain but as *more* capable of being a victim. I wondered whether this tension between "blame and pain" might be a thread running throughout the fabric of moral judgment. Might people generally assume that villainy and victimhood are mutually exclusive, where increased perceptions of vulnerability lead to reduced perceptions of blame, and vice versa?

I had finally stumbled on an intriguing effect—thanks to Carey's nudge—and now I frantically developed studies to test whether judgments of moral responsibility were inversely related to judgments of vulnerability. Together with my adviser, the late Dan Wegner, I asked participants to rate many targets on their capacity for blame and pain, including obvious villains like Hitler, the serial killer Ted Bundy, and the al-Qaeda founder Osama bin Laden. Participants also rated people generally seen as vulnerable, like orphans, victims of date rape, and people with Down's syndrome. To make sure that any differences we found weren't just driven by the famousness of the villains, we rounded out the list of targets with more neutral everyday people, including a network administrator, a teacher, and a bank teller, and two non-villainous celebrities of the day: Britney Spears and Prince Harry.[9]

Wong-Baker FACES® Pain Rating Scale

0	2	4	6	8	10
No Hurt	Hurts Little Bit	Hurts Little More	Hurts Even More	Hurts Whole Lot	Hurts Worst

Figure 8.1: The Wong-Baker pain scale was used to evaluate how much people thought a villain and a victim would suffer if they got cut.

To measure a target's apparent capacity for pain, we asked people to imagine that they stepped on a piece of glass without their shoes on. How much pain would they feel? To answer this question, people circled a "pain face"—ranging from 0 to 10—on the Wong-Baker pain scale, which was developed to help people in the doctor's office express their inner sense of suffering.[10] To measure perceptions of moral blameworthiness, people answered the question "How much blame does this person deserve for the events of their life?"

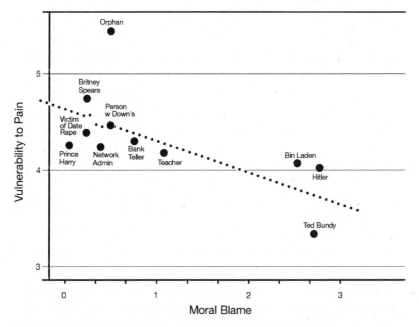

Figure 8.2: People who seem more like villains seem less like victims. As perceptions of blame go up, perceptions of pain go down.

Across these different measures and targets, we found a consistent effect: the more someone seemed like a suffering victim, the less they seemed like a blameworthy villain. In the graph above, you can see the downward-sloping line characteristic of a negative correlation: as perceptions of villainy go up, perceptions of victimhood go down (and vice versa). In our minds, vulnerability seems inconsistent with blame.

Of course, this study used extreme targets—obviously evil wrongdoers and those obviously susceptible to victimization—but other studies revealed the tension between villainy and victimhood in judgments of more everyday people. In one study, we presented participants with two people—Jeffrey and Michael—who both worked at an eco-friendly company but who were planning on polluting the environment to increase profits. Jeffrey took the lead on pushing for these changes and fired an employee who disagreed with them. Michael also agreed with polluting policies but took a more secondary role. In the first part of the study, we simply asked which of the two was more deserving of blame, and unsurprisingly, participants overwhelmingly saw Jeffrey as more of a blameworthy villain.

We predicted that because people saw Jeffrey as a villain, they would also deny his capacity to be a victim, seeing him as less vulnerable to suffering. To assess this, we asked which of the two men—blameworthy Jeffrey or less blameworthy Michael—would feel more pain if scalding-hot coffee was spilled on them. As predicted by moral typecasting, people thought that Jeffrey would suffer less than Michael from the exact same incident. Objectively speaking, someone's evil managerial actions at work are distinct from their sensitivity to burning coffee, and yet people cannot help mentally connecting them, seeing villainy and victimhood as opposing forces.

These studies hint at the two main consequences of moral typecasting. The first is that victims—as non-villains—are seen as less capable of earning blame. The second is villains—as non-victims—are seen as less capable of suffering pain. Sometimes these consequences of moral typecasting are justified: it makes sense that we hold orphans less accountable for their misdeeds than dictators, and that we sympathize more with the plight of orphans than with dictators. But moral typecasting can also blind us to the full humanity of other people, seeing those around us as simplistic moral caricatures.

ESCAPING BLAME

Outrage is one of our most powerful moral feelings. As we saw in chapter 3, we get angry and upset at those who victimize others. This outrage helps to protect ourselves and society by motivating us to punish evildoers, whether by exiling them or locking them in prison. We are especially likely to become outraged and punish those who inflict severe harm—except when a perpetrator convinces us that they are actually a victim.

Think of Cody Posey, who murdered his father, stepmother, and stepsister. When people—and jurors—initially learned about his crime, they were outraged, but soon that outrage turned to sympathy. Upon learning that Cody was brutally abused by his father and stepfamily, people sought to protect him, not punish him. The violence Cody suffered transformed him into a victim, making the harm he perpetrated seem justified and allowing him to escape blame.

When we think about "escaping blame" for wrongdoing, we often think about denial, claiming that you didn't do some kind of nefarious act. Victims can certainly deny their involvement in wrongdoing, but escaping blame as a victim often entails acknowledging the "doing" part of wrongdoing while arguing against the "wrong" part. Cody admitted to the murders but claimed they were justified because of the cruel circumstances.

Victims can acknowledge their misdeeds while excusing their evilness because of their experience of threat, pain, and fear. In the book *Win Your Case,* the successful trial lawyer Gerry Spence outlines seven steps for winning a criminal defense including "becoming the victim," which involves emphasizing the defendant's suffering and recasting the accuser as "callous, cruel, and vindictive." This advice is based on his own experience of judges and juries giving lighter sentences to defendants who successfully prove their victimhood.[11]

Real-life court cases are complex, but our studies provide a more controlled test of the power of victimhood to escape blame. People read a scenario about a man named George who gets paid $600 every week. In the "neutral" condition George uses all his money to buy things, but in the "victim" condition George's supervisor unjustly steals $100 from him and threatens to fire him if he complains.[12]

We described how George was walking down the street when he witnesses a woman dropping a $10 bill. He snatches it up and keeps it, and we asked people to rate how much blame and punishment George deserves. As predicted by typecasting, the victim George was blamed and punished less than the neutral George. Also consistent with typecasting, the more George was seen as sensitive to pain—assessed by another question—the less people wanted to punish him. The more he fit the stereotype of a suffering victim, the less he seemed like a villain.

Another study explored people's reactions to a scenario about two young line cooks working at the same restaurant. They both helped make a dish with peanuts in it, despite having been warned about a customer's nut allergy. The customer then had a life-threatening reaction and almost died. After she recovered, she demanded that one of the negligent cooks get fired; otherwise, she'd sue.

We gave the cooks two different backstories. The "neutral" cook used to work at a hardware store, but the "victimized" cook was hit by a drunk driver, and it took him months to learn how to walk again. Consistent with typecasting, victimhood led to less blame: 69 percent of participants recommended firing the cook without the sad backstory, even though the once-victimized cook had long since recovered. This reveals that moral typecasting is "sticky," just like Hollywood typecasting, with someone's previous moral roles shaping how people see them in the present. Even though the "past victim" was now doing perfectly fine, people still saw him as deserving less blame than someone who was never victimized.

These studies show the power of moral typecasting in controlled experiments, and they also reveal something unexpected. In both scenarios, the "victimized" person was not retaliating against the person who hurt them but was instead harming a *completely different person*. Unlike Cody Posey, who was acting in self-defense to stop his suffering—and perhaps rebalance the scales of justice—the $10 thief and the negligent cook were harming someone else, someone innocent. It seems irrational that long-past victimhood warrants less blame in these cases.

Why should someone escape blame for victimizing the innocent just because they suffered past harm from someone *else*? The answer is moral typecasting: Past suffering changes how we see people's moral character, transforming them from someone capable of earning blame to someone characterized by pain. People sometimes say that "two wrongs don't make a right," but suffering one wrong seems to make committing another wrong more allowable.

In some ways, forgiving victims of their sins makes intuitive sense. If past trauma makes someone more likely to lash out, then perhaps we should give them less blame. On the other hand, does past suffering really prevent someone from taking responsibility for their actions? When someone suffers childhood abuse, should society (not to mention their friends and family) assign them less blame for the cruelty they inflict as an adult?

The exact amount we should forgive the wrongdoing of victims cannot be answered by these scenario studies, or by moral psychology at all. This is a "normative" question about how people *should* assign blame, and—as we touched on earlier—moral psychology provides only "descriptive" answers about how people *do* assign blame. But these studies do reveal the power of victimhood and the allure of moral typecasting.

The deeper reason we feel the tug of moral typecasting has to do with the structure of a typical immoral act. In a standard case of murder, assault, or theft, the person who is being murdered, assaulted, or stolen from is not the person doing the murdering, assaulting, or stealing. In other words, the perpetrator is *not* the victim; these roles are mutually exclusive. In fact, if the perpetrator was the victim within a single immoral act—if the thief was the same as the person being thieved from—then the act is no longer immoral. A one-person theft is simply someone taking money out of their own wallet. Moral typecasting is our mind extending this *either* perpetrator *or* victim dynamic from within single acts to people's general moral character.

A good analogy for this *either-or* perception within any one immoral act is the classic duck-rabbit image, often printed in psychology books. The two possible perceptions of this image are mutually exclusive: when you see it as a duck, you don't see the rabbit, and when you see it as a rabbit, you don't see the duck. Of course, with this plain image, these interpretations can pop back and forth in your mind—rabbit, duck, rabbit, duck—but with more context your perception freezes. In the right-hand panel, the carrot next to the mouth of the rabbit makes it challenging to see the picture as a duck. Learning that someone has been victimized functions the same as the carrot, freezing your perceptions of them as a blameless victim. Of course, if you think hard, you may be able to switch your perceptions back—the victim is really a villain—but people seldom think hard about morality, instead relying on their intuitive perceptions.

Con artists take advantage of this either-or villain-versus-victim tension to bilk people out of money.[13] In one version of a typecasting con, the scammer pretends to be a victim, providing the illusion of suffering to pull at their mark's heartstrings and to make the scammer seem unlike a villain. The scammer might tearfully describe a grievous accident while limping on crutches, or wear a fake cast, just like the serial killer Ted Bundy when he was luring women to murder. Once the mark feels sympathy, it is game over; sympathizing with the scammer blocks people from being suspicious that they might be evil.

In a more sophisticated version of a typecasting con, the scammer convinces the mark that the two of them are working together to defraud a third person (the fake dupe—sometimes a partner of the scammer). Because the mark—the real dupe—feels like a villain, they never stop to consider that they might actually be the victim. Making someone feel like the apex predator pushes away thoughts that they could be prey.

Because victims escape blame, people are incentivized to exaggerate or invent their own victimhood. This can happen in courtrooms,

Figure 8.3: The rabbit-duck figure. Just as seeing a rabbit makes it hard to see the duck, seeing someone as a victim makes it hard to see them as a villain, and vice versa. Just as the appearance of a carrot freezes our perceptions into a rabbit, past victimhood or villainy freezes our moral perceptions of someone into that role.

such as when Harvey Weinstein—the movie producer notorious for sexual assault—came into court limping with a cane. Weinstein hoped to be seen as a victim, an old man suffering from the injustices of age and a weakened body. But Weinstein's victim campaign didn't work, because people had already typecast him as a villain (something he, as a Hollywood producer, might appreciate). It was too little suffering, too late. If anything, people were *more* outraged by his pretending to be a victim; his malingering was interpreted as further evidence of his evilness.

You have certainly witnessed people in your own life use victimhood to escape blame, whether it involves exaggerating their own suffering, or simply bringing up past mistreatment at convenient times. You criticize a friend for saying something cruel, and they start moaning about feeling sick or getting mistreated by their spouse. You accuse a co-worker of stealing an idea, and they whimper about job pressure and their mental health. Importantly, these people may not be *intentionally* using psychological tactics to win you over but may simply intuitively appreciate the power of victimhood to escape blame in moral situations.

I often see moral typecasting at the playground with my kids. As soon as one kid gets in trouble, they immediately emphasize some injury or emotional trauma caused by another kid. I doubt they recognize this as a "strategy"; instead, they are embracing a moral reflex.

Sometimes, however, typecasting is deployed intentionally and maliciously. Entire governments have successfully used moral typecasting to escape blame while advancing their nefarious goals. In a "false flag" operation, a country's military will attack its own troops while pretending to be another country, providing justification for "retaliating" in "self-defense" against that country.

One of the most famous—and successful—false flag operations was implemented by the most famous team of villains, the Nazis. Heinrich Himmler, during September 1939, ordered a small group of German soldiers to disguise themselves in Polish uniforms and then seize a radio station in Gleiwitz, a town that was then near the border of Germany and Poland. These "Polish soldiers" then bragged about their "attack" and broadcast an anti-German tirade, calling for war to begin between Germany and Poland. The Nazis executed some German citizens and left their bodies scattered throughout the radio tower to give the appearance of Polish villainy. Hitler argued that innocent Germans were the victims of Polish ethnic aggression and claimed that Germany had no choice but to take "defensive" action for the "Polish atrocities." He soon invaded Poland.

Although the international community was suspicious of these attacks, this operation gave the Nazis enough perceived victimhood to deflect blame and persuade German citizens to go to war. False flag operations are moral typecasting on the largest and most cynical scale, an extension of our mind's tendency to divide people into two camps: those perpetrating harm and those receiving it. Typecasting means that we not only see victims as blameless but also ignore the pain of those who seem like villains.

IGNORING THE PAIN OF VILLAINS

Jo Cameron cannot feel pain. A cheery seventy-one-year-old from Scotland, she described childbirth as "a tickle" and said that scotch bonnet chili peppers "leave a pleasant glow." After feeling virtually no pain during an entire hip replacement at age sixty-five, she wondered if she might be different from others.[14] Cameron belongs to a rare group of people with a genetic condition called congenital insensitivity to pain with anhidrosis, which makes its bearers feel little to no physical pain. While this may seem like a blessing—no more flinching at vaccines, no more stubbed toes—it is actually a curse.

Many with Cameron's condition do not survive to old age. Pain alerts us to bodily damage and to harmful behaviors we should avoid. Pain keeps our hands off burning stoves and lets us know that our appendix will soon burst. In our evolutionary quest to protect ourselves—discussed in part 1 of the book—physical pain was an essential sensation because it helped us to avoid the dozens of threats that could kill us every day.

Other than a few people like Jo Cameron, all humans possess the capacity to suffer, both physically and emotionally. Sadness, anxiety, and disappointment are useful feelings because they motivate us to avoid the things that cause them, including misfortune, danger, and failure. Whether you are the richest king or the poorest pauper, a technology worker from Sweden or a shaman from an indigenous tribe, no one is a stranger to inner suffering. But just because the vast majority of humanity feels pain does not mean that we always recognize it in others.

As we saw in the last chapter, the problem of other minds can make us guess wrong about the inner experiences of other people. Sometimes, we assume that someone suffers more than they actually do. If you watched Jo Cameron touch a hot stove, you would assume she felt more pain than she actually did. But usually, the bigger problem is underestimating the pain of others, believing that someone suffers little when they are abused, injured, or even tortured. Almost all of us have shrugged when walking by a homeless person filled with distress.

Moral typecasting is one reason why we neglect the pain of others. In the previous section, we saw how victims of harm can seem blameless for wrongdoing. The other half of typecasting is seeing villains—those who harm others—as invulnerable to harm. This half of moral typecasting explains why some people saw the tears of Braden Wallake—the "crying CEO"—as insincere. He harmed his employees by firing them, and now people deny his suffering.

Testing the idea that villains seem insensitive to harm is straightforward. In fact, we already discussed a study that demonstrates this effect, where people saw different targets—some lower on villainy (for example, a teacher) and some higher (for instance, a serial killer)—and then rated how much pain each might feel if they stepped on a piece of glass without shoes. Villains who stepped on glass seemed to feel less pain than other people: the eviler someone seemed, the more their capacity for suffering was denied (see figure 8.2).

Even people who seem mildly evil are seen as less sensitive to pain. In one study, we created a new scenario with characters again named Michael and Jeffrey: Michael persuaded his friend Jeffrey to join him in dining and dashing, leaving a restaurant without paying the bill. When we asked participants who would feel more pain if they both tripped and scraped their hands on the sidewalk, participants thought Michael, the leader, would feel less pain than Jeffrey, the follower, because Michael seemed like more of a villain.

It makes some sense that we feel compelled to deny the suffering of villains. Who wants to empathize with Hitler? But sometimes typecasting can lead us to deny the pain of people many would acknowledge as legitimate victims. This happens when people engage in "victim blaming," convincing themselves that victims are actually villains and therefore undeserving of sympathy. Victim blaming happens with sexual assault, when people ask whether the victim was guilty of wearing something too revealing; with lung cancer, when people ask if the victim smoked; and even with natural disasters, when people ask why the victim lived somewhere dangerous. In all these cases, people try to deny someone's victimhood and see them as responsible for their plight.

Few people like to think of themselves as "victim blamers," and—as we've seen—moral typecasting typically leads us to *not* blame victims. At the same time, there are reasons why we sometimes try to deny people's victimhood. First, our minds strive to provide simple explanations for someone's suffering, ignoring the complex web that often surrounds misfortune. For example, it is much simpler to blame someone's decision to smoke than to acknowledge the many causal factors—including genes, epigenetics, environmental pollutants, and unlucky probabilities—that cause cancerous tumors to grow.

A second reason why we deny other people's victimhood is that the suffering of the innocent is distressing, especially when their victimization makes the world seem unjust.[15] We want victims of lung cancer to have smoked because it keeps the world fair. When a person who has never smoked (and who also eats right and exercises) randomly gets lung cancer, it means that the world is random and cruel, and that *you* could get lung cancer too. No one wants to live in an unfair world, and so our knee-jerk reaction is to blame the victim and maintain our vision of a universe where justice and karma reign.

For many people, this just-world reflex will pass, allowing typecasting to reestablish itself, and leading them to again sympathize with victims. But for other people—most often abusers—intentionally blame the victim. These ruthless individuals use moral typecasting as a weapon, discrediting and gaslighting their victims through a series of steps. The acronym for these steps is DARVO: deny, attack, and reverse victim and offender, and sadly it often works well.

Abusers first deny—to both the victim and other people—that abuse ever took place. They argue that the victim is fabricating their victimization, making up stories in their head, and confusing fantasy with reality. But if that kind of gaslighting fails, then abusers quickly attack the victim, often by claiming that the victim is actually the perpetrator: this is the key element of DARVO, the sneaky move of reversing victim and offender.

Abusers deploy moral typecasting to flip the script, trying to switch who seems like the victim and who seems like the victimizer. They claim that the victim is actually the one perpetrating emotional and physical damage. This gaslighting can be so effective that the victim feels they have committed an act of aggression by simply drawing attention to their abuse.

DARVO is a common strategy. In one study of eighty-nine women who were sexually assaulted in college, almost half said their attackers used these tactics, often with devastating psychological results for them.[16] These victims of sexual assault often doubt their memories of the assault and felt guilty for being attacked. One DARVO expert was the singer R. Kelly, who was sentenced to thirty years in prison for using his fame and power to sexually abuse women and children. More than fifty victims came forward and shared corroborating testimonies about R. Kelly's network of underage sex slaves. But when confronted with these allegations in an interview, he responded by arguing that *he* was the victim, unfairly targeted by these cruel women and unjustly attacked by an unfair media bent on depicting him as the devil.

With the power of DARVO—and typecasting—it can be difficult to make sense of claims of abuse. If both people within a couple are claiming to be abused, whom should we trust? One solution is to rely on statistics, taking the side of the person whose group is more often victimized. For example, women are typically more likely to be harmed by men than vice versa. One in four women will suffer domestic partner violence—usually at the hands of men—and so it makes statistical sense to side with women.

Because our minds seek to simplify the world, it is easy to take this statistical trend—men as perpetrators of violence and women as victims—and generalize it to all men and women. Men become morally typecast as violent harm doers, and women are stereotyped as passive recipients of harm. This gender-based typecasting can be useful because it alerts us to relatively more common situations of men abusing women, but it can also blind us to situations that don't fit this mold.

Imagine there was some abuse between a wife—a five-foot, four-inch, 110-pound homemaker—and her six-foot, two-inch, 190-pound construction worker husband. Who is the victim here? If you were a betting person, the smart money is on the husband abusing the wife. His greater size and strength make him the obvious villain. But there are always exceptions to the rule. The National Domestic Violence Hotline estimates that about 13.8 percent of men have been the victims of severe physical violence at the hands of an intimate partner.[17] While this is approximately one-third of the rate at which women are abused, woman-on-man violence is common enough that many support groups exist to help men grapple with the trauma of abuse. These suffering men often fear coming forward because they correctly intuit that few will believe them.

Studies confirm that people morally typecast others based on gender, believing that men are more likely villains and women are more likely victims. In a paper called "Man Up and Take It,"[18] one study had people read a scenario about creepy behavior between co-workers in a cafeteria. One of the co-workers (either a man or a woman) bent over to grab a fallen fork, and the other co-worker (either a woman or a man) said, "You must get a lot of practice doing that." Participants thought that the same comment would cause less anguish to a man than a woman, and people wanted to punish the man more than the woman for saying it.

Typecasting men as more blameworthy and less vulnerable makes sense in this situation because men are statistically more likely to be sexual harassers, but it also occurs in settings where people should have no gendered expectations, including a short film about geometric shapes. The researchers showed participants a video with two triangles (one green and one orange), where the green triangle appeared to attack the orange one. Participants then rated how much each shape seemed like a victim or a perpetrator and also declared the sex of the triangles by selecting from one of two options: *orange female/green male* or *orange male/green female*.

Although there was nothing about orange or green triangles that made them intrinsically male or female, people had an easy time assigning their sex. Consistent with gender-based typecasting, participants tended to see the orange "aggressor" triangle as male and the victimized green triangle as female. In statistical terms, for every increase in one standard deviation in the perception that the green triangle was a perpetrator, people were 34 percent more likely to say that it was a male. And for every standard deviation increase in the perception that the orange triangle was a victim, people were 50 percent more likely to say that it was a female.

Seeing men as automatic villains can be unfair to them. It is one of the reasons why false accusations of rape can be so sticky, such as in the high-profile case of three Duke lacrosse players—all White men—who in 2006 were accused of sexual assault by the Black exotic dancer they hired to perform at their house. The case gained national attention and sparked intense debates about race, class, and the handling of sexual assault allegations. Initially, the lacrosse players were typecast as obvious villains, and people demanded that they be imprisoned or even hanged. They were rich, White, strong, athletic, and confident—all features that made them seem invulnerable to victimization.

However, the defendants were eventually declared innocent because of inconsistencies in the accuser's statements and a lack of DNA evidence. While the players walked away with a large settlement deal, moral typecasting means that the reputational damage lingers around the Duke lacrosse team. In a documentary on the case, an anonymous player wrote, "Not a month goes by when I am not reminded of the damage those accusations have had on my reputation and the public's perception of my character. Sometimes only time can heal wounds."[19]

False accusations are upsetting and unfair, but they are exceptions to the general rule. Most accusations of rape are true: as best as researchers can estimate, only 2–10 percent of allegations are false.[20] The bigger problem is that women's authentic reports of abuse are often ignored or denied, often because of DARVO. Even with these statistical trends, the truth within situations of abuse can sometimes be murky, but one thing is clear: moral typecasting exerts a powerful pull on our moral judgments.

LESS THAN 100 PERCENT

Moral typecasting is the intuitive urge to see people as *either* 100 percent villains and 0 percent victims *or* 0 percent villains and 100 percent victims. This all-or-nothing division of pain and blame allows us to feel righteous when we excuse the misdeeds of those who suffer or ignore the suffering of those who have harmed others.

But moral typecasting is usually too simple, denying the obvious capacity for pain among those who do wrong and denying the obvious capacity for blame among those who have been harmed. Our moral world is messy, and questions of pain and blame are seldom so cut and dried. People who have done bad often suffer in childhood, and those who have been victimized can sometimes be cruel. We need to acknowledge the existence of both blame and pain.

Of course, there are clear differences between villains and victims. There is no doubt that Adolf Hitler is eviler than Cody Posey. Hitler harmed many more people than Cody, and not in self-defense. Cody also suffered much more than Hitler, being branded by his father and sexually assaulted by his stepmother. But Cody did make the choice to murder three people, and one of those people was his stepsister—a thirteen-year-old child whose mind had also been twisted by Cody's father and stepmother. Cody might have killed the adults in an act of feral desperation, but he could have also felt some smug satisfaction when he pulled the trigger on her.

Likewise, Hitler may be the ultimate villain for all the people he killed, but there was at least one time in his early life when he was the innocent victim of harm. If someone's moral character is the sum of all the times they have harmed others or been harmed themselves, then we might guess that Hitler is 99.9 percent villain and Cody is 97 percent victim. These ratios are a far cry from 50 percent victim and 50 percent villain, but neither are they fully 100 percent or 0 percent. Of course, with extreme villains and victims, we might feel justified in rounding up to 100 percent, but most people in moral situations are much closer to 50–50 than we might like to admit. Almost everyone is motivated by the laudable desire to protect themselves and their families, but humans are also imperfect creatures who can be petty and aggressive, especially when feeling threatened. People are moral mixes. When your spouse gets fired from a job, they are unlikely to be 100 percent victim and 0 percent villain. When your nemesis from the PTA pushes through a policy that benefits their kid, they are unlikely to be 0 percent victim and 100 percent villain. Instead, almost everyone is some blend of victim and villain.

Once we recognize that typecasting is an oversimplification, understanding can take root. We can see glimmers of inner pain behind someone's cruel deeds and recognize some personal responsibility even in someone who greatly suffered.

Escaping the pull of typecasting is hard, but it is possible, even in extreme circumstances. Consider Primo Levi, a Jewish man who was twenty-four years old when he was arrested and thrown onto an overcrowded train to Auschwitz in 1944. In his writing, he recounts many of the brutalities he and his fellow Holocaust victims suffered: starvation, beatings, and hypothermia. He also discusses how watching his fellow prisoners collaborate and cooperate with the Nazi guards helped to disintegrate the simple binary idea of "victims and perpetrators." Levi argues that in this sea of suffering and moral insanity many in the concentration camps inhabited "the gray zone," which defied a tidy black-and-white picture of morality.

Rather than seeing the collaborators as all victims or villains, Levi encourages the reader to appreciate the moral ambiguity in these situations. By placing those who cooperated with the Nazis in order to survive in the "gray zone,"[21] he helps us to withhold simplistic judgments of their deeds and better understand the complicated set of influences affecting them, including their raw desire to survive, their sense of victimization, and their concern for others.

As a trained scientist, Primo Levi knew that the world was complicated and defied obvious categories. One professor summarized Levi's thinking this way: "He believes that reality has the form of a prism, which breaks down beams of light into different colors, none of which can be said to mirror exactly the appearance of the original source of light. The world simply cannot be divided into white and black. There are always numerous accompanying shades of grey in between, and each of us is a grey zoner, in one way or another."[22]

The grey zone invites us to feel some psychological tension about our moral judgments; we can simultaneously believe that someone can suffer and be blameworthy. This is one of the missions of this book: to help us see morality as more of a gradient than a clear line, and to recognize the complexity and trade-offs surrounding moral issues. Holding this complexity within our minds will hopefully provide us with a more accurate and nuanced picture of our fellow human beings.

When we move past the idea that victimhood and villainy are all or nothing, we can better bridge divides and recognize the humanity in people on both sides. In conflict, it is fair to maintain your moral convictions about who is *relatively* more of a victim or *relatively* more of a villain. But seeing someone as "more" victim is truer than seeing them as "all" victim, because it recognizes the messy truth of human morality.

In chapters 10 and 11, we will explore strategies to help us recognize the seeds of victimhood in those we villainize. These strategies are essential because moral understanding is difficult to gain and easily lost; our minds descend into typecasting as easily as water flows downhill.

But before we explore these solutions, we cover one more problem—perhaps the thorniest of them all. Who is a victim and who is a villain can seem obvious, but there is one victim who reigns supreme in its obviousness, whose unjust suffering seems self-evident. That victim is the self.

In Sum

- Just as we typecast Hollywood actors, our moral mind compels us to typecast people, seeing others as either *villains* or *victims*. Typecasting oversimplifies the complex shades within our moral world into stark black and white.
- Normally, we blame villains and worry about the suffering of victims. Typecasting means that we seldom blame victims (because they are *not* villains), and we seldom worry about the suffering of villains (because they are *not* victims).
- Because being a victim helps people escape blame, people often exaggerate their suffering, either subconsciously or deliberately. Abusers also try to convince others (and the person they are abusing) that they are not the villain but the victim, through DARVO (deny, attack, and reverse victim and offender).

- Our minds naturally typecast some groups of people as more likely villains (for example, men) and other groups as more likely victims (for instance, women), but these perceptions can shift. When people are made uncomfortable by the suffering of others, they can sometimes blame the victim.
- In the real world, questions of villainy and victimhood are seldom perfectly black and white. Villains do suffer, and victims often perpetrate harm. In his analysis of collaborators in concentration camps, Primo Levi proposed the idea of "the grey zone," a more complex moral world that mixes victimhood and villainy.

Chapter 9

Suffering: Self-Focused Victimhood

In February 2022, Vladimir Putin invaded Ukraine. He deployed thousands of soldiers into the country, bombing hospitals, killing children, and destroying infrastructure. People in the West saw Putin as an evil dictator, but Putin saw himself as more of a victim. In press conferences, the Russian leader argued that he was left with no choice but to invade Ukraine. He was defending himself and Russia after decades of mistreatment, arguing that "Western elites aren't trying to conceal their goals, to inflict a 'strategic defeat' to Russia." Putin even suggested that the West was to blame for his aggression: "It's they who have started the war. And we are using force to end it."

As the ex-director of the Soviet intelligence force and now Russia's president for life, Putin is no stranger to manipulating language and using propaganda to distort people's perceptions. He was obviously using moral typecasting to spin lies—reversing the perpetrator and victim—and managing the impressions of the Russian soldiers and officials who watched his speech. At the same time, there was almost certainly a kernel of sincerity in his claims: he felt like a victim. Putin is right: he has long been demonized by the West, and so can genuinely feel victimized by "an organized, staged attack on everything Russian."[1]

Putin's feelings of mistreatment might seem impossible to believe. How can someone who acts like a psychopath, killing opponents and poisoning dissidents, be a victim? If moral typecasting nudges us to divide the world into victims and victimizers, it seems obvious that Putin is a victimizer. But to Putin, his victimhood likely seemed obvious.

Some of the most powerful people alive today seem to feel like victims. Despite their wealth and power, they feel chronically mistreated and oppressed—more like the Othered than the Powerful. Larry Ellison, the head of Oracle Corporation and the billionaire who owns the Pacific island of Lanai, felt victimized by the U.S. government when it banned him from flying a MiG-29—a Russian fighter jet—through U.S. airspace. Even Harvey Weinstein, the serial sexual assaulter, felt as though he'd been victimized by the media. He told reporters, "I feel like the forgotten man," because after his crimes became known, no one talked about his work or what he saw as his history of supporting women: "I made more movies directed by women and about women than any filmmaker—and I'm talking about 30 years ago. I'm not talking about now, when it's vogue. I did it first! I pioneered it!"

How can these powerful people, who are so obviously *not* victims (at least to everyone else), feel convinced that they are true victims? One explanation is that, as we saw in the previous chapter on moral typecasting, there are often benefits to claiming victimhood. Although few people want to be victimized, gaining the status of "victim" helps people escape blame after they do harm.

But there is a less cynical explanation for this self-focused victimhood: human minds are fundamentally self-contained and self-focused, and so our suffering seems self-evident.

The problem of other minds means that we never directly feel the pain of other people, but we do powerfully experience our own suffering. If other people's pain is like a whisper on the wind, our own pain is a scream in our ear. The obviousness of our own suffering makes people easily see themselves as victims. Victimhood is egocentric because our minds are egocentric.

EGOCENTRISM

Humans are born egocentric, which means that our self (*ego,* that which feels and thinks) lies at the very center (*centric,* pertaining to the middle point) of our experience. When babies take their first breath, they know only their own sensory experiences, the overwhelming reality of their hunger, sleepiness, or discomfort. Even as they begin to grow and learn about the world, their immediate feelings still define reality. Babies cannot understand the past or the future. Instead, they live as many New Age gurus encourage, experiencing only the "now."

Even as toddlers, kids are rampantly egocentric. They think everyone else shares their taste in food (peanut butter and honey!) and TV shows (cartoons!). They also believe that they are invisible to others when their eyes are covered. They put a blanket over their heads and reason, "Because I can't see you, you can't see me!"

Older kids and adults better understand the disconnection between personal experiences and the external truth of reality. We know that people can still see us even when we close our eyes, and the world "out there" exists even if we cannot see it. Of course, sometimes philosophers still worry about the nature of reality, wondering if the world is all a dream or—as in the movie *The Matrix*—a computer simulation. In one of the oldest formulations of this concern, Descartes asked us to imagine if the world was created by an evil demon with "utmost power and cunning" who has "employed all his energies in order to deceive me."[2]

Descartes wondered whether he could trust his senses or thoughts to reveal the true world: "I shall think that the sky, the air, the earth, colors, shapes, sounds and all external things are merely the delusions of dreams which he has devised to ensnare my judgement. I shall consider myself as not having hands or eyes, or flesh, or blood or senses, but as falsely believing that I have all these things."[3] Descartes also worried that he himself was a figment of his imagination but in the end soothed himself with a career-defining aphorism: *Cogito, ergo sum,* or "I think, therefore I am." He knew he existed because he could experience his own mind. It is a very egocentric proof of human existence.

Older kids might know that the world continues to exist after the lights go out, but still perceive the world from their own perspective. Jean Piaget, the founder of developmental psychology, put a toy model of three mountains in the middle of a room.[4] He had elementary-school-age children inspect the model, noting the different features of each mountain: one mountain had a snowy top, one had a cross, and the other had a little hut on top. After the kids observed the model, Piaget introduced them to a doll and then positioned it somewhere on the model where it would "see" a different view than the child.

Piaget then showed the child ten photos of the mountains taken from various viewpoints and asked which of the photos matched what the doll saw. Would the children be able to de-center their view of the mountains and take the perspective of the doll? Results show that 70–80 percent of children under the age of seven or eight failed the task, picking the picture that matched their own view rather than the doll's view. They could not help being egocentric.

Adults are better at taking other people's perspectives, but we shouldn't be too smug. Studies show that grown-ups are actually just as egocentric as kids when it comes to their initial perceptions, but are better at adjusting those perceptions to match what other people see. This perspective shifting is challenging because it takes effort. It's hard mental work for us humans—as an egocentric species—to appreciate that someone else might see the world differently. When we are unwilling to spend this effort to shift our perspective, like with a political opponent, we can easily fail to appreciate someone's viewpoint.

To demonstrate the tenacity of adult egocentrism, some researchers used a clever setup.[5] The participant sat across from another person, the "director," and between them sat a bookcase divided into a grid of cells. Many of the square cells contained little objects, including

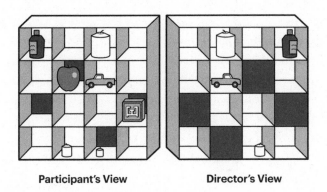

Participant's View   **Director's View**

Figure 9.1: This bookcase holds many different objects. The left side shows the view of the participant, and the right side shows the view of the director. Some objects can be seen by both the participant and the director (the large and medium candles), but some can be seen only by the participant (the smallest candle), because some cells are blocked off on the director's side. In the key trial, the director asks to be given the "small candle," which is really the medium candle from the perspective of the participant. The majority of adults first look at the wrong candle (the smallest), demonstrating egocentrism.

three different candles—a small candle, a medium candle, and a large candle. Crucially, some of these cells were blocked off on the side of the director, hiding the contents from their view. In one of these blocked-off cells sat the smallest candle, which meant that the director couldn't see it. In other words, the director could see only two candles, the medium and the large candles, whereas the participant could see all three candles. This mismatch in knowledge and perception allowed the researchers to test for egocentrism.

The job of participants is to give the director whatever object they ask for—based on the *director's point of view.* For many objects, what the director sees is identical to what participants see. If the director asks for the pickup truck, it is a simple task to find it, grab it, and hand it over. There is only one pickup truck, and it's in a cell that's open at both ends so both of them see it.

But with the candles, the task is more complicated. Because the director cannot see the smallest of the three candles, when they ask for the "small candle," what they really mean is—according to the view of the participant—the *medium* candle. This was the test of egocentrism: Did participants avoid anchoring on their own perspective and give the director the correct medium-sized candle?

People were mostly successful at handing over the right objects. Adults gave the director the medium-sized candle about 83 percent of the time. But 83 percent is still a long way from perfect for such a simple task—just hand over an item!—especially because the grid setup also makes it obvious that the director has a different perspective. If 17 percent of people have difficulty switching their viewpoint when they are trying hard to shift their perspective, just imagine the challenge of understanding someone's different moral position in the heat of a political argument.

Importantly, adults were also initially just as egocentric as kids. The researchers used a camera to examine where participants first looked when they were asked to grab each item. The average adult looked at the wrong/smallest candle at least once before correcting their initial error. About a quarter of adults even first *reached* for the smallest candle, further demonstrating the pull of egocentrism. It takes real mental effort to shift our thoughts and behaviors away from our initial perceptions.[6]

One real-world example of egocentrism is "the curse of knowledge," when experts find it hard to take the perspective of nonexperts. This bias is why network administrators assume that the concepts of packet loss and ping latency are obvious to someone who just wants more reliable internet. Experts assume that other people know as much as they do. The curse of knowledge is an especially big problem for academics because they usually spend their professional lives in a rabbit hole studying a niche topic—whether "British naval history from 1867 to 1898," or "synthetic organometallic chemistry and metal-ligand cooperation," or "mind perception and moral cognition"—where they accumulate technical jargon and develop complicated frameworks.

After decades of study, academics know more about their favored topic than literally anyone else in the entire world, and often forget that other people have never heard of even "basic" concepts they use every day. Shifting perspective away from this egocentric expertise is possible but hard, explaining why academics—including earnest moral psychologists—can struggle to write accessible books.

People are especially egocentric with morality, assuming that their moral convictions capture the objective truth of the moral world. This leads them to assume that everyone else with "good morals" shares their perspective on what is right and what is wrong, including the ultimate source of morality, God.

You might think that God has a very independent—and opaque— perspective on issues like premarital sex and smoking marijuana. As theologians are quick to point out, the mind of God is beyond human comprehension. John Calvin, a leader of the Protestant Reformation, once remarked, "Man with all his shrewdness is as stupid about understanding by himself the mysteries of God, as an ass is incapable of understanding musical harmony."[7]

Unfortunately, the ultimate unknowability of God's moral beliefs actually makes people more egocentric. Without objective evidence about His moral stances, people easily conflate their own perspectives with those of God. In one study, scientists asked people to rate the morals of God and found that people believe that God shares their exact moral positions.[8] If you think using marijuana is permissible, then you think God does too. If you think marijuana destroys communities and harms kids, then you think God has the same opinion.

Most interesting is when researchers put people into an fMRI scanner to look at their brain activation while they pondered the moral beliefs of the Almighty. While making judgments about God's moral sense, people's medial prefrontal cortex was active, a neural region linked to thinking about oneself. In other words, when people think about the mind of God, they anchor on themselves. God may be ultimately unknowable, but this ambiguity paradoxically breeds confidence that His convictions are the same as our own.

People's moral egocentrism also convinces them that millions of others share their political opinions, sometimes leading to disaster. On the right, Roseanne Barr—who had just resurrected her career and was riding high with her new show—tweeted herself into oblivion. She took aim at Valerie Jarrett, an African American woman who served as a senior adviser to Barack Obama during his presidency, tweeting that if the "muslim brotherhood & planet of the apes had a baby=vj [Valerie Jarrett]." People were incensed at her racism, and she lost everything she had worked hard to gain. Roseanne blamed Ambien and alcohol, but egocentrism was also surely responsible, because, as unbelievable as it sounds, she suspected that many others would share her views.

On the left, the CNN commentator Reza Aslan was fired after calling Trump a "piece of shit" on Twitter.[9] The self-described social commentator might have known that cursing out the president of the United States while representing a network notoriously accused of liberal bias could be a problem. But did he guess that his tweet would create so much outrage that he would be fired within the week? Unlikely, because he assumed that many people agreed with him.

Aslan and Barr are different people who made different statements, but both had their careers derailed because they misperceived the minds and moral judgments of other people. Being morally egocentric can be costly for everyday Americans too, like when they make jokes that unexpectedly alienate bosses, co-workers, and friends. People are especially egocentric when it comes to legal trials, where they mistakenly think that impartial observers—like judges and juries—will see moral issues their way.

Despite the popular idea that most lawsuits go to trial, research by legal academics shows that 95 percent of lawsuits do *not*. Instead, they are handled outside the courtroom in private pretrial settlements. Trials are long and costly, and usually they benefit only the lawyers who spend months arguing against each other. If trials are so costly, why do some people opt for them instead of settling? There are likely many reasons, including greed, sunk costs, and the lust for revenge, but one big reason is egocentrism.

If you think you see the moral world as it really is, it's easy to believe that a judge will rule in your favor.[10] In one paper on this topic, a team of German professors argued that "knowledge triggers self-serving interpretations of the case-related information." In other words, people familiar with the situation see the world through self-colored glasses, genuinely believing that others will see the world as they do.[11]

These examples all support the social psychological idea of "naive realism," the egocentric belief that we see the world around us objectively, as it really is. Naive realism means that people who disagree with us must be uninformed, irrational, or biased.

People are naive realists about many things, including thinking that their morals are objectively correct, and their political candidate is objectively the best, but they are especially egocentric when it comes to visceral experiences, such as taste. Consider people who think that pineapple pizza is objectively good, or Australians who think that Vegemite is objectively tasty, or Icelanders who are convinced of the deliciousness of *hákarl,* a fermented/rotten shark meat dish that tastes like urine and causes vomiting, at least among tourists. When you have a strong reaction of "good!" to something in your body, it can be hard to believe that someone else might have the opposite reaction. Like babies in their first year of life, we just *feel* the truth of our visceral experiences, no matter what anyone else says.

But as much as we might feel convinced of the objective reality of good-tasting dishes, there is another visceral experience that reigns supreme in its obvious truth: pain. The overwhelming reality of pain, at least to the experiencer, is why victimhood is so egocentric.

PAIN OVERPOWERS

Throughout the book, we have seen how our minds are fixated on harm when it comes to morality, but there is nothing our mind cares more about than protecting ourselves from concrete physical harm.

To motivate us to avoid harm, we have evolved a powerful physiological signal: pain. Pain is the most aversive sensation that our mind can create; it is so important to our survival that it destroys any other thoughts and feelings.

In the short book *Pain: The Science of Suffering,* Patrick Wall, the British neuroscientist and world expert on pain writes, "Pain captures and monopolizes attention and includes an interruption of any activities not directly related to pain relief."[12] Pain forces people into extreme egocentrism, making them focus on their own bodies and the current moment. Living in the moment might seem good to those seeking Nirvana, but when your present is filled with suffering, living in the now is pure hell.

The sensation of pain typically begins when nerve endings in the periphery of our body are destroyed or irritated, such as by a cut or burn. Then that sensation travels as an electrochemical signal along our nerves until it reaches our spinal cord. Once there, it travels straight up to our brain, first passing through a pain "gate" at the top of our spine before arriving at the ancient brain structure of the thalamus, a hub for sensations that radiates out to the nearby brain regions that create physical experiences. When these various "sensation" areas are activated, people experience the physical qualities that give each instance of pain its unique flavor of suffering, such as burning, throbbing, or cutting.

These sensation regions connect to the "affective regions" of our brain, which are involved in feelings of good and bad. These affective regions help to generate our emotions, from joy to fear, and they do more besides; they help to construct conscious experience. Our consciousness is constantly infused with affect; every moment is colored with some form of feeling, whether good or bad, excited or calm. In some moments, this affective experience may fade to the background, like when we are reading an interesting science book. But when our affect gets amped up, it becomes harder to ignore. If you suddenly got a text from an old lover, your heart would immediately start racing, and your new awareness of these bodily experiences—your affective egocentrism—would make it hard to keep concentrating on this book.

Both positive and negative feelings can captivate our attention, but negative feelings are more powerful. In a comprehensive review of every psychology study involving affective experiences, researchers authoritatively conclude that "bad is stronger than good."[13] Imagine someone offers you a gamble: if a coin flip lands on heads, you gain $1,000, but if it lands on tails, you lose $1,000. Economists point out that this gamble has an "expected value" of zero because you are equally likely to win and lose the same amount of money. And so you should be indifferent toward taking the (zero) risk gamble versus not taking it. Pondering this gamble should feel like pondering whether to start a short walk with your left versus right foot—like nothing.

But the prospect of this gamble *doesn't* feel like nothing; instead, it feels negative. The researchers Tversky and Kahneman (of System 1 and System 2 fame) discovered that the bad feelings we have when contemplating losing $1,000 are twice as strong as the good feelings we have when contemplating winning $1,000. The pain of loss looms larger than the pleasure of gain.

When it comes to physical pain, this affective asymmetry is even stronger. Imagine another coin-flip gamble between the world's most pleasurable versus the world's most painful experience. Heads, have an incredible orgasm on a roller coaster while eating the best possible dessert; tails, excruciating physical torture where someone applies electric shocks to your genitals and also makes you feel like a thousand biting ants are burrowing into your sinuses and that your legs are engulfed in flames. You might agree to this gamble because you assume you will be lucky, but once you have felt the searing power of pain, chances are you would never again flip that coin.

The negative affect we feel when in pain is so powerful that it saturates our entire consciousness with unpleasantness, making everything we think about seem negative, including our forecasts of the future and recollections of the past. It is hard to be optimistic about your future career prospects or fondly reminisce about your childhood when you have a brutal toothache.

Interestingly, although the "physical sensation" and "affective experience" parts of pain are typically linked—like feeling negative because of throbbing pain from stubbing your toe—they can be disconnected. Opioid painkillers dampen only the affective regions of our brain, not the sensation regions, which means that people can still feel the particular sensations of the pain, like throbbing, without it "hurting."[14]

Without painkillers, the affective power of pain continues to capture our attention, making it exceedingly difficult to think rationally. In the framework of System 1 and System 2 that we discussed in chapter 5, pain traps our minds in System 1, destroying our capacity to reason or engage in effortful thought. Some researchers documented this when they asked people to engage in a complex (System 2) cognitive task on a computer.[15] Participants did an "*n*-back" test, where they watch a constant series of flashing letters and press a key each time the current letter is the same as the letter shown *n* times ago—in this case three times ago. So if the letters were *W, U, R, R, U, E, Z,* you would press a key for the second instance of *U,* because it appeared three letters ago.

This task is pretty hard. It taps into System 2 thinking, requiring people to process a constant stream of new information while holding in mind past information (the letter from three letters ago). On some trials, the researchers made it even harder by giving people the painful sensation of burning, courtesy of a thermal probe they attached to the participant's right ankle. They discovered that, unsurprisingly, people's performance was severely impaired when their ankle felt on fire.

In the grid study we discussed above, we saw that it takes effortful thought to overcome our innate egocentrism and take the perspective of others. Because pain knocks out our capacity for reasoning, it makes us doubly egocentric. Suffering not only expands to fill our entire conscious experience, it also prevents us from adjusting away from our own feelings toward someone else's viewpoint. When we hurt, we become convinced that we are obvious victims, which makes it hard to appreciate that others might also feel mistreated. In our minds, feeling pain makes us the only and the ultimate victim.

To quote the American essayist Elaine Scarry, author of *The Body in Pain,* "to have great pain is to have certainty"—certainty of our own victimhood—but "to hear that another person has pain is to have doubt" about their victimhood. People in pain are convinced that they are the "real" victim within a situation. When this conviction is paired with moral typecasting, it makes nuanced conversations about morality all but impossible. Someone who is overwhelmed by the emotional turmoil of grieving or by physical suffering of injury will have a hard time appreciating "both sides" of a conflict and will deny the idea that others might see them as a perpetrator.

Luckily, most people in moral disagreements are not actively in physical pain, but can still be self-focused when it comes to feelings of victimhood. The problem is that any bad feeling—any negative affect like threat, anger, or fear—captures our attention and makes us egocentric. When any two people fight, both will feel frustrated and outraged, and so both will be convinced that they are the true victim. My wife and I have a story of mutual outrage. It happened in our dark bedroom.

It's not what you think. We had just put our kids to bed and were both upstairs, creeping silently. Each of us thought the other had gone downstairs, and both went into our bedroom to grab something. We were looking in different directions in the darkness when we bumped into each other, scaring us both. We angrily demanded the same thing: "Why were you creeping around the room trying to scare me?" Of course, neither of us had *tried* to scare anybody; the two of us were trying not to wake the kids, and innocently bumped into each other in the dark room. But with bodies pumping with adrenaline and minds filled with fear, we couldn't help but focus on the negative feelings that filled our consciousness. Each of us felt as if the other were victimizing us.

After being programmed for millions of years to fear predators and evil people, my wife and I both felt vulnerable in the dark. When we bumped into each other, our first thought wasn't, "This is probably my spouse in my suburban bedroom," but rather, "A predator! A murderer!" It was instantly fight or flight, and our minds took this feeling of threat and immediately transformed it into moral outrage. Each of us felt like a victim, and moral typecasting made the other person seem like a villain. Each of us thought that we were blameless, which meant that all the blame for the collision was pinned on the other.

Although this event was silly, random, and ultimately harmless, it created a tiny moral conflict. Twenty minutes later, after the adrenaline subsided, we laughed about our outrage, but it is also easy to see how this could have kicked off a bigger conflict. After bumping into each other, we could have said terribly unkind things to each other, dredging up old arguments and grudges. These resentful statements would have made each of us feel even more attacked and victimized, and these feelings of victimization would have licensed even more callousness. Who knows how many strained marriages reach their final breaking point after a random experience of physical pain or emotional turmoil suddenly animates lurking feelings of victimhood.

FROM PAIN TO COMPASSION OR SELFISHNESS?

Pain can make you blind to the suffering of others, but shouldn't the general experience of trauma do the opposite, making people more empathic? Empathy is the ability to understand and share the feelings of other people, especially their suffering. Experiencing pain yourself should be helpful for building empathy because it allows you to better appreciate those feelings in others. In *East of Eden,* John Steinbeck wrote, "You can only understand people if you feel them in yourself." It should be easier to appreciate what it is like to be sick or poor if you too have shared that experience.

On the other hand, previous suffering sometimes seems to dull our empathy. People who grow up with trauma can feel the need to shut down their compassion to focus on surviving. Consider David Goggins, a retired Navy SEAL and the author of the immensely popular memoir *Can't Hurt Me,* which explores his childhood of poverty, abuse, and neglect. To cope with this suffering and victimization, Goggins "hardens" himself, becoming physically and mentally tougher and losing his empathy for the weak. His core message is about physical training, but his lack of empathy for weakness is obvious when he writes, "It's so easy to be great nowadays because everyone else is weak." On the suffering of others, the advice he offers is simple: "Stop making excuses. Stop being a victim."[16]

Are most of us more like Steinbeck or Goggins? Does past pain form the foundation for compassion or numb us to the suffering of others? Some psychologists[17] put this question to the test by first asking people about the frequency, severity, and recency of traumatic experiences in six areas: injury/illness, violence, bereavement, relationship events, social-environmental stress, and disasters. They then measured their tendency to feel compassion for others by assessing their agreement with statements like "When I see someone hurt or in need, I feel a powerful urge to take care of them." The data revealed that people who had experienced more severe trauma scored higher on compassion.

Of course, many people talk about how empathic they are, but do these self-reports of compassion translate into behavior? To see if participants would put their money where their mouth is, the researchers included an option at the end of the survey to donate up to $1 to the Red Cross. Whatever they donated would be subtracted from their $1.50 payment for doing the study. Did "compassionate" participants actually give more? Sure enough, people who scored themselves one standard deviation above average on compassion gave 25 cents more. This provides some evidence that traumatic experiences can increase both compassionate feelings and behaviors.

These researchers ran another study where participants worked with a partner on some difficult language comprehension problems from the GRE (the Graduate Record Exam), but—as you might expect by now—the partner was an accomplice of the researchers. The partner pretended to feel sick and begged to quit, but the researcher firmly denied their request, and they grudgingly agreed to stay. The partner and the participant were then sent to separate desks to solve their problems. After the real participant finished their set of problems, they were given the choice either to leave or to stay and help their sick partner, who was struggling to finish up. The researchers again found that people with more severe trauma in their past spent more time helping their struggling accomplice.[18]

Past trauma increases empathy for Red Cross victims and sick research assistants, but does experiencing pain also make you more compassionate toward your enemies? Two researchers put this to the test in an area where empathy seems especially lacking: politics.[19] They brought liberals and conservatives into the lab and measured their sensitivity to pain, both by self-report ratings and by using a pressure algometer, a little metal device that presses into your skin until you report that it becomes painful. After having their general sensitivity to pain assessed, the (now pain-free) participants answered questions about politics.

The results of this study showed that liberals who were especially sensitive to pain (compared with less pain-sensitive liberals) expressed more approval of conservative politicians like Mitch McConnell and Kevin McCarthy and endorsed more conservative stances on issues like antiterrorism policies and criminalizing flag burning. Similarly, pain-sensitive conservatives were more approving of liberal political figures like Nancy Pelosi and Bernie Sanders and had more liberal stances on wealth redistribution and the death penalty.

It might seem strange that the mere tendency to feel pain connects to political empathy, but a harm-based mind offers some explanation. Those who are most attuned to (physically) protecting themselves from pain might recognize that the other side is also motivated by the protection narrative. Importantly, participants in this study were not actively in agony when making judgments about the other side. They were generally sensitive to suffering without being currently trapped in an egocentric prison of pain.

These results suggest that for the average person experiencing pain or past trauma might make you more compassionate, unlike Goggins. But what is true of distant trauma may not apply to more immediate victimization. The power of egocentrism suggests that when people feel victimized in the present, they become more selfish and perhaps seek out ways to right the wrongs they have suffered—even if it wrongs someone else. Researchers ran studies to test this idea and published a paper with a title that gives away the punch line: "Victim Entitlement to Behave Selfishly."[20]

Participants first completed a timed word search on a computer. In one group—the "victim" group—the game was rigged. The word search contained few letters, and they were printed in a large font, so even a quick glance made it obvious that the words participants were supposed to find simply weren't there. These people knew that they were being asked to do an impossible task. To make matters worse, when they tried to use the computer, it froze. They could only futilely click as the timer counted down to zero.

The other group—the "control" group—used a normally functioning game that was also impossible to win, but their matrix of letters contained many more (and much smaller) letters, making it seem likely the target words were present. So, although both groups were doomed to fail, only the victim group felt victimized by a game that was rigged against them.

After the game was over, both the victimized and the control participants played a new game, this time competing against someone else for some prize money. The participant and this new person would race to solve ten different word searches. The researchers asked participants to imagine that in this upcoming game they won seven out of ten of the word searches, and then asked them how they would split $6 of prize money between themselves and their new opponent.

An even split would be $3 each, but remember that participants were told to imagine that they solved more puzzles than their partner— seven versus three—so participants would be on solid ground to take more for themselves, whether a split of $4/$2 (67 percent for themselves) or $5/$1 (83 percent for themselves). Perhaps some participants might even be selfish enough to do a winner-take-all split and keep all $6 for themselves.

The data revealed that participants in the "victim" condition, who were still ruminating over being treated unfairly, were more selfish. Only 8 percent of participants in the "control" condition chose to take all $6 in the second game, while 19 percent of victimized participants kept all the money for themselves. Even though the victimized participants did not objectively lose anything—the first game was just for fun—their feelings of outrage at suffering injustice made them more self-centered and selfish.

Of course, in this study, participants were asked to imagine that they solved more problems than the partner. Perhaps it was easy, in Goggins fashion, to blame them for their "weakness." The real question is whether victimhood licenses someone to take out their outrage on an innocent stranger. Would people pay forward victimization?

The idea of "paying it forward" often comes up with good deeds, like when people at a drive-through window pay for the meal of those behind them, or when charity campaigns argue that one donation will spur on three more donations, creating a flourishing chain of kindness. But my colleagues and I wondered if the reality of paying it forward might be less hopeful. In a series of studies, we investigated whether people were more likely to pay forward kindness or selfishness.[21] The setup was simple and, like the study above, revolved around a participant splitting $6 between themselves and another person. There were two phases.

In the first phase, participants (call them B) were given an envelope filled with some amount of money. They were told that the exact
amount of money depended on what the previous participant (call
them A) decided to do. Participants (B) were told that person A—who
was actually made up by the researchers—was given $6 to split between
themselves and the participant.

The participant (B) would open the envelope to find that person A
was either kind to them (giving them all $6), just fair (giving them a
fifty-fifty split of $3 each), or cruel to them (keeping all the money
for themselves and giving participant B $0). In reality, we seeded the
envelopes with one of these three amounts, creating three randomly
assigned conditions: kindness, fairness, and selfishness.

In the second phase of the study, all participants (B) were given a
new envelope and a fresh $6. They were told that they could split this
new money between themselves (B) and a new future participant (C).
This created a chain of actions through time, with the participants as
the middle link: A gives a split to B, then B gives a split to C. What
did participants do in each condition? Did they similarly pay forward
kindness, fairness, and selfishness from A to C?

We found that those who received the fifty-fifty split of $3 were the
most likely to pay forward the same behavior, on average giving the
next person just a bit more than $3 (specifically $3.38). Interestingly,
those who received a generous amount of $6 did *not* feel compelled to
be similarly kind to the next person. They gave an average of $3.71, an
amount not statistically significantly more than the $3.38 paid forward
in the fairness condition. This suggests that truly generous behavior, at
least in a lab study, gets immediately absorbed. People apparently feel
little guilt when they accept extra money and then fail to pass it on.

But what about the people who got victimized by someone selfish?
Did they—like the generous condition—just absorb the loss and then
make an almost fair split? Far from it. In this condition, the participant (B) gave an average of $1.30 to C—keeping $4.70 of the $6.
This split is statistically significantly more selfish than a fair split of $3.

This study shows that victimization is paid forward more than kindness; when people get screwed over, they feel licensed to screw over
someone else. Of course, there is one seeming silver lining: people did

not victimize the next person quite as badly as they got victimized, giving an average of $1.30 after receiving zero. But when we dug further into this finding, we found that the money splits were "bimodal"; rather than giving the average of $1.30, people instead often opted for complete fairness ($3-$3 split) or complete selfishness ($6-$0 split).

A minority of people took the high road and just offered the next person a fair fifty-fifty split, taking the loss and moving on. But most people in the selfish condition directly passed their feelings of injustice to the next person. If they got zero, they gave zero. When we delved into why this happened, we found that the best predictor of selfishness was participants' emotional experience. When people felt negative emotions after being victimized—reporting feeling distressed and upset—they were more likely to pay forward victimhood. These people egocentrically anchored on their bad feelings after being treated unfairly, and that drove them to treat others unfairly—forging a new link in a chain of suffering that stretched into the future.

When people focus on their own feelings of victimhood, they seldom pause to consider how others might suffer after being victimized by them. Moral typecasting adds to this thoughtlessness by making the victimized people feel blameless for harming others. A real-world example of these chains of selfish victimhood is the looting and rioting that happens after perceived social injustice. For example, when the French government extended the retirement age from sixty-two to sixty-four, creating two more years of work for the typical French person, French citizens were incensed at the unfairness. They could not directly lash out at the politicians who passed the new law, so they took to the streets and destroyed property. Sometimes this property was owned by faceless multinational corporations, but other times it was the mom-and-pop shops of everyday people just trying to make a living. Feelings of victimization created more victimization.

We began this section by asking whether suffering leads people to be compassionate or selfish. The answer is both. Appreciating your own past trauma and being generally sensitive to pain makes you sympathetic to the suffering of others, but feeling pain in the present or stewing in feelings of injustice licenses people to act selfishly. In our egocentric minds, feelings of victimhood can loom so large that they can crowd out concerns for other people. But even if two people experience equal amounts of trauma or injustice, they can differ on how much they feel like victims, because victimhood is often less about what you objectively experience and more about your mindset.

THE VICTIM MINDSET

Some people live with a victim mindset. We all know someone like this, who thinks that the world is out to get them, that anything bad in their life is other people's fault, and that their past struggles make them blameless for the cruelty they inflict on others.

You might think that people with the most powerful victim mindset are those who have suffered extreme trauma. Studies confirm that trauma can leave its mark on your mind. For example, 11 percent of rape victims suffer from post-traumatic stress disorder (PTSD), experiencing intrusive thoughts, difficulty sleeping, and fear of enduring the same trauma.[22] In the original studies of PTSD after World War I—then called shell shock—one researcher estimated that about 20 percent of veterans remained traumatized by the gruesome events they faced, with some frequently suffering from panic attacks and others going catatonic.[23]

But just because someone has suffered trauma in the past, or experiences PTSD in the present, does not mean they have a victim mindset. Even people who have survived extreme events like genocide may not see themselves as victims. The Holocaust survivor Primo Levi, whose thoughts about the grey zone we read in the chapter on typecasting, had clearly been victimized, but his thoughtful discourse about the nuances of morality shows that he didn't *feel* like a victim.

People who have been victimized may acknowledge that they have suffered substantial harm while avoiding a victim *mindset.* But what exactly is a victim mindset, and—if suffering objective trauma is only vaguely related to it—who goes around feeling like a victim? Some scholars from Tel Aviv University wanted to explore this question and developed a twenty-two-question scale designed to measure the "tendency for interpersonal victimhood."[24]

Here are a few statements from the scale, which people rate their agreement with on a scale of 1 (strongly disagree) to 7 (strongly agree):

1. It is important to me that people who hurt me acknowledge that an injustice has been done to me.
2. I think I am much more conscientious and moral in my relations with other people compared to their treatment of me.
3. When people who are close to me feel hurt by my actions, it is very important for me to clarify that justice is on my side.
4. Days after the offense, I am very preoccupied by the injustice done to me.

As with many psychological variables, there is a normal distribution of victim mindsets. The typical person—the fiftieth percentile—is at the midpoint of the scale, at about 4 out of 7, suggesting that they are sometimes preoccupied with feelings of victimhood. The bottom 2.5 percent of people score about 2.4 out of 7: when these people suffer mistreatment at the hands of others, they chalk it up to bad luck or genuine mistakes or provide other charitable interpretations. On the other hand, the top 2.5 percent of people score about 6.6 out of 7. These folks see themselves as constantly receiving injustice and endlessly seek recognition for their feelings of injustice.[25] These self-perceived victims view themselves as more moral than others, and they lack empathy for other people's suffering because they are persistently stewing in their own grievance. Their feelings of victimhood lead them to typecast others as villains, blaming them for anything that goes wrong in their lives.

The scholars who invented this scale explored the attitudes and actions of people with a strong victim mindset. In one study, they had people imagine getting ambiguous feedback from a senior colleague at work, like "It's great that you're passionate about your ideas, but there's a thin line between passion and stubbornness. It can be helpful to consider others' input." Do people see this as encouraging advice or cold criticism? As the researchers predicted, those with a high tendency for interpersonal victimhood saw ambiguous feedback as malicious and driven by cruel intentions. Interestingly, people with victim mindsets did not want to merely avoid their senior colleague, but instead wanted revenge against them.

Another study explored whether these self-perceived victims would act on their thirst for vengeance. Participants were put on the receiving end of a "dictator game," where the dictator (who participants thought was another person but was really a computer program) was given $10 to split between the participant and itself. The researchers programmed the computer to be either very unfair (giving $1 to participants and keeping $9), moderately unfair (giving $3 to participants and keeping $7), or only mildly unfair (giving $4 and keeping $6). Then all participants, no matter how unfairly they were treated, were given the opportunity to retaliate, taking away a percentage of the other "person's" money, ranging from none (the dictator keeps all its money) to all of it (the dictator gets no money). Importantly, this retaliation was pure spite, because taking money away did not benefit the participant in any way.

The researchers found that all people—no matter their level of victim mindset—who were treated very unfairly by the dictator (receiving only $1) felt outraged and yearned for revenge. On average, people in this condition voted to take away 30 percent of the dictator's money. Where the victim mindset really mattered was in cases of mild injustice, where people received $4 out of $10.

The average person in this condition opted to remove only 15 percent of the dictator's winnings (90 cents), but those with a strong victim mindset chose to remove twice as much money—30 percent. This is the same amount of punishment that most people gave in the very unfair condition, when they received only $1. This study reveals that those high in a victim mindset strongly lust for revenge even when only mildly mistreated, and suggests that what separates those with a victim mindset from other people isn't their desire to right obvious wrongs but their tendency to see minor slights as major injustices.

When the researchers looked at what life experiences and personality traits were associated with having a victim mindset, they were surprised to learn that suffering past trauma was *not* correlated with self-perceived victimhood. There are many people who experience trauma in life: more than 70 percent of people report having experienced at least a single traumatic event, and 30 percent of people report four or more, including being mugged, surviving a life-threatening car accident, or experiencing a life-threatening illness. But having been victimized by crime or natural disasters did not reliably lead to developing a victim mindset, suggesting this mindset is less about what actually happens to you and more about your psychological perceptions—like so much of morality.

This research also revealed that people with a strong victim mindset were not especially antisocial or disagreeable, so self-perceived victim-hood is not the same as being generally cantankerous or aggressive. Instead, people with a strong victim mindset often have what's known as an anxious attachment style. Attachment styles, a concept developed by the psychologists John Bowlby and Mary Ainsworth, describe how people emotionally bond and interact with others in relationships. An anxious attachment style involves a high sensitivity to potential threats in relationships, a fear of being abandoned or rejected, and a constant need for reassurance. These feelings of threat are what lead people to see themselves as victims, interpreting interactions as unjust or biased against them. This connection between fear of abandonment and feel-ing victimized can be traced back to our evolutionary past, where being excluded from a group could mean life-threatening danger.[26] Today, even though we're physically safer, this ancient fear can still trigger a deep sense of being unfairly targeted or left out.

A victim mindset can help the anxiously attached by pulling others socially closer, at least at first. Crying about injustice can help someone gain attention, recognition, and compassion, but others may soon grow tired of their overreaction to mild offenses, their self-perceived blamelessness, and their desire for retribution. In this way, a victim mindset can be counterproductive, eventually pushing others away and bringing about the abandonment they fear.

It is worth noting that while those with the strongest victim mind-sets exaggerate the injustices they face, and fixate on their own pain, these people authentically feel that they are suffering. A victim mind-set is associated with poor mental health, including lacking trust in others, ruminating about negative thoughts, and depression. Even if these people are trying to manipulate situations to their advantage—whether consciously or subconsciously—they do not feel advantaged, or even happy.

A strong victim mindset is also common among narcissists, people who are excessively self-centered and have a strong need for admira-tion. Like anxiously attached people, narcissists are insecure, but rather than embracing their victimhood and crying out for help, narcissists project confidence and grandiosity to mask their fear. This confidence is a ruse; narcissists feel deeply victimized from even mild criticism.

Some researchers dissected the daily diaries of narcissists (with their permission) and found that they felt more mistreated by everyday offenses compared with other people.[27] Many narcissists then use these pathological feelings of victimhood to manipulate others into feeling guilty or ashamed. If you happen to point out to narcissists how their actions have hurt you, they'll use DARVO to reverse the situation, claiming that *you* are the perpetrator of harm.

Some Finnish psychologists partnered with the Registered Association for Support for the Victims of Narcissists. They analyzed the "Intimate Relationships Forum" on their website, where there are a hundred threads of messages from spouses venting about life with a narcissist. Common themes in their complaints were their spouse's extreme self-centeredness and reliance on intimidation and physical violence. Narcissists also blame their own flaws and mistakes on their suffering spouses.[28] For example, one spouse of a narcissist wrote, "The usual pattern here is that the narcissist does something that he realizes is wrong; gets feedback for it 'that was wrong'—so what do you know—all the sudden he blames someone else for it and demands an apology for it because he has been hurt." Narcissists are experts in the blame-escaping tactic we read about in the last chapter: become the victim. One study found that this manipulative counter-blame tactic is sadly effective: when people were the targets of a narcissist's DARVO strategy during a confrontation, they tended to walk away blaming themselves.[29]

We started this chapter with the puzzle of how some of the world's most powerful people, like dictators and Hollywood moguls, could feel like victims. Without giving Putin and Harvey Weinstein a stack of questionnaires, we cannot know their inner thoughts, but the science we explored here finds that feelings of victimhood are largely unconnected to objective experiences of suffering. Like the rest of us, world leaders, moguls, and billionaires can all feel like victims if they are insecurely attached or narcissists. Perhaps dictators would feel lower in victimhood if they were hugged more consistently as children.

Thankfully most people we meet in everyday life are neither extreme narcissists nor especially high in a victim mindset. But even average people will use victimhood as a sword and a shield in moral conflicts, cutting down their opponents' claims of suffering while deflecting blame. This is especially true in battles where "us" is pitted against "them." In these situations, we all compete for victimhood.

COMPETITIVE VICTIMHOOD

In the conflict between Israel and Palestine, in the culture clash between liberals and conservatives, and in fights between households at HOA meetings, everyone feels as if their side were the true victim. Egocentrism makes it hard to see beyond our group's feelings of victimhood, especially when there are powerful benefits to being the "real" victim, like escaping blame for wrongdoing and getting to label the other side villains.

The benefits of victimhood do not mean that people *want* to be victimized or harmed. No one wants to suffer. But all things being equal, people and their groups would rather *seem* like victims than villains. In a conflict where each side is doing bad things to the other, the side that earns the title of "victim" gets empathy, while the side that earns the title of "villain" gets disdain, and so groups engage in *competitive victimhood*.[30]

Competitive victimhood can occur between individuals, like when kids fight. When my two daughters—aged six and three—go at each other, it is all aggression and malice. But as soon as someone gets hurt or we parents yell at them, they instantly engage in competitive victimhood. No matter who is actually injured or who started the fight, they both cry and cradle some body part, arguing that the other one is the true aggressor who threw the first punch or insult. Both kids seem to genuinely believe in their victimhood, but both also exaggerate their suffering and downplay their responsibility. The winner of this competition for victimhood should—theoretically—be more likely to receive sympathy and less likely to get a time-out. (In reality, the two kids get told to stop antagonizing each other because the *real* victims are their parents, who must cope with all the chaos.)

For my kids, this sense of victimhood is quickly forgotten when they start playing together again, but with warring social groups competitive victimhood is more entrenched. One of the most famous competitions for victimhood is the Israeli-Palestinian conflict, where both groups have reasonable claims of suffering. Jewish people are one of history's most victimized groups, and endured genocide during the Holocaust. Israel is surrounded by Arab countries and terrorist groups who deny the legitimacy of its statehood, and who have expressed the desire to destroy Israel. These entities frequently act upon that desire through waging war, kidnappings, and bombings. Palestinians are also victimized. Not only are they economically and politically less powerful than Israelis, but Israel frequently seizes Palestinian land and property, controls the movement of Palestinian people, bombs their houses and hospitals, and targets Palestinians in human rights abuses.

Feelings of victimhood color how people view ongoing conflicts, including the legitimacy of terrorism and retaliation. One classic study from the 1980s had Arab, Israeli, and more impartial people watch the same television coverage of the Beirut massacre. Each group came away with starkly different conclusions about how the media treated them. While impartial observers thought the coverage was fair and balanced, pro-Arab and pro-Israeli supporters both felt aggrieved that the media coverage was biased toward the other group, failing to "accurately" represent their side's victimhood.[31]

In an us-versus-them conflict, if your side is the victim, the other side must be a villain. This is convenient because it makes your violent deeds merely acts of self-defense. It also means that harm inflicted on the enemy is not really harmful, because typecasting makes villains seem incapable of suffering. Again, these dynamics are seen most clearly in the conflict between Israel and Palestine. In an article titled "The Role of Victim Beliefs in the Israeli-Palestinian Conflict," one psychologist writes, "In addition to predicting support for future confrontational and violent tendencies toward the other party, victim beliefs can also serve to legitimize past harm-doing against the other group, thereby sustaining and exacerbating the conflict."[32]

Other scholars have noted how competitive victimhood has driven virtually every major intergroup conflict over the last century, including Israelis and Palestinians in the Middle East,[33] Hutus and Tutsis in Rwanda,[34] Catholics and Protestants in Northern Ireland,[35] the war in the Balkans between Serbs and Croats,[36] Pinochet supporters and detractors in Chile,[37] Catalans and Basques in Spain,[38] and Turks and

Armenians.[39] Just as harm is the universal currency of moral judgment, feelings of victimhood are the universal driver of intergroup conflict.[40]

In many conflicts, the question of "true" aggressor and victim is in the eye of the beholder. But some groups actually are more dominant than others. It can take time and perspective to see power structures with clarity, but we can all recognize that Native Americans—who were just minding their own business for thousands of years—were victimized by the more dominant and powerful European settlers. Of course, no one likes feeling like a villain, or being told that they are the descendants of villains, and so competitive victimhood can lead the members of more powerful groups to construct their own narratives of suffering to deflect potential guilt. These narratives often invoke "digressive" claims of victimhood, shifting the conversation away from the issue at hand to another topic where victimhood is easier to claim.

In one study, White Americans read about some White college students getting in trouble for wearing racially insensitive Halloween costumes.[41] In response, some of these participants agreed with the idea that the "true victim" in this whole incident was "the First Amendment and the right to free speech in America." Of course, questions of free speech are legitimately important, and—as we've seen—every moral issue is a complex intersection of trade-offs about harm. But additional studies suggest that these specific claims of victimhood were more of a convenient shield to deflect blame. If complaints about free speech suppression were authentic, these participants should have been concerned about other free speech issues, like freedom of the press, but they were not.

The result of this study does not deny that people can be deeply committed to free speech, nor does it suggest only members of more powerful groups invoke digressive victimhood. Instead, it reveals that knee-jerk claims of suffering can be motivated less by thoughtful convictions and more by competitive victimhood. In any competition for victimhood, people play to win.

Competitive victimhood poisons relations between identity groups and also undermines personal relationships, whether at home or at work. Once two sides are divided by some moral issue—each thinking that they have been unjustly attacked—they both compete for the title of most aggrieved.

The relationships psychologist John Gottman can predict with 93 percent accuracy whether marriages will survive (or die), and his work finds that competitive victimhood spells disaster for romantic relationships. He notes that feelings of defensiveness—which are grounded in a sense of victimhood—are one of the "four horsemen of the apocalypse" that predict the end of marriages. Once people start to list the ways their spouse has been thoughtless, and explain away their own thoughtlessness as justified retaliation, it escalates to clashes that are difficult to defuse.

Studies show that competitive victimhood can encourage aggressiveness between co-workers,[42] but the best place to look at the ills of competitive victimhood is on social media. At the beginning of the COVID pandemic, one pundit tweeted that "social media is where people compete in the victim Olympics,"[43] defending their side's moral position by claiming to be more victimized than the other side. Why are claims of victimhood so ubiquitous on the internet? As we discussed in chapter 4, people express more hostility online than in person because of anonymity and social distance. It is easier to rage at people when you can hide in a mob and when you cannot see the impact of your cruel words.

But there is a more charitable interpretation of why victimhood is so often invoked on social media. The social distance and anonymity of the internet makes it harder to understand other people. In-person conversations allow for small talk that establishes common ground, allowing people to bond over their common love of music or their common dislike of the weather. On the anonymous internet, this initial connection and common ground is hard to find, especially when people immediately start arguing about politics. People might turn to victimhood because it provides a moral currency that everyone can understand. We all have a harm-based mind, and so talking about harm makes sense to everyone.

When we invoke victimhood, it connects to the protection narrative. It suggests to others that we—like them—are concerned with protecting ourselves, our loved ones, and our society. Although egocentrically focusing on our own feelings of suffering can create divides, sharing feelings of victimhood—at least in the right way—may help decrease moral outrage and build respect.

Of course, there may be many ways to create understanding within disagreements. Most people seem to think that the best route to building common ground is by emphasizing facts, rather than feelings of suffering. But most people are wrong.

In Sum

- Humans are egocentric, from the total self-focus of newborns to adults who anchor on their own experiences and tastes. Overcoming this egocentrism is challenging. It takes cognitive effort to understand that other people see the world differently. It is especially hard to understand that some people (and even God) might have different morals from us.
- Egocentrism is especially profound when we are in pain because negative feelings pull our attention inward. When we feel victimized, we feel threatened and angry, which drives us to focus only on ourselves.
- Past experiences of victimization are the foundation for empathy because they allow us to understand the suffering of others. But present feelings of victimhood—when we currently feel aggrieved—blind us to the pain of others and make us feel licensed to act selfishly, even if it means harming innocent others.
- Some people are stuck in a perpetual state of victimhood; they live with a victim mindset. This mindset is not connected to suffering objective trauma but instead driven by the fear of abandonment and by narcissism. People with a victim mindset are genuinely unhappy, but they are challenging to be around. They constantly yearn for special treatment and seethe at the smallest hint of personal injustice.
- Almost all of us have a victim mindset during group conflict. Competitive victimhood magnifies our side's pain and blinds us to the other side's suffering, exacerbating division and spelling disaster for relationships.

PART 3

BRIDGING MORAL DIVIDES

Using Harm for a Better Future

The Myth of Bridging Divides:
Facts Best Bridge Divides

In this book so far, we have deconstructed two popular myths: one about human nature and one about moral psychology. The first myth is that we are a species of predators, not prey. To many, *Homo sapiens* seem like ruthless apex predators bent on destruction. Looking through this dark prism of human nature leads us to see our moral opponents—whether political rivals or disagreeable co-workers—as driven by aggression and a thirst for domination. But while some people are ruthless and power hungry, science suggests that humankind evolved not as predators but as prey. Humans are usually motivated more to protect themselves than to destroy others. When people act aggressively, in the back of their minds they are usually fixated on their own suffering—avoiding harm rather than inflicting it.

The second myth we dispelled was about our moral minds. All moral psychologists agree that morality evolved to help us overcome the challenges of group living, including the threat of other people acting evilly. According to one popular theory, our moral minds are divided into the little rooms of moral "foundations," separate mental compartments that are triggered—or unlocked—by the special keys of their own corresponding moral values (like loyalty or purity). Although discussions about morality involve many different values, and despite obvious diversity across cultures and politics, we have seen how harm is the master key of morality. All of people's moral judgments are fueled by intuitively perceived harm. These perceptions of harm are built off assumptions about who or what is especially vulnerable to mistreatment, which can differ across cultures and politics.

When we recognize that all people share a harm-based moral mind, we gain a new perspective on moral differences. People disagree not because they have over- or underdeveloped mental mechanisms but because they see harm in different ways.

Our shared morality of harm provides the promise of common ground, of bridging divides. Here in this third section, we explore the optimism of a harm-based mind. Not only do our universal concerns about protection explain moral disagreement in the present, but they also give us hope for the future. Acknowledging that we all make moral judgments based on perceptions of victimization allows us to see a glimmer of shared humanity in others, even when we disagree on moral issues. The big question is how we can best nurture this seed of shared humanity to foster greater moral understanding. How can we best bridge moral divides in politics and everyday life?

Perhaps people already know how best to connect across their differences. Evolution has furnished our mind with many useful heuristics, and we might have a good rule of thumb for building respect between those who disagree. To test people's intuitions about bridging divides, our lab—led by my postdoctoral researcher Emily Kubin—asked a representative sample of 251 Americans to imagine "someone who disagrees with you on moral issues," for example, on same-sex mar-

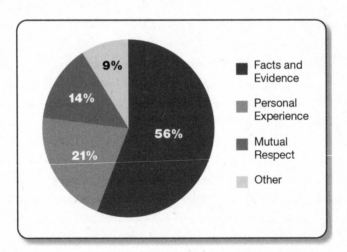

Figure M3.1: Americans reporting on what would make them respect people with different moral beliefs. Most emphasized the importance of facts.

riage or abortion, and then to report "what would make you respect their opinion."

We took their responses, clustered them into themes, and then counted how many people endorsed each theme. The most popular was "facts and evidence" with 56 percent of people believing that they were the best way to increase respect. This majority of people thought that the best route to finding common ground was presenting the raw evidence without any editorializing. These people believe that if we could simply educate people on the real facts of a situation, we would reduce political division. At a distant second and third, people thought that we should emphasize personal experiences (21 percent) or the existence of some mutual respect between disagreeing people (14 percent).

But are these intuitions correct? Do facts and statistics really help to bridge divides? We put these beliefs to the test. In conversations with political opponents, we had people use facts to support their views on guns, taxes, and environmental policy. Our studies suggest that facts are not the best path to understanding; but before we explore these results, it is worth considering why exactly people find facts so appealing.

THE REIGN OF FACTS

How can you know if something is true? This question is the subject of an entire branch of philosophy. It's called epistemology, and the term derives from the Greek word *epistēmē,* which means "knowledge," and in turn derives from the older word *epistasthai,* which means "know," or "know how to do." According to our survey of Americans, people believe epistemology should be based in facts; when something is supported by facts, we know it is true.

Facts were not always so important. Until the rise of modern empiricism several centuries ago, people largely acquired knowledge through nonscientific means like reading sacred texts, sharing stories, and listening to authority figures. For most of recorded history—particularly after Christianity became the official religion of the Roman Empire in the fourth century—religious revelation was also prioritized in epistemology. Because people of the past were mostly illiterate, they couldn't directly read about medicine, cosmology, psychology, or theology, and so had to rely on religious leaders to teach them how the universe was structured and how the mind and body worked. But after more than a thousand years of epistemology dominated by the church, the Enlightenment changed everything.

The Enlightenment was a movement founded on the principles of reason, empiricism, and skepticism of authority. Some famous pre-Enlightenment thinkers like Copernicus, Galileo, and Martin Luther set the stage for this revolution of knowledge. They questioned the Catholic Church's authority over the truth and helped to kick off a centuries-long period of intellectual and social progress that peaked from the late seventeenth to the early nineteenth century. The Enlightenment encouraged people to read for themselves and to directly study and reason about the world. The Royal Society, which remains the oldest scientific academy in existence, was founded in England in 1660 to bring scientists together in pursuit of new knowledge. Its motto: *nullius in verba*—"take nobody's word for it."

The Enlightenment enshrined a new epistemology of *facts,* the set of independently verifiable and objective information about the world. Today, three centuries later, facts still reign supreme, with statistics and science underlying every aspect of society. Data, metrics, and analytics help our economy run more efficiently, allowing businesses to send you targeted ads and then delivering products to your door the next day. Facts reveal how schools should best teach elementary students how to read, how doctors should best treat disease, and how architects should best build ever taller buildings. Our reliance on facts has enabled humanity to progress from the feudal city-states of the eighteenth century to interconnected nations that send astronauts to international space stations.

Of course, you might wonder how well modern people follow the Enlightenment's emphasis on facts. The Enlightenment promoted reason, objectivity, and evidence, but these values seem neglected today, as many seem to ignore the truth when spouting opinions about politics, health, and economics. This is why, according to the psychologist Steven Pinker, we need "Enlightenment now"—the title of one of his books—to reaffirm our commitment to facts.

Pinker argues that the Enlightenment was important because it championed the value of rationality, using the principles of logic and critical thinking to solve problems, overcome our biases, and achieve important societal goals. He sees rationality as an important historical catalyst for developing society's most beneficial human institutions, including science, democracy, and trade. Pinker applauds this progress, saying, "Rationality should be the guiding star for everything we think and do."

I agree that it is important to be rational, and in today's tense political climate it is also important to *seem* rational. When other people seem rational, we treat them with respect. No one wants to have a contentious conversation with someone who lacks logic, who bases their moral judgments on random whims or merely repeats the talking points of television pundits.

Luckily, facts seem like the solution to both being rational *and* seeming rational—a one-two punch against political animosity. If we can all discuss facts, then we can have civil conversations where we can work together to disentangle the truth . . . right?

Unfortunately, our studies show that intuitions about the power of facts are wrong. Facts fail to live up to our expectations. This is the third myth I refute in this book: facts do not best bridge moral divides. Relying on facts may help people *be* rational, but it does not make people *seem* rational, because the facts of the other side seem fake.

Society's Enlightenment-inspired epistemology convinces us that the way to create respect is by throwing facts at your opponent until they submit to your overwhelming rationality, as if their political convictions could be bludgeoned away by statistics. Congressional representatives, political commentators, and social media influencers all treat data like artillery, trying to smash through the enemy's defenses. Viral videos of one side "owning" the other side focus on winning the war of facts. While these videos might make one side feel smug, they rarely change people's minds and certainly fail to foster understanding between political opponents.

Facts fall especially short in this era of fake news where everyone has their own statistics. Modern social media makes it increasingly difficult to distinguish between reliable information and misinformation, and

this allows people to find "data" to support the most extreme of opinions. Today, the very concept of objective truth is being challenged,
undermining the ability of facts to create moral understanding.[1]

Even if we fixed the problems of social media misinformation, the
weakness of facts extends beyond fake news. In moral disagreement,
facts simply provide the wrong kind of truth. Facts are objective information about how the world works, like Galileo showing that both
light and heavy weights fall at equal speed. Unlike gravity, morality
is not objective, even if our moral convictions can feel "objectively"
true. Perhaps we could all agree on the evilness of the Holocaust or the
goodness of a parent's love, but the hot-button issues at the center of
moral debates defy an easy objective answer because they are grounded
in messy trade-offs about perceived harms. In these cases, it is difficult
or even impossible to objectively demonstrate the truth of one's moral
beliefs.

There is no fact that can convince everyone we should prioritize
fetuses over pregnant women or the lives of Black men over the safety
of White police officers. Think back to your own conversations about
morality: when's the last time you had a conversation about a deeply
held moral value and came away from it thinking, "I guess I'm wrong;
their facts were just too good!"? Probably never.

As we will see in the upcoming chapter, when we tested the ability
of facts to bridge divides, they were *not* the best route to mutual understanding. People claimed to want raw statistics, but when our participants received them, they simply shrugged them off. When advocates
of gun control learned a pro-gun-rights statistic—that civilians use
guns to defend themselves more than 989,000 times per year[2]—they
said that this stat failed to capture the whole picture, or wasn't relevant
to the topic at hand, or was biased. When advocates of gun rights
learned that 73 percent of murders in the United States are committed
with firearms,[3] they argued that gun control advocates weren't thinking about the facts correctly, asking in return how many more people
would be killed if good people were forced to give up their guns. Facts
are easily rejected or seen as irrelevant to the deeper moral truth.

Facts fail to foster respect in political discussions because our moral
beliefs are based on intuitions of harm, not objective evidence. Our
moral convictions are founded not on statistics but on feelings of

threat. Of course, facts remain essential for a functioning society and for making good political policies, but to initially connect with people across moral divides, we need something that appears less "objectively" true and more "morally" true. We need stories of suffering.

In Sum

- The third myth is that facts best bridge divides. Ever since the Enlightenment, facts have (rightly) reigned supreme as a source of knowledge.
- The majority of Americans believe that facts are the best way to build respect across moral divides, but they are wrong.

Chapter 10

Understanding: Telling Stories of Harm

Every year on the fourth Thursday of November, Americans gather to share turkey, mashed potatoes, and, increasingly, spite. Thanksgiving brings together family and friends, including people who vote for opposing political candidates and who have different moral convictions. Although major holidays have always had tension humming under the surface, science confirms that these gatherings have become especially antagonistic.

While many Americans were preparing for Thanksgiving in 2020 by going grocery shopping or setting their fantasy football lineups, two researchers were planning a study to see just how polarized family gatherings have become.[1] They recruited Americans who said they would be attending a Thanksgiving dinner and gave them a little after-dinner homework, asking them to record the precise times when they arrived and when they left.

The researchers wanted to know if politically diverse meals (featuring Democrats and Republicans) were shorter than dinners where everyone agreed on politics. In addition to reporting the beginning and end times, participants provided information about each adult at the table: their name, their political affiliation, and their attitude toward Trump.

Together with these data, the researchers also controlled for some key covariates. Covariates are variables that trend (or "covary") with the main variable of interest. In simpler terms, they are factors that researchers consider because they could influence the outcome variable they are measuring. For example, in a study examining the high correlation between the desire to eat ice cream and the desire to drive in a convertible, an important covariate might be "warm weather." If you statistically controlled for this covariate of warm weather the link between ice cream eating and convertible riding would substantially decrease, because it drives both behaviors. But sometimes controlling for covariates can also reveal effects that might otherwise go unnoticed.

One covariate controlled for in the Thanksgiving dinner study was whether the meal was held at a restaurant instead of a home. Restaurant dinners, which accounted for 4 percent of meals, could be several hours shorter than dinners held at a home. It is harder to linger at the table when your server is giving dirty looks. These restaurant dinners also had more political diversity. We know that geographic proximity predicts political similarity: relatives who live on the same city block are more likely to share political views than relatives spread across the state; and relatives who live far from each other are more likely to eat at some restaurant that lies halfway between everyone. After controlling for this and other covariates, the researchers found that dinners with political opponents were an average of twenty-four minutes shorter than dinners where everyone endorsed the same party.

Twenty-four minutes. On the one hand, these results could be worse. People could stand up to leave as soon as Uncle Jesse, the plumber from Missouri, starts to complain about immigrants, or as soon as Cousin Sierra, home from Oberlin College, calls Jesse a neo-Nazi. But twenty-four minutes is about the time it takes to serve and eat pie and ice cream. What hope is there if Americans are willing to skip pie?

Most people have a story about a holiday dinner gone wrong, but does this mean America is hugely and irrevocably polarized? Some experts believe so. One popular measure of perceived polarization comes from the Varieties of Democracy (V-Dem) data set, where five to seven experts on a country's political scene respond to this question: "On a scale of 1 to 4, to what extent is society divided into mutually antagonistic camps in which political differences affect social relationships beyond political discussions?" The expert consensus on America was about 3.8 out of 4, among the highest of any country in the world.[2] But there is no need to panic just yet.

One reason for these negative ratings is a contrast effect; modern political animosity stands out given the relative tranquility of recent American history. Bad things seem especially bad against a background of good. To put things in perspective, let's consider a comparison country. When rating Bosnia, a country that witnessed civil war in the 1990s and where divides are much more entrenched than in America, experts gave it a polarization rating of 3.2, lower than the United States.

This more optimistic rating of Bosnia is hard to square with the realities on the ground. Eboo Patel, founder of a divide-bridging interfaith organization, wrote this about Bosnian daily life: "If you work for the Croat Catholic fire department, you don't respond to the burning buildings of Bosnian Muslims, even if you happen to be closer. And if you work for the Bosnian Muslim fire department, you let the flames engulf Croat Catholic homes."[3]

It may be bad in America, but it's not *that* bad. And even if it is generally bad, people have come back together after much worse, including the Troubles in Northern Ireland and the Rwandan genocide between the Hutus and the Tutsis. Take Bernadette Mukakabera, a Rwandan woman who watched as her Tutsi husband was murdered by Hutus. A decade later, in court, Bernadette faced her husband's killer, Gratien Nyaminani, who offered an apology.

Many of us would have rejected this apology and demanded the harshest sentence available, but she forgave Nyaminani, and her forgiveness persuaded the judge to reduce his initial sentence of nineteen years in jail to two years of community service. Mukakabera's mercy went even further when Nyaminani's daughter started dating her son. Mukakabera saw beyond her lingering prejudice to recognize the growing love between these two young people. She said, "I loved her heart and behavior—this is why I didn't resist her becoming my son's wife."[4]

Bernadette Mukakabera is clearly a special person, special in the same way as Daryl Davis, the Black man from chapter 1 who befriended hundreds of KKK members. I am not arguing that people should be expected to forgive atrocities, but it does put the arguments between conservative Uncle Jesse and progressive Cousin Sierra into perspective. It can be difficult to stay calm while an angry relative lectures you about elections, or when a co-worker fumes about the courts, or when you see your neighbor's aggressive lawn sign. But there is a wide range of toxicity when it comes to toxic polarization, and most of the conflicts we face in our lives are not so extreme that they cannot be overcome.

These final chapters of the book are about how to best bridge moral conflicts. They are far from an authoritative account of conflict resolution, because entire libraries could be filled on soothing conflict. Instead of trying to cover this huge topic, we will focus on how to leverage our harm-based moral minds to connect with others and make them—and ourselves—seem more human.

HIGHLIGHTING HUMANNESS

One of the most powerful drivers of any moral conflict—including civil war and sectarian violence—is dehumanization. Dehumanization is a negative belief that involves, as one scholar puts it, "labelling a group as inhuman, either by reference to subhuman categories . . . or by referring to negatively valued superhuman creatures such as demons, monsters, and satans." Dehumanization can also occur when you view people as mere objects, animals, or even machines, reducing their status to something less than fully human.[5] When you call someone an "animal," a "cockroach," a "beast," a "machine," or a "robot," you are dehumanizing them.

The process of dehumanization starts when you see the other side as fundamentally different from yourself, especially as concerns their minds and morals. Encountering differences is not necessarily bad and can even be exciting, but they can also set the stage for feelings of superiority—and perceptions of inferiority—once conflict arises. Consider how about a third of the world's population eats with their hands, including many people in India and Sri Lanka. To Westerners, this practice seems fun and even quaint. Some high-end ethnic restaurants in New York City offer $100 plates sans utensils where wealthy White Americans can participate in some harmless norm violations.[6]

But to early twentieth-century Westerners with a sense of supremacy and a mission to "civilize" other nations, eating with your hands provided an obvious example of cultural deficiency. The British author Clarence Rook described people who eat with their hands as having "the echo of the beast in their instincts," comparing it to how cavemen once ate.[7] This dehumanization often licensed cruelty or oppression of the "less developed" people.

Any kind of conflict inevitably increases animosity, but dehumanization is one of the most insidious ways to disparage someone, because it strips away their minds and moral status. As we saw in chapter 7 on vulnerability, we give others moral standing based on their mental capacities, and we generally agree that among all creatures and creations humans have the most powerful minds. Scholars throughout history have exalted our species for our exquisite capacity for rationality and our deep capacity for feeling.

Animals might be clever, but only humans can do calculus. Likewise, although animals possess basic affective states—good and bad feelings—only humans possess complex emotions like shame, resentment, love, hope, and disappointment. The specialness of human emotions means that dehumanization often involves denying these capacities to the other side. In one example of dehumanization, a study finds that 59 percent of partisans believe that compared with members of their own party, members of the other party are less capable of feeling rich emotional states.[8]

You can see glimmers of dehumanization in the destruction narrative, where people see their own side's behavior in politics as motivated by protection but see the other side's behavior as motivated by some animalistic predatory instinct. A blatant example of dehumanization is that partisans rate their side as more evolved on the "ascent of man scale" (figure below). This scale is simple, showing people images of apes/humans in various stages of evolution and asking them to place where a target (for example, Democrats) falls on the scale.

On average, people rate the other side as about 30 percent less evolved than their side, not quite equating them with the Taung child, our ancient hominid ancestor, but certainly less developed than *Homo sapiens* (which, by the way, means "wise man" in Latin). We put chimpanzees but not *Homo sapiens* in zoo enclosures, and give basic rights to humans but not gorillas, and so any perception of other people as mere apes is troubling.

Other research shows that partisans engage in dehumanization by seeing the other side as simplified caricatures. In one study, participants saw hundreds of pairs of faces and selected which of the two faces

Figure 10.1: Ascent of man scale. The ape on the left-hand side is slowly evolving into an upright human.

looked more like a conservative or a liberal.[9] The researchers then took all the participants' selections and morphed them together, creating a composite image that reflected the average face that they ascribed to people on the other side versus their own side. As you can see, both conservatives and liberals saw the other side as caricatures, albeit different ones. Conservatives thought liberals looked younger and more naive, and liberals thought conservatives looked grumpy and serious. Both caricatures may be technically human, but each seems stripped of different kinds of thoughtfulness.

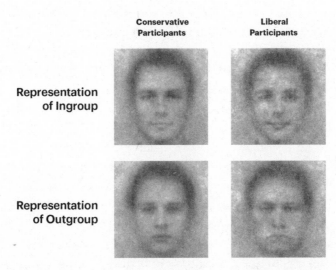

Figure 10.2: The top left quadrant is what conservatives think conservatives look like. The top right is what liberals think liberals look like. The bottom left is what conservatives think liberals look like, and the bottom right is what liberals think conservatives look like.

Research on "humanness"—those elements that seem to make our species special—reveals that people see *Homo sapiens* as possessing two key features, which surprised even the foremost expert on the subject. Nick Haslam is a social psychologist at the University of Melbourne who has studied everything from clinical psychology to bathroom humor. Decades ago, he wanted to investigate how exactly people perceived our species' unique capacities, including the ability to experience rich emotions and to behave rationally. He used two questions to measure perceptions of humanness—one about whether some mental capacity was "uniquely human" and one about whether it was tied to "human nature." He thought of these two terms as synonyms and predicted an extremely high correlation between ratings of them. Instead, people rated them differently, revealing that they tapped two different kinds of humanness. Qualities that participants considered uniquely human were not the same as qualities linked to human nature.

Follow-up research mapped out how people understood these two broad senses of humanness. Uniquely human qualities revolve around rationality and intelligence, including the capacities for politeness and sophistication. These "uniquely human" qualities separate us from other animals and help us rise above their beastly instincts, as Aristotle argued thousands of years ago.[10] On the other hand, "human nature" qualities revolve around emotional depth and warmth toward others, including friendliness and patience. These human nature capacities are seen as somewhat shared with animals, but humans are judged to possess them to a greater degree.

Two kinds of humanness means that people can dehumanize others in two different ways. When people deny others the uniquely human capacities of rationality and intelligence, they see them as savage animals. For obvious reasons, this kind of dehumanization is called "animalistic dehumanization." On the other hand, when people deny others' human nature, they see them as machines or robots, like when Allied propaganda from World War II likened the Germans and the Japanese to cold, killing machines without compassion or pity. This kind of dehumanization is called "mechanistic dehumanization."

If you think back to chapter 7, where we explored perceptions of mind and assumptions of vulnerability, these two senses of humanness neatly map onto the two dimensions of mind perception—being a thinking doer and a vulnerable feeler. Thinking doers are perceived to be rational, and vulnerable feelers are perceived to have rich emotions, so we can say that being a complete human involves being seen to possess the ability for both rational thinking and emotional vulnerability.

In conversations about politics, seeming rational is clearly good, especially within our society that remains rooted in the ideals of the Enlightenment. We all want to look like individuals who respect reason. The benefits of appearing emotionally vulnerable may be less obvious, but there are at least three. First, seeming capable of emotional concern makes it easier to apply the protection narrative versus the destruction narrative. Machines coldly destroy, whereas emotional people compassionately protect. A second benefit of seeming like a vulnerable feeler is that, as we saw in chapter 8 on moral typecasting, vulnerable feelers are less likely to be demonized as villains. If you appear to be a suffering victim of harm, you are less likely to be seen as a callous perpetrator of harm. Finally, seeming vulnerable encourages people to feel empathy, nudging them to resonate with someone's feelings across the eternal gap between two minds.

If we are likely to dehumanize the other side, then the key question is, what intervention can make people seem more human—more rational and more vulnerable—to political opponents? And bonus points if this intervention helps people on the other side better understand opposing moral positions, seeing disagreement not as evidence of evil but as reflecting a different set of assumptions about what might cause suffering. This is a big thorny question, but my team and I had an idea.

We knew from our work that harm was the master key of morality and wondered if harm could make opponents seem more human. Specifically, we predicted that people would see their political opponents as more rational and vulnerable once they learned that they grounded their moral judgments in authentic perceptions of harm, in the genuine desire to protect themselves.

Caring about harm should make people seem rational because there is nothing more logical than trying to avoid harm. As Charles Darwin long ago recognized,[11] it is rational for all animals—whether a squirrel, a single-celled amoeba, or a human being—to try to avoid harm. If someone tells you that they pulled their hand away from a burning stove, you will nod in understanding. We thought that people would also understand when a political opponent described how their moral convictions revolved around protecting themselves from harm.

Being worried about harm should make someone seem not only rational but also vulnerable, the second half of humanness. If they are concerned about suffering harm, then we assume that they must be vulnerable to suffering—why else would they be trying to avoid it? The recognition that someone can be harmed should also facilitate empathy. Evolution programmed each of us to be deeply concerned about being victimized, and so it should be easy for us to resonate with someone else's concerns about being mistreated. We reasoned that harm should especially bridge divides when it is presented in *stories,* not as facts.

STORIES OF HARM TO BRIDGE DIVIDES

In our quest to humanize each other across divides, we need to harness our understanding of the human mind. The Enlightenment shift toward facts helped us build our modern society, but our moral minds predate the Enlightenment by eons. Throughout the history of humanity, we depended on *stories* to learn about the world. When our ancestors gathered around the campfire late at night to talk, they were not discussing statistics but instead telling stories—tales about how best to avoid predators, how to hunt, and how best to make sense of the universe. One expert on evolutionary psychology argues that humans are so defined by our stories that we are "the storytelling animal."[12]

Stories help teach us many things, but they especially focus on how to be moral and how to avoid harm.[13] Today's Disney movies stress that we should care for our friends and be kind to others, and classic fairy tales like "Hansel and Gretel" and "Little Red Riding Hood" contain lessons about the danger of evil strangers.

Although we usually think of kids' stories as happy, they are often quite dark, sacrificing cheerfulness to teach lessons about potential threats, like how lacking self-control can threaten yourself and your family. In *Frozen,* Elsa's inability to rein in her emotions results in mass mayhem: she freezes an entire kingdom, almost kills her sister, and nearly gets herself murdered after being branded a witch. The original version of "Cinderella," written in 1812, sent an unmistakable warning about the wrongness of being cruel to your family. After the long-abused Cinderella slips her dainty foot into a glass slipper and marries the prince, her selfish stepsisters have their eyes pecked out by doves.

Today's stories rarely involve blinding stepsisters, but they are still animated by harm, typically the protagonists' desire to avoid suffering, either for themselves or for their loved ones. This focus on avoiding harm makes the characters lifelike, transforming them from mere characters into three-dimensional human beings. In his book *The Art of Character: Creating Memorable Characters for Fiction, Film, and TV,* David Corbett outlines several guidelines for creating compelling characters, and among the most important is vulnerability—their struggle against some source of suffering, whether physical, situational, or moral. Corbett writes, "When people appear wounded or in need of our help, we are instantly drawn to them—it's a basic human reaction. . . . Vulnerability creates a kind of undertow, pulling us toward a character who is wounded or imperfect, and that attractive force is far more important than whether the character is 'likeable.'"[14] We relate to vulnerable characters because those who experience harm and try to avoid it seem more human. This is why Superman seems unrelatable—invincible, superstrong, and shooting laser beams out of his eyes—until you understand that he can suffer just like the rest of us. He is sad about losing his biological parents, is powerless to kryptonite, and worries about Lois Lane.

Seeing fictional characters as full human beings is a worthy goal for writers; it is also our goal for bridging divides. Work from our lab,[15] led by my postdoctoral researcher Emily Kubin, finds that harm-focused stories help us respect and humanize our political opponents. In one experiment, we had an experimenter grab two passersby on campus and have them talk about the divisive issue of guns. One of these passersby was actually an accomplice of ours, a female research assistant pretending to be walking around. This accomplice always took the opposite view on guns from our real participant. If the participant said they were pro–gun control, the confederate was pro–gun rights. While these two people debated the morality of guns, we recorded the audio to later analyze how much the participant treated the accomplice as rational and with respect.

Everyone in the study had a contentious conversation about guns, but we randomly assigned people to two conditions. Because most people put so much stock in its ability to create common ground, one condition focused on facts. The other condition focused on stories. In the "facts" condition, the accomplice grounded her opposing moral position in objective knowledge, arguing, "I believe this because I have read many books and governmental reports on gun policy, so my factual knowledge has really made me feel strongly about this."

In the "story" condition, the accomplice used personal experiences of harm to ground her opinion. When she was pro–gun rights, she said, "I believe this because my mom was able to protect herself with her gun when someone attacked her," and when she was pro–gun control, she said, "I believe this because my mom was hospitalized after being hit by a stray bullet."

This study design allowed us to compare the divide-bridging effectiveness of emphasizing facts versus telling personal stories of harm, but we ran into a problem: participants were usually *too* respectful. These conversations were not social media shouting matches between anonymous trolls but instead in-person discussions between a campus visitor and a young woman who was both positive and outgoing— essential traits for a research assistant whose main job is to speak with strangers. While this civility was refreshing, it made it difficult to re-create the tense political interactions we wanted to study.

To turn up the heat in the conversation, we tweaked the design by having our research assistant accomplice insult the participant. Once the participant stated their position on guns, she said, "I don't know how you can call yourself an American if you don't think that guns" either "hurt people and communities" or "keep our communities safe," depending on what side she was criticizing. Then our accomplice proceeded to ground her beliefs in either facts or stories of harm. The tweak worked: there were no screaming matches, but insulting people's moral position made them less courteous.

After we collected and analyzed 153 conversations about guns, the data were clear. Compared with emphasizing facts, sharing personal stories about harm better bridged divides. When a separate team of research assistants rated the recordings of the conversations, they judged that the storytelling accomplice, compared to the fact-launching accomplice, was treated as more rational (5.2 for stories versus 4.3 for facts on a 7-point scale) and with more respect (5.9 versus 5.2), and people also seemed more willing to interact with her (5.9 versus 5.2). If you want to have more civil conversations, your best bet is to ground your moral beliefs in experiences of harm.

Sharing personal experiences instead of facts improved cross-partisan perceptions by about 0.7 to 0.9 on a 7-point scale. This may not seem like a giant effect, but it is actually quite substantial. Psychologists use a statistical term called Cohen's d to measure "effect sizes," which tells us the power of our interventions to effect change. Cohen's d can range from 0 (no effect) to 0.2 (a small effect) to 0.5 (a medium effect) to 0.8 or bigger (a large effect).

Depending on the context, even small effects can be meaningful in the real world. The most classic example is aspirin, which has a small effect size ($d = 0.12$) for reducing the risk of heart attacks,[16] but this effect was judged significant enough to end the study; the medical community thought the drug was too beneficial to withhold from the placebo group and so they gave aspirin to all participants.[17] Even small effect sizes can make a life-or-death difference for thousands of people.

Compared with emphasizing facts, telling personal stories about harm had a medium effect size (average Cohen's $d = 0.47$) in increasing perceptions of rationality, respect, and the willingness to interact with political opponents. This effect size is not only bigger than the impact of aspirin but also stands out in the messiness of behavioral science interventions. When a massive team of researchers replicated twenty-eight famous psychology findings, they found that their effect sizes tended to be small, with a median Cohen's d of 0.15[18]—much smaller than the power of telling stories of harm.

It is also worth noting that our studies aimed to build respect by sharing personal experiences, *not* to persuade others to change their minds. In many political conversations, people often seek to alter people's beliefs, but we sought the more basic goal of getting people to speak more civilly. Before you can be persuaded by someone, you must respect them, and respect between political opponents is at historic lows. We wanted a route to encourage the civil conversations that are necessary for a functioning democracy, where people who disagree can still discuss issues with each other.

One limitation of our on-campus study where people spoke about guns is that our accomplice did not provide specific facts, or share real experiences, so a follow-up study used both actual facts and real stories of harm. We pulled facts from www.justfacts.com, a site that lists statistics about gun violence from reputable sources like annual reports and federal data sets. We reported two of these stats earlier: 73 percent of murders in the United States are committed with firearms (perhaps supporting a pro-gun-control argument), and civilians use guns to defend themselves 989,000 times per year (perhaps supporting a pro-gun-rights argument). These statistics were about harm—since that's what morality is grounded in—but we suspected that they lacked the moral weight of stories involving suffering.

To get real stories of harm, we asked people online to volunteer their experiences with guns, and then got a separate group of participants to rate these stories on how much harm they involved. This gave us stories that contained either mild, medium, or severe harm. We obtained stories that supported both gun control and gun rights; here are some examples of the pro-gun-control experiences. Mild harm: "I experienced a neighbor who has guns and he got really upset about something and then he fired his gun randomly up in the sky. Nobody got hurt, but there is a possibility that he would do it again and he might hurt somebody." Medium harm: "I had practiced many times for what to do if there was an active shooter on campus. I should be able to go to school without this worry. I also went to see the *Batman* film on the same night that someone had shot up the theater at another location." And severe harm: "I had a friend who was shot and murdered by a gun. The person who killed him was able to get that gun without having a proper background check."

As we predicted, stories of severe harm—on both sides of the debate—best fostered perceptions of rationality and feelings of respect between political opponents. Everyone can appreciate moral convictions grounded in stories of obvious victimization. We were also surprised to discover that personal stories of mild harm were more effective at fostering respect than deploying facts, even when those facts seemed so powerful (at least to us researchers). But our participants, like people everywhere, seem to be desensitized to the impact of statistics. They are just the angry background buzz of political divides and easily ignored. A person's story of suffering, however, demands attention.

Our studies also reveal the power of harm-based stories in places filled with toxic partisanship, like the YouTube comments section, where people seem to delight in random cruelty. We programmed a software script to scrape 300,978 comments across 194 videos about abortion by both pro-choice and pro-life advocates. In some of these videos, people argued for their position by emphasizing facts, like statistics about unplanned pregnancies, the number of abortion clinics in a state, and details about the funding of Planned Parenthood. In other videos, people grounded their moral position in personal experiences, walking viewers through their own abortion and their feelings about it.

We then used a computer program called LIWC (pronounced "Luke") to analyze these comments. LIWC stands for Linguistic Inquiry Word Count, and it tallies up the words people use to provide an insight into their psychology. One of my favorite findings from LIWC is that couples who often use the word "you" in their relationships are more likely to break up. You'd think that focusing on the other person in a relationship would predict better relationship quality, but using second-person pronouns correlates with more criticism and blame, like "You are such a slob. You just expect me to clean up after you," or "You are always working. Work is more important to you than your family." This is why psychologists often teach people in therapy to use "I" statements to convey their feelings in a way that's more about subjective experiences.

Beyond specific words, LIWC also counts broader language categories, and for our study on YouTube comments we focused on two: emotional tone and sociality. Emotional tone is the general meanness or kindness of the language, and we used the algorithm to identify positive words like "happy" and "grateful" and negative words like "upset" and "angry," to get an overall vibe of the comments. Emotional tone is important for bridging divides because respectful conversations are more positive, or at least less negative.

The second language category we searched the comments for was sociality, which captures the amount of "affiliative language" within text, indicating how much people want social connection, bonding, or cooperation. When the algorithm detected affiliative language, it was usually in a sentence with a positive emotional tone, with words like "friend," "family," and "together," or in sentences that used inclusive pronouns like "we," "us," and "our." This variable tells us how much people want to interact with another person, which is also important for bridging divides. When we ran the numbers, we found that comments were both more positive and more affiliative when videos discussed people's own stories rather than summarized statistics.

We wondered if the same benefits of harm-based stories would hold in another tough setting: when guests were being questioned—and often grilled—by news show anchors like Wolf Blitzer and Bill O'Reilly. We collected 145 transcripts of interviews from both CNN and Fox News across three different time points: 32 from 2002–4, 72 from 2008–10, and 41 from 2015–17. We used these multiple time points to ensure our results generalized across different political moments.

A team of research assistants rated how much the guests on these shows grounded their moral positions in facts versus personal stories about suffering. For example, one politician who emphasized facts when discussing the importance of economic changes said, "We've seen the unemployment rate fall from its peak of 6.3 percent now down to 5.7. We've seen about 250,000 more jobs created since the summer. That's not enough." Another politician who spoke about the same topic discussed personal experiences instead: "I can speak from personal experience myself. My husband has been unemployed. He is a very smart educated man. And the jobs just aren't there. We are true middle class, and the middle class is suffering."

Our research assistants also coded whether the anchors treated the guests as rational. Did the program hosts constructively engage with their guests and give them time to say their message, or did they snort derisively and then shout over them? Our analyses found that the more guests talked about personal stories of harm versus facts, the more they were treated as rational.

Stories of harm not only increase respect but also decrease dehumanization. In other studies,[19] we showed participants Facebook posts from political opponents, some of which argued for their position with facts alone, while others used stories. We asked participants political tolerance questions, like "how willing would you be to have this individual live next door?" or ". . . date your son or daughter?," and also measured their tendency to dehumanize their political opponent, both mechanistically ("they are mechanical and cold, like a robot") and animalistically ("they lack self-restraint, like an animal"). Facebook users who grounded their political stances in personal stories of harm (compared with facts) were afforded more tolerance and dehumanized less.

Across dozens of studies, we consistently find that sharing personal stories of harm is a powerful way to bridge moral and political divides, whether in online surveys, analyses of news interviews, YouTube comments sections, simulated Facebook posts, and in-person conversations. Because we humans have harm- and story-based minds, narratives of suffering are key to fostering respect across politics—an insight that can help real-world moral conflicts.

REAL-WORLD STORYTELLING

Narrative 4 is a nonprofit organization founded to help people see the humanity of the other side, even across unimaginable differences. One of its founders is the novelist Colum McCann, an Irish author who won the National Book Award for his book *Let the Great World Spin,* an allegory about the 9/11 attacks. McCann is known for his empathic writing and for his ability to take a nuanced perspective of people on either side of conflicts.

One day, McCann was at a retreat with several other authors and the executive director of the Aspen Writers' Foundation, Lisa Consiglio. They were trying to explore the depths of each other's experiences and decided to do a story exchange, an exercise where two partners tell each other a story, and then they switch, retelling their partner's story. Crucially, you have to retell the story in the *first person.* If I told you the story of me getting stranded in the frozen wilderness of northern Canada, you would retell the story as if it happened to you, using "I" and "me," and infusing it with your own feelings and impressions to make the experience your own.

Participating in these story exchanges brought many of the authors to tears, and McCann and Consiglio realized that they had stumbled on a powerful method for building empathy across divides. I witnessed one Narrative 4 exchange in person and was impressed by its power to immediately connect people. Reliving someone's experience for yourself—especially with them sitting right next to you—directly connects you to their mind, their life, and their perspective, fostering moral understanding.

In the hardest test of story exchanges, Narrative 4 paired two people with completely opposite stances on guns. Todd Underwood is a staunch advocate of gun rights. He collects guns and is the founder of the United Gun Group, a firearms e-commerce website where George Zimmerman sold the gun that killed Trayvon Martin. Underwood claims to "own an arsenal of guns" and, prior to the interview, described the movement to restrict access to guns as "a lot of misinformation by people who are completely uneducated, making an emotional decision, and trying to justify it intellectually."

Todd's conversation partner was Carolyn Tuft, who was shot in a mass shooting in a mall in Salt Lake City. Her fifteen-year-old daughter was shot too. Although Tuft survived with lead poisoning from the three bullets shot point-blank into her lower back, her daughter died. Now Carolyn is an activist for gun control, saying that even "if I would have had a gun in every pocket, there is not one thing I could have done."

The whole exchange is worth watching, but its most emotional moment is when Underwood retells Tuft's experience of losing her daughter. He speaks about the pain of losing Tuft's daughter as if she were his own, and how the loss still haunts him today, how it robbed him of who he used to be. By the end of his first-person retelling of Tuft's story, Underwood is sobbing. Tuft reaches out to Underwood and touches his hand, a compelling moment of humanness across moral differences.

It wasn't just Underwood who understood Tuft. She also came to appreciate his capacity for vulnerability and rationality, because his story was also grounded in harm. He ran his gun sales website to support himself and his family because of a disability that makes it difficult to work outside his home.

If, instead of sharing and retelling stories, Tuft and Underwood had launched sets of facts at each other, moral understanding would have been much more elusive. Even though facts might be "objective," shoving statistics at each other fails to dispel the aura of irrationality and the lack of vulnerability that surrounds political opponents.

The power of harm-based stories and the weakness of facts in moral conversations does not mean that facts are unimportant. Facts are essential to every aspect of life, especially in determining the best policies for society. As a scientist, I have based my entire career on facts. But our findings show that facts are best presented only after building some initial respect with a person on the other side, and that respect is easiest to build with harm-based storytelling. Ideally, the story will be about the issue under discussion, but not everyone has a poignant story about a hot-button issue. One good place to start is telling a general story about yourself, about your background and how your experiences shaped your beliefs. No one goes through life without some suffering or tribulations, and so these stories can touch on these elements.

Importantly, there are some rules for using stories to bridge divides. The first rule of telling—and listening to—stories is to strive for *understanding*, not persuasion. Studies find that presenting stories primarily to persuade can backfire,[20] because people can easily see when others are on the offensive, and then quickly become defensive. Instead of trying to change someone's opinion, make it clear that your aim for the conversation is to understand each other.[21] You can even explicitly say, "I'd like to try to understand your perspective." This might seem corny, but making obvious your goal of understanding is a powerful way of creating goodwill.

The second rule of stories is that they should not be confused with facts. Facts are objective pieces of information without a point of view. That's the whole point of facts: they do not depend on who is talking about them. The theory of gravity is a fact no matter who you are or what identity groups you belong to. Stories are not facts. They have a point of view; they happen to someone in particular. When you tell a story, emphasize that it is an experience from *your* perspective, and that it could help someone understand that perspective.

The third rule of stories is that we must *listen* to other people's stories. Too often in conversation, we focus only on our own irritation while the other person is talking. Instead of engaging with their thoughts and beliefs, we simply rehearse what we will say to counteract their points.

People easily recognize when we are not listening to them. Our social minds are finely tuned to the subtlest of behavioral cues. I tell students in my classes that I can see if they're cheating—looking at each other's tests—even if they sit at the very back of the room, because humans are amazingly good at detecting what people are paying attention to. It's obvious when a student is furtively glancing at their neighbor's exam. Likewise, it's obvious when your conversational partner isn't paying attention, when their eyes are glazed over and they're distantly nodding, ruminating on their own feelings. People tell stories because they want to be heard and understood, and so you need to try to hear and understand.

These three rules are not really separate; they all revolve around the goal of seeking understanding rather than persuasion. Understanding requires (1) genuinely trying to understand, (2) recognizing that stories—unlike facts—are special tools to create human understanding, and (3) making the effort to truly listen to someone else's story, so that you can understand them.

One final reason that stories are so good at bridging divides is that they involve us opening up to other people. They take something from deep within us and then gift it to another person. The mere act of telling a story—especially a story of harm—is a feat of vulnerability, showing that we want to trust someone and that we want them to trust us. Although vulnerability helps us connect with opponents, it is hard to become vulnerable with an "opponent."

This is the paradox of being vulnerable—what is best at bridging divides is hardest to do. How can we reap the benefits of vulnerability when human nature makes us fear being vulnerable? How can we open ourselves up without feeling open to attack? In the next chapter, we will explore three simple steps to help.

In Sum

- Most people think facts best help bridge moral divides, but they do not. Facts give the wrong kind of truth for moral conversations, and in political arguments we disagree about which facts are true and relevant.
- A major driver of conflict is dehumanization. Seeing the other side as less than human—as irrational and invulnerable—licenses cruelty toward them. The best way to make each other seem fully human is by telling stories of harm. Not only do stories of harm resonate with our ancient harm-based minds,

but worrying about avoiding harm makes us seem both rational and vulnerable.

- Studies find that stories of harm foster perceptions of rationality and respect across moral divides, whether on social media, on cable news, in op-eds, or in face-to-face conversations. Once stories of harm have created mutual understanding, facts can be useful.
- For our stories of harm to be effective, we must focus on using them for understanding, not for "winning" some debate. It is also important to listen to other people's stories of harm.

Chapter 11

Hope: Opening Up

Stories of harm can help us bridge divides, in part because they make us seem vulnerable, providing evidence of our humanity. But actually sharing these stories—becoming vulnerable—is hard. Millions of years of evolution have made us fear being attacked. Just as we cannot imagine baring our necks to a hungry predator, we cannot imagine being emotionally vulnerable with someone who might attack us for our moral beliefs. This is the *paradox of vulnerability*. The best way to connect with the other side is also the most difficult.

Luckily, there are hundreds of organizations that are experts in resolving this paradox. I have worked with a number of them, each with hopeful names like Beyond Conflict, Over Zero, the National Institute for Civil Discourse, More in Common, and the One America Movement. They sometimes employ scientists, but their staffs are mostly practitioners—patient, open-minded people dedicated to bridging divides.

Many of these groups have drawn inspiration from the organization Essential Partners, a pioneer in the anti-polarization and conflict-mediation space. Essential Partners has developed many frameworks to build trust, and their employees are experts at detecting and defusing the many bombs that lurk within moral disagreements. Essential Partners has facilitated discussions between police and Black communities in the South, between angry factions in evangelical churches, and between refugees and residents in Jordan.

Essential Partners was started by Laura Chasin in 1989, who before then was working as a therapist at the Family Institute in Cambridge,

Massachusetts. She was developing new techniques for bringing families back together, which mostly focused on using narratives, helping people to tell—and listen to—the stories of their loved ones.

One day at home, Chasin was flipping through the channels and landed on a talk show, a precursor to *Jerry Springer*, where a charismatic host set up a contentious conversation. The setup was not "Who's the Father?" or "She's Been Cheating!" but rather a discussion about abortion. Just like now, abortion was a hot-button issue in the 1980s, and the plan was to have two pro-life advocates and two pro-choice advocates debate for half an hour. The host clearly wanted some conflict to boost ratings.

Chasin looked at the setup of the stage through her eyes as a family therapist and guessed that the conversation would go poorly, just as intended. Each group was on its own side of the stage, like two small infantry units in opposing trenches. Then the host stood between them in no-man's-land and opened the debate with a prompt like "tell us why your side is good and the other side is evil"—framing the disagreement in the starkest moral terms. Within two minutes, the discussion had devolved into a shouting match with each side spitting insults at the other.

Chasin realized she could actually bridge moral divides with her experience as a family therapist, but she was hesitant to shift her focus away from the families she was helping. Then a man walked into two women's health clinics in Brookline, Massachusetts, and shot two people. The community cried out for a response to the violence and for more understanding across politics, so she stepped in. Chasin created Essential Partners to help address this conflict and others like it. She thought of people on either side of a moral issue as a fractured family, which provides a more productive frame for conversations than mediating between "opponents." In her discussion groups, Chasin focused on the relationships between the participants, encouraging people to understand where the other side is coming from and nudging them to recognize that everyone has legitimate worries and fears.

Chasin recognized that a key element of good relationships—in families and otherwise—is the willingness to be vulnerable. But people are only willing to be vulnerable when they know that others are motivated to understand them and value their mutual connection. Psychology has a name for the conditions that create the willingness to be vulnerable: "psychological safety," a telling term given that people are motivated to avoid harm.[1] Conversational settings feel "psychologically safe" when people can share their thoughts and feelings without fear of rejection or attack, when people are convinced that others are not predators out to destroy them.

Creating a psychologically safe environment is hard in family therapy because most people have decades of emotional baggage with their relatives. But it can be even harder to encourage vulnerability with political opponents who seem to disagree with our deepest moral convictions. To allow for vulnerability, Chasin and her colleagues at Essential Partners focus on setting up the physical and emotional space to encourage (but never demand) openness.

Unlike the stage of that ill-fated talk show, Essential Partners does not segregate the two sides of the conflict across the room or even on opposing sides of the table. Instead, they sit the group around a circle (no head of the table because that connotes more power), making sure to alternate people from each position so that everyone is sandwiched between those supporting the other side. This positioning prevents discussants from making mini coalitions with their in-group members. Structuring conversations so that they move around a circle also helps everyone feel as if they have a turn to share their perspective.

Decades before our lab tested the power of personal narratives to bridge divides, Essential Partners was using storytelling to build connection across differences. Across hundreds of projects in fractured communities, they also discovered that the most effective stories often revolve around concerns about threats and experiences of past suffering. These harm-based stories seemed to humanize people, illustrating to their opponents that they have the capacity to feel and think.

Beyond sharing stories of harm, the facilitators at Essential Partners encourage people to highlight the moral concern or value that sits at the heart of conflict for them. This allows others to see that they are indeed moral people who care about ethical values. They also invite people to see the complexity within the other side's values and perceptions of harm, revealing hidden depth and—hopefully—room for common ground. In a conversation about abortion, these discussions might reveal that your political opponents are concerned about both "freedom" and "compassion" and care about both the health of a mother and the rights of a fetus but are conflicted about how to best prioritize these different concerns.

Facilitators also invite people to consider the complexity within their own values. They probe whether there might be an inner tension within someone's moral position, some lurking dissonance. Again in a conversation about abortion, a pro-life person might volunteer that they feel some internal conflict when it comes to abortion for people who are raped, or a pro-choice person might volunteer that they feel some psychological tension when it comes to aborting a later-term fetus, especially if there is no medical reason prompting that decision. The moral beliefs of most individuals are more nuanced than their political party's platforms, and hinge on delicate trade-offs involving relative perceptions of harm.

Being guided to introspect into your own moral complexity helps people step out of an all-or-nothing view of good and evil—a caricature of a moral world populated with 100 percent victims versus 100 percent villains. It also helps to foster a "psychologically safer" environment as discussion participants recognize that both they and others have some uncertainty about morality and politics, increasing their collective vulnerability.

These vulnerability-increasing techniques of Essential Partners are very effective, but to work well, they require an expert facilitator. This is why Essential Partners is still in business thirty-five years later, even after Chasin's unexpected death a decade ago. It is simply hard for people trapped in a cycle of conflict to open up to each other. You need firm guardrails to make sure that conversations do not veer off the road into shouting matches and personal attacks. But there are so few expert facilitators and so many of us who want to better understand. Might there be an easy framework for better bridging divides in conversations?

Could there be three simple steps for more moral understanding in discussions? I asked this question of John Sarrouf, one of the most essential partners of Essential Partners. We were having a Zoom call one lovely spring afternoon. My window was open, the birds were chirping, and the internet was on fire with arguments about abortion, trans rights, mass shootings, and federal budgets.

Sarrouf has smiling eyes, tall hair, and impeccable diction from his training as a theater actor. He became a thespian to reveal the force and complexity of human experience, but like Chasin he felt the call to apply his unique skills to bridging divides. Although Sarrouf is still a member of the storied Actors' Equity Association, he broke from full-time acting to do a master's in dispute resolution at the University of Massachusetts before directing university programs on having difficult conversations. He now co-directs Essential Partners, trying to connect people across moral divides.

Sarrouf and I have worked together at conferences dedicated to moral understanding, where I talk about the latest science and he discusses the real-world practices of building connection. He has a good sense of humor and laughed when I asked him for three easy steps for healing America and the rest of the world from the intractable conflicts wrought by toxic polarization. I knew it was a glib question that was impossible to answer, but Sarrouf was willing to try. He overflows with optimism—what else nudges someone to become a professional theater actor and then devote their life to moving people through humanity's worst conflicts?

He suggested many tips for resolving the paradox of vulnerability and for bridging divides in conversations, but because three is a nice number, I have grouped these points together into a triad. For better discussions about morality and politics we need to *connect, invite,* and *validate,* which together spell "civ," the first three letters of "civil," which is how our conversations should be.

TIP 1: CONNECT

Family therapy is all about (re)building relationships and emotionally (re)connecting with people. Before you start talking about charged issues, you need to relate to someone as a person. The whole goal of bridging divides is to see someone as a full human being, and human beings are much more than just their political beliefs.

As we learned in chapter 1, many people are part of the "exhausted majority" and feel that their political leanings are mostly unimportant to who they really are. Even if you are someone who cares deeply about politics, you also care about a lot of other things. You are worried about your friend in the hospital; you are excited about an upcoming vacation; you are preoccupied with a big project at work; you are wondering if you should get another pet or maybe a new car. Most of our inner lives (at least when we are not doomscrolling on social media) have very little to do with national politics, and so the first step to having a conversation about controversy is to kick the controversy down the road. Start with the nonpolitical; talk about your life.

Many people dread even banal conversations, but we massively underestimate how we will enjoy them. Researchers from the University of Chicago, including Juliana Schroeder and Nick Epley, went to commuter rail stations outside Chicago and surveyed commuters waiting for the train. They asked people how they felt about striking up a conversation with a stranger versus sitting on the train in solitude. Most said that talking to someone else would overall be a negative experience and that solitude would be more enjoyable. The researchers then put this intuition to the test, getting some train commuters to have conversations and allowing others to enjoy their solitude. After their trip into the city, the commuters filled out a survey about how much they enjoyed their trip and then mailed it back to the university.

When the researchers opened these envelopes, they were surprised by the results. Those who had conversations with strangers enjoyed their commute the most, even if they were introverts.[2] People were also wrong about their experience of solitude, reporting that it felt negative—as negative as they thought having a conversation would be.

Making small talk with a stranger on the train seems different from talking to a political opponent, but small talk is a good first step to better conversations about morality. Even if someone disagrees with us on a divisive issue, we likely have many other similarities, and small talk helps to uncover that common ground. Perhaps they cheer for the same sports team, or have the same kind of pet, or share your niche interest in mycology—all topics you can discuss to "connect" before broaching politics.

One study confirmed that first connecting over shared interests and identities created better conversations between political opponents.[3] Researchers used an online matching algorithm to pair participants who disagreed about politics but shared some other interests. For example, Joseph and James might be told that they have opposite stances on wealth redistribution but were told (truthfully) that they were born in the same city, liked the same types of movies, and both really enjoyed hiking. This helped situate their political differences as just one difference among many similarities, which increased the participants' ratings of closeness to each other, which in turn made them more receptive to their partner's opposing political views.

Even if (you think) you really dislike small talk with strangers, there are proven methods to improve conversations. In the same way that we underestimate how much we will enjoy chatting with strangers, we also underestimate the power of asking questions and focusing on our discussion partner.

In one study, psychologists brought 215 pairs of people into their lab to "get to know someone else" over an online chat platform.[4] Half the participants were instructed to ask a few questions about the other person (no more than four), and the other half were instructed to ask *a lot* of questions (at least nine). For example, if someone in the conversation said, "I'm planning a trip to Canada," someone in the "few questions" condition might say, "Cool, I've never been to Canada," whereas someone in the "many questions" condition might say, "Cool, have you ever been there before?" After chatting for fifteen minutes, both participants then rated how much they liked their conversation partner, and also tried to guess how much they were liked by them.

Participants were surprised by how the conversations went, especially those who asked many questions. People thought that their partner would prefer them to ask fewer questions—it's a conversation, not an inquisition!—but this intuition was wrong. They were liked best when they asked a lot of questions, especially follow-up questions, like "Could you tell me more about that?" because it demonstrates genuine interest in what the other person is saying. (Asking questions also helps you get a date; in another study, the researchers found that those who asked more questions at a speed-dating event got more invitations for a second date.)

Asking questions is a great way to connect with people, but we fail to appreciate this because we think about asking questions from the wrong perspective—imagining conversations from the outside, instead of the inside. These same researchers found that those observing conversations rate the question answerers as more likable because they're talking more. All that speaking makes them seem like the star of the show. But *watching* a conversation is very different from *having* a conversation, and when we are talking with someone else, we like to be able to share our thoughts and feelings. There's nothing more affirming than someone who is trying to understand your perspective by asking good questions.

Asking questions is important to building connection, but asking *deep* questions is even better because—as Sarrouf says—conflict tends to flatten people, transforming them into a two-dimensional cutout of a person rather than a full-fledged person. The building blocks of meaningful relationships are meaningful conversations, where you go beyond small talk to ask about someone's core experiences, beliefs, and desires. Asking someone deep questions combats "flattening" by giving your partner a chance to showcase their emotional and cognitive depth, reminding us that they are fully human.

You might bristle at the suggestion to ask strangers more intimate questions. After all, we all know someone who shares too much personal information. Maybe you're at a party having a good time, bantering about work with colleagues, and then someone steps in and hauls the conversation toward their profound anxiety after a recent breakup. You feel awkward and start looking for an exit. Studies show that these uncomfortable experiences loom large in our minds, giving us the stereotype that deep personal topics ruin conversations. But this stereotype is wrong. Deep conversations about profound topics are less awkward and more enjoyable than we imagine—especially when they involve asking questions instead of self-centered monologues.

In one study, people talked either to strangers or to people they were close with and were told to either make superficial chitchat or discuss profound issues.[5] In the superficial chitchat condition, people talked about their local city, the recent weather, and their latest holiday. In the deep conversations, people asked each other about the last time they cried, what they were most grateful for, or what they most wanted to know about their future.

The results show that people generally overestimated the awkwardness of having any kind of conversation with strangers, replicating the findings of the Chicago train study. But people especially overestimated the awkwardness of having meaningful conversations with strangers.

Most people were actually delighted to open up about their hopes and dreams and consistently felt more connected to their conversation partner after discussing deep rather than shallow topics. Obviously, there are limitations to the conclusions of this study. It still might be bad to ask your partner, "What's the most hopeless you've ever felt?" while playing a summer cornhole game, but even here science says that this question will be received much better than you imagine. When you are teetering on the edge about whether to discuss something deep, take the plunge.

The strategy of asking deep questions also works with political opponents, helping us to see them less as caricatures and more as full human beings. One study randomly assigned two political opponents to have an online conversation about politics (gun control) or to just talk about the meaning of life.[6] *Both* types of conversations, political and nonpolitical, significantly reduced participants' dislike for each other. But the people who talked about the meaning of life saw an even greater benefit, becoming less likely to describe each other as "mean" and "closed-minded" and more likely to describe each other as "intelligent" and "patriotic." Another study found the same result with video calls between political opponents: talking to an opponent about their vision of the "ideal day" dramatically reduced animosity toward them.[7]

Talking with someone—especially when you ask them deeper questions—is a simple but surprisingly powerful way to connect with them, but there is an important caveat. When trying to connect, you should actually be *trying* to connect, not amassing information that can be marshaled against them later. To build moral understanding, we must strive for understanding and not domination. Once someone realizes that you have an "understanding" attitude, forming a connection is easier, and they will be more likely to accept when you *invite* them, the second letter of "civil."

TIP 2: INVITE

After establishing an initial connection with someone, you might want to discuss politics, that uncomfortable constellation of morals, values, and perceived harm. Rather than launching into a tirade about your political convictions, take a cue from the power of asking questions: invite them to share their perspective.

The word "invite" is the key. Not demand, not force. There is a psychological phenomenon called reactance, which describes when people rebel against social pressure. If you have ever told a three-year-old to do something and then watched as they did the exact opposite—just to spite you—you've witnessed reactance. No one should feel compelled to discuss their feelings, especially when the goal is making people feel understood.

One example of political reactance was found in a sample of German citizens during an election campaign.[8] When these people had politics forced into their day—for example, encountering a political attack ad while online shopping—they reacted by withdrawing from politics, intentionally avoiding any additional information about the election. Just as nobody wants to have political propaganda forced on them, few people are excited when, in the break room, a co-worker demands to know their thoughts on abortion. Instead of forcing politics on people, you should engage in "invitational rhetoric," extending an offer to understand someone's views.[9]

It starts with a proposal, not an assault. To delve into challenging topics, you can explicitly ask, "Can I ask you about something?" or even "Is this a good time to ask about something?" This might sound artificial, but is very useful because it puts the conversational ball in their court. It allows your partner to decline if they are not feeling ready to talk about politics. Importantly, even if they decide to pass on politics, your invitation establishes that you are interested in listening instead of lecturing, and this will help them feel more at ease and more open to chatting later.

An invitation reveals that the purpose of your conversation is understanding. Sarrouf says that "purpose is primary," which means that people—with our big social brains—are very sensitive to *why* someone wants to have a conversation. If you are inviting them to share their perspective, it signals your intention to learn. When I asked Sarrouf to be more concrete about how an invitation might unfold, he deftly demonstrated, first asking me to imagine we had voted for different candidates: "Kurt, could I ask you something about this last election? And the reason why I want to have this conversation is because I've read a lot about it, and there's a lot I don't really understand. I know you voted differently than I did, and I don't really understand, and I want to understand." You can see that his invitation to me literally mentioned the word "understand" three times, unambiguously revealing his intention.

Ideally, after your invitation, they will tell you about their perspective, and help you understand where they're coming from. Keep in mind that they might not have read a book on moral understanding, and so they might say things that you find offensive. They might not ground their opinions in universally understood stories of harm, and instead fire facts at you. But you can be confident that inviting them to share their perspective will make them less antagonistic than they could be. They will find it hard and uncomfortable to put their feelings and thoughts into words, but know this: that they appreciate the opportunity to be understood, to be *heard.*

After sharing themselves with you, they will feel vulnerable, which is why the next step is *validate,* the third letter in "civil."

TIP 3: VALIDATE

After you connect with someone and then invite them to share their perspective, they will hopefully tell you about their moral positions, and their principles, reasons, and perceptions behind those positions. Now they stand in an uneasy place, wondering what's going to happen. Are you going to attack them, using your newfound insights about their hopes and beliefs to better pierce their soft spots? To foster civil dialogue, you need to assuage these fears. You need to let your partner know that you value them and the understanding they've now provided. You must validate their perspective.

Validation means acknowledging that the other person genuinely holds their moral convictions and believes that those convictions help to safeguard themselves, their loved ones, and society. It means acknowledging that the other person is trying their best to do right, be good, and protect the vulnerable. Validation is *not* about agreement but about recognizing someone's perspectives and their good intentions.

The validation stage is also a chance for you to connect what they said with how it affected you. Remember the problem of other minds? How we can never get inside the minds of others to truly know their thoughts and feelings? The problem of other minds is especially thorny when discussing contentious issues because it's easy to misinterpret what people say, thinking that they intend something cruel when they're just having difficulty putting messy feelings into words.

Sarrouf says that you need to "close the gap" between what they intended to say and the impact of their words on you. Part of validation is detailing your own experience: how their feelings and stories affected you. You could mention how you feel sympathy with something they said, like a story of suffering. You could also say how something they said made you thoughtful or even upset; it is okay to be honest if you are angry, so long as you stick to your own feelings. Use "I" statements like "I feel . . ." rather than "you" accusations like "You are . . . !"

Resist the urge to insult. In contentious conversations it is easy to get outraged; that's the nature of moral disagreement. The trick is to use your feelings as an opportunity to help your conversational partner understand you, giving them feedback to better comprehend the impact of their words. You are striving for mutual understanding not mutual destruction.

It is not easy to make someone feel that their perspective is valued, especially in political conversations, but some researchers wondered if an AI chatbot might be able to help.[10] They trained it to be an expert in moral understanding, and it made real-time conversational recommendations so that people felt more understood. In one study, participants texted with a partner about gun control, and for some of them the chatbot first intercepted their message and offered helpful ways to reframe it. Participants had the option of using the reframed message or keeping the original.

In one real conversation from this study, a gun control supporter starts by saying, "Guns kill an unacceptable number of people every year. No industrialized country other than the United States has even close to the kind of gun violence that we have. I think that we need far stricter gun laws in the U.S. to prevent this kind of violence. Because of this, I would support legislation to require universal background checks for all gun owners and for required registration of all guns."

Then the pro-gun supporter first writes, "You communist! Having guns is an important part of my life as an American. It's one of the reasons I'm proud to be in this country. And I feel a million x safer when I have my gun with me." But this message was intercepted by the chatbot and rephrased as "Thank you for telling me that. Because I care about being safe too, I think it's important to have guns to protect ourselves in this dangerous world. Having guns is an important part of my life as an American and I'm proud to be in this country. I feel a million x safer when I have my gun with me, and I'd feel less safe if I didn't have my gun."

This reframing was more validating, expressing gratitude for sharing their opinion—"Thank you for telling me that"—even if that initial message was aggressive. The reframed message also emphasizes concerns of harm. The chatbot figured out that the best way to make people feel understood is by recognizing their feelings of threat, like when it writes about a "dangerous world" and feelings of safety. Validation is best achieved when it recognizes that people's behavior is described by the *protection narrative*. These conversational changes were effective: participants who used the validating chatbot had higher-quality conversations (as reported by the participants) and ended up having more respect for their opponents' opinions.

When you have more validating conversations, you may find yourself being more open to someone's moral stance. Understanding can pave the way for appreciation, but remember, the initial goal of these difficult conversations is understanding, not persuasion. As we have discussed, a diversity of opinions—moral pluralism—is necessary for a functioning democracy, and so you should feel empowered to stick to your moral convictions, just as your conversational partner should feel free to stick with theirs. You can acknowledge that someone's moral beliefs—and their perceptions of harm—are authentically held without agreeing with them.

These three tips for more CIVil conversation—connect, invite, and validate—will not make conversations about controversial issues easy, but they will make them *easier,* and that is important for our under-standing and for democracy.

In Sum

- There is a paradox of vulnerability. Opening up with stories of harm helps to bridge divides, but it is hard to open up to moral "opponents." This paradox can make us paralyzed at the crossroads of connection, torn between the power of sharing our suffering and the desire for self-protection.
- An expert at bridging divides, John Sarrouf from Essential Part-ners provides three lessons for connecting across differences. These lessons can be summarized with the acronym CIVil conversations.
- The *c* is for "connect." Before we talk politics, we must first connect on a human level. There are many ways to bond with people, including talking about shared hobbies or discussing your hopes and dreams. Asking many (deep) questions—especially follow-up questions—is a good way to build com-mon ground, but the questions must be geared toward genuine understanding.
- The *i* is for "invite." Extending an invitation to others to share their perspective helps avoid reactance; no one likes being forced to be vulnerable. When asking someone for their thoughts and views, remember that "purpose is primary." You must empha-size that your goal for the conversation is understanding.
- The *v* is for "validate." When someone opens up to you, you must make them feel understood and valued. Validating is not agreeing, but authentically listening to someone. Try to "close the gap" between what they intended to say and how their words affected you. One good route to validating: acknowledg-ing your shared desire for protection.

Epilogue

Humility: Always Learning

Every year, I teach a course on "moral understanding" to college students. When I tell this to my colleagues, many wish me luck, as if I were going on a risky mission into enemy territory. Many people have written off students as too easily triggered to have their beliefs challenged, and as too angry and fragile to engage in civil discourse.

The goal of this course is to educate students about our moral minds and the roots of our divisions, and they learn about the concepts in this book, especially how differing perceptions of harm underlie moral disagreement. An important part of the course involves practicing difficult conversations about contentious issues. Students learn skills for better discussions and then go out into the real world to talk with people who disagree with them.

I always knew this would be a challenging course to teach, and friends warned me that I might be "canceled." These warnings echoed in my head when I looked at the course website a week before the start of the semester. I panicked when I realized that I made a clerical error that could doom the course.

I have poor attention to detail. Without my fantastic editor, there would be hundreds of typos in this book, and there are likely still some, despite his best efforts. Even when the stakes are high, I will miss crucial things. Ages ago, when I applied to graduate school, my application to Stanford laid out my plans to be advised by a faculty member who had left the department years earlier. (I didn't get an interview.)

As I looked at my course website, I was disappointed but not surprised to discover I had listed my course as Psyc 572 instead of the actual course number, Psyc 574. I was only off by two, but what a difference that made.

Psyc 574 was my course: the Science of Moral Understanding. Psyc 572 was Theoretical and Empirical Perspectives on Sex and Gender Differences. Both were upper-level psychology courses, but while mine emphasized "difficult moral disagreements (e.g., abortion, euthanasia) and . . . how best to bridge them," Psyc 572 emphasized "understanding gender as a social psychological construct." This mistake not only made me look careless but created a dilemma for the students. They were allowed to switch out of my class, but upper-level psychology classes at UNC fill up so quickly that there were no other open classes. If they wanted enough credits to graduate, they were stuck with me.

I figured that while both liberals and conservatives would get excited about Psyc 574, it was likely only committed progressives who would be excited to dive into the social construction of gender. And if I were to believe the stereotypes on social media, these especially progressive students might be especially likely to get outraged.

Rather than folks from both the left and the right, I ended up with a very left-leaning class of mostly twenty-two-year-olds. But here's the thing: Despite the mix-up, I was less worried than you might think. I had led other classes where we tackled heated issues, and I always found the students excited for frank conversation. Of course, leading these classes always required setting up ground rules for discussion and easing students into hot-button topics, but I never had someone walk out or try to cancel me.

My worries completely evaporated during the first week of class. The students were engaged and eager to learn about the roots of moral disagreement. When pro-choice students were assigned to be pro-life in a debate, they marshaled the very best arguments of the other side. I was proud.

I was especially proud of how they translated those skills into their real-world conversations about morality. One discussion focused on how much racism comes from the structure of social systems versus the hatred of individuals. Some had conversations with roommates or friends with similar opinions, but to my surprise other students decided to have these talks in "hard mode," approaching their MAGA-supporting parents or grandparents or, in the case of one student, a frat boy.

When reflecting on her discussion, she wrote, "I decided to have a conversation with a White fraternity boy on vacation about racism (that was a funny sentence). As I suspected, he believes in the 'bad apples' phenomenon"—that racism is driven by a few bad people and not the structure of systems, as she believed.

This conversation evolved into a back-and-forth about policing and race. My student thought that the police were not all bad but deeply influenced by a racist history and an unfair set of laws. My student shared with the fraternity brother how even young children can be influenced by racist systems, with Black children showing racial preferences for White dolls over Black dolls.

The fraternity brother brought up that his uncle is a police officer, and how his love and respect for him make it difficult to see how all cops might be inadvertently racist. Throughout this conversation, my student wrote that she "engaged patiently and was an active listener, making sure I didn't personally offend his loved one while still remaining firm in my argument. Mutual understanding wasn't fully achieved; however, I feel like we both left the conversation having more empathy towards one another than when I initiated."

I hadn't expected these short conversations to create this much empathy. Of course, some discussions got derailed, but none seemed to make any relationship worse off, and no one regretted having them. The crucial point is that all my students went into the conversations with the motivation to better *understand* their partner, not to win. Because of this, many came away with a deeper understanding of those on the other side. Some even came away with deeper friendships.

Here's an excerpt from one of my favorite responses: "I decided to have respectful and kind discourse with my roommate who is republican. I consider myself to be pretty far left winged." After detailing more background, she writes, "This conversation went actually extremely well overall because I employed a morally humble approach by treating her with moral regard and verbally and physically expressing my attentiveness to her moral opinion, rather than trying to shut her down for a very strong opinion of hers that was polar opposite to mine. There were points in the conversation where I didn't know as much as her on a specific issue, or she challenged a misconception of mine with facts about what republicans actually believe in, which allowed me to acknowledge my own moral fallibility. The conversation, rather than going south like some previously did, ended up in us hugging and agreeing that it was super interesting to listen to how someone else sees the world and how refreshing it is that the conversation didn't happen over social media/text, where things tend to escalate behind a screen. We ended up going to get dinner that night, because we appreciated each other's time spent discussing and I feel really great overall about applying moral humility now to my personal life!"

This example is only a single story, but it is enough to give me hope when I think about political division today. In her reflection, the phrase "moral humility" keeps popping up. This is an idea I try to foster in my class, and I believe that her morally humble mindset helped the conversation go well.

Moral humility is the ability to acknowledge that you may not know everything about moral issues while still staying true to your convictions. It is not about giving up faith in your values but instead recognizing the validity of other people's moral convictions—that other people can still be authentically moral even if their morals are different from your own. For this student, moral humility meant recognizing that her roommate had a valid perspective and possessed some knowledge that she lacked, while also appreciating that she had some misconceptions about the other side.

Ultimately, this whole book is about moral humility. Moral humility is rejecting the easy idea that people who disagree with you are motivated to destroy. Moral humility is also about recognizing that the differences between our side and their side are less deep than they seem. We and our "opponents" have the same moral minds, with all of our moral judgments growing out of the same concerns about avoiding, preventing, and rectifying harm.

Moral humility is also about recognizing that we have something to learn from those who disagree with us. This lesson may be very specific. By talking to someone on the other side, we might learn only about the mind and morals of that one person. But often, the understanding is broader, allowing us to better recognize the humanity of those who disagree with us, and hopefully nudging us toward the belief that moral differences are essential to a strong democracy.

MORAL UNDERSTANDING

Moral understanding is hard won, and can be easily lost, especially because of the allure of the three myths debunked in this book. Myth 1 is that humans are more predators than prey. This misconception about human nature poisons our perceptions of our political opponents, who we wrongly assume want to watch the world burn. Fortunately, the truth is that people are more prey than predators; we are less motivated to destroy and more motivated to protect ourselves and society.

Myth 2 touches on the idea that people with different politics have deeply different minds. One theory suggests that liberals care only about direct physical and emotional harm and the harm of unfairness, while conservatives care about these concerns plus "harmless" morality like loyalty to group members, respecting authorities, and protecting purity. But the notion of "harmless wrongs" is a myth, grounded in the misconception that harm is an objective fact. It is not.

When it comes to our moral psychology, harm is a matter of perception. Everyone's moral judgments are grounded in intuitive perceptions of victimization, and moral differences arise from different assumptions about who or what is especially vulnerable to victimization. Despite our different moral stances, this shared focus on harm provides common ground with our opponents, which can help us bridge divides.

To best harness this common ground and connect across political disagreement, we need to let go of a third myth: that facts are the best way to achieve moral understanding in contentious conversations. Ever since the Enlightenment, facts have (understandably) held a privileged position in our society, but our minds are better suited to connect over stories, especially those that center on suffering. Sharing stories of harm is more effective at bridging divides than launching statistics at our opponents. When we combine this advice with practitioner-tested steps for having better dialogues—connect, invite, and validate—conversations with political opponents go much better than expected.

This book has been about the psychology of our moral disagreements, because I believe that understanding the mind is crucial to understanding our human condition—and we are all humans, no matter our moral positions. When we appreciate how our minds work, it is easier to sit with the central tension of moral conflict: that other people can disagree with you and still be good people. Like my family in Nebraska, people can vote for different candidates and still be caring, compassionate, and moral people.

Despite having different moral convictions, people on the other side still care about their loved ones and still feel threatened by the modern world. In fact, it is *because* people care about their loved ones and feel threatened that they hold fast to their moral convictions. People with different politics might disagree with you about how best to protect society from harm, but we all genuinely care about preventing victimization.

Whether in politics or everyday life, most of us are trying our best to uphold morality. It can be hard to remember this, especially when someone insults you on social media, comparing your side to the Nazis—or when someone corners your car in a dark loading dock, like when I was a teenager on the way to the movies that night. But everyone—even the man who slapped me around—wakes up in the morning striving to do right. Each of us shares a human nature built upon detecting threat and a morality focused on preventing harm, and each of us wants our experiences of suffering to be heard.

It is true that many of us today are outraged. But most of us want to be less outraged, and understanding the truth about our moral minds will help.

Acknowledgments

It would be outrageous not to acknowledge the many people who helped with this book.

Thanks to my agent, Max Brockman, for always thinking big, for encouraging me to write this book, and for his constant guidance. Thanks to my editor, Edward Kastenmeier, for his faith that the ideas here are important, and for his patience, perseverance, and vision as he shaped a thought-provoking book that balances science and stories. Thanks to my research assistants, Will Blakey and Sam Pratt. Will was in the trenches with me for the hardest parts, and I couldn't think of a better comrade, helping me to think through ideas, sketch out studies, check drafts, revise paragraphs, propose structures, find stories, stress test controversial sections, and connect all the dots. Sam helped get the book over the finish line, providing thoughtful edits and good perspectives, polishing up crucial sections with precision and speed, and helping to get all the i's dotted and t's crossed in the text and in the production process.

Thanks to the folks who read and offered honest and thoughtful comments on previous drafts, helping to save me from my curse of (limited) knowledge: Molly Worthen, Josh Abrams, and Chad Woolf. Thanks also to Kevin House for making beautiful figures.

Thanks to Chris Howard-Woods and Lisa Kwan at Pantheon for their work on the book, and thanks to the Penguin Random House Speakers Bureau, especially Kim Ingenito, for representing me for talks to help spread the ideas. Thanks to Bret Simmons and Kaya Stanley at TEDx Reno for giving me the chance to talk about these ideas, and to Daniel Jones, Nathan Christ, and Devon Eifel at FreeThink for making a compelling video about this work.

Thanks to my PhD students, postdocs, and lab managers past and present, whose research and hard work provides the foundation for much of this book: Chelsea Schein, Neil Hester, Amelia Goranson, Josh Jackson, Rachel Hartman, Sam Abrams, Connon O'Fallon, Danica Dillion, Jonathan Keeley, Simone Tang, Peter Schmidt, Emily Kubin, Kyra Kapsaskis, Stephen Anderson, Cameron Doyle, Yochanan Bigman, Andrew Vonasch, Frank Kachanoff, Nich Dimaggio, and Carlos Rebollar. Also thanks to new lab additions for the work you'll do: Madhulika Shastry, Sharlene Fernandes, and Helen Devine.

Thanks to the many funders and program officers who supported this work, including Steve Breckler at the National Science Foundation; Virginia Cooper at Templeton; and especially Hussein Hussein, Nicole Gordon, Nik Walker, and Branden Polk at Stand Together, who helped me create the Center for the Science of Moral Understanding. And thanks to all the affiliates of the center who helped to make it a vibrant place for research and ideas.

Thanks to everyone at the New Pluralists and many practitioner organizations for helping to support this work and make it matter for the real world. At New Pluralists: Lauren Higgins, Uma Viswanathan, and Alison Grubbs. At One America Movement: Sarah Beckerman, Rachel Schmelkin, and Chandra Whetstine. At More in Common: Julia Coffin. At Beyond Conflict: Jasmine Ramsey. At Over Zero: Laura Livingston. At Greater Good Science Center: Jason Marsh. At The Village Square: Liz Joyner.

Thanks to my colleagues in UNC Social Psych for their camaraderie: Keith Payne, Keely Muscatell, Paschal Sheeran, Barb Frederickson, Sara Algoe, and Julian Rucker.

Thanks to the folks at Ohio State, especially Gifford Weary, Duane Wegener, Russ Fazio, Rich Petty, Lisa Libby, Steve Spencer, Dylan Wagner, Ken Fujita, and Baldwin Way for creating a welcoming department and for an amazing opportunity to expand the impact of these ideas.

Thanks to all the friends for their support through chaos. At Carolina: Mike Christian, Jess Christian, Alex Miller, Jillian Dempsey, Jonah Berger, Jordan Etkin, Steve Buzinski and Kym Weed, Dave Rose, Adrian Bischoff and Margaret Sheridan, Jason and Rebecca Goldsmith, and David and Shannon English. Grad school and before: Karim Kassam, Carey Morewedge, Ryan Darrach, Modupe Akinola, Adam Waytz, and Kevin Lewis (whose close reading of the manuscript caught tons of typos).

Thanks to the many amazing undergrad research assistants and students in my classes, including Peyton Miyares and Belinda Woodard, for giving me hope for the future.

Thanks to Dan Wegner, for teaching me how to think and write, and to Lisa Barrett and Nick Epley for continued mentorship.

Thanks to my parents and family for your love: Ann and Phil Clarke,

Mark and Louise Gray, Sue and Steve Lindquist, and Kim Lindquist and Joe Caprio.

Thanks to my two incredible kids, Iris and Ida, for keeping daily life interesting and full of love.

And of course, thanks to my amazing wife, Kristen Lindquist, for being the best partner I could imagine. I'm so glad we sat next to each other on that plane from Memphis.

Notes

INTRODUCTION: Swerve: The Power of Harm

1. YouGov, "Have You Lost Any Friendships Because of Differences in Opinion Related to the COVID-19 Pandemic?"
2. Binder, *Polarized We Govern?*, "Political Opponents Accept Blatant Moral Wrongs, Fueling Partisan Divides."
3. Reilly, "Read Hillary Clinton's 'Basket of Deplorables' Remarks About Donald Trump Supporters."
4. Manchester, "Conservative Writer Calls Democratic Party an 'Evil Institution.'"
5. Puryear et al., "People Believe Political Opponents Accept Blatant Moral Wrongs, Fueling Partisan Divides."
6. Schein and Gray, "Theory of Dyadic Morality."
7. Jones et al., "Exposure to Descriptions of Traumatic Events Narrows One's Concept of Trauma."

Chapter 1: WAR: IS UNDERSTANDING BETRAYAL?

1. *The Matt Walsh Show*, March 7, 2023, https://www.mediamatters.org/media/4001834.
2. Ali, W. August 4, 2022. "If Dems Fought an All-Out Culture War, They'd Win." Daily Beast. https://www.thedailybeast.com/if-democrats-fought-an-all-out-culture-war-against-republicans-theyd-win.
3. Puryear et al., "People Believe Political Opponents Accept Blatant Moral Wrongs, Fueling Partisan Divides."
4. Williamson, "Christmas Truce."
5. Weintraub, *Silent Night*.
6. ANES, "Independent Analysis of American National Election Survey."

7. Hartman, Hester, and Gray, "People See Political Opponents as More Stupid Than Evil."

8. Ibid.

9. Kemmelmeier, "Is There a Relationship Between Political Orientation and Cognitive Ability?"

10. Woessner, Maranto, and Thompson, "Is Collegiate Political Correctness Fake News?"

11. Carl, "Cognitive Ability and Political Beliefs in the United States."

12. Ibid.; Jedinger and Burger, "Do Smarter People Have More Conservative Economic Attitudes?"

13. Kahan, Peters, Dawson, and Slovic, "Motivated Numeracy and Enlightened Self-Government."

14. Puryear et al., "People Believe Political Opponents Accept Blatant Moral Wrongs, Fueling Partisan Divides."

15. Goya-Tocchetto et al., "Partisan Trade-Off Bias."

16. Amira, Wright, and Goya-Tocchetto, "In-Group Love Versus Out-Group Hate."

17. Womick and King, "Right-Wing Authoritarianism and Anti-Asian Prejudice in Response to the COVID-19 Pandemic in the United States."

18. Waytz, Young, and Ginges, "Motive Attribution Asymmetry for Love vs. Hate Drives Intractable Conflict."

19. Pasek et al., "Misperceptions About Out-Partisans' Democratic Values May Erode Democracy."

20. Ramos Salazar, "Negative Reciprocity Process in Marital Relationships."

21. Ripley, *High Conflict.*

22. Yourish et al., "Inside the Apocalyptic Worldview of 'Tucker Carlson Tonight.'"

23. Berry and Sobieraj, *Outrage Industry.*

24. Sobieraj and Berry, "From Incivility to Outrage."

25. Moore-Berg et al., "Exaggerated Meta-perceptions Predict Intergroup Hostility Between American Political Partisans."

26. Landry et al., "Reducing Explicit Blatant Dehumanization by Correcting Exaggerated Meta-perceptions."

27. Ahler and Sood, "Parties in Our Heads."

28. *Toward a More Responsible Two-Party System.*

29. Kalmoe and Mason, "Lethal Mass Partisanship."

30. Pasek et al., "Misperceptions About Out-Partisans' Democratic Values May Erode Democracy."

31. Davis, "Why I, as a Black Man, Attend KKK Rallies."

32. Broockman and Kalla, "Durably Reducing Transphobia."

33. Strohminger, Knobe, and Newman, "True Self."

MYTH 1: The Myth of Human Nature

1. Henrich and Muthukrishna, "What Makes Us Smart?"
2. Abramson, "Our Brains Are Stuck in the Stone Age."
3. World Health Organization, *Obesity and Overweight.*
4. Stiner, Barkai, and Gopher, "Cooperative Hunting and Meat Sharing 400–200 Kya at Qesem Cave, Israel."
5. Darwin, *Narrative of the Surveying Voyages of His Majesty's Ships* Adventure *and* Beagle.
6. Gayley, "Compassionate Treatment of Animals."
7. Ben-Dor, Sirtoli, and Barkai, "Evolution of the Human Trophic Level During the Pleistocene"; Roopnarine, "Humans Are Apex Predators"; Suraci et al., "Fear of Humans as Apex Predators Has Landscape-Scale Impacts from Mountain Lions to Mice."
8. Young, "Evolution of the Human Hand."
9. Lieberman, *Exercised.*
10. Wrangham, *Catching Fire.*
11. Brink, *Imagining Head-Smashed-In.*
12. Harari, *Sapiens.*
13. Dart, *Adventures with the Missing Link.*
14. Dart, *"Australopithecus africanus."*
15. Garwin and Lincoln, *Century of "Nature."*
16. Tennyson, *In Memoriam A. H. H.*
17. Freud, *Civilization and Its Discontents.*
18. Wrangham, "Two Types of Aggression in Human Evolution."

Chapter 2: PREY: THE NEW HUMAN NATURE

1. Ruark, *Horn of the Hunter.*
2. Ritchie, "Did Humans Cause the Quaternary Megafauna Extinction?"
3. Roach et al., "Elastic Energy Storage in the Shoulder and the Evolution of High-Speed Throwing in Homo."
4. Harcourt-Smith, "First Hominins and the Origins of Bipedalism."
5. Hart and Sussman, *Man the Hunted.*
6. Wilkins et al., "Evidence for Early Hafted Hunting Technology."
7. Henrich, *Secret of Our Success.*
8. Falk, *Primate Diversity.*
9. Jordania, *Why Do People Sing?*
10. Lovejoy, "Evolution of Human Walking."
11. Lieberman, *Exercised.*

12. Morin and Winterhalder, "Ethnography and Ethnohistory Support the Efficiency of Hunting Through Endurance Running in Humans."
13. Pattison, "Born to Run?"
14. Ibid.
15. Liebenberg, "Persistence Hunting by Modern Hunter-Gatherers."
16. Pickering and Bunn, "Endurance Running Hypothesis and Hunting and Scavenging in Savanna-Woodlands."
17. Boaz et al., "Large Mammalian Carnivores as a Taphonomic Factor in the Bone Accumulation at Zhoukoudian."
18. Hart and Sussman, *Man the Hunted*.
19. Evans et al., "Microcephalin, a Gene Regulating Brain Size, Continues to Evolve Adaptively in Humans."
20. Goodall, "Infant Killing and Cannibalism in Free-Living Chimpanzees."
21. Tutin, McGrew, and Baldwin, "Social Organization of Savanna-Dwelling Chimpanzees, *Pan troglodytes verus,* at Mt. Assirik, Senegal."
22. Tsukahara, "Lions Eat Chimpanzees."
23. Hart, "Primates as Prey."
24. Martins and Harris, "Movement, Activity, and Hunting Behaviour of Leopards in the Cederberg Mountains, South Africa."
25. Nakazawa et al., "Leopard Ate a Chimpanzee."
26. Dart, "*A Note on the Taungs Skull.*"
27. Brown, *Eagles of the World*.
28. Berger and Clarke, "Eagle Involvement in Accumulation of the Taung Child Fauna"; Berger and McGraw, "Further Evidence for Eagle Predation of, and Feeding Damage on, the Taung Child."
29. Gabunia et al., "Dmanisi and Dispersal."
30. Hart and Sussman, *Man the Hunted*.

Chapter 3: SOCIAL: THE RISE OF MORALITY

1. Stevens et al., "Motion Dazzle and Camouflage as Distinct Anti-predator Defenses."
2. De Vos and O'Riain, "Sharks Shape the Geometry of a Selfish Seal Herd."
3. Maynard Smith and Harper, *Animal Signals*.
4. Henrich, *Secret of Our Success*.
5. Timmermann, "Quantifying the Potential Causes of Neanderthal Extinction."
6. Henrich, *Secret of Our Success;* Norenzayan et al., "Cultural Evolution of Prosocial Religions."
7. van der Bijl and Kolm, "Why Direct Effects of Predation Complicate the Social Brain Hypothesis."

8. Seidensticker and Lumpkin, *Great Cats.*
9. Dunbar, "Social Brain Hypothesis and Its Implications for Social Evolution."
10. Ringelmann, "Recherches sur les moteurs animés."
11. Endicott, "Peaceful Foragers."
12. Pinker, *Better Angels of Our Nature.*
13. Ferguson, "Pinker's List."
14. Gómez et al., "Phylogenetic Roots of Human Lethal Violence."
15. Everett, *Don't Sleep, There Are Snakes.*
16. Ibid.
17. Alfano, Cheong, and Curry, "Moral Universals."
18. Fukuyama, *Trust.*
19. Lieberman and Smith, "It's All Relative."
20. Alvarez, Ceballos, and Quinteiro, "Role of Inbreeding in the Extinction of a European Royal Dynasty."
21. Daly and Wilson, "Some Differential Attributes of Lethal Assaults on Small Children by Stepfathers Versus Genetic Fathers."
22. Curtis, *Habsburgs.*
23. Vilas et al., "Is the 'Habsburg Jaw' Related to Inbreeding?"
24. Alvarez, Ceballos, and Quinteiro, "Role of Inbreeding in the Extinction of a European Royal Dynasty."
25. Alshaikhli, Killeen, and Rokkam, "Hemophilia B"; Rogaev et al., "Genotype Analysis Identifies the Cause of the 'Royal Disease.'"
26. Haidt and Joseph, "Intuitive Ethics."
27. Curry, "Morality as Cooperation."
28. Janoff-Bulman, Sheikh, and Baldacci, "Mapping Moral Motives."
29. Gelfand et al., "Differences Between Tight and Loose Cultures."
30. Matsumura, "Moral Economy as Emotional Interaction."
31. Podolefsky, "Contemporary Warfare in the New Guinea Highlands."
32. Fiske and Rai, *Virtuous Violence.*
33. Nisbett and Cohen, *Culture of Honor.*
34. Meyer, *Highland Scots of North Carolina.*
35. McCorkle, "Personal Precautions to Violence in Prison."
36. Gambetta, *Codes of the Underworld.*
37. Fehr and Gächter, "Altruistic Punishment in Humans."
38. Ibid.
39. Uehara et al., "Fate of Defeated Alpha Male Chimpanzees in Relation to Their Social Networks"; Whyte, "Chimps Beat Up, Murder, and Then Cannibalise Their Former Tyrant."
40. Boehm, *Hierarchy in the Forest.*

Chapter 4: DANGEROUS: IGNORING OUR OBVIOUS SAFETY

1. Ronson, "How One Stupid Tweet Blew Up Justine Sacco's Life."
2. Wessels, *Myth of Progress.*
3. Acemoglu and Restrepo, "Tasks, Automation, and the Rise in U.S. Wage Inequality."
4. Everett, *Don't Sleep, There Are Snakes.*
5. David, *Fashion Victims.*
6. Crowley, Smyth, and Murphy, "Emigration to North America in the Era of the Great Famine," 214.
7. World Meteorological Organization, "Weather-Related Disasters Increase over Past 50 Years, Causing More Damage but Fewer Deaths."
8. Skenazy, "Suburban Mom Handcuffed, Jailed for Making 8-Year-Old Son Walk Half a Mile Home."
9. Campbell and Manning, *Rise of Victimhood Culture;* Lukianoff and Haidt, *Coddling of the American Mind;* Twenge, *iGen.*
10. CDC, "Youth Risk Behavior Survey Data Summary & Trends Report: 2011–2021."
11. McGrath and Haslam, "Development and Validation of the Harm Concept Breadth Scale."
12. Katz, "Poor Haitians on a Mud Diet."
13. Yiend and Mathews, "Anxiety and Attention to Threatening Pictures."
14. Adams and Kleck, "Perceived Gaze Direction and the Processing of Facial Displays of Emotion."
15. Adams et al., "Effects of Gaze on Amygdala Sensitivity to Anger and Fear Faces."
16. Gómez et al., "Phylogenetic Roots of Human Lethal Violence."
17. "50 of the Most Dangerous Cities in the World," *USA Today.*
18. Brenan, "Worry About Crime in U.S. at Highest Level Since 2016."
19. Levari et al., "Prevalence-Induced Concept Change in Human Judgment."
20. Jones et al., "Exposure to Descriptions of Traumatic Events Narrows One's Concept of Trauma."
21. Jones and McNally, "Does Broadening One's Concept of Trauma Undermine Resilience?"
22. Jones, "Neurotic Treadmill."
23. Dückers, Alisic, and Brewin, "Vulnerability Paradox in the Cross-National Prevalence of Post-traumatic Stress Disorder."
24. McNally, "Expanding Empire of Psychopathology."
25. Mastroianni and Gilbert, "Illusion of Moral Decline."
26. Yuan et al., "Did Cooperation Among Strangers Decline in the United States?"

27. Singer, *Animal Liberation.*

28. "Prozac for Puppy?," ABC News.

29. Turner, "Year of Outrage."

30. Friedersdorf, "Reflections on a Year of Outrage."

31. Ellison et al., "Anonymity and Aggressive Driving Behavior."

32. Brady et al., "Emotion Shapes the Diffusion of Moralized Content in Social Networks."

33. Grubbs et al., "Moral Grandstanding in Public Discourse."

34. Lin et al., "Association Between Social Media Use and Depression Among U.S. Young Adults."

35. Schwartz, "Dungeons & Dragons Prison Ban Upheld."

36. Puryear, Vandello, and Gray, "Moral Panics on Social Media Are Fueled by Signals of Virality."

MYTH 2:   The Myth of the Moral Mind

1. Haidt, Bjorklund, and Murphy, "Moral Dumbfounding."

2. Royzman, Kim, and Leeman, "Curious Tale of Julie and Mark."

3. Ibid.

4. Stanley, Yin, and Sinnott-Armstrong, "Reason-Based Explanation for Moral Dumbfounding."

5. Haslam, "Concept Creep."

Chapter 5: LEGACY: A RECENT HISTORY OF HARM

1. Hamlin, Wynn, and Bloom, "Social Evaluation by Preverbal Infants."

2. Turiel, *Development of Social Knowledge.*

3. Henrich, Heine, and Norenzayan, "Weirdest People in the World?"

4. Shweder, Mahapatra, and Miller, "Culture and Moral Development."

5. Carter, "7 Reasons No One Does Funerals Like the South."

6. Shweder, "Relativism and Universalism."

7. Shweder et al., "'Big Three' of Morality (Autonomy, Community, Divinity) and the 'Big Three' Explanations of Suffering."

8. Shweder, "Psychology of Practice and the Practice of the Three Psychologies."

9. Turiel, Killen, and Helwig, "Morality."

10. Turiel, *Development of Social Knowledge.*

11. Shweder et al., "'Big Three' of Morality (Autonomy, Community, Divinity) and the 'Big Three' Explanations of Suffering."

12. Haidt and Joseph, "Intuitive Ethics."

13. Haidt, *The Righteous Mind.*
14. Barrett and Satpute, "Large-Scale Brain Networks in Affective and Social Neuroscience."
15. Cushman and Young, "Patterns of Moral Judgment Derive from Nonmoral Psychological Representations."
16. Graham et al., "Mapping the Moral Domain."
17. Ibid.
18. Haidt, "Emotional Dog and Its Rational Tail."

Chapter 6: INTUITIVE: THE NEW HARM

1. Shweder, "Relativism and Universalism."
2. Gendler, "Alief and Belief."
3. Cushman et al., "Simulating Murder."
4. Barnes-Holmes et al., "Using the Implicit Association Test and the Implicit Relational Assessment Procedure to Measure Attitudes Toward Meat and Vegetables in Vegetarians and Meat-Eaters"; Ordóñez and Benson, "Decisions Under Time Pressure"; Rand et al., "Social Heuristics Shape Intuitive Cooperation."
5. Gray, Schein, and Ward, "Myth of Harmless Wrongs in Moral Cognition."
6. Ibid.
7. Schein, Ritter, and Gray, "Harm Mediates the Disgust-Immorality Link."
8. Gray and Schein, "The Myth of the Harmless Wrong."
9. Bryant, *Anita Bryant Story.*
10. Uhlmann and Zhu, "Acts, Persons, and Intuitions."
11. Royzman, Kim, and Leeman, "Curious Tale of Julie and Mark."
12. Chakroff et al., "From Impure to Harmful"; DeScioli, Gilbert, and Kurzban, "Indelible Victims and Persistent Punishers in Moral Cognition"; Stanley, Yin, and Sinnott-Armstrong, "Reason-Based Explanation for Moral Dumbfounding."
13. Graham et al., "Moral Foundations Theory."
14. Rottman, Young, and Kelemen, "Impact of Testimony on Children's Moralization of Novel Actions."
15. Ochoa, "Template Matching and Moral Judgment."
16. Dalin-Kaptzan, "Most Punctual Countries in the (On-Demand) World."
17. Gelfand et al., "Differences Between Tight and Loose Cultures."
18. Hirota, Nakashima, and Tsutsui, "Psychological Motivations for Collectivist Behavior"; Takamatsu et al., "Moralization of Japanese Cultural Norms Among Student Sojourners in Japan"; Zhai, "Values of Deference to Authority in Japan and China."

Chapter 7: VULNERABILITY: EXPLAINING POLITICAL DIFFERENCES

1. Gray, *Men Are from Mars, Women Are from Venus.*
2. Mehl et al., "Are Women Really More Talkative Than Men?"
3. Meterko and Cooper, "Cognitive Biases in Criminal Case Evaluation."
4. Hergovich, Schott, and Burger, "Biased Evaluation of Abstracts Depending on Topic and Conclusion."
5. Haidt, *Righteous Mind.*
6. 2004 Republican Party Platform: A Safer World and a More Hopeful America.
7. Frankovic, "Americans Are Patriotic—but Differ on What That Means."
8. Pew Research Center, "Party Identification Among Religious Groups and Religiously Unaffiliated Voters."
9. Frimer, Tell, and Motyl, "Sacralizing Liberals and Fair-Minded Conservatives."
10. Frimer, Tell, and Haidt, "Liberals Condemn Sacrilege Too."
11. Harrington, "Liberals More Likely to Cry Than Conservatives."
12. Ochoa, "Template Matching and Moral Judgment."
13. Chalmers, "Consciousness and Its Place in Nature."
14. Hastorf and Cantril, "They Saw a Game."
15. Caplan, McCartney, and Sisti, *Health, Disease, and Illness.*
16. Guillory, "Pro-slavery Arguments of Dr. Samuel A. Cartwright."
17. Douglass, "What to the Slave Is the Fourth of July?"
18. Descartes, "Animals Are Machines."
19. Gray, Gray, and Wegner, "Dimensions of Mind Perception."
20. Lovejoy, *Great Chain of Being.*
21. Dennett, *Kinds of Minds.*
22. Govrin, *Ethics and Attachment.*
23. O'Toole, "3-Year-Old Taken to Syracuse Hospital After She Eats Marijuana Candy."
24. Womick et al., "Moral Disagreement Across Politics Is Explained by Different Assumptions About Who Is Most Vulnerable to Harm."
25. Ibid.
26. Harris et al., "Global Maps of Twenty-First Century Forest Carbon Fluxes"; "Rainforest," *National Geographic.*
27. Hughes et al., "Global Warming and Recurrent Mass Bleaching of Corals."
28. Pew Research Center, "As Economic Concerns Recede, Environmental Protection Rises on the Public's Policy Agenda."
29. Joselow and Sotomayor, "House GOP Passes Energy Package with Eye on Gas Prices, 2024."
30. Denning, "Drilling for Oil on the Moon."
31. Gashaw, "In God We Trust."
32. Fahmy, "Key Findings About Americans' Belief in God."

33. Weinandy, *Does God Suffer?*
34. Rooney, "Suffering and the Teachings of Jesus Christ."
35. Gray, Schein, and Ward, "Myth of Harmless Wrongs in Moral Cognition."
36. Smith, "Just One-Third of U.S. Catholics Agree with Their Church That Eucharist Is Body, Blood of Christ."
37. Cowen, *Big Business.*
38. "In Their Own Words, Owners Explain How Tax Increases Would Harm Their Businesses."
39. Pierson et al., "Large-Scale Analysis of Racial Disparities in Police Stops Across the United States."
40. Mapping Police Violence, *2023 Police Violence Report.*
41. Federal Bureau of Investigation Crime Data Explorer.
42. Thune, "Demonizing and Defunding Police Has Consequences."
43. Jost, "Quarter Century of System Justification Theory."
44. Beauvoir, *Second Sex.*
45. Ordoñez, "What a Second-Term Trump Immigration Agenda Might Look Like."
46. Wellons, "Affirmative Action Is Still an Effective and Necessary Tool."
47. Dirks, "Affirmative Action Divided Asian Americans and Other People of Color."
48. Hughes, "10 Notes on the End of Affirmative Action."
49. Guzman and Kollar, *Income in the United States.*
50. Fryer, "Empirical Analysis of Racial Differences in Police Use of Force."
51. Lemieux, "Is Being a Cop So Dangerous?"
52. Marx and Engels, *Communist Manifesto.*
53. King, "Letter from Birmingham Jail."
54. Locke, *Second Treatise of Government.*
55. Ingraham, "Laura Ingraham: 'Because You're a Minority, You Get Special Standards, Special Treatment.'"
56. Continetti, "Battle of Woke Island."
57. Kendi, *How to Be an Antiracist.*

Chapter 8: BLAME: MORAL TYPECASTING

1. Diver, "Journal Reveals Hitler's Dysfunctional Family."
2. Larson, "Canyon of Secrets"; Monacelli, "Why Did Cody Posey Kill His Family?"
3. Sousa et al., "Longitudinal Study on the Effects of Child Abuse and Children's Exposure to Domestic Violence, Parent-Child Attachments, and Antisocial Behavior in Adolescence."
4. Godwin, "Meme, Counter-meme."

5. Perry and Grubbs, "How Americans Polarize Around Historical Figures."

6. Steele, "Moral Typecasting Explains Evaluations of Undocumented Immigrants."

7. Ibid.

8. Dennett, *Kinds of Minds*.

9. Gray and Wegner, "Moral Typecasting."

10. Garra et al., "Validation of the Wong-Baker FACES Pain Rating Scale in Pediatric Emergency Department Patients."

11. Spence, *Win Your Case*, 162.

12. Gray and Wegner, "To Escape Blame, Don't Be a Hero—Be a Victim."

13. Konnikova, *Confidence Game*.

14. Murphy, "At 71, She's Never Felt Pain or Anxiety."

15. Lerner, *Belief in a Just World*.

16. Brown, "Women's Narratives of Trauma: (Re)storying. Uncertainty, Minimization and Self-Blame."

17. Domestic Violence Hotline, "Domestic Violence Statistics."

18. Reynolds et al., "Man Up and Take It."

19. Zenovich, "Fantastic Lies."

20. Lisak et al., "False Allegations of Sexual Assault."

21. Levi, *The Drowned and the Saved*.

22. Klein, "Primo Levi."

Chapter 9: SUFFERING: SELF-FOCUSED VICTIMHOOD

1. "Putin Compared the Attack on Russian Culture in the West with the Events in Hitler's Germany."

2. Descartes, *Meditations on First Philosophy with Selections from the Objections and Replies*.

3. Ibid.

4. Piaget and Inhelder, *Psychology of the Child*.

5. Keysar et al., "Taking Perspective in Conversation."

6. Keysar, Lin, and Barr, "Limits on Theory of Mind Use in Adults."

7. Calvin, *Commentaries on the Book of the Prophet Jeremiah and the Lamentations*.

8. Epley et al., "Believers' Estimates of God's Beliefs Are More Egocentric Than Estimates of Other People's Beliefs."

9. Guo, "CNN Cut Ties with Reza Aslan for Calling Trump a 'Piece of Shit.'"

10. Hippel and Hoeppner, "Biased Judgements of Fairness in Bargaining"; Komlik, "Egocentric Perceptions and Self-Serving Bias in Negotiations."

11. Babcock et al., "Biased Judgments of Fairness in Bargaining."

12. Wall, *Pain*.

13. Baumeister et al., "Bad Is Stronger Than Good."

14. Price, Von der Gruen, Miller, Rafii, and Price, "A Psychophysical Analysis of Morphine Analgesia."

15. Moore, Keogh, and Eccleston, "The Interruptive Effect of Pain on Attention."

16. Goggins, *Can't Hurt Me.*

17. Lim and DeSteno, "Suffering and Compassion."

18. Ibid.

19. Lee and Ma, "Pain Sensitivity Predicts Support for Moral and Political Views Across the Aisle."

20. Zitek et al., "Victim Entitlement to Behave Selfishly."

21. Gray, Ward, and Norton, "Paying It Forward."

22. Kilpatrick, *Mental Health Impact of Rape.*

23. Winter, *Cambridge History of the First World War,* vol. 1, *Global War.*

24. Gabay et al., "Tendency for Interpersonal Victimhood."

25. Ibid.

26. Moore, Keogh, and Eccleston, "The Interruptive Effect of Pain on Attention."

27. McCullough et al., "Narcissists as 'Victims.'"

28. Määttä, Uusiautti, and Määttä, "Intimate Relationship in the Shadow of Narcissism."

29. Harsey, Zurbriggen, and Freyd, "Perpetrator Responses to Victim Confrontation."

30. Noor et al., "When Suffering Begets Suffering."

31. Vallone, Ross, and Lepper, "Hostile Media Phenomenon."

32. Vollhardt, "Role of Victim Beliefs in the Israeli-Palestinian Conflict."

33. Burkhardt-Vetter, "Reconciliation in the Making."

34. Vollhardt and Bilali, "Role of Inclusive and Exclusive Victim Consciousness in Predicting Intergroup Attitudes."

35. Brewer and Hayes, "Victimhood Status and Public Attitudes Towards Post-conflict Agreements"; Noor et al., "On Positive Psychological Outcomes."

36. Rupar et al., "General Inclusive Victimhood Predicts Willingness to Engage in Intergroup Contact."

37. Noor et al., "On Positive Psychological Outcomes."

38. Rupar et al., "General Inclusive Victimhood Predicts Willingness to Engage in Intergroup Contact."

39. Demirel and Eriksson, "Competitive Victimhood and Reconciliation"; Uluğ et al., "How Do Conflict Narratives Shape Conflict- and Peace-Related Outcomes Among Majority Group Members?"

40. Gray and Kubin, "Victimhood: The Most Powerful Force in Morality and Politics."

41. Danbold, Onyeador, and Unzueta, "Dominant Groups Support Digressive Victimhood Claims to Counter Accusations of Discrimination."

42. Aquino and Bradfield, "Perceived Victimization in the Workplace"; Jockin, Arvey, and McGue, "Perceived Victimization Moderates Self-Reports of Workplace Aggression and Conflict"; Mackey et al., "Victim and Culprit?"

43. Bischoff (@EBischoff), "Beginning to see a pattern."

MYTH 3: The Myth of Bridging Divides

1. Vernon, "Science in the Post-Truth Era."

2. Agresti, Smith, and Reynolds, "Gun Control Facts."

3. Ibid.

Chapter 10: UNDERSTANDING: TELLING STORIES OF HARM

1. Frimer and Skitka, "Are Politically Diverse Thanksgiving Dinners Shorter Than Politically Uniform Ones?"

2. McCoy and Press, *What Happens When Democracies Become Perniciously Polarized?*

3. Patel, "America's Hidden Strength."

4. Bucyana, "Rwanda Genocide."

5. Haslam, "Dehumanization."

6. Wang, "At These Hot New York Restaurants, Eating with Your Hands Is the Point."

7. Rook, "Art of Eating."

8. Martherus et al., "Party Animals?"

9. Petsko and Kteily, "Political (Meta-)Dehumanization in Mental Representations."

10. Aristotle, *Nicomachean Ethics.*

11. Darwin, *Origin of Species.*

12. Gottschall, *Storytelling Animal.*

13. Haven, *Story Proof.*

14. Corbett, *Art of Character.*

15. Kubin et al., "Personal Experiences Bridge Moral and Political Divides Better Than Facts."

16. Leucht et al., "How Effective Are Common Medications."

17. Steering Committee of the Physicians' Health Study Research Group, "Final Report on the Aspirin Component of the Ongoing Physicians' Health Study."

18. Klein et al., "Many Labs 2."

19. Kubin, Gray, and von Sikorski, "Reducing Political Dehumanization by Pairing Facts with Personal Experiences."

20. Appel, "Affective Resistance to Narrative Persuasion."

21. Hussein and Tormala, "Undermining Your Case to Enhance Your Impact."

Chapter 11: HOPE: OPENING UP

1. Newman, Donohue, and Eva, "Psychological Safety."
2. Epley and Schroeder, "Mistakenly Seeking Solitude."
3. Balietti et al., "Reducing Opinion Polarization."
4. Huang et al., "It Doesn't Hurt to Ask."
5. Kardas, Kumar, and Epley, "Overly Shallow?"
6. Rossiter, "Similar and Distinct Effects of Political and Non-political Conversation on Affective Polarization."
7. Santoro and Broockman, "Promise and Pitfalls of Cross-Partisan Conversations for Reducing Affective Polarization."
8. Marcinkowski and Došenović, "From Incidental Exposure to Intentional Avoidance."
9. Foss and Griffin, "Beyond Persuasion."
10. Argyle et al., "Leveraging AI for Democratic Discourse."

Bibliography

ABC News. "Prozac for Puppy? More American Pets Are Prescribed Psychiatric Drugs." ABC News, Feb. 6, 2012.

Abramson, Ashley. "Our Brains Are Stuck in the Stone Age." *Elemental,* Feb. 5, 2020. elemental.medium.com.

Acemoglu, Daron, and Pascual Restrepo. "Tasks, Automation, and the Rise in U.S. Wage Inequality." *Econometrica* 90, no. 5 (2022): 1973–2016. doi:10.3982 /ECTA19815.

Adams, Reginald B., Heather L. Gordon, Abigail A. Baird, Nalini Ambady, and Robert E. Kleck. "Effects of Gaze on Amygdala Sensitivity to Anger and Fear Faces." *Science* 300, no. 5625 (2003): 1536. doi:10.1126/science.1082244.

Adams, Reginald B., and Robert E. Kleck. "Perceived Gaze Direction and the Processing of Facial Displays of Emotion." *Psychological Science* 14, no. 6 (2003): 644–47. doi:10.1046/j.0956-7976.2003.psci_1479.x.

Agresti, James D., Reid K. Smith, and William T. Reynolds. "Gun Control Facts." Just Facts, Nov. 15, 2023. www.justfacts.com.

Ahler, Douglas J., and Gaurav Sood. "The Parties in Our Heads: Misperceptions About Party Composition and Their Consequences." *Journal of Politics* 80, no. 3 (2018): 964–81. doi:10.1086/697253.

Alfano, Mark, Marc Cheong, and Oliver Scott Curry. "Moral Universals: A Machine-Reading Analysis of 256 Societies." *Heliyon* 10, no. 6 (2024): e25940. doi:10.1016/j.heliyon.2024.e25940.

Alshaikhli, Alfarooq, Robert B. Killeen, and Venkata R. Rokkam. "Hemophilia B." StatPearls, Oct. 29, 2023. www.ncbi.nlm.nih.gov.

Alvarez, Gonzalo, Francisco C. Ceballos, and Celsa Quinteiro. "The Role of Inbreeding in the Extinction of a European Royal Dynasty." Edited by Marc Bauchet. *PLoS ONE* 4, no. 4 (2009): e5174. doi:10.1371/journal.pone.0005174.

Amira, Karyn, Jennifer Cole Wright, and Daniela Goya-Tocchetto. "In-Group Love

Versus Out-Group Hate: Which Is More Important to Partisans and When?" *Political Behavior* 43, no. 2 (2021): 473–94. doi:10.1007/s11109-019-09557-6.

ANES. "Independent Analysis of American National Election Survey." Accessed July 20, 2023. electionstudies.org.

Appel, Markus. "Affective Resistance to Narrative Persuasion." *Journal of Business Research* 149 (2022): 850–59. doi:10.1016/j.jbusres.2022.05.001.

Aquino, Karl, and Murray Bradfield. "Perceived Victimization in the Workplace: The Role of Situational Factors and Victim Characteristics." *Organization Science* 11, no. 5 (2000): 525–37. doi:10.1287/orsc.11.5.525.15205.

Argyle, Lisa P., Christopher A. Bail, Ethan C. Busby, Joshua R. Gubler, Thomas Howe, Christopher Rytting, et al. "Leveraging AI for Democratic Discourse: Chat Interventions Can Improve Online Political Conversations at Scale." *Proceedings of the National Academy of Sciences* 120, no. 41 (2023): e2311627120. doi:10.1073/pnas.2311627120.

Aristotle. *Nicomachean Ethics.* Translated by W. D. Ross. Lexington, Ky.: World Library Classics, 2009.

Babcock, Linda, George Loewenstein, Samuel Issacharoff, and Colin Camerer. "Biased Judgments of Fairness in Bargaining." *American Economic Review* 85, no. 5 (1995): 1337–43.

Balietti, Stefano, Lise Getoor, Daniel G. Goldstein, and Duncan J. Watts. "Reducing Opinion Polarization: Effects of Exposure to Similar People with Differing Political Views." *Proceedings of the National Academy of Sciences* 118, no. 52 (2021): e2112552118. doi:10.1073/pnas.2112552118.

Barnes-Holmes, Dermot, Louise Murtagh, Yvonne Barnes-Holmes, and Ian Stewart. "Using the Implicit Association Test and the Implicit Relational Assessment Procedure to Measure Attitudes Toward Meat and Vegetables in Vegetarians and Meat-Eaters." *Psychological Record* 60, no. 2 (2010): 287–305. doi:10.1007/BF03395708.

Barrett, Lisa Feldman, and Ajay Bhaskar Satpute. "Large-Scale Brain Networks in Affective and Social Neuroscience: Towards an Integrative Functional Architecture of the Brain." *Current Opinion in Neurobiology* 23, no. 3 (2013): 361–72.

Baumeister, Roy F., Ellen Bratslavsky, Catrin Finkenauer, and Kathleen D. Vohs. "Bad Is Stronger Than Good." *Review of General Psychology* 5, no. 4 (2001): 323–70. doi:10.1037/1089-2680.5.4.323.

Baumeister, Roy F., and Mark R. Leary. "The Need to Belong: Desire for Interpersonal Attachments as a Fundamental Human Motivation." *Psychological Bulletin* 117, no. 3 (1995), 497–529. https://doi.org/10.1037/0033-2909.117.3.497.

Beauvoir, Simone de. *The Second Sex.* New York: Vintage Books, 1989.

Ben-Dor, Miki, Raphael Sirtoli, and Ran Barkai. "The Evolution of the Human Trophic Level During the Pleistocene." *American Journal of Physical Anthropology* 175, no. S72 (2021): 27–56. doi:10.1002/ajpa.24247.

Berger, L. R., and R. J. Clarke. "Eagle Involvement in Accumulation of the Taung Child Fauna." *Journal of Human Evolution* 29, no. 3 (1995): 275–99. doi:10.1006/jhev.1995.1060.

Berger, L. R., and W. S. McGraw. "Further Evidence for Eagle Predation of, and Feeding Damage on, the Taung Child." *South African Journal of Science* 103, no. 11–12 (2007): 496–98.

Berry, Jeffrey M., and Sarah Sobieraj. *The Outrage Industry: Political Opinion Media and the New Incivility.* Reprint, Oxford: Oxford University Press, 2016.

Binder, Sarah A. *Polarized We Govern?* Center for Effective Public Management, Brookings, May 27, 2014. www.brookings.edu.

Bischoff, Eric (@EBischoff). "Beginning to see a pattern. Social media is where people compete in the victim olympics. There's a division for everyone." Twitter, July 21, 2020, 8:52 p.m. twitter.com/EBischoff/status/12857393805194 40386?s=20.

Boaz, Noel, Russell Ciochon, Xu Qinqi, and Jinyi Liu. "Large Mammalian Carnivores as a Taphonomic Factor in the Bone Accumulation at Zhoukoudian." *Acta Anthropologica Sinica* 19 (2000).

Boehm, Christopher. *Hierarchy in the Forest: The Evolution of Egalitarian Behavior.* Cambridge, Mass.: Harvard University Press, 2001.

Brady, William J., Julian A. Wills, John T. Jost, Joshua A. Tucker, and Jay J. Van Bavel. "Emotion Shapes the Diffusion of Moralized Content in Social Networks." *Proceedings of the National Academy of Sciences* 114, no. 28 (2017): 7313–18. doi:10.1073/pnas.1618923114.

Brenan, Megan. "Worry About Crime in U.S. at Highest Level Since 2016." Gallup, April 7, 2022. news.gallup.com.

Brewer, John D., and Bernadette C. Hayes. "Victimhood Status and Public Attitudes Towards Post-conflict Agreements: Northern Ireland as a Case Study." *Political Studies* 61, no. 2 (2013): 442–61. doi:10.1111/j.1467-9248.2012.00973.x.

Brink, Jack W. *Imagining Head-Smashed-In: Aboriginal Buffalo Hunting on the Northern Plains.* Edmonton: Athabasca University Press, 2008.

Broockman, David, and Joshua Kalla. "Durably Reducing Transphobia: A Field Experiment on Door-to-Door Canvassing." *Science* 352, no. 6282 (2016): 220–24. doi:10.1126/science.aad9713.

Brown, Catarina. "Women's Narratives of Trauma: (Re)storying. Uncertainty, Minimization and Self-Blame," *Narative Works* 3, no. 1 (2013). https://doi.org /10.7202/1062052ar.

Brown, Leslie. *Eagles of the World.* New York: Universe Books, 1977.

Bryant, Anita. *The Anita Bryant Story: The Survival of Our Nation's Families and the Threat of Militant Homosexuality.* Old Tappan, N.J.: Revell, 1977.

Bucyana, Yves. "Rwanda Genocide: 'I Forgave My Husband's Killer—Our Children Married.'" BBC News, April 23, 2022. www.bbc.com.

Burkhardt-Vetter, Olga. "Reconciliation in the Making: Overcoming Competitive Victimhood Through Inter-group Dialogue in Palestine/Israel." In *The Politics of Victimhood in Post-conflict Societies: Comparative and Analytical Perspectives,* edited by Vincent Druliolle and Roddy Brett, 237–63. Cham: Springer International Publishing, 2018. doi:10.1007/978-3-319-70202-5_10.

Calvin, John. *Commentaries on the Book of the Prophet Jeremiah and the Lamentations.* Vol. 1. Translated by John Owen. Edinburgh: Calvin Translation Society, 1850. Accessed September 16, 2024. https://www.ccel.org/ccel/c/calvin/calcom 39/cache/calcom39.pdf.

Campbell, Bradley, and Jason Manning. *The Rise of Victimhood Culture: Microaggressions, Safe Spaces, and the New Culture Wars.* Cham: Palgrave Macmillan, 2018.

Caplan, Arthur L., James J. McCartney, and Dominic A. Sisti, eds. *Health, Disease, and Illness: Concepts in Medicine.* Washington, D.C.: Georgetown University Press, 2004.

Carl, Noah. "Cognitive Ability and Political Beliefs in the United States." *Personality and Individual Differences* 83 (2015): 245–48. doi:10.1016/j.paid.2015.04.029.

Carter, Maria. "7 Reasons No One Does Funerals Like the South." *Country Living,* Jan. 21, 2018. www.countryliving.com.

CDC. "Youth Risk Behavior Survey Data Summary & Trends Report: 2011–2021." 2023.

Chakroff, Alek, Pascale Sophie Russell, Jared Piazza, and Liane Young. "From Impure to Harmful: Asymmetric Expectations About Immoral Agents." *Journal of Experimental Social Psychology* 69 (2017): 201–9. doi:10.1016/j .jesp.2016.08.001.

Chalmers, David J. "Consciousness and Its Place in Nature." In *Blackwell Guide to Philosophy of Mind,* edited by Stephen P. Stich and Ted A. Warfield, 1–45. Malden, Mass.: Blackwell, 2003.

Continetti, Matthew. "The Battle of Woke Island." *National Review,* April 7, 2018. www.nationalreview.com.

Corbett, David. *The Art of Character: Creating Memorable Characters for Fiction, Film, and TV.* New York: Penguin Books, 2013.

Cowen, Tyler. *Big Business: A Love Letter to an American Anti-hero.* New York: St. Martin's Press, 2019.

Crowley, John, William Smyth, and Michael Murphy. "Emigration to North America in the Era of the Great Famine, 1845–55." In *Atlas of the Great Irish Famine,* edited by John Crowley, William Smyth, and Michael Murphy. New York: New York University Press, 2012.

Curry, Oliver Scott. "Morality as Cooperation: A Problem-Centered Approach." In *The Evolution of Morality,* edited by Todd K. Shackelford and Ranald D.

Hansen, 27–51. Cham: Springer International, 2016. doi:10.1007/978-3
-319-19671-8_2.

Curtis, Benjamin. *The Habsburgs: The History of a Dynasty.* London: Bloomsbury, 2013.

Cushman, Fiery, Kurt Gray, Allison Gaffey, and Wendy Berry Mendes. "Simulating Murder: The Aversion to Harmful Action." *Emotion* 12, no. 1 (2012): 2–7. doi:10.1037/a0025071.

Cushman, Fiery, and Liane Young. "Patterns of Moral Judgment Derive from Nonmoral Psychological Representations." *Cognitive Science* 35, no. 6 (2011): 1052–75. doi:10.1111/j.1551-6709.2010.01167.x.

Dalin-Kaptzan, Zahava. "The Most Punctual Countries in the (On-Demand) World." *Bringg,* Nov. 28, 2016. www.bringg.com.

Daly, Martin, and Margo I. Wilson. "Some Differential Attributes of Lethal Assaults on Small Children by Stepfathers Versus Genetic Fathers." *Ethology and Sociobiology* 15, no. 4 (1994): 207–17. doi:10.1016/0162-3095(94)90014-0.

Danbold, Felix, Ivuoma N. Onyeador, and Miguel M. Unzueta. "Dominant Groups Support Digressive Victimhood Claims to Counter Accusations of Discrimination." *Journal of Experimental Social Psychology* 98 (2022): 104233. doi:10.1016/j.jesp.2021.104233.

Dart, Raymond A. "A Note on the Taungs Skull." *South African Journal of Science* 26 (1929).

———. *Adventures with the Missing Link.* New York: Harper, 1959.

———. "*Australopithecus africanus:* The Man-Ape of South Africa." *Nature* 115, no. 2884 (1925): 195–99. doi:10.1038/115195a0.

Darwin, Charles. *Narrative of the Surveying Voyages of His Majesty's Ships* Adventure and Beagle, *Between the Years 1826 and 1836, Describing Their Examination of the . . . Circumnavigation of the Globe.* Vol. 1. London: Henry Colburn, 1839.

———. *The Origin of Species.* New York: P. F. Collier, 1909.

David, Alison Matthews. *Fashion Victims: The Dangers of Dress Past and Present.* London: Bloomsbury Visual Arts, 2017.

Davis, Daryl. "Why I, as a Black Man, Attend KKK Rallies." TEDxNaperville, TED Talk, Nov. 2017. www.ted.com.

Demirel, Cagla, and Johan Eriksson. "Competitive Victimhood and Reconciliation: The Case of Turkish–Armenian Relations." *Identities* 27, no. 5 (2020): 537–56. doi:10.1080/1070289X.2019.1611073.

Dennett, Daniel C. *Kinds of Minds: Toward an Understanding of Consciousness.* New York: Basic Books, 1997.

Denning, Liam. "Drilling for Oil on the Moon." *Bloomberg,* July 9, 2023. www.bloomberg.com.

Descartes, René. "Animals Are Machines." In *Environmental Ethics: Divergence and*

Convergence, edited by Susan J. Armstrong and Richard G. Botzler, 281–85. New York: McGraw-Hill, 1993. dhaydock.org.

———. *Meditations on First Philosophy with Selections from the Objections and Replies.* Translated by Mike Moriarty. Oxford: Oxford University Press, 2008.

DeScioli, Peter, Sarah Gilbert, and Robert Kurzban. "Indelible Victims and Persistent Punishers in Moral Cognition." *Psychological Inquiry* 23, no. 2 (2012): 143–49.

De Vos, Alta, and M. Justin O'Riain. "Sharks Shape the Geometry of a Selfish Seal Herd: Experimental Evidence from Seal Decoys." *Biology Letters* 6, no. 1 (2010): 48–50. doi:10.1098/rsbl.2009.0628.

Dirks, Sandhya. "Affirmative Action Divided Asian Americans and Other People of Color. Here's How." NPR, July 2, 2023.

Diver, Krysia. "Journal Reveals Hitler's Dysfunctional Family." *Guardian,* Aug. 4, 2005. www.theguardian.com.

Domestic Violence Hotline. "Domestic Violence Statistics." Hotline. Accessed Aug. 2, 2023. www.thehotline.org.

Douglass, Frederick. *Narrative of the Life of Frederick Douglass, an American Slave.* London: Collins, 1851.

———. "What to the Slave Is the Fourth of July?" 1852. https://www.pbs.org/wgbh/aia/part4/4h2927t.html.

Dückers, Michel L. A., Eva Alisic, and Chris R. Brewin. "A Vulnerability Paradox in the Cross-National Prevalence of Post-traumatic Stress Disorder." *British Journal of Psychiatry* 209, no. 4 (2016): 300–305. doi:10.1192/bjp.bp.115.176628.

Dunbar, R. I. M. "The Social Brain Hypothesis and Its Implications for Social Evolution." *Annals of Human Biology* 36, no. 5 (2009): 562–72. doi:10.1080/03014460902960289.

Ellison, Patricia A., John M. Govern, Herbert L. Petri, and Michael H. Figler. "Anonymity and Aggressive Driving Behavior: A Field Study." *Journal of Social Behavior and Personality* 10, no. 1 (1995): 265–72.

Endicott, Kirk. "Peaceful Foragers: The Significance of the Batek and Moriori for the Question of Innate Human Violence." In *War, Peace, and Human Nature,* edited by Douglas P. Fry, 243–61. New York: Oxford University Press, 2013. doi:10.1093/acprof:oso/9780199858996.003.0012.

Epley, Nicholas, Benjamin A. Converse, Alexa Delbosc, George A. Monteleone, and John T. Cacioppo. "Believers' Estimates of God's Beliefs Are More Egocentric Than Estimates of Other People's Beliefs." *Proceedings of the National Academy of Sciences* 106, no. 51 (2009): 21533–38. doi:10.1073/pnas.0908374106.

Epley, Nicholas, and Juliana Schroeder. "Mistakenly Seeking Solitude." *Journal of Experimental Psychology: General* 143 (2014): 1980–99. doi:10.1037/a0037323.

Evans, Patrick D., Sandra L. Gilbert, Nitzan Mekel-Bobrov, Eric J. Vallender, Jeffrey R. Anderson, Leila M. Vaez-Azizi, et al. "Microcephalin, a Gene Regulating

Brain Size, Continues to Evolve Adaptively in Humans." *Science* 309, no. 5741 (2005): 1717–20. doi:10.1126/science.1113722.

Everett, Daniel L. *Don't Sleep, There Are Snakes: Life and Language in the Amazonian Jungle.* New York: Vintage, 2009.

Fahmy, Dalia. "Key Findings About Americans' Belief in God." Pew Research Center, April 25, 2018. www.pewresearch.org.

Falk, Dean. *Primate Diversity.* New York: W. W. Norton, 2000.

Federal Bureau of Investigation Crime Data Explorer. Federal Bureau of Investigation, 2022. cde.ucr.cjis.gov.

Fehr, Ernst, and Simon Gächter. "Altruistic Punishment in Humans." *Nature* 415, no. 6868 (2002): 137–40. doi:10.1038/415137a.

Ferguson, R. Brian. "Pinker's List: Exaggerating Prehistoric War Mortality." In *War, Peace, and Human Nature: The Convergence of Evolutionary and Cultural Views,* edited by Douglas P. Fry, 112–31. New York: Oxford University Press, 2013. doi:10.1093/acprof:oso/9780199858996.003.0007.

Fiske, Alan Page, and Tage Shakti Rai. *Virtuous Violence: Hurting and Killing to Create, Sustain, End, and Honor Social Relationships.* Cambridge, U.K.: Cambridge University Press, 2014. doi:10.1017/CBO9781316104668.

Foss, Sonja K., and Cindy L. Griffin. "Beyond Persuasion: A Proposal for an Invitational Rhetoric." *Communication Monographs* 62, no. 1 (1995): 2–18. doi:10.1080/03637759509376345.

Frankovic, Kathy. "Americans Are Patriotic—but Differ on What That Means." YouGov, July 3, 2018. today.yougov.com.

Freud, Sigmund. *Civilization and Its Discontents.* Austria: Internationaler Psychoanalytischer Verlag Wien, 1930.

Friedersdorf, Conor. "Reflections on a Year of Outrage." *Atlantic,* Dec. 30, 2018.

Frimer, Jeremy A., and Linda J. Skitka. "Are Politically Diverse Thanksgiving Dinners Shorter Than Politically Uniform Ones?" *PLoS ONE* 15, no. 10 (2020): e0239988. doi:10.1371/journal.pone.0239988.

Frimer, Jeremy A., Caitlin E. Tell, and Jonathan Haidt. "Liberals Condemn Sacrilege Too: The Harmless Desecration of Cerro Torre." *Social Psychological and Personality Science* 6, no. 8 (2015). doi.org/10.1177/1948550615597974.

Frimer, Jeremy A., Caitlin E. Tell, and Matt Motyl. "Sacralizing Liberals and Fair-Minded Conservatives: Ideological Symmetry in the Moral Motives in the Culture War." *Analyses of Social Issues and Public Policy* 17, no. 1 (2017): 33–59. doi:10.1111/asap.12127.

Fryer, Roland G. "An Empirical Analysis of Racial Differences in Police Use of Force." *Journal of Political Economy* 127, no. 3 (2017). https://doi.org/10.1086/701423.

Fukuyama, Francis. *Trust: The Social Virtues and the Creation of Prosperity.* New York: Free Press, 1996.

Gabay, Rahav, Boaz Hameiri, Tammy Rubel-Lifschitz, and Arie Nadler. "The Tendency for Interpersonal Victimhood: The Personality Construct and Its Consequences." *Personality and Individual Differences* 165 (2020): 110134. doi:10.1016/j.paid.2020.110134.

Gabunia, Leo, Susan C. Antón, David Lordkipanidze, Abesalom Vekua, Antje Justus, and Carl C. Swisher III. "Dmanisi and Dispersal." *Evolutionary Anthropology: Issues, News, and Reviews* 10, no. 5 (2001): 158–70. doi:10.1002/evan .1030.

Gambetta, Diego. *Codes of the Underworld: How Criminals Communicate.* Princeton, N.J.: Princeton University Press, 2011.

Garra, Gregory, Adam J. Singer, Breena R. Taira, Jasmin Chohan, Hiran Cardoz, Ernest Chisena, et al. "Validation of the Wong-Baker FACES Pain Rating Scale in Pediatric Emergency Department Patients." *Academic Emergency Medicine* 17, no. 1 (2010): 50–54. doi:10.1111/j.1553-2712.2009.00620.x.

Garwin, Laura, and Tim Lincoln, eds. *A Century of "Nature": Twenty-One Discoveries That Changed Science and the World.* Chicago: University of Chicago Press, 2003.

Gashaw, Amen. "In God We Trust: How American Christianity Became Republicanism." *Harvard Political Review,* Jan. 9, 2021. harvardpolitics.com.

Gayley, Holly. "The Compassionate Treatment of Animals." *Journal of Religious Ethics* 45, no. 1 (2017): 29–57. doi:10.1111/jore.12167.

Gelfand, Michele J., Jana L. Raver, Lisa Nishii, Lisa M. Leslie, Janetta Lun, Beng Chong Lim, et al. "Differences Between Tight and Loose Cultures: A 33-Nation Study." *Science* 332, no. 6033 (2011): 1100–1104. doi:10.1126 /science.1197754.

Gendler, Tamar Szabo. "Alief and Belief." *Journal of Philosophy* 105, no. 10 (2008): 634–63.

Godwin, Mike. "Meme, Counter-meme." *WIRED,* Oct. 1, 1994. www.wired.com.

Goggins, David. *Can't Hurt Me: Master Your Mind and Defy the Odds.* N.p.: Lioncrest, 2018.

Gómez, José María, Miguel Verdú, Adela González-Megías, and Marcos Méndez. "The Phylogenetic Roots of Human Lethal Violence." *Nature* 538, no. 7624 (2016): 233–37. doi:10.1038/nature19758.

Goodall, Jane. "Infant Killing and Cannibalism in Free-Living Chimpanzees." *Folia Primatologica* 28, no. 4 (1977).

Gottschall, Jonathan. *The Storytelling Animal: How Stories Make Us Human.* Boston: Mariner Books, 2013.

Govrin, Aner. *Ethics and Attachment: How We Make Moral Judgments.* London: Routledge, 2018. doi:10.4324/9781315114286.

Goya-Tocchetto, Daniela, Aaron C. Kay, Heidi Vuletich, Andrew Vonasch, and Keith Payne. "The Partisan Trade-Off Bias: When Political Polarization Meets

Policy Trade-Offs." *Journal of Experimental Social Psychology* 98 (2022): 104231. doi:10.1016/j.jesp.2021.104231.

Graham, Jesse, Jonathan Haidt, Matt Motyl, Peter Meindl, Carol Iskiwitch, and Marlon Mooijman. "Moral Foundations Theory: On the Advantages of Moral Pluralism over Moral Monism." In *Atlas of Moral Psychology,* edited by Kurt Gray and Jesse Graham, 211–22. New York: Guilford Press, 2018.

Graham, Jesse, Brian A. Nosek, Jonathan Haidt, Ravi Iyer, Spassena Koleva, and Peter H. Ditto. "Mapping the Moral Domain." *Journal of Personality and Social Psychology* 101, no. 2 (2011): 366–85. doi:10.1037/a0021847.

Gray, Heather M., Kurt Gray, and Daniel M. Wegner. "Dimensions of Mind Perception." *Science* 315, no. 5812 (2007): 619.

Gray, John. *Men Are from Mars, Women Are from Venus: The Classic Guide to Understanding the Opposite Sex.* New York: Harper, 2012.

Gray, Kurt, and Emily Kubin. "Victimhood: The Most Powerful Force in Morality and Politics." *Advances in Experimental Social Psychology* 70 (2024): 137–220. https://doi.org/10.1016/bs.aesp.2024.03.004.

Gray, Kurt, Chelsea Schein, and Adrian F. Ward. "The Myth of Harmless Wrongs in Moral Cognition: Automatic Dyadic Completion from Sin to Suffering." *Journal of Experimental Psychology: General* 143 (2014): 1600–1615. doi:10.1037/a0036149.

Gray, Kurt, Adrian F. Ward, and Michael I. Norton. "Paying It Forward: Generalized Reciprocity and the Limits of Generosity." *Journal of Experimental Psychology: General* 143 (2014): 247–54.

Gray, Kurt, and Daniel M. Wegner. "Moral Typecasting: Divergent Perceptions of Moral Agents and Moral Patients." *Journal of Personality and Social Psychology* 96, no. 3 (2009): 505–20. doi:10.1037/a0013748.

———. "To Escape Blame, Don't Be a Hero—Be a Victim." *Journal of Experimental Social Psychology* 47, no. 2 (2011): 516–19. doi:10.1016/j.jesp.2010.12.012.

Grubbs, Joshua B., Brandon Warmke, Justin Tosi, A. Shanti James, and W. Keith Campbell. "Moral Grandstanding in Public Discourse: Status-Seeking Motives as a Potential Explanatory Mechanism in Predicting Conflict." *PLoS ONE* 14, no. 10 (2019): e0223749. doi:10.1371/journal.pone.0223749.

Guillory, James Denny. "The Pro-slavery Arguments of Dr. Samuel A. Cartwright." *Journal of the Louisiana Historical Association* 9, no. 3 (1968): 209–27.

Guo, Jeff. "CNN Cut Ties with Reza Aslan for Calling Trump a 'Piece of Shit.'" *Vox,* June 9, 2017.

Guzman, Gloria, and Melissa Kollar. *Income in the United States: 2022.* U.S. Census Bureau, Sept. 12, 2023. www.census.gov.

Haidt, Jonathan. "The Emotional Dog and Its Rational Tail: A Social Intuitionist Approach to Moral Judgment." *Psychological Review* 108, no. 4 (2001): 814–34.

————. *The Righteous Mind: Why Good People Are Divided by Politics and Religion.* New York: Pantheon Books, 2012.

Haidt, Jonathan, Fredrik Björklund, and Scott Murphy. "Moral Dumbfounding: When Intuition Finds No Reason." MS, University of Virginia, Aug. 10, 2000.

Haidt, Jonathan, and Craig Joseph. "Intuitive Ethics: How Innately Prepared Intuitions Generate Culturally Variable Virtues." *Daedalus* 133, no. 4 (2004): 55–66.

Hamlin, J. Kiley, Karen Wynn, and Paul Bloom. "Social Evaluation by Preverbal Infants." *Nature* 450, no. 7169 (2007): 557–59. doi:10.1038/nature06288.

Harari, Yuval Noah. *Sapiens: A Brief History of Humankind.* New York: Harper, 2015.

Harcourt-Smith, William H. E. "The First Hominins and the Origins of Bipedalism." *Evolution: Education and Outreach* 3, no. 3 (2010): 333–40. doi:10.1007/s12052-010-0257-6.

Harrington, Elizabeth. "Liberals More Likely to Cry Than Conservatives." *Washington Free Beacon,* July 13, 2016. freebeacon.com.

Harris, Nancy L., David A. Gibbs, Alessandro Baccini, Richard A. Birdsey, Sytze De Bruin, Mary Farina, et al. "Global Maps of Twenty-First Century Forest Carbon Fluxes." *Nature Climate Change* 11, no. 3 (2021): 234–40. doi:10.1038/s41558-020-00976-6.

Harsey, Sarah J., Eileen L. Zurbriggen, and Jennifer J. Freyd. "Perpetrator Responses to Victim Confrontation: DARVO and Victim Self-Blame." *Journal of Aggression, Maltreatment, and Trauma* 26, no. 6 (2017): 644–63. doi:10.1080/10926771.2017.1320777.

Hart, Donna. "Primates as Prey: Ecological, Morphological, and Behavioral Relationships Between Primate Species and Their Predators." PhD diss., Washington University in St. Louis, 2000. www.proquest.com.

Hart, Donna, and Robert W. Sussman. *Man the Hunted: Primates, Predators, and Human Evolution.* New York: Westview Press, 2005.

Hartman, Rachel, Neil Hester, and Kurt Gray. "People See Political Opponents as More Stupid Than Evil." *Personality and Social Psychology Bulletin* 49, no. 7 (2023). doi:10.1177/01461672221089451.

Haslam, Nick. "Concept Creep: Psychology's Expanding Concepts of Harm and Pathology." *Psychological Inquiry* 27, no. 1 (2016): 1–17.

————. "Dehumanization: An Integrative Review." *Personality and Social Psychology Review* 10, no. 3 (2006): 252–64.

Hastorf, Albert H., and Hadley Cantril. "They Saw a Game: A Case Study." *Journal of Abnormal and Social Psychology* 49 (1954): 129–34. doi:10.1037/h0057880.

Haven, Kendall. *Story Proof: The Science Behind the Startling Power of Story.* Westport, Conn.: Libraries Unlimited, 2007.

Henrich, Joseph. *The Secret of Our Success: How Culture Is Driving Human Evo-*

lution, Domesticating Our Species, and Making Us Smarter. Princeton, N.J.: Princeton University Press, 2015.

Henrich, Joseph, Steven Heine, and Ara Norenzayan. "The Weirdest People in the World?" *Behavioral and Brain Sciences* 33, no. 2–3 (2010): 61–83.

Henrich, Joseph, and Michael Muthukrishna. "What Makes Us Smart?" *Topics in Cognitive Science,* April 22, 2023. doi:10.1111/tops.12656.

Hergovich, Andreas, Reinhard Schott, and Christoph Burger. "Biased Evaluation of Abstracts Depending on Topic and Conclusion: Further Evidence of a Confirmation Bias Within Scientific Psychology." *Current Psychology* 29, no. 3 (2010): 188–209. doi:10.1007/s12144-010-9087-5.

Hippel, Svenja, and Sven Hoeppner. "Biased Judgements of Fairness in Bargaining: A Replication in the Laboratory." *International Review of Law and Economics* 58 (2019): 63–74. doi:10.1016/j.irle.2019.02.001.

Hirota, Shinichi, Kiyotaka Nakashima, and Yoshiro Tsutsui. "Psychological Motivations for Collectivist Behavior: Comparison Between Japan and the U.S." *Mind and Society* 22, no. 1–2 (2023): 103–28. doi:10.1007/s11299-023-00298-y.

Huang, Karen, Michael Yeomans, Alison Wood Brooks, Julia Minson, and Francesca Gino. "It Doesn't Hurt to Ask: Question-Asking Increases Liking." *Journal of Personality and Social Psychology* 113, no. 3 (2017): 430–52. doi:10.1037/pspi0000097.

Hughes, Coleman. "10 Notes on the End of Affirmative Action." *Coleman's Corner,* June 29, 2023. colemanhughes.substack.com.

Hughes, Terry P., James T. Kerry, Mariana Álvarez-Noriega, Jorge G. Álvarez-Romero, Kristen D. Anderson, Andrew H. Baird, et al. "Global Warming and Recurrent Mass Bleaching of Corals." *Nature* 543, no. 7645 (2017): 373–77. doi:10.1038/nature21707.

Hussein, Mohamed A., and Zakary L. Tormala. "Undermining Your Case to Enhance Your Impact: A Framework for Understanding the Effects of Acts of Receptiveness in Persuasion." *Personality and Social Psychology Review* 25 (2021): 229–50. doi:10.1177/10888683211001269.

Ingraham, Laura. "Laura Ingraham: 'Because You're a Minority, You Get Special Standards, Special Treatment.'" Media Matters, Jan. 23, 2019. www.media matters.org.

"In Their Own Words, Owners Explain How Tax Increases Would Harm Their Businesses." NFIB, Feb. 1, 2022. www.nfib.com.

Janoff-Bulman, Ronnie, Sana Sheikh, and Kate G. Baldacci. "Mapping Moral Motives: Approach, Avoidance, and Political Orientation." *Journal of Experimental Social Psychology* 44, no. 4 (2008): 1091–99. doi:10.1016/j.jesp.2007.11.003.

Jedinger, Alexander, and Axel M. Burger. "Do Smarter People Have More Conservative Economic Attitudes? Assessing the Relationship Between Cognitive

Ability and Economic Ideology." *Personality and Social Psychology Bulletin* 48, no. 11 (2022): 1548–65. doi:10.1177/01461672211046808.

Jockin, Victor, Richard D. Arvey, and Matt McGue. "Perceived Victimization Moderates Self-Reports of Workplace Aggression and Conflict." *Journal of Applied Psychology* 86 (2001): 1262–69. doi:10.1037/0021-9010.86.6.1262.

Jones, Payton J. "The Neurotic Treadmill: Decreasing Adversity, Increasing Vulnerability?" PhD diss., Harvard University, 2021. dash.harvard.edu.

Jones, Payton J., David E. Levari, Benjamin W. Bellet, and Richard J. McNally. "Exposure to Descriptions of Traumatic Events Narrows One's Concept of Trauma." *Journal of Experimental Psychology: Applied* 29, no. 1 (2023): 179–87. doi:10.1037/xap0000389.

Jones, Payton J., and Richard J. McNally. "Does Broadening One's Concept of Trauma Undermine Resilience?" *Psychological Trauma: Theory, Research, Practice, and Policy* 14, no. S1 (2022): S131–39. doi:10.1037/tra0001063.

Jordania, Joseph. *Why Do People Sing? Music in Human Evolution.* Edited by Alexander Jordania. Tbilisi: Logos, 2011.

Joselow, Maxine, and Marianna Sotomayor. "House GOP Passes Energy Package with Eye on Gas Prices, 2024." *Washington Post,* March 30, 2023.

Jost, John T. "A Quarter Century of System Justification Theory: Questions, Answers, Criticisms, and Societal Applications." *British Journal of Social Psychology* 58, no. 2 (2019): 263–314. doi:10.1111/bjso.12297.

Kahan, Dan M., Ellen Peters, Erica Cantrell Dawson, and Paul Slovic. "Motivated Numeracy and Enlightened Self-Government." *Behavioural Public Policy* 1, no. 1 (2017): 54–86. doi:10.1017/bpp.2016.2.

Kalmoe, Nathan P., and Lilliana Mason. "Lethal Mass Partisanship: Prevalence, Correlates, and Electoral Contingencies." NCAPSA American Politics Meeting, 2019.

Kardas, Michael, Amit Kumar, and Nicholas Epley. "Overly Shallow? Miscalibrated Expectations Create a Barrier to Deeper Conversation." *Journal of Personality and Social Psychology* 122, no. 3 (2022): 367–98. doi:10.1037/pspa0000281.

Katz, Jonathan M. "Poor Haitians on a Mud Diet." *Los Angeles Times,* Feb. 3, 2008.

Kemmelmeier, Markus. "Is There a Relationship Between Political Orientation and Cognitive Ability? A Test of Three Hypotheses in Two Studies." *Personality and Individual Differences* 45, no. 8 (2008): 767–72. doi:10.1016/j.paid.2008.08.003.

Kendi, Ibram X. *How to Be an Antiracist.* New York: One World/Random House, 2019.

Keysar, Boaz, Dale J. Barr, Jennifer A. Balin, and Jason S. Brauner. "Taking Perspective in Conversation: The Role of Mutual Knowledge in Comprehension." *Psychological Science* 11, no. 1 (2000): 32–38. doi:10.1111/1467-9280.00211.

Keysar, Boaz, Shuhong Lin, and Dale J. Barr. "Limits on Theory of Mind Use in Adults." *Cognition* 89, no. 1 (2003): 25–41. doi:10.1016/S0010-0277(03)00064-7.

Kilpatrick, Dean. *Mental Health Impact of Rape.* National Violence Against Women Prevention Research Center, 2000. Accessed Aug. 7, 2023. mainweb-v.musc.edu.

King, Martin Luther, Jr. "Letter from Birmingham Jail." April 16, 1963. letterfromjail.com.

Klein, Ilona. "Primo Levi: The Drowned, the Saved, and the 'Grey Zone.'" *Brigham Young Scholars Archive,* 1990.

Klein, Richard A., Michelangelo Vianello, Fred Hasselman, Byron G. Adams, Reginald B. Adams, Sinan Alper, et al. "Many Labs 2: Investigating Variation in Replicability Across Samples and Settings." *Advances in Methods and Practices in Psychological Science* 1, no. 4 (2018): 443–90. doi:10.1177/2515245918810225.

Komlik, Oleg. "Egocentric Perceptions and Self-Serving Bias in Negotiations: Fairness, Dynamics, and Ethics." *Journal of Intercultural Management and Ethics* 4, no. 3 (2021): 61–70.

Konnikova, Maria. *The Confidence Game: Why We Fall for It . . . Every Time.* New York: Viking, 2016.

Kubin, Emily, Kurt J. Gray, and Christian von Sikorski. "Reducing Political Dehumanization by Pairing Facts with Personal Experiences." *Political Psychology* 44, no. 5 (2023): 1119–40. doi:10.1111/pops.12875.

Kubin, Emily, Curtis Puryear, Chelsea Schein, and Kurt Gray. "Personal Experiences Bridge Moral and Political Divides Better Than Facts." *Proceedings of the National Academy of Sciences* 118, no. 6 (2021): e2008389118. doi:10.1073/pnas.2008389118.

Landry, Alexander P., Jonathan W. Schooler, Robb Willer, and Paul Seli. "Reducing Explicit Blatant Dehumanization by Correcting Exaggerated Meta-perceptions." *Social Psychological and Personality Science* 14, no. 4 (2023): 407–18. doi:10.1177/19485506221099146.

Larson, John. "Canyon of Secrets." NBC News, May 7, 2006.

Lee, Spike W. S., and Cecilia Ma. "Pain Sensitivity Predicts Support for Moral and Political Views Across the Aisle." *Journal of Personality and Social Psychology* 125, no. 6 (2023): 1239–64. doi:10.1037/pspa0000355.

Lemieux, Pierre. "Is Being a Cop So Dangerous?" Econlib, July 7, 2020. www.econlib.org.

Lerner, Melvin. *The Belief in a Just World: A Fundamental Delusion.* New York: Springer, 1980.

Leucht, Stefan, Bartosz Helfer, Gerald Gartlehner, and John M. Davis. "How Effective Are Common Medications: A Perspective Based on Meta-analyses of Major Drugs." *BMC Medicine* 13, no. 1 (2015): 253. doi:10.1186/s12916-015-0494-1.

Levari, David E., Daniel T. Gilbert, Timothy D. Wilson, Beau Sievers, David M. Amodio, and Thalia Wheatley. "Prevalence-Induced Concept Change in Human Judgment." *Science* 360, no. 6396 (2018): 1465–67. doi:10.1126/science.aap8731.

Levi, Primo. *The Drowned and the Saved.* New York: Vintage International, 1989.

Liebenberg, Louis. "Persistence Hunting by Modern Hunter-Gatherers." *Current Anthropology* 47, no. 6 (2006): 1017–26. doi:10.1086/508695.

Lieberman, Daniel. *Exercised: Why Something We Never Evolved to Do Is Healthy and Rewarding.* New York: Vintage Books, 2021.

Lieberman, Debra, and Adam Smith. "It's All Relative: Sexual Aversions and Moral Judgments Regarding Sex Among Siblings." *Current Directions in Psychological Science* 21, no. 4 (2012): 243–47. doi:10.1177/0963721412447620.

Lim, Daniel, and David DeSteno. "Suffering and Compassion: The Links Among Adverse Life Experiences, Empathy, Compassion, and Prosocial Behavior." *Emotion* 16, no. 2 (2016): 175–82. doi:10.1037/emo0000144.

Lin, Liu Yi, Jaime E. Sidani, Ariel Shensa, Ana Radovic, Elizabeth Miller, Jason B. Colditz, et al. "Association Between Social Media Use and Depression Among U.S. Young Adults." *Depression and Anxiety* 33, no. 4 (2016): 323–31. doi:10.1002/da.22466.

Lisak, David, Lori Gardinier, Sarah C. Nicksa, and Ashley M. Cote. "False Allegations of Sexual Assault: An Analysis of Ten Years of Reported Cases." *Violence Against Women* 16, no. 12 (2010): 1318–34. doi:10.1177/1077801210387747.

Locke, John. *Second Treatise of Government* (chapter VI, section 61), 1689.

Lovejoy, Arthur O. *The Great Chain of Being: A Study of the History of an Idea.* Cambridge, Mass.: Harvard University Press, 1976.

Lovejoy, C. Owen. "Evolution of Human Walking." *Scientific American* 259, no. 5 (1988): 118–25.

Lukianoff, Greg, and Jonathan Haidt. *The Coddling of the American Mind: How Good Intentions and Bad Ideas Are Setting Up a Generation for Failure.* New York: Penguin Books, 2019.

Määttä, Marju, Satu Uusiautti, and Kaarina Määttä. "An Intimate Relationship in the Shadow of Narcissism: What Is It Like to Live with a Narcissistic Spouse?" *International Journal of Research Studies in Psychology* 1, no. 1 (2012). doi:10.5861/ijrsp.2012.v1i1.28.

Mackey, Jeremy D., Jeremy R. Brees, Charn P. McAllister, Michelle L. Zorn, Mark J. Martinko, and Paul Harvey. "Victim and Culprit? The Effects of Entitlement and Felt Accountability on Perceptions of Abusive Supervision and Perpetration of Workplace Bullying." *Journal of Business Ethics* 153, no. 3 (2018): 659–73. doi:10.1007/s10551-016-3348-7.

Manchester, Julia. "Conservative Writer Calls Democratic Party an 'Evil Institution.'" *Hill,* March 3, 2019. thehill.com.

Mapping Police Violence. *2023 Police Violence Report.* policeviolencereport.org.

Marcinkowski, Frank, and Pero Došenović. "From Incidental Exposure to Intentional Avoidance: Psychological Reactance to Political Communication During the 2017 German National Election Campaign." *New Media and Society* 23, no. 3 (2021): 457–78. doi:10.1177/1461444820902104.

Martherus, James L., Andres G. Martinez, Paul K. Piff, and Alexander G. Theodoridis. "Party Animals? Extreme Partisan Polarization and Dehumanization." *Political Behavior* 43, no. 2 (2021): 517–40. doi:10.1007/s11109-019 -09559-4.

Martins, Quinton, and Stephen Harris. "Movement, Activity, and Hunting Behaviour of Leopards in the Cederberg Mountains, South Africa." *African Journal of Ecology* 51, no. 4 (2013): 571–79. doi:10.1111/aje.12068.

Marx, Karl, and Friedrich Engels. *The Communist Manifesto.* London: Workers' Educational Association, 1848.

Mastroianni, Adam M., and Daniel T. Gilbert. "The Illusion of Moral Decline." *Nature* 618, no. 7966 (2023): 782–89. doi:10.1038/s41586-023-06137-x.

Matsumura, Keiichiro. "Moral Economy as Emotional Interaction: Food Sharing and Reciprocity in Highland Ethiopia." *African Studies Quarterly* 9, no. 1–2 (2006).

Maynard Smith, John, and David Harper. *Animal Signals.* New York: Oxford University Press, 2004.

McCorkle, Richard C. "Personal Precautions to Violence in Prison." *Criminal Justice and Behavior* 19, no. 2 (1992): 160–73. doi:10.1177/009385489201 9002004.

McCoy, Jennifer and Benjamin Press. *What Happens When Democracies Become Perniciously Polarized?* Carnegie Endowment for International Peace, Jan. 18, 2022. carnegieendowment.org.

McCullough, Michael E., Robert A. Emmons, Shelley Dean Kilpatrick, and Courtney N. Mooney. "Narcissists as 'Victims': The Role of Narcissism in the Perception of Transgressions." *Personality and Social Psychology Bulletin* 29, no. 7 (2003): 885–93. doi:10.1177/0146167203029007007.

McGrath, Melanie J., and Nick Haslam. "Development and Validation of the Harm Concept Breadth Scale: Assessing Individual Differences in Harm Inflation." *PLoS ONE* 15, no. 8 (2020): e0237732. doi:10.1371/journal.pone.0237732.

McNally, Richard J. "The Expanding Empire of Psychopathology: The Case of PTSD." *Psychological Inquiry* 27, no. 1 (2016): 46–49. doi:10.1080/1047840X .2016.1108168.

Mehl, Matthias R., Simine Vazire, Nairán Ramírez-Esparza, Richard B. Slatcher, and James W. Pennebaker. "Are Women Really More Talkative Than Men?" *Science* 317, no. 5834 (2007): 82. doi:10.1126/science.1139940.

Meterko, Vanessa, and Glinda Cooper. "Cognitive Biases in Criminal Case Evaluation: A Review of the Research." *Journal of Police and Criminal Psychology* 37, no. 1 (2022): 101–22. doi:10.1007/s11896-020-09425-8.

Meyer, Duane. *The Highland Scots of North Carolina, 1732–1776.* Chapel Hill: University of North Carolina Press, 1987.

Monacelli, Antonia. "Why Did Cody Posey Kill His Family? Murder on a New Mexico Ranch." *CrimeWire,* Nov. 7, 2023. thecrimewire.com.

Moore-Berg, Samantha L., Lee-Or Ankori-Karlinsky, Boaz Hameiri, and Emile Bruneau. "Exaggerated Meta-perceptions Predict Intergroup Hostility Between American Political Partisans." *Proceedings of the National Academy of Sciences* 117, no. 26 (2020): 14864–72. doi:10.1073/pnas.2001263117.

Morin, Eugène, and Bruce Winterhalder. "Ethnography and Ethnohistory Support the Efficiency of Hunting Through Endurance Running in Humans." *Nature Human Behaviour,* May 13, 2024, 1–11. doi:10.1038/s41562-024-01876-x.

Murphy, Heather. "At 71, She's Never Felt Pain or Anxiety. Now Scientists Know Why." *New York Times,* March 28, 2019.

Nakazawa, Nobuko, Shunkichi Hanamura, Eiji Inoue, Masato Nakatsukasa, and Michio Nakamura. "A Leopard Ate a Chimpanzee: First Evidence from East Africa." *Journal of Human Evolution* 65, no. 3 (2013): 334–37. doi:10.1016/j.jhevol.2013.04.003.

National Geographic. "Rainforest." education.nationalgeographic.org.

Newman, Alexander, Ross Donohue, and Nathan Eva. "Psychological Safety: A Systematic Review of the Literature." *Human Resource Management Review* 27, no. 3 (2017): 521–35. doi:10.1016/j.hrmr.2017.01.001.

Nisbett, Richard E., and Dov Cohen. *Culture of Honor: The Psychology of Violence in the South.* New York: Westview Press, 1996.

Noor, Masi, Rupert Brown, Roberto Gonzalez, Jorge Manzi, and Christopher Alan Lewis. "On Positive Psychological Outcomes: What Helps Groups with a History of Conflict to Forgive and Reconcile with Each Other?" *Personality and Social Psychology Bulletin* 34, no. 6 (2008): 819–32. doi:10.1177/0146167208315555.

Noor, Masi, Nurit Shnabel, Samer Halabi, and Arie Nadler. "When Suffering Begets Suffering: The Psychology of Competitive Victimhood Between Adversarial Groups in Violent Conflicts." *Personality and Social Psychology Review* 16, no. 4 (2012): 351–74. doi:10.1177/1088868312440048.

Norenzayan, Ara, Azim F. Shariff, Will M. Gervais, Aiyana K. Willard, Rita A. McNamara, Edward Slingerland, et al. "The Cultural Evolution of Prosocial Religions." *Behavioral and Brain Sciences* 39 (2016): e1.

Ochoa, Nicolas Restrepo. "Template Matching and Moral Judgment: A New Method and Empirical Test." *Poetics* 92 (2022): 101643. doi:10.1016/j.poetic.2021.101643.

Ordoñez, Franco. "What a Second-Term Trump Immigration Agenda Might Look Like." *All Things Considered,* NPR, Feb. 11, 2024.

Ordóñez, Lisa, and Lehman Benson. "Decisions Under Time Pressure: How Time Constraint Affects Risky Decision Making." *Organizational Behavior and Human Decision Processes* 71, no. 2 (1997): 121–40. doi:10.1006/obhd.1997.2717.

O'Toole, Katie. "3-Year-Old Taken to Syracuse Hospital After She Eats Marijuana Candy; Parents Charged." *Syracuse,* Feb. 17, 2022. www.syracuse.com.

Pasek, Michael H., Lee-Or Ankori-Karlinsky, Alex Levy-Vene, and Samantha L. Moore-Berg. "Misperceptions About Out-Partisans' Democratic Values May Erode Democracy." *Scientific Reports* 12, no. 1 (2022): 16284. doi:10.1038/s41598-022-19616-4.

Patel, Eboo. "America's Hidden Strength." Persuasion, May 16, 2022. www.persuasion.community.

Pattison, Kermit. "Born to Run? Endurance Running May Have Evolved to Help Humans Chase Down Prey." *Science,* May 13, 2024. doi:10.1126/science.zmxb8it.

Perry, Samuel, and Joshua B. Grubbs. "How Americans Polarize Around Historical Figures" (unpublished manuscript, 2024).

Petsko, Christopher D., and Nour S. Kteily. "Political (Meta-)Dehumanization in Mental Representations: Divergent Emphases in the Minds of Liberals Versus Conservatives." *Personality and Social Psychology Bulletin,* July 7, 2023. doi:10.1177/01461672231180971.

Pew Research Center. "As Economic Concerns Recede, Environmental Protection Rises on the Public's Policy Agenda." Feb. 13, 2020. www.pewresearch.org.

———. "Party Identification Among Religious Groups and Religiously Unaffiliated Voters." April 9, 2024. www.pewresearch.org.

Piaget, Jean, and Bärbel Inhelder. *The Psychology of the Child.* New York: Basic Books, 1969.

Pickering, Travis Rayne, and Henry T. Bunn. "The Endurance Running Hypothesis and Hunting and Scavenging in Savanna-Woodlands." *Journal of Human Evolution* 53, no. 4 (2007): 434–38. doi:10.1016/j.jhevol.2007.01.012.

Pierson, Emma, Camelia Simoiu, Jan Overgoor, Sam Corbett-Davies, Daniel Jenson, Amy Shoemaker, et al. "A Large-Scale Analysis of Racial Disparities in Police Stops Across the United States." *Nature Human Behaviour* 4, no. 7 (2020): 736–45. doi:10.1038/s41562-020-0858-1.

Pinker, Steven. *The Better Angels of Our Nature: Why Violence Has Declined.* New York: Viking, 2011.

Podolefsky, Aaron. "Contemporary Warfare in the New Guinea Highlands." *Ethnology* 23, no. 2 (1984): 73–83. doi:10.2307/3773694.

Price, D. D., A. Von der Gruen, J. Miller, A. Rafii, and C. Price. "A Psychophysical Analysis of Morphine Analgesia." *Pain* 22, no. 3 (July 1985), 261–69. https://doi.org/10.1016/0304-3959(85)90026-0.

Puryear, Curtis, Emily Kubin, Chelsea Schein, Yochanan Bigman, Pierce Ekstrom and Kurt Gray. "People Believe Political Opponents Accept Blatant Moral Wrongs, Fueling Partisan Divides." *PNAS Nexus* 3 (2024). https://doi.org/10.1093/pnasnexus/pgae244.

Puryear, Curtis, Joseph A. Vandello, and Kurt Gray. "Moral Panics on Social Media Are Fueled by Signals of Virality." *Journal of Personality and Social Psychology* (2024). Accessed April 15, 2024. https://dx.doi.org/10.1037/pspa0000379.

"Putin Compared the Attack on Russian Culture in the West with the Events in Hitler's Germany." *Izvestia,* March 25, 2022. iz.ru.

Ramos Salazar, Leslie. "The Negative Reciprocity Process in Marital Relationships: A Literature Review." *Aggression and Violent Behavior* 24 (2015): 113–19. doi:10.1016/j.avb.2015.05.008.

Rand, David G., Alexander Peysakhovich, Gordon T. Kraft-Todd, George E. Newman, Owen Wurzbacher, Martin A. Nowak, et al. "Social Heuristics Shape Intuitive Cooperation." *Nature Communications* 5, no. 1 (2014): 3677. doi:10.1038/ncomms4677.

Reilly, Katie. "Read Hillary Clinton's 'Basket of Deplorables' Remarks About Donald Trump Supporters." *Time,* Sept. 10, 2016.

Republican Party Platform: A Safer World and a More Hopeful America. August 30, 2004. Retrieved from https://www.presidency.ucsb.edu/documents/2004-republican-party-platform.

Reynolds, Tania, Chuck Howard, Hallgeir Sjåstad, Luke Zhu, Tyler G. Okimoto, Roy F. Baumeister, et al. "Man Up and Take It: Gender Bias in Moral Typecasting." *Organizational Behavior and Human Decision Processes* 161 (2020): 120–41. doi:10.1016/j.obhdp.2020.05.002.

Ringelmann, Max. "Recherches sur les moteurs animés: Travail de l'homme." *Annales de l'Institut National Agronomique* 12 (1913): 1–40.

Ripley, Amanda. *High Conflict: Why We Get Trapped and How We Get Out.* New York: Simon & Schuster, 2021.

Ritchie, Hannah. "Did Humans Cause the Quaternary Megafauna Extinction?" Our World in Data, Nov. 30, 2022. ourworldindata.org.

Roach, Neil T., Madhusudhan Venkadesan, Michael J. Rainbow, and Daniel E. Lieberman. "Elastic Energy Storage in the Shoulder and the Evolution of High-Speed Throwing in Homo." *Nature* 498, no. 7455 (2013): 483–86. doi:10.1038/nature12267.

Rogaev, Evgeny I., Anastasia P. Grigorenko, Gulnaz Faskhutdinova, Ellen L. W. Kittler, and Yuri K. Moliaka. "Genotype Analysis Identifies the Cause of the 'Royal Disease.'" *Science* 326, no. 5954 (2009): 817. doi:10.1126/science.1180660.

Ronson, Jon. "How One Stupid Tweet Blew Up Justine Sacco's Life." *New York Times,* Feb. 12, 2015.

Rook, Clarence. "The Art of Eating." *Marlborough Express,* July 13, 1909. paper spast.natlib.govt.nz.

Rooney, Rev. Donald J. "Suffering and the Teachings of Jesus Christ." *Claritas: Journal of Dialogue and Culture* 4, no. 2 (2015): 18–25.

Roopnarine, Peter D. "Humans Are Apex Predators." *Proceedings of the National Academy of Sciences* 111, no. 9 (2014): E796. doi:10.1073/pnas.1323645111.

Rosenthal, Marina N., and Jennifer J. Freyd. "From DARVO to Distress: College Women's Contact with Their Perpetrators After Sexual Assault." *Journal of Aggression, Maltreatment, and Trauma* 31, no. 4 (2022): 459–77. doi:10.1080/10926771.2022.2055512.

Rossiter, Erin. "The Similar and Distinct Effects of Political and Non-political Conversation on Affective Polarization." 2023. erossiter.com.

Rottman, Joshua, Liane Young, and Deborah Kelemen. "The Impact of Testimony on Children's Moralization of Novel Actions." *Emotion* 17, no. 5 (2017): 811–27. doi:10.1037/emo0000276.

Royzman, Edward, Kwanwoo Kim, and Robert F. Leeman. "The Curious Tale of Julie and Mark: Unraveling the Moral Dumbfounding Effect." *Judgment and Decision Making* 10, no. 4 (2015): 296–313.

Ruark, Robert. *Horn of the Hunter.* Garden City, N.Y.: Doubleday, 1953.

Rupar, Mirjana, Magdalena Bobowik, Maitane Arnoso, Ainara Arnoso, and Johanna Ray Vollhardt. "General Inclusive Victimhood Predicts Willingness to Engage in Intergroup Contact: Findings from Bosnia-Herzegovina and the Basque Country." *Journal of Applied Social Psychology* 52, no. 2 (2022): 71–84. doi:10.1111/jasp.12835.

Santoro, Erik, and David E. Broockman. "The Promise and Pitfalls of Cross-Partisan Conversations for Reducing Affective Polarization: Evidence from Randomized Experiments." *Science Advances* 8, no. 25 (2022): eabn5515. doi:10.1126/sciadv.abn5515.

Schein, Chelsea, and Kurt Gray. "The Theory of Dyadic Morality: Reinventing Moral Judgment by Redefining Harm." *Personality and Social Psychology Review* 22, no. 1 (2018): 32–70. doi:10.1177/1088868317698288.

Schwartz, John. "Dungeons & Dragons Prison Ban Upheld." *New York Times,* Jan. 26, 2010.

Seidensticker, John, and Susan Lumpkin. *Great Cats.* Emmaus, Pa.: Rodale Press, 1991.

Shweder, Richard A. "The Psychology of Practice and the Practice of the Three Psychologies." *Asian Journal of Social Psychology* 3, no. 3 (2000): 207–22. doi:10.1111/1467-839X.00065.

———. "Relativism and Universalism." In *A Companion to Moral Anthropology,* edited by Didier Fassin, 85–102. Hoboken, N.J.: John Wiley & Sons, 2012.

Shweder, Richard A., Manamohan Mahapatra, and Joan G. Miller. "Culture and Moral Development." In *The Emergence of Morality in Young Children,* edited by Jerome Kagan and Sharon Lamb, 1–83. Chicago: University of Chicago Press, 1987.

Shweder, Richard A., Nancy C. Much, Manamohan Mahapatra, and Lawrence Park. "The 'Big Three' of Morality (Autonomy, Community, Divinity) and the 'Big Three' Explanations of Suffering." In *Morality and Health,* edited by Allan M. Brandt and Paul Rozin. New York: Routledge, 1997.

Singer, Peter. *Animal Liberation.* New York: Random House, 1975.

Skenazy, Lenore. "Suburban Mom Handcuffed, Jailed for Making 8-Year-Old Son Walk Half a Mile Home." *Reason,* Nov. 16, 2022. reason.com.

Smith, Gregory A. "Just One-Third of U.S. Catholics Agree with Their Church That Eucharist Is Body, Blood of Christ." Pew Research Center, Aug. 5, 2019. www.pewresearch.org.

Sobieraj, Sarah, and Jeffrey M. Berry. "From Incivility to Outrage: Political Discourse in Blogs, Talk Radio, and Cable News." *Political Communication* 28, no. 1 (2011): 19–41. doi:10.1080/10584609.2010.542360.

Sousa, Cindy, Todd I. Herrenkohl, Carrie A. Moylan, Emiko A. Tajima, J. Bart Klika, Roy C. Herrenkohl, et al. "Longitudinal Study on the Effects of Child Abuse and Children's Exposure to Domestic Violence, Parent-Child Attachments, and Antisocial Behavior in Adolescence." *Journal of Interpersonal Violence* 26, no. 1 (2011): 111–36. doi:10.1177/0886260510362883.

Spence, Gerry. *Win Your Case: How to Present, Persuade, and Prevail—Every Place, Every Time.* New York: St. Martin's Press, 2005.

Stanley, Matthew L., Siyuan Yin, and Walter Sinnott-Armstrong. "A Reason-Based Explanation for Moral Dumbfounding." *Judgment and Decision Making* 14, no. 2 (2019): 120–29. doi:10.1017/s1930297500003351.

Steele, Rachel R. "Moral Typecasting Explains Evaluations of Undocumented Immigrants." *Journal of Social and Political Psychology* 11, no. 1 (2023): 348–61. doi:10.5964/jspp.5617.

Steering Committee of the Physicians' Health Study Research Group. "Final Report on the Aspirin Component of the Ongoing Physicians' Health Study." *New England Journal of Medicine* 321, no. 3 (1989): 129–35. doi:10.1056/NEJM198907203210301.

Stevens, Martin, W. Tom L. Searle, Jenny E. Seymour, Kate L. A. Marshall, and Graeme D. Ruxton. "Motion Dazzle and Camouflage as Distinct Anti-predator Defenses." *BMC Biology* 9 (2011): 81. doi:10.1186/1741-7007-9-81.

Stiner, Mary C., Ran Barkai, and Avi Gopher. "Cooperative Hunting and Meat Sharing 400–200 Kya at Qesem Cave, Israel." *Proceedings of the National Academy of Sciences* 106, no. 32 (2009): 13207–12. doi:10.1073/pnas.0900564106.

Strohminger, Nina, Joshua Knobe, and George Newman. "The True Self: A Psychological Concept Distinct from the Self." *Perspectives on Psychological Science* 12, no. 4 (2017): 551–60. doi:10.1177/1745691616689495.

Suraci, Justin P., Michael Clinchy, Liana Y. Zanette, and Christopher C. Wilmers. "Fear of Humans as Apex Predators Has Landscape-Scale Impacts from Mountain Lions to Mice." *Ecology Letters* 22, no. 10 (2019): 1578–86. doi:10.1111/ele.13344.

Takamatsu, Reina, May Cho Min, Lina Wang, Wenzhen Xu, Norihito Taniguchi, and Jiro Takai. "Moralization of Japanese Cultural Norms Among Student Sojourners in Japan." *International Journal of Intercultural Relations* 80 (2021): 242–49. doi:10.1016/j.ijintrel.2020.12.001.

Tennyson, Alfred. *In Memoriam A. H. H.* London: E. Moxon, 1850.

Thune, John. "Demonizing and Defunding Police Has Consequences." John Thune U.S. Senator for South Dakota, July 16, 2021. www.thune.senate.gov.

Timmermann, Axel. "Quantifying the Potential Causes of Neanderthal Extinction: Abrupt Climate Change Versus Competition and Interbreeding." *Quaternary Science Reviews* 238 (2020): 106331. doi:10.1016/j.quascirev.2020.106331.

Toward a More Responsible Two-Party System: A Report. American Political Science Association: Committee on Political Parties, 1950. archive.org/details/towardmorerespon0000amer.

Tsukahara, Takahiro. "Lions Eat Chimpanzees: The First Evidence of Predation by Lions on Wild Chimpanzees." *American Journal of Primatology* 29, no. 1 (1993): 1–11. doi:10.1002/ajp.1350290102.

Turiel, Elliot. *The Development of Social Knowledge: Morality and Convention.* Cambridge, U.K.: Cambridge University Press, 1983.

Turiel, Elliot, Melanie Killen, and Charles C. Helwig. "Morality: Its Structure, Functions, and Vagaries." In *The Emergence of Morality in Young Children,* edited by Jerome Kagan and Sharon Lamb, 155–243. Chicago: University of Chicago Press, 1987.

Turner, Julia. "The Year of Outrage." *Slate,* Dec. 17, 2014.

Tutin, C., William McGrew, and P. Baldwin. "Social Organization of Savanna-Dwelling Chimpanzees, *Pan troglodytes verus,* at Mt. Assirik, Senegal." *Primates* 24 (1983): 154–73. doi:10.1007/BF02381079.

Twenge, Jean. *iGen: Why Today's Super-Connected Kids Are Growing Up Less Rebellious, More Tolerant, Less Happy—and Completely Unprepared for Adulthood—and What That Means for the Rest of Us.* New York: Atria Books, 2017.

Uehara, Shigeo, Mariko Hiraiwa-Hasegawa, Kazuhiko Hosaka, and Miya Hamai. "The Fate of Defeated Alpha Male Chimpanzees in Relation to Their Social Networks." *Primates* 35, no. 1 (1994): 49–55. doi:10.1007/BF02381485.

Uhlmann, Eric Luis, and Luke [Lei] Zhu. "Acts, Persons, and Intuitions: Person-Centered Cues and Gut Reactions to Harmless Transgressions." *Social Psychological and Personality Science* 5, no. 3 (2014). doi:10.1177/1948550613497238.

Uluğ, Özden Melis, Brian Lickel, Bernhard Leidner, and Gilad Hirschberger. "How Do Conflict Narratives Shape Conflict- and Peace-Related Outcomes Among Majority Group Members? The Role of Competitive Victimhood in Intractable Conflicts." *Group Processes and Intergroup Relations* 24, no. 5 (2021): 797–814. doi:10.1177/1368430220915771.

USA Today. "50 of the Most Dangerous Cities in the World." July 24, 2019.

Vallone, Robert P., Lee Ross, and Mark R. Lepper. "The Hostile Media Phenomenon: Biased Perception and Perceptions of Media Bias in Coverage of the Beirut Massacre." *Journal of Personality and Social Psychology* 49, no. 3 (1985): 577–85. doi:10.1037/0022-3514.49.3.577.

van der Bijl, Wouter, and Niclas Kolm. "Why Direct Effects of Predation Complicate the Social Brain Hypothesis: And How Incorporation of Explicit Proximate Behavioral Mechanisms Might Help." *BioEssays: News and Reviews in Molecular, Cellular, and Developmental Biology* 38 (2016). doi:10.1002/bies.201500166.

Vernon, Jamie. "Science in the Post-truth Era." *American Scientist* (2017). https://www.americanscientist.org/article/science-in-the-post-truth-era.

Vilas, Román, Francisco C. Ceballos, Laila Al-Soufi, Raúl González-García, Carlos Moreno, Manuel Moreno, et al. "Is the 'Habsburg Jaw' Related to Inbreeding?" *Annals of Human Biology* 46, no. 7–8 (2019): 553–61. doi:10.1080/03014460.2019.1687752.

Vollhardt, Johanna R. "The Role of Victim Beliefs in the Israeli-Palestinian Conflict: Risk or Potential for Peace?" *Peace and Conflict: Journal of Peace Psychology* 15, no. 2 (2009): 135–59. doi:10.1080/10781910802544373.

Vollhardt, Johanna Ray, and Rezarta Bilali. "The Role of Inclusive and Exclusive Victim Consciousness in Predicting Intergroup Attitudes: Findings from Rwanda, Burundi, and DRC." *Political Psychology* 36, no. 5 (2015): 489–506. doi:10.1111/pops.12174.

Wall, Patrick. *Pain: The Science of Suffering.* New York: Columbia University Press, 2002.

Wang, Andy. "At These Hot New York Restaurants, Eating with Your Hands Is the Point." *Forbes,* Jan. 26, 2024.

Waytz, Adam, Liane L. Young, and Jeremy Ginges. "Motive Attribution Asymmetry for Love vs. Hate Drives Intractable Conflict." *Proceedings of the National Academy of Sciences* 111, no. 44 (2014): 15687–92.

Weinandy, Thomas Gerard. *Does God Suffer?* Notre Dame, Ind.: University of Notre Dame Press, 2000.

Weintraub, Stanley. *Silent Night: The Remarkable Christmas Truce of 1914.* London: Simon & Schuster, 2014.

Wellons, Tonia. "Affirmative Action Is Still an Effective and Necessary Tool." *Contexts* 18, no. 1 (2019): 80. doi:10.1177/1536504219830685.

Wessels, Tom. *The Myth of Progress: Toward a Sustainable Future.* Rev. ed. Hanover, N.H.: University Press of New England, 2013.

Whyte, Chelsea. "Chimps Beat Up, Murder, and Then Cannibalise Their Former Tyrant." *NewScientist,* Jan. 30, 2017. www.newscientist.com.

Wilkins, Jayne, Benjamin J. Schoville, Kyle S. Brown, and Michael Chazan. "Evidence for Early Hafted Hunting Technology." *Science* 338, no. 6109 (2012): 942–46. doi:10.1126/science.1227608.

Williamson, Henry. "The Christmas Truce." 1914. Accessed March 9, 2023. www.worldwar1.com.

Winter, Jay, ed. *The Cambridge History of the First World War.* Vol. 1, *Global War.* Cambridge, U.K.: Cambridge University Press, 2014. doi:10.1017/CHO9780511675669.

Woessner, Matthew, Robert Maranto, and Amanda Thompson. "Is Collegiate Political Correctness Fake News? Relationships Between Grades and Ideology." EDRE Working Paper No. 2019-15, May 6, 2019. doi:10.2139/ssrn.3383704.

Womick, Jake, Daniela Goya-Tocchetto, Nicolas R. Ochoa, Carlos Rebollar, Kyra Kapsaskis, Samuel Pratt, et al. "Moral Disagreement Across Politics Is Explained by Different Assumptions About Who Is Most Vulnerable to Harm." PsyArXiv, March 26, 2024. doi.org/10.31234/osf.io/qsg7j.

Womick, Jake, and Laura A. King. "Right-Wing Authoritarianism and Anti-Asian Prejudice in Response to the COVID-19 Pandemic in the United States." *Journal of Applied Social Psychology* 53, no. 12 (2023): 1202–13. doi:10.1111/jasp.13007.

World Health Organization. *Obesity and Overweight,* March 1, 2024. www.who.int.

World Meteorological Organization. "Weather-Related Disasters Increase over Past 50 Years, Causing More Damage but Fewer Deaths." Aug. 31, 2021. wmo.int.

Wrangham, Richard W. *Catching Fire: How Cooking Made Us Human.* New York: Basic Books, 2009.

———. "Two Types of Aggression in Human Evolution." *Proceedings of the National Academy of Sciences* 115, no. 2 (2018): 245–53. doi:10.1073/pnas.1713611115.

Yiend, Jenny, and Andrew Mathews. "Anxiety and Attention to Threatening Pictures." *Quarterly Journal of Experimental Psychology A: Human Experimental Psychology* 54A, no. 3 (2001): 665–81. doi:10.1080/02724980042000462.

YouGov. "Have You Lost Any Friendships Because of Differences in Opinion Related to the COVID-19 Pandemic?" Aug. 5, 2021. today.yougov.com.

Young, Richard W. "Evolution of the Human Hand: The Role of Throwing and Clubbing." *Journal of Anatomy* 202, no. 1 (2003): 165–74. doi:10.1046/j.1469-7580.2003.00144.x.

Yourish, Karen, Weiyi Cai, Larry Buchanan, Aaron Byrd, Barbara Harvey, Blacki
    Migliozzi, et al. "Inside the Apocalyptic Worldview of 'Tucker Carlson
    Tonight.'" *New York Times,* April 30, 2022.

Yuan, Mingliang, Giuliana Spadaro, Shuxian Jin, Junhui Wu, Yu Kou, Paul A. M.
    Van Lange, et al. "Did Cooperation Among Strangers Decline in the United
    States? A Cross-Temporal Meta-analysis of Social Dilemmas (1956–2017)."
    Psychological Bulletin 148, no. 3–4 (2022): 129–57. doi:10.1037/bul0000363.

Zenovich, Marina, dir. "Fantastic Lies." *30 for 30,* ESPN, March 20, 2016.

Zhai, Yida. "Values of Deference to Authority in Japan and China." *Interna-
    tional Journal of Comparative Sociology* 58, no. 2 (2017): 120–39. doi:10.1177
    /0020715217694078.

Zitek, Emily, Alexander Jordan, Benoît Monin, and Frederick Leach. "Victim
    Entitlement to Behave Selfishly." *Journal of Personality and Social Psychology* 98
    (2010): 245–55. doi:10.1037/a0017168.

Index

Page numbers in *italics* refer to illustrations.

Illustration Credits

matting adapted from Kurt Gray et al., "The Affective Harm Account (AHA) of Moral Judgment: Reconciling Cognition and Affect, Dyadic Morality and Disgust, Harm and Purity," *Journal of Personality and Social Psychology* 123, no. 6 (2022): 1199–222. Reprinted with permission.

173 Figure 7.1: Rights received from Alamy Images.

176 Figure 7.2: From H. M. Gray, K. Gray, and D. M. Wegner, "Dimensions of Mind Perception," *Science* 315, no. 5812 (2007). Reprinted with permission from AAAS.

187 Figure 7.3: From J. Womick et al., "Moral Disagreement Across Politics Is Explained by Different Assumptions About Who Is Most Vulnerable to Harm," PsyArXiv, March 26, 2024. Reprinted with permission. (*Figure adapted by Kevin House*)

201 Figure 8.1: Wong-Baker FACES Foundation (2022). Wong-Baker FACES Pain Rating Scale. Retrieved May 18, 2023, with permission from www.WongBaker FACES.org.

201 Figure 8.2: Original data and figure from Gray and Wegner, "Moral Typecasting," *Journal of Personality and Social Psychology* 96, no. 3 (2009): 505–20. (*Figure adapted by Kevin House*)

206 Figure 8.3: Original figure from Joseph Jastrow, "The Mind's Eye," *Popular Science Monthly,* Jan. 1899, 299–312. (Public Domain). (*Figure adapted by Kevin House*)

221 Figure 9.1: From B. Keysar, D. J. Barr, A. Balin, and J. S. Brauner, "Taking Perspective in Conversation: The Role of Mutual Knowledge in Comprehension," *Psychological Science* 11, no. 1 (2000): 32–38. Reprinted with permission. (*Figure adapted by Kevin House*)

250 Figure M3.1: Original data and figure from E. Kubin, C. Puryear, C. Schein, and K. Gray, "Personal Experiences Bridge Moral and Political Divides Better Than Facts," *Proceedings of the National Academy of Sciences* 118, no. 6 (2021). (*Figure adapted by Kevin House*)

261 Figure 10.1: From N. Kteily, E. Bruneau, A. Waytz, and S. Cotterill, "The Ascent of Man: Theoretical and Empirical Evidence for Blatant Dehumanization," *Journal of Personality and Social Psychology* 109, no. 5 (2015): 901–31. Reprinted with permission.

261 Figure 10.2: From C. Petsko and N. Kteily, "Political (Meta-)Dehumanization in Mental Representations: Divergent Emphases in the Minds of Liberals Versus Conservatives," *Personality and Social Psychology Bulletin,* July 7, 2023. Reprinted with permission. (*Figure adapted by Kevin House*)

A Note About the Author

KURT GRAY is a professor of psychology and neuroscience at the University of North Carolina at Chapel Hill, where he directs the Deepest Beliefs Lab and the Center for the Science of Moral Understanding. His findings have been featured in *The New York Times, The Economist, Scientific American,* and *Wired.* He is a regular guest on *Hidden Brain* and other podcasts and has spoken at multiple TEDx events. Gray is the co-author of the book *The Mind Club: Who Thinks, What Feels, and Why It Matters.*

A Note on the Type

This book was set in Adobe Garamond. Designed for the Adobe Corporation by Robert Slimbach, the fonts are based on types first cut by
Claude Garamond (ca. 1480–1561). Garamond was a pupil of Geoffroy
Tory and is believed to have followed the Venetian models, although
he introduced a number of important differences, and it is to him that
we owe the letter we now know as "old style." He gave to his letters an
elegance and feeling of movement that won him an immediate reputation
and the patronage of Francis I of France.

Composed by North Market Street Graphics, Lancaster, Pennsylvania

Printed and bound by Berryville Graphics, Berryville, Virginia

Designed by Betty Lew